THE WEST IN RUSSIA AND CHINA

Holy Russia, Empire of the Middle, what have they done to you,
and what have you done to yourselves?　　　PETRU DUMITRIU, *Incognito*

VOLUME 2

THE WEST IN RUSSIA
AND CHINA

Religious and Secular Thought in
Modern Times

DONALD W. TREADGOLD

Institute for Comparative and Foreign Area Studies
University of Washington

VOLUME 2
CHINA, 1582–1949

CAMBRIDGE
At the University Press
1973

Published by the Syndics of the Cambridge University Press
Bentley House, 200 Euston Road, London NW1 2DB
American Branch: 32 East 57th Street, New York, N.Y.10022

© Cambridge University Press 1973

Library of Congress Catalogue Card Number: 72-78886

ISBNs

0 521 08555 1 hard cover
0 521 09726 6 paperback

Composed in Great Britain
by Alden & Mowbray Ltd
at the Alden Press, Oxford

Printed in the United States of America

For Catherine

The sun of those dead heroes has long since set; but their record is before me still. And, while the wind whistles under the eaves, I open my book and read; and lo! in their presence my heart glows with a borrowed fire.

WEN T'IEN-HSIANG, facing death on refusing allegiance to the Mongols in a prison of Kublai Khan, 1280

CONTENTS

Preface   *page* ix

Foreword to volume 2: the high culture of Old China   xiii

Map of China   xxii

1 CHRISTIAN HUMANISM: THE JESUITS (1582–
1774)   1
The earliest Sino-European contacts; the coming of Ricci; the
Chinese Apostolate of Ricci (1589–1610); the China Mission under
Schall and others (1610–1666); Verbiest and the Rites Controversy
(1666–1722); the last decades of the Jesuit Mission (1689–1774);
conclusion

2 CHRISTIAN PIETISM: THE FUNDAMENTALIST
PROTESTANTS (1807–1900)   35
Introduction; Morrison's Mission (1807–1834); Legge and the Term
Controversy; Protestantism and T'ai-p'ing Christianity; Timothy
Richard and the reform movement; conclusion

3 CHRISTIAN MODERNISM: SUN YAT-SEN (1895–
1925)   70
Introduction; the rise of modernism in the West; modernism super-
sedes fundamentalism in China; Sun Yat-sen and the early Kuomintang; conclusion

4 SYNCRETISM: K'ANG YU-WEI, T'AN SSU-
T'UNG, AND LIANG CH'I-CH'AO (1890–1929)   99
Introduction; the revolution in Chinese education; K'ang Yu-wei;
T'an Ssu-t'ung; Liang Ch'i-ch'ao

5 LIBERALISM: TOWARD THE MAY FOURTH
INCIDENT (1898–1923)   123
Introduction; Yen Fu; Lu Hsün and the rejection of the Chinese
tradition; the circle of *The New Youth*: Ch'en Tu-hsiu and Hu Shih;
the May Fourth Incident; conclusion

6 SOCIALISM: ANARCHISM (1907–1922) AND
MARXISM–LENINISM (1920–1949)   142
Introduction; the Anarchists in Paris and Tokyo; the anti-religious
movement; the formation of the Chinese Communist Party; literary

debates (1920–1936); philosophical debates (1923–1937); the nationalists' eclecticism (1925–1949); the rise of Communism; conclusion

7 THE WEST AND THE CHINESE TRADITION   164

CONCLUSION: THE WEST IN RUSSIA AND CHINA 173
The secularization of the West; a comparison of Western intellectual
influences in Russia and China; totalitarianism; the prospects for
cultural pluralism; conclusion

Abbreviations   196

Notes   197

Additional bibliography   236

Index   240

PREFACE

This book endeavors to trace the development of Western thought in Russia and China through its chief phases. In writing it I have used many secondary works, but in many cases I have also gone to the sources – especially in those areas where secondary treatments are inadequate or non-existent, but not only in such areas. The claim that this book might have to the attention of readers rests not mainly in the information that it brings for the first time to the attention of specialists, though it does contain some such information, but rather in the new way that it attempts to interpret material much of which has been previously known. It seeks to achieve a synthesis without being exhaustive; many significant figures or groups are touched on lightly or not at all, and much of the historical significance of some figures and groups discussed may lie outside the discussion of them to be found here.

The book is intended not as history of philosophy (for which one may consult Fung Yu-lan's and V. V. Zenkovsky's works on China and Russia respectively), history of culture (C. P. Fitzgerald and James H. Billington provide introductions), history of science (Joseph Needham and Alexander Vucinich), or history of religion (here there are no one-volume manuals, though there are histories of churches, which are not the same thing), but as history of thought – of ideas that had some public impact, and specifically ideas of Western origin.

History of religious thought is prominent in the story up to the point where it ceased to be prominent in Russian and Chinese reality. Religious connections with the West are not the subject investigated, before or after that point; for example, the Chinese Roman Catholic community after the eighteenth century, though it was considerably larger than the Chinese Protestant one, receives next to no attention. When matters outside of thought within the field of religion are referred to, the purpose is to explain the limits of the influence or simply the negative effects of religious thought in the given instance. The non-religious thought studied is chiefly of the kind associated with belief in and commitment to a goal (or goals), and in fact much of it was not only chronologically but logically connected with the religious ideas that had been enunciated earlier. Obviously, not all ideas transmitted from the West to Russia and China are examined; obviously, the ideas studied here were important ones.

I have sought to avoid posing the problem as one of the direct causal relation of a given Western work or thinker on a given Russian or Chinese. Limited inquiries of such a kind have produced and will doubtless produce interesting and useful studies. However, here attention is drawn rather to the way certain trends of Western thought took hold in Russia and China and were developed in an institutional context quite different from the one in which they originated.

The reader will not find in this book an evaluation of any thinker or group of thinkers as unequivocally beneficent or pernicious. Christians, liberals, and socialists (including Communists) may all find here ample ground for both praise and blame of themselves or others. However, the objective has been first to understand what happened. There is room for differing evaluations of what happened and how it happened, and my own will be evident before the end of the book.

It is possible that some readers whose interest is confined chiefly to the contemporary world may impute their own feelings to me and accuse me of projecting attitudes of the present into the past. Of course Communist rule in Russia and China is a fact of overwhelming importance, and its recency (despite the difference between 1917 and 1949) makes dispassionate evaluation difficult. If one likes Communism, one may argue that our story is of the indispensable preparation for the victory of the good in two great countries; if one dislikes it, one may hold that the story shows an uninterrupted march toward disaster. The background of Communism in Russia and China today needs to be understood, and if someone wishes to read this book in order to learn more about it, I have no objection. My aim, however, has been to trace the course of Western thought, in Russia and China, distributing attention in a defensible manner among periods and phases, comparing developments in the two countries. Some of the comparison is not explicit; often studying events in one country has affected my approach to events in the other.

The question of the extent to which Russia and China are comparable ought to be distinguished from the question of whether they are similar. Benjamin I. Schwartz has well said, 'the question of whether Russian culture has or has not been part of or "affiliated" with the culture of the West remains unanswered. But there can be no doubt about the separate evolution of Chinese culture.'[1] Equally, it may be added, there can be no doubt that the same major phases of Western thought and many of the same individual ideas and thinkers were influential in both countries, and there thus seems good reason to explore the ways in which the reception of Western thought was similar or different in Russia and China. There exist divergent views on the degree to which state and society in Russia were like state and society in China. My own views on the issue will appear, for what they are worth, but the possible usefulness of a comparison of cultural development does not depend on any particular view of that problem.

One attitude of mine that will be prominent in the exposition to follow is sympathy for solutions of the West–East cultural confrontation that represent what I call 'syncretism'. In using the term I have in mind several men I have known, of whom I shall mention three: the Very Rev. Georges Florovsky,

Hsiao Kung-ch'üan, and the late Hsia Tsi-an. Each of the three – two now living, one dead – was deeply rooted in his own cultural tradition and also found firm footing in that of the West as well. They also taught me something of what heights culture has reached in Russia and China, not so much by their formal instruction (though in two of the three cases that was also helpful) as by their persons and their lives.

I thank the following in particular for assistance: The Far Eastern and Russian Institute (now renamed Institute for Comparative and Foreign Area Studies), its two successive directors, George E. Taylor and George Beckmann, and my colleagues in the Russian and East European Seminar and the Modern Chinese History Project Colloquium at the University of Washington – the members of each group read and criticized every chapter in their field of interest in draft (sometimes more than one) form; Marc Raeff; Fr Francis A. Rouleau, SJ; Oswald P. Backus; Gustave Alef; my colleagues and the staff at Toyo Bunko, Tokyo; my colleagues and the staff at the Institute of History of the USSR Academy of Sciences, Moscow; the staffs of the Lenin State Library, the Central State Archive of Literature and Art (TsGALI), and of the Central State Archives of Old Documents (TsGADA), all in Moscow; Gordon B. Turner and the American Council of Learned Societies; Bryce Wood and the Social Science Research Council; the Guggenheim Foundation; John K. Fairbank and the rest of the SSRC Committee on Exchanges with Asian Institutions. Mr and Mrs Wong Young-tsu assisted me with the translation of numerous Chinese materials, but I take full responsibility for the cases in which I may have overridden their superior judgment. Mrs George Fisher has patiently and flawlessly typed the entire manuscript in several successive versions. More personal indebtedness I shall not attempt to discharge here.

The Wade–Giles system of romanization of Chinese and the Library of Congress systems of transliteration from Russian and Ukrainian have been used, with certain modifications. I have tried not to allow consistency to make usage foolish in any given instance, and I have used more modifications in the text than in footnotes. Not everyone will like all the decisions of this kind I have made, but I would be grateful if such decisions could be distinguished from errors.

D.W.T.

January 1972

FOREWORD TO VOLUME 2

THE HIGH CULTURE OF OLD CHINA

That which is bestowed by Heaven is called man's nature; the fulfillment of this nature is called the Way; the cultivation of the.Way is called culture.

Chung Yung (the Confucian classic often called Doctrine of the Mean)

Civilization in China had come into existence at least as early as 2000 BC. Historic times can be dated to roughly 1600 BC, with the beginning of the Shang (called by its successors the Yin) dynasty. Only in the last half-century has modern archeology confirmed, to the skeptics' surprise, the validity of the traditional Chinese record of that period. In Shang times there was an organized state and a system of writing clearly recognizable as an early form of the present-day Chinese characters (used also in Japan, Korea, and until recently Vietnam). It is by far the oldest writing system in the world, a fact which accounts for part of the depth of feeling of cultural continuity to be found among the Chinese.

The high culture of China dates from the Chou dynasty (traditional dates, 1122–256 BC), which overthrew the Shang. As in contemporary Greece and India, there was in middle and late Chou China a great outpouring of thought and literature. Various strands came to be distinguished: Confucianist, Taoist, and others of what was called with considerable exaggeration the 'Hundred Schools'. Confucius (K'ung-fu-tzu, 551–479 BC) was the greatest figure of the period; in his career he was a frustrated politician, who while seeking a position as adviser to a great ruler seems to have spent much of his life as a teacher. Appealing for the revival of a semi-mythical tradition, in fact he espoused ethical conduct in government and in other aspects of life. Confucian wisdom is best reflected in six books more or less directly connected with the Master himself. The clearest impression of Confucius as a man and teacher comes from the *Analects* (*Lun Yü*), a collection of anecdotes probably compiled by his students after his death. The Five Classics, a later term, include four books which Confucius himself may have edited, preserved, praised, or otherwise transmitted: the *Book of Changes* (*I Ching*), a manual of divination based on 64 hexagrams; the *Book of Documents* (*Shu Ching*), containing speeches and other material (some of it now known to be forged) composed partly in support of Chou legitimacy; the *Book of Poems* (*Shih Ching*); and the *Spring and Autumn Annals* (*Ch'un Ch'iu*), recording events in the small state of Lu from 722 to 481 BC. The fifth of the classics is the *Book of Rites* (*Li Chi*), a later compilation mostly of ritual documents. Two other sets of basic Confucian writings were drawn up much later. The Thirteen Classics counted the *Spring and Autumn Annals* as three works rather than one because of three 'commentaries' (one of which, the *Tso Chuan*, was originally unrelated to it) that were usually appended, and added two writings similar to the *Book of Rites* and four other works: the *Analects* (*Lun Yü*) of Confucius, the book called *Mencius* (*Meng-tzu*), the *Book of Filial Piety* (*Hsiao Ching*), and the *Erh Ya*, a sort of proto-dictionary. The Four Books listing was an attempt to provide in brief compass the essence of Confucianism and became the central curriculum of later-day classical studies. They included two sections from the *Book of Rites* called The Great Learning (*Ta Hsüeh*) and Doctrine of the Mean (*Chung Yung*), the *Analects*, and the *Mencius*. Of all these, the two most closely connected with Confucius himself, aside from the *Analects*, are the *Spring and Autumn Annals*, by which he said he would be remembered, and the *Book of Changes*, which delighted him in his last years. The one which most shaped Confucian doctrine in later centuries was the *Mencius*.

The basis of Confucianism is to be found in the exaltation of certain virtues which the *chün-tzu* ('the superior man') should practice. They included *jen* (love of humanity or benevolence), *shu* (reciprocity, refraining from doing to others what one does not like, Confucius's 'negative Golden Rule'), *i* (righteousness), and others; the *chün-tzu* should also cultivate *wen* (culture) and *li* (the rules of proper behavior). Such ethical teachings soon became the foundation of rearing and judging the officialdom that the Han and later dynasties needed to govern their vast domains.

Confucius had many successors, the most notable of whom was Mencius (372–289 BC). He developed the less authoritarian side of Confucian teaching, contending that human nature was good, that the welfare of the people was the ruler's proper concern, and that if he lost sight of it he lost the 'Mandate of Heaven' and thereby his title to rule. A competing strain of Confucian thought was set forth by Hsün-tzu (*c.* 300–237 BC), who held that human nature was evil, but that a rigorous education, free from superstitious elements, could correct the defect. Hsün-tzu's pessimism regarding human nature is close to that of Legists (*Fa-chia*), whose doctrines were most systematically set forth in the writings of Han-fei-tzu. Their school furnished much of the ideology that was employed by Ch'in Shih Huang-ti, who overthrew the 'warring states' and founded the Empire in 221 BC. The Legists held that the ruler should correct the evil in man by a code of legal rules precisely formulated and strictly enforced and could govern properly only through autocracy. Though the Legist school was near to the Confucianism of Hsün-tzu in some respects, it was alien to the essential humanism of Confucianism in practice; Ch'in Shih Huang-ti showed as much by sequestering Confucian books and slaughtering Confucian scholars.

Next to Confucianism in importance among the schools of Chou times was Taoism. It was strongly mystical, but sought union not with any deity but with nature, and may reflect pre-Confucian animist beliefs and practices of the Chinese and possibly also of non-Chinese peoples. It repudiated Confucius's concern with human society and focused on the individual's relation to the natural universe. The basic texts, perhaps composed in the third century BC, were the *Book of the Way and Power* (*Tao Te Ching*), attributed to a probably mythical 'Old Master' or Lao-tzu, and the *Chuang-tzu*. The Taoist sage, as hermit or ruler, was to seek the Way by 'doing nothing' (*wu wei*), by which was meant coming close to something like what was in the West called a 'state of nature', where the primitive and unspoiled man and the universe live in harmony. Despite Taoism's probable origin in opposition to Confucianism, the two coexisted easily in Chinese society and even in the same individual.

There is no need to discuss here other Chou schools, such as the *yin-yang* thinkers, who viewed all things as generated by the interaction of the *yang* (male, active, light, etc.) principle and the *yin* (female, passive, dark); the 'Five Elements' school, who derived all things from combinations of earth, metal, fire, wood, and water; and the school of Mo-tzu, who were utilitarian and on those grounds stressed the need of propitiating the spirits and advocated universal love (rather than the hierarchical order of human relations developing in Confucianist thought). Such schools either disappeared (as did that of Mo-tzu) or had only limited effects on the later Chinese tradition.

The astonishing cultural pluralism of Chou times yielded to a narrower spectrum of ideas and beliefs by the time of the Han dynasty. The Ch'in had burned Confucian books and practiced Legism; during the Han, Confucian teachings revived but Legism left its mark on imperial administration at least. The symbiotic result has been termed by James Legge an 'imperial Confucianism' in which Confucian doctrines were adapted to the requirements of the state bureaucracy. Confucius posthumously realized with a vengeance his wish to advise rulers, though it is not clear that he would have approved the way that his ethical precepts were applied over the millennium and a half that followed.

Taoism retained much popularity as a mystical philosophy, and in the second century a loosely organized religious Taoism appeared. In 444 an emperor of the T'o-pa Wei dynasty (not Chinese but proto-Mongol) was even induced to proclaim Taoism the state religion, and in the eighth century under the T'ang dynasty it received powerful imperial patronage. Thereafter it sank to become more or less permanently a major ingredient of Chinese popular religion and a source of inspiration to some poets and painters. Combining in curious ways superstition and proto-science, Taoists also contributed substantially to China's scientific and even technological development. As both philosophy and religion, however, Taoism was soon overshadowed by Buddhism.

Buddhism was the first current of thought of clearly foreign origin to have a major impact on China. It derived from the Indian prince Siddhārtha Gautama of the fifth century BC, who left behind the doctrine that the suffering in life, which is due to desire, can be eliminated by the proper sort of spiritual self-discipline, the objective being the achievement of the ultimate transcendence of the world (or annihilation of the individual) in Nirvāna. How this basically straightforward doctrine (if accompanied by such difficulties as to limit its successful practice to a few and by such mysteries as to defy rational discourse about them) became transformed, in one line of development, into mass salvation cults, need not be explained here.

During the first centuries AD Buddhism appeared in China. Various sects spread gradually, by way of Indian and then Chinese translators and missionaries; we know of nearly 200 Chinese who traveled to India from the third to the eighth centuries to learn more about Buddhism, constituting 'the first great student migration of East Asian history'.[1] Not only China but all Asia south of Siberia and east of Persia felt the effects of the expansion of Buddhism deeply during much of this period. The T'o-pa Wei supported it in the north for a time, but the apogee of Chinese Buddhism came only in the eighth century under the T'ang emperors. Buddhism was not an exclusive religion, and its growth was partly due to its willingness to acknowledge varying degrees of validity in, and indeed to incorporate elements from, Taoist and Confucianist teachings. Neither was it very much concerned about consistency or orthodoxy in doctrine. Though the Hīnayāna ('Lesser Vehicle') or Theravāda ('doctrine of the Elders') tendency had been subjected to examination by a series of ecclesiastical councils, the Mahāyāna ('Greater Vehicle') trend had not. The most influential sects in China were of Mahāyāna derivation: the T'ien-t'ai (named after a mountain where the founder of the sect established a temple), which did not exist at all in India, a school which attributed ultimate wisdom to the Lotus sutra; the Hua-yen (Flower Garland); the Ch'an (from Sanskrit *dhyāna*; in Japan, Zen) school of meditation; and the Ching-t'u (Pure Land). The first two sects required greater knowledge and sophistication, and were thus limited to an elite; the latter two offered easier salvation to the masses.

Although Buddhism was 'fully and triumphantly established throughout China' in the eighth century, by the 840's it had been criticized and blamed sufficiently for some of the mid-T'ang problems so that the emperor could order a thoroughgoing destruction of shrines, confiscation of lands, and secularization of clergy.[2]

A revival of Confucianism ensued, but the effects of Buddhism were not easily to be brushed aside. Neo-Confucianism, as the revived form in the Sung period has come to be called, drew on Buddhist categories and tried to satisfy human needs which Buddhism strove to meet in restating Confucian precepts. This was the method of Ou-yang Hsiu (1007–70) and others whose work was synthesized by Chu Hsi (1130–1200). The pre-Buddhist meaning of *li* as merely rational order was replaced in his teaching by the meaning of a pan-absolute in the Mahāyāna Buddhist sense; the opposition of *li* to *ch'i* (material force) paralleled the Buddhist opposition of *li* to *shih* (facts or events).[3] Chu Hsi emphasized the gradualist path to knowledge of *li*, as a number of Buddhist sects had done in their search for enlightenment, but it was a rational and scholarly path based on study of the Confucian classics. It was Chu Hsi who first identified 'Four Books' as the basic classical canon, therewith adding the *Mencius* to it. Accompanied by Chu Hsi's commentaries, these texts became official orthodoxy and the foundation of the examination system from the Yüan dynasty to 1905, when the system was abolished.

As the school of *li* faltered, however, by Ming times, a new version of neo-Confucianism emerged from the so-called school of *hsin* or mind in the writings of Wang Yang-ming (1472–1529). Called a 'Buddhist in disguise', Wang carried his emphasis on innate knowledge, in contradistinction to Chu Hsi's stress on the principle of things external to the mind, to the point of subitism – opening the way to a moment of sudden enlightenment which seemingly made long and painful study superfluous.

What Arthur Wright calls the 'appropriation' of (certain aspects of) Buddhism by neo-Confucianism paradoxically facilitated the defection of the upper classes from Buddhism, but Buddhism among the lower classes did not weaken. It joined Taoist and other elements to produce 'an almost undifferentiated popular religion'[4] that to this day has not been given a universally recognized name. The orthodoxy of the examination system governed the literati, though it did not prevent their exploring ideas other than Chu Hsi's version of Confucianism, in thought or even in writing. But there was no attempt at all to make the neo-Confucian ethical system replace Buddho-Taoist worship among the masses, and Buddhist and other terminology was used in 'Confucianizing' Taiwan and other areas in the eighteenth and nineteenth centuries because such terms were 'more readily understandable' to the people.[5]

The result of the Confucian revival, in the Sung and Yüan periods, was thus to produce a great cultural gulf between the literate, perhaps non-religious, neo-Confucian scholar-gentry (*shen-shih*) and the illiterate, religious and indeed superstitious, Buddho-Taoist (with not a few Confucian borrowings) peasantry. Buddhist or Buddho-Taoist elements were fundamental in a number of secret societies which threatened or even overthrew dynasties, from the founding of the White Lotus Society in the twelfth century onward.[6] Sung despotism witnessed the beginning of the conversion of neo-Confucianism, which started as a protest against the existing order, into a 'state-sponsored system of thought for keeping in humbled silence the very ones who might have protested'.[7] Confucian virtues were related rigorously to the needs of the centralized state; for example, loyalty (*chung*) was given the new meaning of blind devotion to the ruler, requiring the official of a fallen dynasty to withdraw into permanent retirement.[8]

The conversion of neo-Confucianism into a new and sterner version of 'imperial Confucianism', the ideology of a state bureaucracy, did not occur in a year or a century, nor was Confucianism thereby deprived of all critical or possibly even subversive elements. In the late Ming period the school of philosophers who were mainly ex-officials centering in the Tung-lin Academy (founded in 1604 at Wusih in the lower Yangtse Valley) carried on an intellectual and moral crusade against corruption that after a time achieved a fleeting success (1620–2).[9] A few decades later Huang Tsung-hsi (1610–95) composed 'the most enduring and influential Confucian critique of Chinese despotism' in his work *A Plan for the Prince* (*Ming-i Tai-fang Lu*).[10]

Under the Ch'ing dynasty several thinkers, some of whom were Ming loyalists, took up critical positions in their writings. The school of Han Learning invoked the authority of the commentators of the Han period, close to the time when the classics were composed, against what were regarded as the mistakes of Sung and Ming thought. Its chief representative was Ku Yen-wu (1613–82), who attacked the subjectivity and the willingness to dispense with learning that he found in the school of Wang Yang-ming and even what he considered the sterility of the Chu Hsi school; he also criticized the over-centralization of the Ming state. Scholars of the school of Han Learning developed a method called *k'ao-cheng* (search for evidence, or 'empirical research') for examining the authenticity of ancient texts. Yen Jo-chü's (1636–1704) demonstration that the Old-Text portion of the *Book of Documents* was a forgery provided the sensation of this movement, but there were other important discoveries and much useful work in the humanities generally.

There were also thinkers who, agreeing with the Han school's critique of Sung and Ming learning, were critical of the Han scholars' apparent willingness to leave aside difficult practical problems and absorb themselves in literary ones. Such men included Yen Yüan (1635–1704), who attacked the Sung thinkers for having been influenced by Taoist and Buddhist notions. 'Probably the greatest thinker and scholar of the Ch'ing dynasty',[11] Tai Chen (1724–77) pursued the attack on Sung and Ming thought, denying the sharp distinction that had been made between *li* and *ch'i* and the contention that the *li* could be grasped by meditation alone. True understanding could come only through relating thought to practical affairs. Tai Chen by his first-rate scholarly method showed his indebtedness to the Han school even though he thought it mistaken to be content with literary studies alone. Another notable scholar who benefited from the achievements of the Han school but critically questioned the commentators of the Han period was Ts'ui Shu (1740–1816), who counseled beginning with the one classic most incontrovertibly a source of Confucius's views, the *Analects*.

Despite the gifted critics of the Ch'ing period, neo-Confucianism withstood the challenges they offered. The prestige of the Chu Hsi tradition was successfully maintained, and subsequent trends attracted the adherence of such luminaries as the great governor-general, Tseng Kuo-fan, of the mid-nineteenth century.

Less influential (at least until the late nineteenth century) was the New Text school, which revived a debate as old as the Han dynasty. After the fall of the short-lived Ch'in, the question had arisen of restoring the canon of the Confucian classics burned by order of the First Emperor. The first to be reconstructed were called the New Texts – so-called from the fact that they were written in the characters of the Ch'in-Han period. Near the close of the Earlier Han period (AD 25) another set was assembled, supposedly having been found sealed in the walls of Confucius's home; they were called Old Texts because they were written in the characters of the Chou period. The New Text school in Han times was associated with Tung Chung-shu and others who made use of *yin-yang* ideas and attached importance to prognostication and apocryphal writings, while the Old Text school sought to expel superstition and recover the pristine image of Confucius as an ethical teacher. During the reign of Wang Mang (AD 9–23) the minister Liu Hsin was able to bestow official approval on the Old Texts, but the Kuang-wu emperor, founder of the Later Han, having thrown out the usurper, established the New Texts in their place. Nevertheless supporters of the Old Texts came forward again in the first and second centuries AD, and by the time of division (420) of China into Northern and Southern dynasties the New Texters were defeated and silenced.

Not until the eighteenth century did the New Text school revive in the study by Chuang Ts'un-yü (1719–88) of one of its central documents, the Kung-yang commentary on the *Spring and Autumn Annals*. Through Liu Feng-lu (1776–1829), Kung Tzu-chen (1792–1841), and Wei Yüan (1794–1856) to K'ang Yu-wei (1858–1927) the assault on the Old Texts broadened and deepened. K'ang wished not to remove religious elements from Confucianism but to strengthen them; at the same time, he wished to depict Confucius as a political and social reformer.

In his book on Ch'ing thought Liang Ch'i-ch'ao distinguishes four stages of 'liberation through the revival of [increasingly remote] antiquity':

(1) the revival of Sung and liberation from the thought of Wang Yang-ming (of the Ming period; apparently he has in mind Ku Yen-wu and others);

(2) the revival of T'ang and Han and liberation from the thought of Ch'eng Hao and Chu Hsi (of the Sung period; apparently Tai Chen and others);

(3) the revival of Earlier Han and liberation from the thought of Hsü Shen and Cheng Hsüan (of the Later Han period; apparently Chuang Ts'un-yü, Wei Yüan, and K'ang Yu-wei);

(4) the revival of pre-Ch'in antiquity, and liberation from all commentaries (apparently Liang Ch'i-ch'ao himself and T'an Ssu-t'ung).

Liang adds that the process 'could not stop' there, but had to go on until it brought liberation from Confucius and Mencius.[12] Apparently 'liberation from Confucius' was intended to refer not to the uncompromising anti-Confucian movement of the early Republican period but to the position Liang himself had reached when he declared that while he loved Confucius, he loved truth more.

By the time of Liang Ch'i-ch'ao in the twentieth century China was deeply involved in the encounter with the West (and also Japan, which played an important part in mediating Western influence on China), on every level from technological and military to philosophical and religious. From the moment of the arrival in 1582 of the first Westerners in China, the Jesuits, the possibility of significant cultural interaction had come to exist. Indeed there was more such interaction in the seventeenth and eighteenth centuries than many have thought. What is remarkable, however, is the extent to which the high culture of old China remained, at least until about 1900, preoccupied with questions set by her own tradition.

That tradition was, as suggested by the preceding glimpse of a few of its features, far richer than the orthodox neo-Confucianism of the Ch'ing period, far more diverse than Confucianism itself, far broader than the literature of the Confucian, Buddhist, and Taoist writers and the innumerable commentaries and essays on the ethical, philosophical, and religious questions they raised. Especially before the persecution of 841–5, Zoroastrianism, Manicheanism, and the Nestorian version of Christianity also existed in China, though chiefly important among non-Chinese peoples; Judaism kept small bands of adherents until the nineteenth century; Islam has lasted from T'ang times until the present, with millions of followers in the western regions of the country and elsewhere.

Many of China's cultural achievements outside religion and philosophy have been derived from their inspiration. In the magnificent T'ang period, there was clear Buddhist influence on music, sculpture (in which Buddhist borrowings from Greece may be seen in form though scarcely in spirit), painting, and calligraphy – that art especially characteristic of China, in which esthetics and meaning were blended. Taoism's preoccupation with nature contributed to the landscape painting of the Sung period, which was never to be surpassed in its artistic quality. Taoist hedonism inspired one of China's greatest poets, Li Po in the T'ang era, as Confucian imperatives governed the thinking of his friend, the equally great poet Tu Fu. The notion that the artist and writer might be expected also to be a statesman, and vice versa, which was fully shaped by Sung times, owed something to both Confucianism and Taoism.

Other arts developed more on their own. The Sung period saw the art of ceramics, which lacked obvious religious inspiration, carried to its height of perfection in Chinese annals. In the Yüan period the writing of dramas and prose tales in the vernacular became noteworthy. Under Ming the great popular novels *The Water Margin* or *All Men are Brothers* (*Shui-hu chuan*) and *Golden Lotus* (*Chin P'ing Mei*) were produced, under the Ch'ing *The Dream of the Red Chamber* (*Hung-lou meng*). From Han times the writing of history had been an honored art, beginning with the work of Ssu-ma Ch'ien

(d. about 85 BC) and the standard dynastic history of the Earlier Han by Pan Ku (d. AD 92); 'standard' histories were written for each dynasty and came to number twenty-five.[13] Religious or philosophical influences were not absent from any of the arts; but such influences varied greatly in intensity, and the high culture of China offers a heterogeneous treasury containing all sorts of surprising riches.

Nevertheless the problems which the Chinese tradition set for itself can be characterized as of certain kinds and not others. Those problems were at root moral problems. As Fung Yu-lan writes, the methods of Chinese thinkers were 'not primarily for the seeking of knowledge, but rather for self-cultivation; [they were]...not for the search of truth, but for the search of good'.[14] In many ways old Russian culture and old Chinese culture were dissimilar, but in this respect they were alike. The category of truth was of much less importance than the categories of goodness – which was of over-arching significance – and beauty – which was less clearly articulated in theory but of major significance in Chinese cultural life. That is to say, old Chinese thought, like old Russian thought, may be said to have been Hebraic rather than Hellenic, Biblical rather than patristic in spirit. True, that is not to distinguish the thought of the two peoples very sharply from all others; for while there was more than one 'Israel' in world history, there was only one Greece, both literally and figuratively. (This contention is designed to refer to intellectual history, not to argue where or how God made Himself manifest to man.)

The ineluctable introduction of the category of truth by the West offered a difficulty to Chinese thinkers. There were other difficulties in the realm of thought; in more tangible and material fields, they were manifold, seemingly almost infinite. In the nineteenth and twentieth centuries China stood in the immediate shadow of Western political and military power. China had known conquering barbarians many times before. Long ago Mencius had said: 'I have heard of men using the doctrines of our great land to change barbarians, but I have never yet heard of any being changed by barbarians.'[15] As far as the 'barbarians' of Chou times were concerned, he was right, and in the eyes of many nineteenth-century Chinese he was still right, for the memory of the ascendancy of Buddhism had grown dim. In fact, China had had little to fear from the power of India when it accepted Indian ideas, though many suggested that the ideas and the religion were to be feared and rejected. Facing the power of the West, China had little time to reflect. To confront, at the same time and in the same hands, superior force and, if not a superior culture, at least one equally high, was a new experience for the Chinese. The Chinese response was complex; it has already had great implications for the whole planet; its final form is not yet clear. The 'cultivation of the Way' that played such a part in Chinese culture may still have its lessons to teach the Chinese and the rest of humanity.

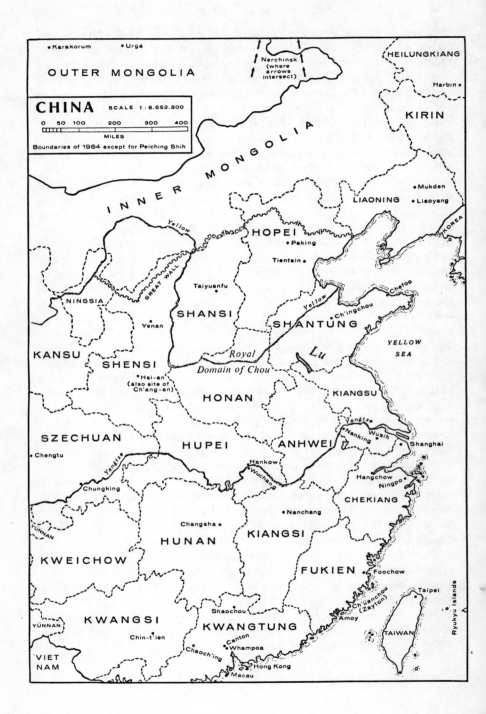

- Karakorum   • Urga

OUTER MONGOLIA

HEILUNGKIANG

Harbin •

CHINA SCALE 1:6,652,800

0 50 100   200   300   400

MILES

Boundaries of 1964 except for Peiching Shih

Nerchinsk
(where
arrows
intersect)

I N N E R   M O N G O L I A

KIRIN

• Mukden
• Liaoyang

LIAONING

Yellow

HOPEI

• Peking

Tientsin •

Chefoo

KOREA

NINGSIA

GREAT WALL

Taiyuanfu •

SHANSI

Yellow

Ch'ingchou •

SHANTUNG

YELLOW
SEA

KANSU

SHENSI

Yenan •

• Hsi-an
(also site of
Ch'ang-an)

*Royal
Domain of Chou*

Lu

HONAN

KIANGSU

SZECHUAN

• Chengtu

HUPEI

ANHWEI

Yangtze

• Nanking Wusih

• Shanghai

Chungking •

Yangtze

Hankow •
Wuchang

Hangchow •
Ningpo •

CHEKIANG

• Nanchang

YUNNAN

Changsha •

HUNAN

KIANGSI

KWEICHOW

FUKIEN

• Foochow

YUNNAN

Chin-t'ien •

KWANGSI

Shaochou •

KWANGTUNG

Ch'üanchou
(Zayton)

Amoy

Taipei •

Ryukyu Islands

VIET
NAM

Chaoch'ing •

Canton •
• Whampoa

• Hong Kong

Macau •

TAIWAN

I

CHRISTIAN HUMANISM: THE JESUITS (1582–1774)

So Paul stood up in full view of the Areopagus, and said, Men of Athens, wherever I look I find you scrupulously religious. Why, in examining your monuments as I passed by them, I found among others an altar which bore the inscription, To the unknown God. And it is this unknown object of your devotion that I am revealing to you...he is not far from any one of us; it is in him that we live, and move, and have our being; thus, some of your own poets have told us, For indeed, we are his children...some mocked, while others said, We must hear more from thee about this...But there were men who attached themselves to him and learned to believe, among them Dionysius the Areopagite; and so did a woman called Damaris, and others with them.

Acts 17.22–34 (Ronald Knox trans.)

THE EARLIEST SINO-EUROPEAN CONTACTS

It is not certain when men living in the Mediterranean world came to know of China, and the Chinese to know of states and cultures in the West. It was formerly thought, especially in the nineteenth century, that the Jews had had relations with the Chinese long before the birth of Christ. The Protestant missionaries attached great importance to the single Biblical text, Isaiah 49.12, on which this belief rested. Modern scholarship, however, is inclined to doubt that the Isaiah text refers to China at all.[1] Certain misty traditions of the Christians of India hold that St Thomas the Apostle or some of his followers reached China. Some surviving accounts are not convincing, since they refer to 'Camballe' (Cambaluc or Khanbaliq) and to voyages thence on Chinese vessels; they could scarcely therefore have been written earlier than the thirteenth century.[2] Although 'St Thomas' Christians are reliably reported to have been in South India by the sixth century,[3] no connection of theirs with China can be demonstrated.

If the Jews did not know China, the Greeks might have. G. F. Hudson's study indicates his belief that Aristaeus of Proconnesus, author of a poem called the *Arimaspea*, had actually visited 'the lands north of the T'ien-shan' in the seventh century BC – the borderlands of China if not China proper – and Hudson devotes a good deal of space to an attempt to show that the Hyperboreans whom Herodotus, crediting Aristaeus, mentions were the Chinese.[4] More recent scholarship, however, remains skeptical.[5]

The first visitors from the Mediterranean appear to have reached China in AD 166, coming from the Rome of Marcus Aurelius Antonius.[6] The reality of this mission has been questioned, partly because no known Roman or Byzantine documents mention it or any other mission to or from China.[7] Hudson concludes that the Romans of 166, 226, and 284 were merchants 'assuming an official status to further their ends'. China certainly knew of Rome (or at any rate the Oriental part of the Roman Empire), calling it Ta Ch'in, and later (beginning with the embassy of 643) Fu Lin.[8] That mission was probably the first official contact between Europe and China. Hudson lists Byzantine embassies in 667, 711, 719, 742, and 1081 – perhaps not all from the emperors but from local officials. But none of these contacts came to much, probably in part because of the decline of the silk trade. From the first century BC until the sixth century AD the silk trade had flourished, through Persian and other middlemen; but about 553, silk moth eggs were smuggled into Byzantium, and the Mediterranean area was soon producing its own silk. Travel was difficult, and trade was no longer of vital importance.

Yet it was during the early centuries of the Byzantine Empire that the first cultural influences from the Greco-Roman world reached China, with the great expansion of Nestorian Christianity through Central Asia. The existence of Nestorianism in China was long forgotten, and rediscovered only in 1625 when a monument was found near Hsi-an in Shensi. Dated 781, the monument recorded the establishment of clergy in Ch'ang-an in 635. Christianity is not mentioned by name. The reference is to the 'illustrious' (or perhaps 'luminous') religion (*ching chiao*); but the referent is Nestorian Christianity beyond any doubt.[9]

The question of what the adjective 'Nestorian' means in this connection need not detain us. Nestorius did not found any church, and his followers in the Middle East did not apply the term 'Nestorian' to themselves. However, the belief in distinctively Nestorian doctrines in China is amply attested by such sources as the *Book of Jesus the Messiah*, probably dating from 637.[10] Nestorianism was tolerated by the T'ang rulers, but it seems to have been confined to Turkic peoples such as the Uighurs and not to have spread among the Chinese. After the T'ang period it declined and almost disappeared. Moule declares that there is no evidence that Christian communities survived in China to the eleventh and twelfth centuries;[11] nevertheless one man whom he himself mentions, Rabban Sauma, provides at least a fragment of such evidence, since he was born in Peking. Rabban Sauma was dispatched by the Mongols at Baghdad with a mission to the pope in 1287, meeting Philip IV of France and Edward I of England (in Gascony), and received a cordial welcome at the court of Pope Nicholas IV.[12]

It was the migration westward of the Mongols that brought the first envoys from China to the continent of Europe. Chinese ambassadors had visited Ferghana in 128 BC and Mesopotamia in AD 97, obtaining thereby some notion of the Mediterranean world which was never entirely lost thereafter, but no embassy reached Europe until a group of Alan Christians at the court of the last Yüan emperor sent one to the pope at Avignon in 1338. On the eve of the

Mongol conquests, the eastward drive of Europeans which was the Crusades intensified their interest in the Near East and areas beyond. When Genghis Khan and his successors sent their armies westward, winning every battle up through Liegnitz (1241), the Crusaders had occupied Constantinople and set up a Latin Empire there.

The papacy of course wished to convert all pagan barbarians, including the Mongols; but it developed a special enthusiasm for converting the Mongols, since they were threatening the rear of the Muslims in Palestine.[13] The Council of Lyon (1245), after hearing a report on the Mongols from Russian bishops, decided to send a mission to Karakorum. Thereupon the first of a series of Franciscan missionary-diplomats, Friar John of Plano Carpini, made his way to the Mongol capital, arriving back in Kiev in 1247, but attained no diplomatic objectives. The Seventh Crusade, led by Louis IX (St Louis) of France, prompted further efforts to concert operations against the Muslims. In 1249 Louis sent the Dominican Andrew of Longjumeau to Karakorum; in 1253 he sent the Franciscan William of Ruisbroek. Courtesies were exchanged, but little else.

When Kublai Khan established himself in Cambaluc (Peking) in 1264, the Mongols showed hospitality and interest in Europeans. The first visitors to the emperor there were the Venetian merchants Polo in 1265 or 1266. The emperor asked the pope through them for one hundred learned missionaries; the brothers Nicolò and Maffeo transmitted his message. Pope Gregory X sent two Dominicans, who started for China but turned back. Thereby one of history's great opportunities may have been missed, for although missionaries reached Cambaluc in 1294 to stay for some time, it was in response to no such grand imperial invitation as that of thirty years previously. The brothers Polo did return to Cambaluc, arriving in 1275 accompanied by Nicolò's son Marco. They remained seventeen years, returning to astonish Europe with one of the greatest travel accounts of all time.[14]

When the Polos were returning to Europe for good they must have passed Friar John of Montecorvino on the sea route from Ormuz, Persia, to China. He was dispatched as a missionary by Pope Nicholas IV in 1289, reaching Cambaluc in 1294. The Mongols had proclaimed the Yüan dynasty in China in 1279, having finally defeated the southern Sung forces, and had in 1289 established a governmental office to deal with Christian clergy called the Ch'ung-fu-ssu. At this point the Christian clergy were presumably entirely Nestorian, for none of the Franciscans up till then had remained in China or baptized anyone, let alone created any indigenous clergy. However, the new bureau now acquired some Catholics to deal with. Another friar joined John in 1303. In 1307 the pope elevated John to be Archbishop of Cambaluc and sent seven bishops to assist him. Three of them died *en route* and one turned back, but three arrived, and three more were dispatched in 1312. The result was that the archbishop was able to strengthen the mission in Cambaluc and begin a new one at 'Zayton' (the Arab name for Ch'üanchou in Fukien, then a great port). When he died in China in 1328, there were several thousand Roman Catholic Christians in China.

Most seem, however, to have been from among the Turkic peoples, notably the subjects of an Öngüt prince whom both John and Marco Polo call 'the good King George'; they were converted from Nestorianism to Roman Catholicism. Mass was celebrated in the Turkic language of this people. This was the summit of the attainments of the Franciscan mission, but it is doubtful that it had any significant relation to the Chinese. Even the first Roman Catholic church built in China, built by John before 1300, has proven to have been in the Öngüt capital, near the boundary separating Outer and Inner Mongolia and not, as often supposed, in or near Cambaluc.15

The death of John of Montecorvino occurred about the same time as that of Andrew of Perugia, bishop of Zayton. A successor was appointed in 1333, but he apparently never reached China. The embassy already mentioned of the last Yüan emperor to Avignon, in 1338, among other things asked that another head of the mission be dispatched. Benedict XII in response sent a last group of Franciscans, headed by John of Marignolli. They traveled with the Mongol envoys, reaching Cambaluc in 1342. Marignolli left three or four years later and returned to Avignon in 1353 with a further request from the emperor for more missionaries. The Black Death had just wreaked havoc in Europe; all clergy were in short supply; there was thus no response from the papacy. Titular successors to John of Montecorvino were appointed until 1426, but none reached China.

In 1368 an indigenous dynasty, that of the Mings, replaced the Mongol Yüan dynasty. From the first its monarchs were far less cosmopolitan than the Mongols. The Franciscan missions came to an end; when the Jesuits arrived both the Nestorian and Roman Catholic communities of the Chinese Empire for all practical purposes were extinct.16 The discovery of the Nestorian stele in 1625 came as such a surprise that its authenticity was disputed for a long time. Still more astonishing, the Franciscans who returned to China shortly after the Jesuits had penetrated it had no knowledge of their predecessors in their own order.17

The Nestorians in China may have had only modest aims; we know so little about them that we can only speculate. As for the Franciscans, their aims were ambitious, their resources limited, the difficulties they faced enormous. Their methods, however, were not those apt to overcome the obstacles in their path even under the relatively tolerant Yüan emperors, let alone the xenophobic Mings. Their style was that of bold and uncompromising evangelism. Thus William of Ruisbroek, ushered into the presence of Batu, khan of the Golden Horde in southern Russia, *en route* to the east, promptly told him that unless he became a Christian he would not go to heaven but be eternally damned.18 Fortunately for the friar, Batu only smiled tolerantly, though his courtiers raised a protesting clamor. It was not the sort of approach that could have been expected to win the Chinese, especially their literati, and did not. In fact, the report of Fra Peregrino da Castello indicates that the Franciscans (at least up to 1318) did not know any Chinese, and preached through two interpreters – which languages were used we do not know.[19]

In 1933 the missionary Mostaert discovered Nestorian Christians among the Erküt tribe of Ordos Mongols.[20] But this remains an isolated instance. The first Jesuit in China, Matteo Ricci, succeeded in locating one community of people who were reputedly Christians (as well as several communities who were certainly Jews).[21] However, he failed to find out anything about their origin. It is significant that Father Nicolas Trigault, in his Latin version of the Ricci journals, after discussing the faint traces of previous Christianity the Jesuits had encountered, mentions as a possible antecedent not Olopen, the Syrian Nestorian missionary (of whom he did not know, since the monument of 781 was not discovered for a decade after he wrote), nor John of Montecorvino (of whom, as noted, even the contemporary Franciscans did not know), but only St Thomas and the Indian legends of his mission in China.[22]

The finding of the monument near Hsi-an in 1625 created a sensation. The sources make clear the joy and pride with which Chinese Christians acknowledged proof that their 'new' faith was old in China;[23] the Jesuits recognized the value of the discovery. Much later the Protestants rejoiced in its existence, feeling little of the animus toward the largely vanished Nestorian sect which their more militant spirits directed toward Roman Catholics.[24] Timothy Richard was drawn to pondering its significance, and persuaded himself that it not only indicated an early penetration of Christianity into China but reflected Christian influences that must have reached Japan in such a way as to help produce what he called 'higher Buddhism' there.[25]

However, the missionaries of modern times generally entered China without consciousness that they were building on foundations of pre-sixteenth century predecessors, and indeed nothing of those foundations seems to have remained. If any Chinese Christian communities survived into modern times, they have not been found (with the single exception reported by Ricci) and played no part in history. Before the arrival of the Jesuits there were at times some Christians in the Chinese Empire, but very few Chinese Christians, and none who to our knowledge made the slightest impact on the thought and culture of China.

THE COMING OF RICCI

The towering figure of Matteo Ricci has been amply studied, though his name may have been better known to the literate public of the eighteenth century than to that of the twentieth. Pasquale D'Élia celebrates him as a fellow national: 'The human source from which flows the good that the Catholic Church does in China today is a worthy son of Italy, Father Matteo Ricci.'[26] The American Jesuit, Fr Dunne, sees his chief merit as the application to China of what Dunne regards as the Catholic Church's ancient policy of accommodation.[27] Another Jesuit, Fr Gallagher, sees Ricci as the true discoverer of China in modern times.[28] One writer approaching his subject from the standpoint of the secular historian of science, Joseph Needham, flatly terms him 'one of the most remarkable and brilliant men in history'.[29]

Ricci was an admirable Italian, distinguished Jesuit, brilliant accommodator, and the West's first Sinologist; his work also marks the beginning of the story of Western thought in China. This did not mean that he came with the notion that the West was superior to China. On the contrary he came as China's first immigrant in the modern sense – a foreigner who entered the country with the resolve of living the rest of his life there and becoming a member of the Chinese community in dress, manners, language, and culture, at the same time as he strove, with the other members of the Society of Jesus and of the Roman Catholic Church, to convert China to Christianity. In the process of seeking to do these things, he did much to transmit Western learning to the Chinese.

It was from the Europe of the High Renaissance that Ricci came, and he owed his high intellectual attainments to the training he had received from the educational institutions of his Society. The Society of Jesus, whose foundation reflected Ignatius of Loyola's belated recognition of the consequences of his own youthful ignorance and narrowness, was intended as a means of mobilizing the full resources of Western culture in the service of the Roman Church. Its success was well reflected in the stature of Ricci's teachers at Rome, the mathematician Christopher Clavius and the gifted Robert Bellarmine, as well as in the prodigious achievements of Ricci himself – indeed, in the brilliantly perceptive manner in which Ricci and a few others worked out missionary methods applicable to the non-Western world, especially to the great Asian civilizations of China, Japan, and India.

Not all Jesuits had Ricci's ability or vision; a number of non-Jesuit Roman Catholic missionaries did share his enlightened outlook. But for the most part the Ricci approach to China was the Jesuit approach; its foundations he himself derived from the Society, while his fellow Jesuits by and large followed the particular paths his genius worked out. Ricci individually and the Jesuits as a group in Asia (and Africa and Latin America) had to overcome much ignorance and hostility within the Church, and in the end their methods were repudiated and the China mission destroyed largely as a result of such ignorance and hostility. It may be argued that there was a potential flaw in the Society from the start: it was to be a missionary organization which would be both disciplined (as previous orders had been) and intellectual (as none were before). If the perceptions of the gifted minds concerned came into conflict with orders from above, either the perceptions must be ignored or the orders disobeyed. What happened, in the case of China, was that the Jesuits, having to choose, obeyed the orders and thus destroyed the fruits of their own work.

The new missionary era accompanying the Age of Discovery had begun with the Portuguese in the saddle. Armed with full papal authorization in

Africa, Asia (except for the Philippines, where the Spaniards enjoyed the same privileges, as they also did in Western Latin America), and Brazil, the Portuguese had begun in India to set the first patterns of the new Christian missions. It was a pattern of attempting to turn indigenous converts into second-class Portuguese citizens and second-class Christians; there was no willingness to compromise with or even study seriously Indian culture or religions. The Spaniards did the same as their rivals, in the Philippines producing permanent mass Christianization and in Spanish America permanent Hispanicization as well, leaving little trace of earlier cultures in either case.

After the Society of Jesus was founded in 1540, its leadership immediately experimented with a different approach in Ireland (1542) and Ethiopia. But both countries had been Christian for more than a millennium; Asia was a quite different problem, with the minor exception of the Malabar Christians of India. The Portuguese in India, whose center was the see of Goa (captured 1510, a bishopric from 1534, an archbishopric from 1558), were introduced, with the arrival of St Francis Xavier[30] in 1542, to a new kind of missionary strategy. It was one of patience, charity, and Christian love; but it was not yet the developed main current of Jesuit strategy, for Xavier chose to work with the poor, outcasts, and children rather than with the well-educated and powerful.

In Japan, which Xavier reached in 1549, such methods were to work reasonably well.[31] This was something of a paradox, for Xavier was chagrined and disappointed to find that the Japanese emperor was by no means absolute in his power and that the feudal organization was the basis of Japanese society. Nevertheless this lack of centralization provided just the opportunity the Roman Catholic missionaries needed who were following Xavier's lead, and the number of converts grew rapidly. By 1583 there were about 150,000 Roman Catholic Christians in Japan; in 1606 750,000; in 1614, after the first persecutions, there were still almost 300,000.[32] By the 1630's, however, Christianity was almost extinct in Kyushu, its former stronghold; by 1641 there remained only the Protestant Dutch, who had not pressed missionary activity, at Deshima as a link with the West. With that exception, Tokugawa Japan had withdrawn into complete seclusion, which would be ended only by Perry in the nineteenth century.

Xavier, however, at length concluded that the Japanese, whose character excited his boundless admiration, could be converted only by way of knowledge of the culture of China which had so influenced Japan, and decided China was therefore the key. In 1552 he died on an island southwest of Canton, vainly attempting to reach the mainland of China. The forceful personality and impressive character of the 'Apostle of the Indies' left an inspiring example, but Xavier's approach was essentially pre-Jesuit, and it offered no solution to the problem of forcing the formidable, seemingly impregnable barriers erected against foreigners by Ming China.

There was, after the Portuguese settled on the Macau peninsula in 1557, a territorial base for missionary work in China, but it proved not easy to use successfully. During the fifteen years following the death of Xavier, a scattering of Jesuits (Melchior Nunes Barreto in 1555, Juan Bautista Ribera in 1565), Dominicans (Gaspar da Cruz, 1556), and Augustinians (Martin de Rada and Jerónimo Marin, 1575) reached the mainland but failed to accomplish anything. The two Jesuits concluded that conversion of the Chinese could not be achieved except by the use of force, and none of these men except de Rada made any effort to study China seriously.

The Jesuit strategy which proved successful began to be laid out by Alessandro Valignano, the Italian who as Visitor of all Jesuit missions in the Far East sailed from Lisbon and arrived in India in 1574, went on to Macau in 1577, and remained in the Far East until his death in 1606. Though he underestimated Indian civilization, he followed Xavier in his high estimate of Japanese culture and his belief that China must be penetrated before success could be hoped for in Japan. As a first step, he summoned priests from Goa to study Chinese in Macau. In 1579 Michele Ruggieri arrived, and in 1582 came Matteo Ricci.

Ricci had left his home in Macerata for Rome at the age of sixteen, in 1568, to study jurisprudence at the university there. In 1571 he entered the Society of Jesus and after about a year of novitiate took his vows and became a student at the Collegio Romano. There he studied humanities and philosophy from 1572 to 1577. Volunteering for Far Eastern missions, he then went to Coimbra and studied briefly there before sailing from Lisbon in 1578. He had been four years in India, studying theology and being ordained priest. Up to 1582 he had therefore had twelve years of the best education then available, but no instruction on China.[33]

Valignano's strategy of penetrating China by 'a confrontation with the intellectual aristocracy on its own level of language, social customs and superior talent'[34] had found two apparently promising instruments. In fact only Ricci fully realized the promise; Ruggieri never became very proficient in Chinese and, finding that the China mission overtaxed his powers, returned in 1588 to Rome to request the pope to send an embassy to the Chinese emperor and remained in Italy until his death in 1607.

At Macau Ricci immediately proved his fitness for the task assigned him. He made rapid progress in Chinese studies, despite the fact that other Jesuits on Macau were far from sympathetic and repeatedly interfered. Already in 1584 in collaboration with Ruggieri he published a translation of the Ten Commandments (*Tsu-ch'uan T'ien-chu Shih-chieh*); it was the first Christian publication in the Chinese language. During 1582 Ruggieri was admitted to the mainland three times: once on an official errand, the second time as one given permission (soon revoked) to establish a settlement, the third on another official visit, in the course of which permission to settle was refused. Then abruptly the two missionaries were invited to establish themselves at present-day Chaoch'ing, arriving in September 1583. Ricci returned to Macau on a visit for the last time in 1592, but he never left China thereafter.

On the advice of the sympathetic viceroy of the two provinces of Kwang-tung and Kwangsi, Ricci and Ruggieri adopted the dress of Buddhist monks. In 1585 they built a small church. When a new viceroy was named, Ricci, with another Jesuit, had to move to Shaochou. By the time he visited Macau in 1592, he had discovered several important facts. Very early he realized how dependent the Jesuit missions would be on the attitude of the officialdom, since their buildings were repeatedly invaded by marauders incited by Buddhist priests or simply impelled by the search for loot and excitement, and judgment of the culprits would affect the Jesuits' future prospects. Gradually Ricci came to suspect that in Ming China (and the same remained true under the Ch'ing) no single person, even the emperor, would ever make a clear ruling either that they could or could not stay and do their work in peace. However, he perceived that if the Jesuits could sufficiently influence the scholar-gentry, an atmosphere would be created in which they could expect to be generally received with sympathy. The basic documents of the Chinese culture of which the scholar-gentry were custodians were the Confucian classics. Thereupon Ricci determined to master them as a means of approaching the literati on terms of equality. Valignano approved his intention. Shortly after returning from Macau, Ricci changed the dress of the Buddhist monks for that of the Confucian scholars and began to study to be one of the latter.

This was not conceived of as a masquerade. It was the duty of the Christian missionary to become an inhabitant (the idea of 'citizen' reflects more ex-plicitly political conceptions, perhaps, but Ricci's view approached this) of China not merely in the sense of extended or even permanent residence, but in the psychological and cultural sense. It was not a Western Church in China that he wished to establish, but a Chinese Church that was part of the univer-sal Church; his aim was 'not simply to establish a certain number of Christian communities on the fringes of a hostile society; it was rather to build a Sino-Christian civilization'.[35] Ricci was always ready to approach Chinese culture with an attitude of respect and a desire to identify elements in it consonant with Christianity as well as those not positively discordant. He was deter-mined not to demand Westernization of the Chinese converts whom he hoped to make. Christ had not been a Chinese; neither had He been an Italian (or any other kind of European); the same was true of the Apostles and many saints and Fathers of the Church.

Ricci's aim was to convert the Chinese to Christianity. In order to do so, he was willing to use all the resources of European learning and science at his or his fellow Jesuits' command. In the event it worked both ways, logically and chronologically. Some Chinese were converted as a result of their initial admiration for Western knowledge, some gained at least bits of the latter after conversion, to which regard for the character of the Jesuits had led them; and the result was the beginning of the impact of Western thought on China.

Ricci's policy has been called one of 'accommodation', and it is an apt term. It was criticized many times during the past three and a half centuries by anti-intellectual and ardently (perhaps misguidedly) democratic persons and groups. One ingredient of his policy seemed to Ricci's critics to be that of working 'from the top down', assuming the literati to be on top. John J. Considine employed this phrase; George H. Dunne challenged it, arguing that 'there is no indication that Ricci hoped to make Christians of the academicians as a whole'.[36] Arnold H. Rowbotham, though far from unsympathetic to the Jesuits, speaks of their 'truckling to officials' and calls the gifts they often made to functionaries 'bribery'.[37] The same kind of revulsion at Jesuit methods in China was felt by many of the Protestant evangelical missionaries of the nineteenth century, partly because their tradition was one distrustful of too much learning.[38]

In fact Ricci and his brethren performed the *k'o-t'ou* (which Western ambassadors later, with the honor of their governments at stake, refused to do), presented gifts, observed the rules of returning visits very soon after they were made (in Peking this almost exhausted Ricci), and in general conformed to Chinese custom whenever Christian belief was not at stake, but only personal dignity as Westerners conceived of it. Such behavior created good impressions. The prisms, sundials, clocks, maps, and other technical novelties included among gifts to officials or displayed to visitors aroused curiosity and a desire to investigate further.

However, Ricci's significant successes were gained by different means, precisely the means that Valignano and he had planned; those means were intellectual. He began with Western culture: cartography and geography first, then mathematics and astronomy, then philosophy and theology via the tracts he himself and others wrote in Chinese; and then he was prepared to proceed to the arena of Chinese culture, starting with the classics and commentators, laboring for the clarification of the Confucian tradition itself, relating Western ideas to it, accepting what a Christian could accept and being prepared to explain why a Christian could not accept other things, trying to discern truth in the Chinese tradition and to distinguish it from theological error and scientific falsehood.

THE CHINESE APOSTOLATE OF RICCI (1589-1610)

It was in Shaochou, where the mission had moved in 1589, that Ricci acquired his first real Chinese friend and pupil, Ch'ü T'ai-su, moving gradually from science to theology, discussing every point at length as they went. The obstacle to Ch'ü's conversion, as it was in so many cases thereafter, was concubinage – but not in this instance because his Chinese friend desired to keep more than one woman. His wife had died, but he could not for a time bring himself to marry his low-born concubine. (In 1605, nevertheless, he finally did so.)

In 1595 Ricci made his first attempt to reach Peking in the company of a friendly official. The tense atmosphere engendered by the Japanese invasion of Korea was a hindrance, however; Ricci got no farther than Nanking, from there having to flee to Nanchang. The latter was a city much frequented by scholars, and there for the first time he came into contact with the literary societies or 'academies' which gave rise to the nationwide Tung-lin movement, whose aims were reformist.[39] In Nanchang he composed his first original work in Chinese, *On Friendship* (*Chiao-yu lun*), published without his authorization although he was happy with its publication.[40] As he wrote at the time, 'in order to publish anything I have to get permission from so many of our people that I cannot do anything. Men who are not in China and cannot read Chinese insist upon passing judgment.'[41] The treatise won wide acclaim.

In 1598 Ricci headed for the capital again, accompanied by another high official. This time he reached the city; but the atmosphere had not improved, his friends who were now in office in Peking dared not receive or assist him, and he decided to leave. Intending to make but a brief visit to Nanking, he there met a warm reception, won a great success in an argument with a renowned Buddhist monk at a dinner in his own honor, and decided to stay for a time. Here he revised his map of the world, first drawn up in 1584, with China in the center. A copy of the map reached Shanghai, and it induced Hsü Kuang-ch'i to come to Nanking in 1600 to meet Ricci. Four years earlier Hsü had seen Ricci's original map and become interested in both Western science and theology. Paul Hsü, as he was later baptized, was the first and greatest of Ricci's scholar-converts from Tung-lin circles.[42]

In 1600 Ricci's third try for Peking at last succeeded. Although his party became embroiled for a time with a powerful and deceitful eunuch and was detained, he finally managed to present his gifts for the Wan-li emperor, and in May 1601 was released from detention on the unspoken understanding that he was to be allowed to remain in Peking. Apparently he never left it again before his death in 1610.

Ricci never succeeded in seeing the Wan-li emperor, but he still established his mission on a firm basis in the capital. He made distinguished scholar-converts, chief among them Li Chih-tsao who was, like Ch'ü T'ai-su and Hsü Kuang-ch'i, attracted to Ricci through Western science and whom Ricci ranked with Hsü alone as a Chinese able fully to master Euclid, though he was less saintly and more worldly than Hsü. For years Li worked with Ricci, collaborating in writing volumes on geography, mathematics, astronomy, and also theology. It was Li who published new editions of Ricci's *The True Doctrine of the Lord of Heaven* (*T'ien-chu Shih I*)[43] and *On Friendship*. As in the case of Ch'ü T'ai-su, monogamy was for Li a difficulty; he yielded only in 1610, and was baptized Leo Li. Hsü, Li, and (Michael) Yang T'ing-yün were dubbed 'the three pillars of the early Church' (*k'ai-chiao san-ta chu-shih*). Michael Yang was not Ricci's convert but Lazzaro Cattaneo's. He was baptized in 1611, after Ricci's death, after dismissing a second wife and after intellectual struggles over the doctrine of the Incarnation, which he along with a number of other Chinese scholars found difficult to reconcile with his ideas of the majesty of God.

From 1598 to 1603 Ricci was superior of the China mission under the direction of Macau; after 1603 he answered directly to the vice-provincial in Japan. As superior he was beset with many problems: Chinese jealousy, lack of comprehension, and fear of him, his religion, and above all of other Western barbarians who might come after him; the slowness and obtuseness of many of his fellow Jesuits who often failed to support him in Macau, other stations in Asia, and Rome; the clumsiness, ignorance, and misguided zeal of members of other Roman Catholic orders, who felt the kind of revulsion at Ricci's methods common among poorly educated Christians then and later; and the greediness and cruelty of certain Westerners representing secular state governments – for example the Spaniards who massacred the inhabitants of Manila in 1603, the Dutch who pirated a ship laden with silk in which the Jesuits had an interest in Macau in 1604 or those who attacked Macau in 1622 (after Ricci's death), and were driven off only by dint of the use of cannon supervised by three Jesuit fathers. When Ricci died in 1610, there were four small chapels in the Chinese Empire, each attached to a Jesuit residence; there were perhaps 2,500 Chinese Roman Catholics, many from the educated class; 8 out of the 16 Jesuits in China were Chinese,[44] though none of the latter was yet a priest.

There is no evidence that Ricci felt disappointment at these results. He did not underestimate the task of converting China, believed it would take a long time, and never wavered in the conviction that he had found the right way to bring it about. His memoirs, completed shortly before his death,[45] bespeak his admiration for the Chinese people despite his consciousness of the social evils present among them. In the latter he includes divination, slavery, the drowning of female infants, suicide, castration to produce eunuchs for imperial service, alchemy, and the search for physical immortality on earth. Concerning their culture, he declares, 'of all the pagan sects known to Europe, I know of no people who fell into fewer errors in the early ages of their antiquity than did the Chinese'. They began by worshipping Heaven (*T'ien*) and the Most High God (*Shang-ti*), and had no gods who were patrons of vices, unlike the Greeks, Romans, or Egyptians. He denies that the Confucianists worshipped their ancestors or Confucius himself, and praises their insights. As for Buddhism, like Timothy Richard later (but with more caution) he believed that Buddhism contained influences from the West and that it had 'actually caught a glimpse of light from the Christian Gospels'.[46] However, he lamented the confusion and degradation that had overtaken both Buddhism and Taoism in China.

In his memoirs can be discerned Ricci's view of the relation between Chinese culture and Christianity which led Paul Li (Li Ying-shih) to say of the latter: 'It does away with idols and completes the law of the literati.'[47] The sentence sums up Ricci's mission admirably; it could serve as an epitome of both the way a good Chinese could accept conversion to Christianity and the way a properly trained Western missionary ought to present the Christian religion in China. Ricci's own skill in doing so deserves illustrating. In *The True Doctrine of the Lord of Heaven*, he wrote:

Our Lord of Heaven (*T'ien-chu*) is shown in the ancient classics to be the Most High God (*Shang-ti*). In the *Doctrine of the Mean* Confucius is quoted as saying, 'The rites used at the sacrificial altars are to serve the Most High God.' Chu Hsi commented, 'He refrains from mentioning the Lord Earth in order to save words.' I think Confucius understood that if one thing is mentioned, it cannot be considered two; why should he have wished to save words? In the chapter Chou Sung of the *Shang Shu* it is said, 'Wu Wang depended on his own strength; there is no one who could surpass him. Did he not achieve success and peace; the Most High God made him monarch'... In looking through the classics one by one, one may learn that the Most High God differs from the Lord of Heaven only in the name given him.⁴⁸

He thus adopted the idiom of the Chinese scholar, discussed the same texts he did, and yet set forth Christian doctrine in the course of doing so.

Numerous Chinese who did not become converts were not only impressed by Ricci and his teachings, but also influenced by them. Hsieh Chao-chih wrote of Ricci (or Li Ma-tou, the name by which he has passed into Chinese annals), 'This man understands the literary art; in Confucian elegance he is no different from a Chinese... I am very pleased by his ideas, since they are close to those of the literati, and he is more concerned with advising men than they are...'⁴⁹ Another scholar who befriended the Jesuits without becoming a convert, Chou Yüan-piao, replied to a letter of Ricci's thus:

I received a letter from Kuo Yang-lao [Lazzaro Cattaneo] and was overjoyed. I also received your letter; it is as if I were on an island seeing an extraordinary man. A few of your brother [priests] desire on the basis of the teaching of the Lord of Heaven to influence China; this aim of theirs is good and sincere. As I endeavor to fathom its inner meaning, that teaching is not contrary to the words of our country's sages, but our sages and Confucian scholars go into greater detail. Are you willing to agree that they are not at odds with one another? As for those differences which exist in minor matters, they lie in the realm of customs. You have been reading the *Book of Changes*; in it *ch'ien* is used to mean Heaven; thus we do know Heaven. I do not know whether you agree with me.⁵⁰

Still another, Wang T'ing-na, wrote a poem about Ricci:

> There is a man from the Far West who knows the Way,
> He concerns himself more about literature and thought than we;
> In the spirit of his thought there is neither Buddhism nor Taoism,
> His spirit is his own and yet like that of the Confucian scholar.⁵¹

Several scholars thus accepted Ricci's view that the Confucian classics contained not only ethical truth acceptable to all mankind including Christians, but also the beginnings of a cosmogony and even theology consonant with Christian conceptions. This was true of non-Christians as well as Christian converts. Of course, Ricci had his critics and opponents. Some even undertook to challenge his science; Wei Chün wrote,

We need not discuss other points, but just take for example the position of China on the map. He [Ricci] puts it not in the center but to the West and inclined to the North. This is altogether far from the truth, for China should be in the center of the world, which we can prove by the single fact that we can see the North Star resting at the zenith of the heaven at midnight...Those who trust him say that the people in his country are fond of traveling afar, but such an error as this would certainly not be made by a widely-traveled man.[52]

Note that even in attacking him, Wei Chün pays tribute to Ricci's influence ('those who trust him...'). The substance of Wei's observations is most charitably to be passed over without comment, and there were of course more sophisticated challenges to Ricci. There was also some simple jealousy. When a tomb was selected for him outside of Peking, a eunuch taunted one of the Chinese Jesuit brothers: 'Tell me, what is this mysterious potion possessed by your master, with which he so completely captivates the minds of so many men?' The brother replied: 'My Master has virtue and education and books, and the law of the Most High God, which he preaches on all occasions, and really, there is no more powerful concoction than that for captivating the minds of the great.'[53]

Ricci's 'concoction' had indeed proved its power; it remained to be seen whether his strategy could be applied as he envisaged over the necessary decades or perhaps centuries. He anticipated continuing obstacles from the Chinese side; it is doubtful if he expected the kind of furor among Roman Catholics in the West which was in fact to wreck their own mission in the 'rites controversy' – and also to stifle the influence of Western thought on China for a crucial century afterward.

THE CHINA MISSION UNDER SCHALL AND OTHERS (1610–1666)

During the half-century that followed Ricci's death, the Jesuits registered two notable achievements: ascendancy in the governmental calendrical bureau as a result of their demonstrated astronomical prowess, and successful survival of the fall of the Ming dynasty and the foundation of its successor, the Ch'ing. Simultaneously the first clouds of the approaching storm appeared as the critics of the Jesuits in Peking obtained the ear of more than one pope.

The Jesuits' astronomical successes were, considering the strength of the vested interests which they jeopardized, remarkably easy. In December 1610, after the imperial astronomers made an error in predicting an eclipse, Paul Hsü was instrumental in obtaining a decision by the emperor to entrust the reform of the Chinese calendar to the Jesuits. Under pressure of court intrigues, in 1616 the decision was withdrawn. However, after the arrival in Peking of the astronomically talented Johann Schall von Bell (discussed below), Hsü was able to raise the issue again. In 1629 he prevailed on the new Ch'ung-chen emperor to appoint him to take charge of calendrical reform, assisted by the Jesuits. They dominated the Bureau of the Calendar (Li Chü, renamed Ch'in T'ien Chien before the end of the reign) from 1629 to 1774[54] and beginning with Schall Jesuits were also titular heads of the Bureau during the whole period except for 1664-9.

There has been some controversy over the character of the Jesuit contribution to Chinese natural science and particularly mathematics and astronomy. The two 'most important features in European astronomy at the time', declares Needham, were the telescope and the Copernican heliocentric theory.[55] The Jesuits introduced the former but, he writes, 'after some hesitations, they held back' the latter. Duyvendak goes further to assert that during this period Chinese scholars were 'never...faced with the appalling vision of the "T'ien-hsia" flying through space as a mere speck of dust'.[56] D'Élia has produced sources to show clearly that Duyvendak is in error and that, on the contrary, Chinese works of the Jesuits as early as 1637 contain accounts of the heliocentric theory, although in those works they purport not to accept it.[57] D'Élia also points to the zeal with which the Jesuits propagated in China many of Galileo's discoveries which he had made by means of the telescope. At issue here is of course the condemnation of Galileo by the Church – or, more accurately, the condemnation of heliocentrism by the Holy Office in connection with the Galileo case in 1616 and the sentence against Galileo personally which was passed in 1633. This was presumably the reason for the Jesuits' failure to teach heliocentrism in China, since Ricci's old teacher, Clavius, had written to Galileo in 1610 that Jesuit astronomers 'had confirmed all his discoveries'[58] and we are entitled to assume that many Jesuits knew that the scientific evidence in favor of heliocentrism was overwhelming.

Needham points out that there were no direct implications for the problem of calendrical reform in the Jesuits' policy of not publicly espousing heliocentrism, as the Ptolemaic and heliocentric systems are mathematically strictly equivalent.[59] It may be added in defense of the consequences of that Jesuit policy that the Copernican system, chiefly because it retained the notion of circular motion in the heavens (though Kepler discovered elliptical motion, and Galileo probably knew of his discoveries, even Galileo did not attempt to revise Copernicus accordingly), still had its defects, and astronomy has long since ceased to hold that the sun (any more than the earth) was in the center of the universe or 'stood still'. Moreover, Chinese astronomy, like the Ptolemaic system, was geocentric and it would have been difficult to persuade the Chinese of heliocentrism. Such remarks, however, do not meet the fundamental issue. The issue is not one of supposed conflict between religion and science; St Augustine, St Thomas Aquinas, and other authorities had long held that the Bible could not be used to establish scientific fact, and there was no justification in the Holy Office's so doing in the decision of 1616, in Roman Catholic tradition or in the view of many influential contemporaries, including

Cardinal Barberini (later Pope Urban VIII). A modern Roman Catholic commentator writes, 'the theologians' treatment of Galileo was an unfortunate error; and, however it might be explained, it cannot be defended'.[60] But the problem was that the Jesuits, many of them knowing of the theological 'error' and the scientific fallaciousness of the Holy Office's decision, still were bound to obey it. The potential conflict between the intellectual pursuit of truth and discipline, already noted in the Society of Jesus, already was visible from the perspective of the Peking Fathers in 1616. At that time it did little damage in China; but in a few decades the conflict was to erupt there with fatal consequences.

When it comes to assessing the overall achievements of the Jesuits in China in the realm of science,[61] Needham notes among their faults their underestimation of the general state of 'the sciences in China', which may be partly ascribed to the fact that at the time, as he himself brings out, there were few Chinese who were familiar with the scientific achievements of their own relatively remote past; which means that Needham is chiefly saying that the Jesuits were unaware of much of the history of Chinese science (not of the science of their period), since it had been largely forgotten. He also declares that 'the Jesuits, with all their brilliance, were a strange mixture, for side by side with their science went a vivid faith in devils and exorcisms' – he has in mind passages from Ricci's diary.[62] Here one may urge a little caution. Where Christian and non-Christian priests once sought to drive out 'devils' today psychiatrists try to drive out complexes (or whatever name they give to the temporary mental states they hope to cure); however, the techniques of neither can thus far claim certain efficacy, while the analysis of the two groups (terminology aside) may not necessarily be mutually exclusive. More relevant may be the fact that no corpus of superior psychiatric knowledge was available in the sixteenth century and rejected or neglected (as was the case, as just noted, in astronomy).

The Jesuits, of course, were not primarily astronomers. Conscious of their own limitations, they repeatedly begged Rome for astronomical assistance and asked Galileo himself for aid. He never responded, apparently out of pique at the attitude of certain Jesuit critics of his in Rome (unfortunately Clavius's attitude was not shared by, for example, Bellarmine). The Jesuits had to do the best they could, which was quite enough to silence their competitors in China of the day and maintain their ascendancy in the calendrical office. Altogether, as Needham persuasively writes, 'if the bringing of the science and mathematics of Europe was for them a means to an end, it stands for all time nevertheless as an example of cultural relations at the highest level between two civilisations theretofore sundered'.[63]

After 1629 (except for 1664–9) the Jesuits' position in the calendrical bureau was firm, but they did not thereby always enjoy smooth relations with the imperial power or escape all persecution. Most serious was the fact that the Ming dynasty was showing signs of disintegration, and the problem was posed of what policies the Jesuits should follow if the dynastic cycle was about to revolve.

Already in 1617 Ricci's immediate successor as chief of the mission, Nicolò Longobardo, was confronted with a real threat when an imperial edict ordered the expulsion of the Jesuits from China. The man behind this rather abrupt act was Shen Ch'üeh, vice-president of the Board of Rites in Nanking. For months he had been persecuting Christians himself, and though he had been boldly and for a time effectively opposed by Paul Hsü, he prevailed in the edict of 1617. Fortunately for the Jesuits the edict was not fully enforced, and though some of them suffered physically and spiritually, the result was nothing more than a few difficult years. During some of them important literary work was done, especially in Hangchow, especially by Giulio Aleni, who earned the sobriquet of 'the Western Confucius' after he had proved himself a worthy pupil as well as the favorite of Yang T"ing-yün.

Reinforcements arrived in 1619. Nicolas Trigault had been sent back to Europe six years earlier to secure them, and had embarked in Portugal with twenty-two priests. Unfortunately he reached Macau with only four, but at least two of them, Johann Schreck (Terrentius) and Johann Adam Schall von Bell (T'ang Jo-wang), were men of towering stature, gifted in mathematics and astronomy as well as letters. After the unexpected and sudden death of Terrentius, Schall was in 1630 appointed to the Bureau of the Calendar. In a short period all three of the Chinese 'pillars' of the Church died: in 1627 Michael Yang, in 1630 Leo Li, in 1633 Paul Hsü. The Jesuits keenly felt their loss.

However, the Ch'ung-chen emperor (1628–44) still favored them, and in 1642 he called on Schall to manufacture cannon for the defense of Peking. During the 1630's two great threats to Ming power had arisen: a multitude of rebel ('bandit') leaders, chief of them Li Tzu-ch'eng, from Shensi, who was approaching Peking in the early 1640's, and the Manchus. From the first years of the century the tribal chieftain Nurhaci had begun expanding his power, and in 1616 had proclaimed himself first emperor of the Chin dynasty (later renamed Ch'ing). In 1621 he established a new capital at Liaoyang on the Liaotung peninsula. Repeated Chinese efforts to resist the Manchus failed, and when the rebel Li Tzu-ch'eng was marching on Peking, the Manchus awaited the lot of *tertius gaudens*. Schall's efforts were to no avail. The cannon were used not against Li but, as it turned out, against the emperor himself by his own eunuchs, who were trying to control a crowd in which the emperor had sought to hide himself. In 1644 Li took the capital, and the emperor hanged himself, ending the Ming dynasty.

At that moment, however, it was not completely clear that the end had come. There were still Ming troops who chose to ally themselves with the Manchus against the Chinese rebels. Li was defeated, the Manchus entered Peking, and a boy emperor was proclaimed with the reign title Shun-chih. Two Ming princes tried to continue the struggle, one in Fukien and in Chekiang. The latter adventure lasted only a few months, but the Fukien regime held out for a time, and some Jesuits served it. The T'ang Wang, its leader, immediately summoned the Jesuit Francesco Sambiasi to take office. Sambiasi came to Fukien, but refused the appointment. In 1646 the T'ang Wang was captured and executed by the Ch'ing forces, but his cause was taken up by another prince, the Kuei Wang, whose chief assistants were Christians. He was proclaimed emperor in Chaoch'ing, as it happened the site of Ricci's first establishment on the mainland. His fortunes waxed and waned. In the meantime the Christian eunuch Achilles P'ang T'ien-shou, one of his close advisers, brought the Jesuit Andreas Koffler into the court. Koffler converted the Kuei Wang's wife and baptized her as Anna, his mother as Maria, his father's legal wife as Helena, his baby son as Constantine.

This fleeting pseudomorphosis of Byzantium in Southern China ended in tragedy. The dowager empress Helena wrote letters to the pope and the general of the Society of Jesus asking for help, and Achilles P'ang wrote another to the pope; one Michel Boym was dispatched as messenger with them.[64] Although he was amply supplied with proof of the authenticity of his errand, he was attacked as a fraud and ignored by the papacy for three years. At last Alexander VII received him, and he hastened back, to find that Helena had been dead for some time. The Kuei Wang was in the process of being driven into Burma, whence he and his son Constantine were extradited and then strangled in 1662. Boym died in 1659, one more victim of the inability of the Jesuits in China to get the attention of authorities in Rome.

The Jesuits did not, however, count heavily on the success of the posterior Mings; they tried to prepare for the possibility of Manchu victory as well. Adam Schall was the only foreigner to remain in Peking during the fighting. From the outset he won Manchu favor, and within months of their capture of Peking he was appointed director of the calendrical bureau, after refusing six times.

Schall subsequently made achievements denied to Ricci, of whom he was a worthy successor.[65] He had entered the Jesuit order in 1607 in Köln, attended the German College in Rome 1608–11, completed his studies in 1617, and accompanied Trigault to the Far East. He had aimed to prepare the way for conversion of the last Ming emperor by first making converts of a number of eunuchs and women of the palace, from 1632 on. Apparently the Ch'ung-chen emperor was impressed and did not impede but even seems to have facilitated Schall's efforts.[66] The overthrow of the Mings, however, meant that he had to make a new start.

During the next seventeen years Schall developed a truly remarkable friendship with the young Shun-chih emperor, who used to visit him frequently and stretch out on Schall's bed with a book. The young man insisted that Schall adopt as his own grandson the five-year-old son of his majordomo, who was devoted to Schall though none too discreet about repeating Schall's sharp judgments of other people. The emperor came to call Schall 'Ma-fa', a Manchu phrase meaning 'Honorable Father', used by a son to a father or a pupil to a master.[67] Schall was awarded repeated honors until in 1658 he became Imperial Chamberlain, mandarin of the first class, first division. The missionary believed that the emperor had accepted much of Christian teaching, and that monogamy alone stood between him and conversion. In the last three years of the emperor's life, however, Schall encountered difficulties. Eunuchs and Ch'an (Zen) Buddhist monks gained in influence, and the emperor became infatuated with his half-brother's wife. Moreover, two Jesuits in Peking had mounted a campaign against Schall: the Portuguese Gabriel de Magalhães and the Sicilian Ludovico Buglio. They carried their charges, which dealt with his calendrical work and his acceptance of court titles, as well as with his personal morals, to Rome. However, the charges endangering his scientific work were dismissed, and by 1657 the judgment vindicating Schall had reached China. The emperor, who despite his turn in another direction had retained his love and respect for Schall, died in 1661.

Once again Schall had to contend with new imperial authority, this time with little success. In the first years of the new K'ang-hsi reign, a powerful courtier, Yang Kuang-hsien, attempted to destroy Schall. At length Yang secured the condemnation of Schall, his assistant Ferdinand Verbiest, and (with poetic justice) Schall's antagonists Magalhães and Buglio. Schall was sentenced to death, the others to imprisonment. A great earthquake and fire seem to have given Schall's defenders courage, and the four Jesuits were released. Schall died not long afterwards, in 1666.

During his last months Schall indited a confession of faults which were doubtless real ones. He had been too cavalier with his superiors, too harsh with some of his fellows, too mild with his servant. Certainly he was less saintly than Ricci, less patient with fools, less cautious about adopting Chinese customs that risked disharmony with his religious precepts. His achievements, however, were enormous. He triumphantly justified the astronomical science of the West, on which the Jesuits had staked so much; the challenge to it of Yang Kuang-hsien proved only temporarily successful. Finally, Schall had come near to converting a reigning emperor. The situation seemed favorable indeed for Christianity in China. In 1663 the Visitor da Gama reported that there were 114,000 Christians in the empire; in 1664 the vice-provincial, Le Fèvre, wrote that 'the Manchus allow the Gospel to be preached with the same freedom which prevails in Europe'.[68] It was a rather flat statement. The Manchus were still capable of seizing Schall and sentencing him to death (though he was, as noted, pardoned); some risks still attended the preaching of Christianity in China. So were there risks in Europe for any given priest or preacher, if he was a Catholic in a Protestant state or a Protestant in a Catholic state. The fact was that in China no significant impediments were being offered to the propagation of Christianity, at least by those who followed Ricci's policies. That, however, proved to be a crucial qualification in the following decades.

VERBIEST AND THE RITES CONTROVERSY (1666–1722)

Schall's successor as leading spirit of the mission was Ferdinand Verbiest (Nan Huai-jen), who was already serving as his assistant.[69] A great Fleming followed the great Italian and the great German who had led the mission thus far. Born in 1623, he had entered the Jesuit novitiate at Malines and studied at Louvain and Courtrai. At the age of twenty-two he decided to be a missionary, and in 1647 made an effort to go to Latin America. Having been unsuccessful, he continued studies at Brussels, Rome, and Seville, where he finished his theological work. In 1657 he embarked for China at the summons of Schall with 14 other missionaries, 7 of whom died *en route* to Macau. After six months in Shensi he was called to Peking by Schall in 1660. The Shun-chih emperor died the next year, and Verbiest shared in the subsequent persecutions of Christians. In 1668, however, the young K'ang-hsi emperor dissolved the regency, and Verbiest was given the opportunity to demonstrate his astronomical prowess and, dramatically predicting where the shadow of a marker would fall on a plank, was ordered to repeat his success in the presence of the emperor. As a result he was entrusted with the supervision of the calendar in 1669. The emperor allowed 25 missionaries detained at Canton to return to the provinces, raised a monument to the dead Schall, and made himself Verbiest's pupil in various studies.

Verbiest thus rapidly developed an intimacy with the K'ang-hsi emperor paralleling that of Schall's with the Shun-chih emperor; indeed it was carried even further. Not only his knowledge of astronomy but his engineering skill was called upon. He repaired Schall's cannon and manufactured new ones, worked out a means of safely transporting enormous blocks of granite across the weak Marco Polo Bridge, constructed fountains that set bells ringing at fixed times and pumps to bring water into the palace, and performed many technical and scientific tasks while in attendance upon the indefatigable young emperor. He was rewarded with high office and the ennobling of his ancestors. If the emperor had not been so insistent on his accompanying him on his manifold journeys, Verbiest might have lived beyond the age of sixty. He died exhausted in 1688, too soon to see two events for which he had helped pave the way: the Treaty of Nerchinsk between China and Russia in 1689 and the edict of 1692 granting religious toleration to Chinese Christians.

It was during Verbiest's tenure in Peking that the storm gathered which was to undo much of the Jesuits' work and to shatter forever Ricci's dream of conversion of China through the Confucian literati. The conflict was one among Roman Catholic Westerners; Chinese and Manchus, including the emperor himself, took a part, but were not permitted to have a say in the crucial disputes, and resentment at that fact was one factor in the outcome. The conflict was partly political and partly intellectual. The political side, if it may be so called, involved chiefly the rivalry between the Jesuits and the mendicant orders, especially Franciscans and Dominicans, but also the

Jesuits' disputes with the more fundamentalist Jansenists, the papacy and its various subordinate agencies in Rome being summoned to decide the validity of charges and counter-charges. The intellectual side[70] involved three particular issues, all hinging on the degree of truth to be assigned to parts of Confucian doctrine and the respect to be accorded Chinese cultural tradition. The first was whether to permit certain ceremonies in honor of Confucius; the question was related to whether Confucian ethics were to be judged more or less consonant with Christianity. The second was whether to permit reverence toward the familial dead by way of prostrations, offerings of incense, food, and so forth (often called 'ancestor worship'). The 'Rites' which figured in the controversy were chiefly these two, honoring Confucius and the familial dead. The third issue on the intellectual side was the so-called 'term question': whether to interpret certain words employed in the Confucian classics, chiefly *T'ien* (heaven) and *Shang-ti* (the Lord Above), as consonant with the Christian idea of God – in other words, whether to credit the ancient Chinese with a monotheistic belief. There was no doubt in the minds of any of the missionaries that the 'Rites' had become entwined with superstitious practices and notions. The question was, were they separable from the latter? Ricci had in his pragmatic of December 1603, which had been approved by Valignano, authorized the two Rites, while his other writings had interpreted the two classical Chinese terms *T'ien* and *Shang-ti* as referring to God.

The political and intellectual sides of the intra-Catholic conflict, as they have been described, were related, at least in this respect: conversion of the mandarins, a highly educated and fastidious group of men, accustomed to treating (often with some justification) the culture of outsiders as inferior, was at best an intricate and hazardous enterprise, requiring the greatest consistency, discipline, and restraint from the missionaries. A few reckless acts or statements could instantly imperil the whole enterprise. The clumsiness of the mendicants, who scorned the Jesuits' notion of intellectual apostolate, constantly endangered the latter. After 1631 the Jesuits were particularly embarrassed by Spanish friars from the Philippines, boat loads of whom would periodically wash up on the coast, march through the streets of the nearest town preaching 'Christ crucified' at the top of their lungs in Latin which was promptly interpreted by a native; the result was apt to be anger from the Chinese hearers and arrest by the civil authorities. The Jesuits were, because of these and other less dramatic incidents, anxious to prevent the mendicant Franciscans and Dominicans from flooding into China.

In 1585 Gregory XIII had upheld Valignano's pleas on this issue; but Clement VIII in 1600, Paul V in 1608, and Urban VIII in 1633 had opened the way for the mendicant orders to enter China. Decade after decade, in consequence, the mendicants would, through their own maladroitness, get themselves into trouble with Chinese authorities, thereupon often calling on the irritated Jesuits for help in getting out. Still more serious a danger, however, was the mendicant orders' repeated indictment of the Jesuits to Rome.

The first challenge was contained in a letter of the Dominican Juan Bautista Morales of 1639, in which he attacked Jesuit methods of accommodation.[71] In brief, the charges were that the Jesuits did not impose the obligation of fasting on the Chinese, that they did not use all the prescribed forms in baptizing women, that they did not declare that Confucius was in hell, that they did not insist on monogamy, and they did not proclaim the doctrine of the Crucifixion. The first three charges were true, the second two false. The Congregation for the Propagation of the Faith (*de Propaganda Fide*, created in 1622 as a means of removing mission policy from the hands of the Spaniards and Portuguese and centralizing it in Rome) did not ask the Jesuits (whom Morales shrewdly refrained from mentioning by name) to reply, but condemned the practices specified (some of them thus involving the 'Rites'), and Innocent X upheld the decision in 1645.

A Jesuit, Martino Martini, was thereupon sent to Rome to try to show that Morales's description of the Rites and of Jesuit practice was not accurate. This time the case was transferred to the Holy Office. The result was that Alexander VII, in 1656, in effect reversed the previous decision and approved the Ricci position.[72] Especially after this, the majority of Franciscans, some Dominicans (among them the first Chinese bishop, Gregorio Lopez or Lo Wen-tsao, Vicar Apostolic of Nanking), and numerous Augustinians (led by Bishop Alvaro Benevente) accepted the Ricci methods in most respects. A decree of Clement IX in 1669, concluding an appeal by the Dominican Juan Polanco against that of 1656, left it unchanged.[73]

The Jesuit position was, however, soon challenged by a new ecclesio-political force, the French secular priests of the Missions Etrangères (organized in 1684). In 1659 the pope consecrated three bishops for China, chief among them François Pallu. In transmitting to Pallu the instructions of the Secretary of *Propaganda Fide*, the archivist wrote: 'Beware of the Jesuits, principally the Portuguese, hide your plans from them until you reach the Indies, but keep on friendly terms with them in other respects.'[74] One of the other bishops chosen, Lambert de la Motte, wrote: 'It is to be wished that no more Jesuits should remain in the Indies, for they have corrupted the Gospel: I realised that God wished that the Society be humiliated.'[75]

Malcolm Hay in his study *Failure in the Far East* seeks to prove that an anti-Jesuit conspiracy of Jansenists was at work throughout the final phase of the Rites Controversy. The study has been criticized for inaccuracy and oversimplification, no doubt with justice. However, it seems clear enough from the sources Hay cites that the newly dispatched missionaries had far from open minds at least in respect to the political side of the conflict. Pallu reached the Far East in 1674, but was arrested in Manila by the Spaniards and returned to Rome without visiting Japan or China. That did not prevent him from reporting at length to the pope on Far Eastern missions and bitterly attacking them. As a result, the pope imposed a new oath of obedience to the Vicars Apostolic, raising problems of conflict with civil allegiance as well as the exemption from episcopal jurisdiction previously granted by the papacy to the major religious orders. In 1683 Verbiest wrote to Bishop Lopez that if the Chinese government ever heard about any oaths of obedience, it might mean the end of the whole China mission.[76]

Bishop Pallu finally landed in China, at Amoy, in January 1684, but he died in October without getting out of Fukien province. His successor as administrator of the China mission was Charles Maigrot, Vicar Apostolic (but not bishop) of Fukien. On 26 March 1693 he promulgated an order condemning the teachings of Ricci, forbidding the rites honoring Confucius and the familial dead, and prohibiting the use of the terms *T'ien* and *Shang-ti* for God. The timing of this order was spectacularly ill-advised; it followed by just a year the imperial edict of toleration, itself climaxing over a hundred years of the painstaking and patient work of the Jesuits. At the same time, however, it came when the K'ang-hsi emperor was most ready to support the Jesuits. In 1700 the latter presented an exposition of their understanding of the meaning of the rites to the highest Chinese authority, namely the emperor himself; he responded on 30 November by confirming the accuracy of their interpretation *in toto*: 'there is not a word which needs changing'.

The action of the Jesuits in appealing to the emperor infuriated the critics of the Ricci policies, both then and since. Arnold Rowbotham writes that 'it would seem to an impartial observer that by appealing to the head of a "heathen" nation for interpretation of a matter which was still *sub-judice* at Rome the Jesuits had committed an act of indiscretion which was not likely to allay bitterness or to bring nearer the solution of the problem'.[77] K. M. Panikkar, a fiercely anti-Western Indian nationalist, here becomes solicitous of the sensibilities of the pope, who 'naturally felt that in a matter concerning faith and doctrine, the Jesuits were appealing to an authority outside the church in order to force his own hand'.[78] Marshall Broomhall, an evangelical Protestant, writes: 'Strange as it may seem, while the Jesuits in Europe were upholding the infallibility of the Pope in their conflict with the Jansenists, in China, on the contrary, they denied that the Pope had any power or authority to determine the meaning of a single Chinese word.'[79] Such non-Catholic authors seem to have invented a Roman Catholic doctrine to the effect that the papacy possesses some special competence in matters of fact concerning the customs of distant lands.[80]

One would in any event think that non-Catholic scholars might be concerned about the substance of the dispute (since Catholic scholars are prohibited from discussing it) as well as the question of the proper procedure to be followed within the Roman Church. On this issue, modern scholarship has much to say in the Jesuits' favor. Joseph Needham has recently declared:

The texts thus said one thing and the Neo-Confucian commentaries said something quite different. . . In the first case Chinese thought needed only a minimum of revealed religion to assume the status of Catholic Christianity; in the second China was a land of atheists and agnostics. We can see now that to a large extent Ricci was right, and if the Jesuits had persisted in interpreting the ancient texts along these lines ultimate historical researches would have justified them.[81]

Of course Ricci and his successors did persist, to the outer limits of what their discipline required and, some would say, beyond. They had, however, been constantly harassed not merely by people who took a different view but by amateur, indeed incompetent, Sinologists among the courtiers of the papacy and newly-arrived missionaries in China. It is scarcely to be wondered at that they attempted to establish once and for all, through Chinese authority, facts about Chinese culture fundamental to the dispute to which they were party – a dispute on which hung the future of the Church in China.

It did the Jesuits no good to submit the K'ang-hsi emperor's opinion to Rome. On 20 November 1704 Clement XI signed a decree confirming Maigrot's order of 1693. However, he had already sent to China a legate, Charles Thomas Maillard de Tournon, Patriarch of Antioch, charged with studying part of the facts at first hand.[82] The preconceptions Tournon brought to the task were demonstrated by the fact that in passing through India in 1704, without knowing anything of Indian history, religions, or languages, he issued a condemnation of the so-called 'Malabar rites', acceptance of which had eased the task of such great Jesuits in India as Roberto di Nobili. In 1705 Tournon reached Canton, and was told that an official welcome awaited him in Peking. A prolonged struggle between his party and the Jesuits ensued, but one for which the former was ill-prepared.

Maigrot was summoned from Fukien to assist Tournon, and a fateful interview with the emperor occurred. The question was Maigrot's competence on matters of fact concerning Chinese culture. The unfortunate Maigrot proved unable to repeat a passage from the classics at the emperor's request (upon which the emperor himself repeated several pages of the work), unable to read three of the four characters on a scroll hanging behind the throne, unable to recognize Ricci's Chinese name or to state that he had read Ricci's *The True Doctrine of the Lord of Heaven*. In rage and frustration, he bellowed that the emperor was an atheist and China a land of atheists, then refused to retract the statements. The emperor subsequently wrote of Maigrot: 'A man in this empire who should show such ignorance would move the hearers to laughter. Not understanding the sense of the Books he cannot say what they contain, as he affirms.'[83] By the time he had written this, the emperor had banished Maigrot and two other members of the Tournon mission, who there-upon returned to Europe.

Maigrot made himself ridiculous; Tournon did not do much better. He lost his temper a few weeks after the Maigrot interview and shouted at the Jesuit Father Anton Thomas, declaring: 'If the devils had come to Peking from hell, they could not have done worse things against the Religion and the Holy See than the Jesuits have done. The Emperor is your slave, who speaks and acts only according to your suggestions. I advise you and all the Fathers of your Society to leave China.' He scorned the whole intellectual apostolate of the Jesuits, acknowledging sarcastically that 'we cannot compete with them in the art of making clocks, playing the violin, checking the Calendar, and making jam for the Emperor's table.'[84] It was made clear that there was nothing further for him to do in Peking, so he returned to the south. *En route* he stopped at Nanking and repeated, in a letter to the missionaries, the major points of the Maigrot order of 1693 on the Rites and the terms for God. The emperor thereupon ordered his arrest, holding him to be in defiance of the imperial will, and he was handed over to the Portuguese in Macau, where he was imprisoned and died in 1710.

Even then all was not lost. In December 1706 the emperor ordered that all missionaries were to be queried regarding their acceptance of the 'practices of Ricci'; if they responded affirmatively, they might receive a residence certificate and remain in China; otherwise they were to be expelled. The Peking Jesuits, the Portuguese clergy, the Franciscan bishop in Peking, the Augustinian vicar apostolic of Kwangsi, and others ignored Tournon's letter and awaited a ruling from Rome. In March 1715 Clement XI, in the constitution *Ex illa die*, reiterated the 1693 prohibitions of Maigrot. Even then the Jesuits, with the support of the emperor, delayed submission. The papacy thought it prudent to send still another legate to China, and in 1719 dispatched George Ambrose de Mezzabarba, Patriarch of Alexandria. He was a diplomat as Tournon was not, and sought to soften the force of *Ex illa die* by granting eight 'permissions' abrogating secretly and partially some of its strictures. They were satisfactory to no one, and were soon repudiated by the papacy. Benedict XIV, in the constitution *Ex quo singulari* of 1742, renewed the Maigrot strictures and prescribed an oath to be taken by all Roman Catholic missionaries in China.[85]

The Rites Controversy was at an end. So was the Jesuits' chance of converting the Chinese. It is difficult to fix the precise moment at which hope vanished; perhaps the death of the K'ang-hsi emperor in 1722 is the crucial event, for he supported the Peking Fathers to the last. His son, the Yung-cheng emperor, took a very different line. He revived and reaffirmed the 'Sacred Edict' of 1691 by which Christianity had been branded 'uncanonical'; thus the 1692 edict of toleration was ignored, and active if sporadic persecution of the remaining Christians followed. In 1726 it was reported that out of the 7,000 Christians in Peking, more than half had apostatized, including nearly all the literati. It is not surprising that latter-day Chinese writers,[86] soberly discussing their forefathers of the sixteenth and seventeenth centuries, feel compelled to defend them against 'charges' of having been Christians and converts at the hands of Westerners who in their own day, before the disastrous intervention of the papacy, were widely accepted as friends of China—converts to a religion which was then regarded by many, including the emperor himself, as compatible with much of the Chinese traditional culture if not specifically (to use Paul Li's phrase) 'completing the law of the literati'.

THE LAST DECADES OF THE JESUIT MISSION (1689–1774)

Paying tribute to Ricci, Schall, and Verbiest, Rowbotham writes that after the death of the last of these three great men 'the cause of Christianity was steadily to lose ground in the capital until its final disappearance with the missionaries who upheld it'.[87] This is a statement of doubtful accuracy. The previous pages should already have made clear that the Peking Fathers were in no serious difficulty with the Chinese during the opening decades of the Rites Controversy. Probably not until the K'ang-hsi emperor's order of 1706 that missionaries pledge adherence to the 'practices of Ricci' or be expelled was there any serious question about whether the Peking mission was to continue and whether Christianity was to enjoy as before official patronage; probably not until the emperor died in 1722 was at least the latter question answered. George H. Dunne is therefore doubtless right when he writes that the forty years following 1671 (the year of the restoration to the provinces of the missionaries exiled in 1664) 'saw the fortunes of the mission rise to their highest point'.[88] In other words, from the 1670's to the 1710's may be taken to be the period at which not only did the prospects for continued conversions seem brightest, but when the intellectual impact, on Christian and non-Christian Chinese alike, reached its peak.

The Treaty of Nerchinsk between Russia and China was concluded in 1689. Its diplomatic significance need not be explored here; it was important in that it was the first treaty made by China with a foreign power on the basis of equality, and to that extent reflected the impact of the West, particularly its newly formulated ideas of international law; even the language of the final text, which was Latin, mirrored a conception of foreign relations which was totally new to China. It was therefore logical that the Jesuits, who had contributed so much to making known such conceptions in China (and had done something of the sort in Russia also, as discussed in earlier chapters), should take a prominent part in the negotiations. Verbiest, before he died, was instrumental in arranging that Thomas Pereira be named to the Chinese delegation, and the latter was accompanied by Jean François Gerbillon, newly arrived in China. Verbiest hoped for two outcomes, which depended on both Russia's and China's being more or less satisfied with the result of the negotiations: he wished the overland route through Siberia and Moscow to be made available to the Jesuits, in place of the sea route endangered by the Dutch maritime ascendancy of the seventeenth century;[89] and he desired the position of the Peking Fathers to be made more secure. Not merely in assuring a mutually acceptable outcome but in conducting the negotiations, the Jesuits played an important part, as 'documentators and interpreters' at a time when neither Russians nor Chinese knew anything much about the other but when the Jesuits had reasonably good information on both, and also as intermediaries and negotiators.[90] Although the chief Russian negotiator, F. A. Golovin, was profuse in his acknowledgment of the Jesuits' assistance and 'heaped favors on them',[91] the Russian attitude to the Jesuits was just in the process of changing, for reasons more weighty than the outcome at Nerchinsk,[92] and the overland route remained beyond their grasp.

It indeed appears as if the gratitude of the Manchus, especially of Prince Songgotu (So-e-t'u), the chief negotiator, was a factor in the imperial decree of 22 March 1692, granting religious toleration to the Chinese Christians. However, it may be too categorical to term this edict simply 'a reward for their [the Jesuits'] services'.[93] Their services to Russia did not coincide with rising favor towards them in Moscow; their services to China crowned almost a century of hard labor in Peking in which their prestige had, with a few ups and downs, mounted rather steadily. The decree reads in part:

[The Jesuits] are in charge of astronomy and the [Bureau of the Calendar]... They have applied themselves assiduously to the founding of canon and the making of war armaments, which were used in the recent internal disturbances. When they were sent to Nipchou [Nerchinsk] with our ambassadors to arrange a treaty of peace with the Muscovites, they succeeded in bringing these negotiations to a successful conclusion. They have, therefore, rendered great service to the empire. The Europeans in the provinces have never been accused of any misdemeanor or of having caused any disorder. The doctrines that they teach are not evil nor are they capable of leading the people astray or of causing disturbances... We must, then... permit everyone to go to [the Christian churches]... to worship God, without fear of molestation...[94]

This decree, given the changeable character of Chinese law,[95] might not have been expected to endure forever. The immediate prospects, however, were bright. Soon afterward, the Jesuit prescription of quinine for an illness of the emperor that was apparently malaria was efficacious. In 1693, in consequence, the Fathers were permitted to move into the Imperial City, where they built a beautiful church consecrated in 1703.

The three lonely titans who had in succession led the mission were gone, but in their place were a number of gifted Jesuits and Catholic laymen: Fr Filippo Maria Grimaldi, director of the Bureau of the Calendar; Thomas Pereira (d. 1708), who had extraordinary musical gifts and was chosen by the emperor to teach him Western music, who originated the writing of music by characters, who distinguished himself at Nerchinsk, and had other talents; Jean François Gerbillon (d. 1707), who in twelve months had mastered both Manchu and Chinese in order to act as a successful diplomat at Nerchinsk, and was tutoring the emperor in philosophy and geometry; the layman Giovanni Gherardini, who was conducting a school of oil painting in Peking, and whom the emperor tried his best to dissuade from returning to Europe in 1704; the lay brother Rhodes, who was imperial apothecary, with the right to accompany the emperor on his journeys; Frs Joachim Bouvet (d. 1732) and

Claude de Visdelou (d. 1737), who gave mathematical instruction to the crown prince; at least six other fathers were of comparable distinction in the arts or sciences.[96]

When the K'ang-hsi emperor was followed by his son, the Yung-cheng emperor (1722–35) and the latter by his son, the Ch'ien-lung emperor (1736–96), Jesuits were no longer used as advisers and diplomats, but their knowledge and skill kept them still at court until the abolition of the Society of Jesus in 1773 by the papal decree *Dominus ac redemptor*. Among the Jesuits of this era were Antoine Gaubil (d. 1759), perhaps the greatest Jesuit sinologist, elected member of the Imperial Russian Academy of Sciences and the Royal Society in London, and supervisor of the Imperial College where noble Manchu youths were trained for the diplomatic service; Dominique Parennin (d. 1741), admired by Voltaire, inspirer of the cartographic survey from which came the great atlas of China (1735) that was the first based on scientific observations made *in situ*; J. H. M. de Prémare, who despite his dubious 'Figurist'[97] opinions was a great scholar of the Chinese classics; Joseph Castiglione, court painter from 1715 to 1765, who with Michel Benoît constructed several buildings in the Western style in the Yüan-ming-yüan or Summer Palace – these, the main monuments left by the Jesuits, were through another historical irony destroyed by other Westerners, British and French soldiers, in the war of 1860. There were others worthy of note up to Augustin de Hallerstein, director of the Bureau of the Calendar who died in 1774, prostrated by the shock of learning of the worldwide suppression of the Society of Jesus by Clement XIV the previous year.

Chinese Christians were making important contributions to culture. The 'three pillars' were long dead. One convert, Lo Wen-tsao, a Dominican who took the name Gregorio Lopez, in 1674 had been made vicar apostolic of Nanking and titular bishop of Basileus; he died in 1691 in Macau, just before news arrived that he had been named first bishop of Nanking. He was one of those to appeal for reconfirmation of the earlier brief of Paul V's of 1615 approving the use of Chinese as a liturgical language, and was rather crudely rebuffed by the *Propaganda Fide*.[98] The refusal of Rome to countenance the liturgy in Chinese was an obstacle to the possibility of bringing Chinese scholars into the priesthood. It is true that Rome permitted ordination of older Chinese who had had theological training in their own language provided that they learn enough Latin by rote to administer the sacraments, but though the literati might have found that not difficult, they may well have felt some repugnance at making use of that concession.

The only Chinese bishop until the twentieth century was thus not a Jesuit, but a number of Chinese did enter the Society of Jesus. The first Chinese Jesuit to become a priest, Cheng Wei-hsin, who took the name Emmanuel de Siqueira, accompanied Alexandre de Rhodes to Europe in 1645 and was ordained, after the full fourteen years of Jesuit schooling, probably in 1663 at the age of thirty (as compared with Bishop Lopez, ordained at the age of forty-four after only three years' study). Obviously he possessed extra-ordinary linguistic gifts, learning Armenian well enough to pass as an Armenian among the Turks when they were seeking to detain him, and being selected to teach European youth in the Roman College for three years. His chance to enter into the China mission effort came only in 1669, when he was already very ill, and he died in 1673, too early to use his unusual ability fully, though thirty years later he was being venerated along with Étienne Fabre (Le Fèvre) as a saint among Peking Christians.[99] In 1688 three Chinese Jesuits were ordained priests by Bishop Lopez, one of whom was a scholar, Wu Li, one of the great artists of the Ch'ing period.[100] There were a few later ordinations. Father Rouleau comments, however, that 'finding candidates from among the Christian scholar class who possessed the necessary qualifications [to be unmarried or widowered, to promise celibacy, to be of exceptional moral life] was a problem that even the most articulate defenders of [a Chinese] clergy and liturgy confessed to be practically insoluble'.[101] Some who were not scholars were ordained. But whatever the dimensions of this problem, it did not in the seventeenth century rank as one of the major obstacles to the growth of the Chinese Church.

Among the Chinese Christians were members of the imperial family. One, Prince Te P'ei, wrote in the eighteenth century, when it was no longer wise to profess Christianity openly:

What heaven has bestowed upon us is the greater thing; what we have received from our fathers and mothers is the lesser thing. The greater thing is eternal; the lesser thing is only temporary. Man has these two things; if he follows the lesser and forgets the greater, he cannot meet the standard of the universe.[102]

Ch'en Yüan comments, 'in sum, he covertly recognizes that beyond fathers and mothers there is a Heavenly Father'.

There were many literati who met and were influenced by the Jesuits without necessarily becoming converts. Thus Huang Ching-fang wrote concerning Giulio Aleni in the mid-seventeenth century:

I judge concerning Mr Ai Szu-chi [Aleni], from meeting him, that he is respect-ful and sincere, pure-hearted and humble, indeed has the manner of a great scholar, and thus deserves respect. Ah! He has acquired the manner of a great scholar; he especially respects those who translate important books; he has come eighty thousand li. In contrast, we recline at ease and eat our fill, do not venture a glance at the outside world, and shamelessly and minutely criticize their [Westerners'] strengths and weaknesses. Is that not something to be ashamed of?[103]

Among them were men deeply influenced by the scientific learning the Jesuits brought with them. For example, the mathematician Mei Wen-ting wrote to a friend, Hsüeh I-fu, who was a close collaborator of the Polish missionary and mathematician Jean-Nicolas Smogułęcki:

I look at European learning,
   At times I devoted myself to it.
Reflecting on it, I forgot to sleep and eat;
   Its hidden meaning penetrated my spirit.
I regret that I inhabit a high mountain,
   Where I rarely encounter strange books.
I want to pursue study in them,
   But what I learn from them is difficult to reconcile with what I
                                          have known.
How can I desert the literati
   And instead pursue Western thoughts?
If I wish for a time to study problems of the calendar,
   People will say I am disloyal to old traditions.
If I am to behave uprightly in this world
   How can I become different in the end from what I was at the start?
Only in my later years have I begun to receive your letters,
   And they clearly lift the veil, as if from my mind.
I have no need to serve Jesus,
   And yet I can study Western books exhaustively.
I understand that one who consults T'an Tzu[104]
   Does not betray the spirit of men of olden times.
Would that I could walk in your footsteps
   So that I could be your student and that my eyes could be opened![105]

The joint work of Smogułęcki and Hsüeh had real significance, introducing 'spherical trigonometry and logarithms into China';[106] and Mei himself did important work in popularizing the new Western mathematics. Attracted powerfully by Western science, less so or not at all by Christianity, he well illustrates the intellectual impact of the China mission outside of religion.

The official Ming dynastic history, composed in a later era, of anti-Christian and anti-Western feeling, states: 'After Ma-tou [Ricci] came to China, a number of other priests followed him. In Nanking a certain Wang Feng-su [Alfonso Vagnani] preached Christianity to deceive our people. From among the gentry (shih ta-fu) and the common people there were many who were attracted to it...'[107] In this account there is no suggestion of the fact that the China mission was destroyed not by Chinese, but by Europeans, and that in the climactic phase of the struggle which brought about destruction the Jesuits were given unequivocal support by many Chinese, common people, scholars, and the emperor himself.

CONCLUSION

The Jesuit achievement in China in early modern times is summed up by an aggressive Chinese nationalist of the twentieth century who is a bitter critic of contemporary Christian missions:

The Jesuits have given China the best of what contemporary Europe could give, and they have interpreted the spirit of China in a way that no Chinese could have improved upon. They came to China essentially as students and servants, true to the spirit of their faith, not as missionaries of a 'superior' religion or as 'civilisers' like their modern successors.[108]

Their achievement was great indeed. But there was not only achievement, but also an opportunity – one whose realization, to a greater or lesser degree, would have changed world history. The Jesuits of the sixteenth and seventeenth centuries had an opportunity to convert the Chinese Empire – possibly to gain imperial patronage and widespread popular support, as the Buddhists had done in China in the early centuries of the Christian era, more likely to win an influential segment of the literati and a small if growing fraction of the ordinary people, as Roman Catholics did in Viet Nam.

What was before 1715 not merely a possibility but a reality was the establishment of a footing for a Chinese Christian civilization – not one that renounced or apologized for the Confucian tradition, but one that built on it with all its strengths and weaknesses, one that did not indiscriminately borrow Western ideas or techniques but used them in advancing a philosophically worked-out syncretist position. A significant number of Chinese intellectuals had decided that Confucianism should be purified of later accretions, as Ricci had indicated, and that it could thus be harmonized with Western science and learning and also with the Christian religion.

After the Rites Controversy and finally the Yung-cheng emperor's edict of 1724 banning Christianity, this kind of syncretist searching on the cultural level became impossible. In fact a number of Chinese Christian families retained their Christianity until modern times – the family of Paul Hsü is only one example. However, thereafter Roman Catholicism was reduced to tallying baptisms. It could not play a further role in the cultural realm comparable to the one Ricci and his successors had given it in China. Chinese intellectuals might ponder the worth of syncretism in private, and that was all. Syncretism in the form of a combination of a purified Confucianism with Western learning and Roman Catholic Christianity was discredited. A Chinese Christian culture could hope for successful growth only if the literati regarded it as a respectable alternative, whether or not they became converts or students of it in various ways. Many had already come so to regard it. However, if they were to continue to do so, the Jesuits themselves must continue to work in the cultural field and to earn the respect the literati might accord anyone with sound knowledge and appreciation of Chinese civilization. The Peking Jesuits understood that, and their opponents did not, and in comparison to those facts all the particular events of the Rites Controversy, the rudeness and adroitness of this or that person or agency pale to insignificance. The essence of the imbroglio is exemplified in the passing vignette of poor Maigrot attempting in vain to read a few Chinese characters to the emperor. He was ignorant of China; he did not care for China (under pressure shouting that it was a land of atheists, which even the non-Christian literati had come under Jesuit influence to regard as an insult); and yet he undertook to dictate to China.

It is difficult to maintain that this point has been fully understood. Row-botham writes that if the Jesuit position had been accepted by the papacy, the Catholic Church in China might have lost its identity and 'become merged in the relatively formless chaos of native philosophical thought'– as, for example, Nestorianism had been.[109] This statement fails to do justice to traditional Chinese culture, reflects an underestimation of the abilities of the Jesuits, neglects the fact that Nestorianism never really entered into an en-counter with Chinese culture at all, and does not take account of the fact that Christianity is not culture-bound, as its progress from Judea through Hellen-ized Egypt and Greece to Persia and India, Africa, and the Western Hemi-sphere may suggest. Individual Christians and even Christian institutions may have been culture-bound, but Christianity is not.[110] The Jesuits in Peking knew that it was not and acted on their knowledge, perhaps more successfully than any other Christians in history. In their psychological make-up feelings of national rivalry *vis-à-vis* fellow Europeans was not always absent, little as it is to be seen in the best of the Jesuits, but feelings of antipathy or condescension *vis-à-vis* the Chinese left virtually no trace at all.

The opportunity that existed for the preservation and growth of syncretism was destroyed, through one of the great ironies of world history, by Western Christians, specifically by the papacy. Much too late to retrieve the damage, in December 1939, a decree of the *Propaganda Fide* in effect acknowledged that the K'ang-hsi emperor had been right in approving the Jesuits' under-standing of the Chinese rites in 1700.[111]

As a result Roman Catholic Christianity had growing and great influence on a number of Chinese thinkers – if not long enough for it to leave deep marks on the written corpus of Chinese thought, for a number of decades – but these traces eroded and almost disappeared in the decades following the K'ang-hsi reign. To be sure, they did not disappear entirely. Ricci's work, *The True Doctrine of the Lord of Heaven*, was incorporated into the Ch'ien-lung compendium of classics; so was Emmanuel Diaz's short astronomy, with references to Christian belief omitted. By 1631 Jesuits had published at least 340 works, most of them Christian apologetics but many dealing with other aspects of Western culture (including science, to be discussed shortly).[112]

It is difficult to say what the effects of these works, indirectly or directly, may have been. Fr Bernard has contended that the Jesuits had substantial influence on the Tung-lin school of philosophers during the late Ming period and the 'Han learning' of the Ch'ing. He holds that Leo Li, Paul Hsü, and Michael Yang were at various times presidents of the Tung-lin academy at Wusih; that certain members of the school, fleeing from the Mings to Japan, there 'devoted their enforced leisure' to a return to Han texts; and that most of the scholars who adhered to 'the neo-Han school' of the later eighteenth and nineteenth century 'passed through the discipline of the mathematical sciences brought to China by the Jesuits'.[113] H. G. Creel writes that the Jesuits asserted that the metaphysics of neo-Confucianism had been derived not from Confucius but from Buddhism; that since they were in contact with some Chinese scholars who opposed neo-Confucianism, 'it appears possible that the Chinese philosophical movement may have been influenced, in some degree, by this criticism by alien observers. It also appears that the Chinese philosophers took over, from the Jesuits, scientific [that is, scholarly] techniques in such fields as that of linguistics, which played a role of some importance in their movement.'[114]

The whole thrust of the philosophical work of Ricci and his successors and the basis of the Jesuit position in the Rites Controversy lay in a challenge to the Sung neo-Confucian commentators and an effort to direct attention to the original texts. It should thus be no surprise if it were to be shown that their work had some impact on Ku Yen-wu and the school of 'Han Learning' – though in the aftermath of the Rites Controversy there was ample reason for Chinese writers not to mention any such debt. Whether Jesuit influence on modern Chinese philosophy was marginal or substantial, it deserves further careful study.[115]

As for science, the Jesuits' impact remained visible, though diminishing, until the next encounter with the West in the nineteenth century. Liang Ch'i-ch'ao has asserted that 'since the last phase of the Ming..., when Matteo Ricci and others introduced into China what was then known as Western learning, the method of scholarly research had changed [under pressure] from without. At first only astronomers and mathematicians credited [the new method] but later on it was gradually applied to other subjects'.[116] He documents Jesuit influence on a number of Chinese scientists and sciences of the time. A few influences were long lasting. For example, Paul Hsü's agricultural encyclopedia remained in use until our own day; logarithmic tables produced by Jesuit effort were reproduced in the Ch'ing-shih kao (1917–24). The K'ang-hsi Jesuit atlas, completed in 1717 and 'not only the best map which had ever been made in Asia, but better and more accurate than any European map of its time',[117] was used thereafter. Verbiest introduced the thermometer. Much of the calendrical and astronomical knowledge brought was never lost. More could be added on particular scientific practices or techniques, but it would lie outside the realm of this study.

If the mission had not been destroyed from without, there seems no reason to suppose that Western science and Christian humanism might not have advanced together, the popularity of the one enhancing the reception of the other. The possibility of the development of a Chinese Christian civilization lay open, whether or not that would have been dependent on the conversion of the majority of the people. As these paths were blocked as a result of the action of the papacy, China may have been done much harm; the harm that the West may have sustained is also worth considering.

As a consequence of Jesuit reports and in connection with the echoes of the Rites Controversy in Europe, there was much attention paid to China in the West in the seventeenth and eighteenth centuries. Such cosmopolitan thinkers as Leibniz dreamed of institutional anchors for Chinese–Western relations in the sphere of the arts and sciences.[118] The image of the Celestial Empire which became current inspired European political economists, jurists, and essayists of all kinds to re-examine old ideas and formulate new ones. But in the late eighteenth century China was once again forgotten, and the encounter of 1840 was almost a rediscovery of the other on the part of both China and the West. The difference was that the West was apt to think, by the early nineteenth century, that it was superior to China in power, wealth, and civilization. It was a quite different attitude from that characteristic of Europe of the High Renaissance.

Rowbotham concludes that 'the Jesuits and their opponents – as well as those in control in Rome – brought about the temporary [sic] ruin of the Faith in China'.[119] This is much like saying that 'Napoleon and Venice' brought about the ruin of Venice; of course the Venetians made mistakes, but it was Napoleon who ended Venetian independence. The victim is always human, but that does not exonerate the predator. The Jesuits' opponents brought them down, and whatever one thinks of the prospects of the China mission in the eighteenth century, that is no ground for misstating what happened.

When the West returned to China, a few missionaries as well as many traders were present, but the military power of the Western states was in the foreground from the start of the new phase. The Chinese might well recall the words of the Yung-cheng emperor to a missionary:

You want all Chinese to become Christians. Your Law demands it, I know. But in that case what will become of us? Shall we become subjects of your king? The converts you make recognize only you in time of trouble. They will listen to no other voice but yours. I know that at the present time there is nothing to fear, but when your ships come by the thousands then there will probably be great disorder...[120]

These words were uttered after the Rites Controversy had ended. Perhaps the emperor was too polite to recall his father's experience and to say, 'You have already been compelled to obey the dictates of a foreign potentate whose trusted advisers had no sympathy for China. The Pope has no divisions, but supposing he had, or supposing one of the European monarchs appears at our borders with his armies, what then?' To that unasked question, the nineteenth century was to give the answer.

When a Western traveler visited the former cathedral of the Jesuits in 1865, he found little that was especially remarkable at the spot, only 'the memories that it evokes of a time when it seemed that Christianity must spread its rays (rayonner) to the whole of China'.[121] It was then only memories that remained; and yet when such lives as those of Verbiest, Schall, and Ricci, who showed an apostolic vision comparable to that of St Paul among the Athenians, have touched our planet, the memories can never quite be effaced.

CHRISTIAN PIETISM: THE FUNDA-MENTALIST PROTESTANTS (1807–1900)

We have several very interesting inquirers; one intends to move nearer the chapel, so that his whole family may come to worship and especially that his children may come to our school. Also a young man has recently come out very boldly for Christ.

> A missionary in Wuchang, a city of 400,000,
> reporting no converts for 1903

INTRODUCTION

The foremost historian of Protestant and perhaps of all Christian missions in China writes,

Since Christianity necessarily runs counter to so much that is an integral part of Chinese culture and, if its inward spirit is caught and its essential experience shared by many of the Chinese, would largely reshape that culture...it is obvious that in China it can have no easily won triumph... [1]

In contrast Matteo Ricci, writing over three centuries earlier, had held:

China is very different from other lands and peoples, because the Chinese are a people that is wise, given to letters and little given to war, of great intellectual talent, and is now more than ever doubtful of its own religions or superstitions; and thus it would be easy, as I firmly believe, to convert an innumerable multitude of them in a short time. [2]

How is the difference between the two views, one reflecting the outlook of most Protestant missionaries of the nineteenth century, the other mirroring the Jesuits' approach of an earlier period, to be explained? No doubt the changed historical circumstances constitute part of the explanation. Chinese hostility provoked by the establishment of Westerners on Chinese soil through the use of superior military and economic power – as contrasted with the confident attitude of the Ch'ing regime in the seventeenth century toward the Westerners then in the Pacific – certainly conditioned the missionaries' evaluation of the difficulty of their task. Nevertheless Latourette here is not discussing power relations, but is seeking to characterize Chinese culture and its relation to Christianity. Had Chinese culture changed? In some ways, yes. However, the changes that had actually occurred in Chinese culture are far less important in explaining the difference between the two evaluations cited

35

than the differences between the Christian humanism of the Jesuits and the Christian pietism of the fundamentalist Protestants who made up the great bulk of the missionaries of the nineteenth century – who were through most of that period for good or ill almost the sole channel through which the influences of Western culture reached the Chinese.

Despite the divisions introduced into European culture by the Protestant Reformation and Catholic Reform (in which the formation of the Society of Jesus was an important part), the Jesuits were relatively little concerned with advancing one thread of thought as against another; and Protestant humanists such as Leibniz and Wolff recognized the fact. To the Jesuits nothing human was alien, even though discipline might occasionally limit (as in the case of Copernican teachings, discussed above) the ideas they could overtly support and propagate. To the Protestant pietists, despite notable exceptions, almost everything human outside of their own religious beliefs was apt to be regarded with suspicion at best, contempt and hatred at worst. Even the truly exceptional men such as Timothy Richard had a formidable burden of previous training from which they had to disengage themselves in order to arrive, by trial and error and against implacable opposition from their colleagues, at a conception of their intellectual obligations as missionaries which Ricci had had from virtually the moment he set foot on the Chinese mainland.

Latourette accurately writes:

Since Protestant foreign missions arose largely out of the Pietist and Evangelical movement, with few if any exceptions missionaries were agreed that becoming a Christian involved an experience of conversion. Missionaries were unanimous in the conviction, too, that true conversion must be the introduction to a definite type of life, a life in which spiritual and moral transformation was being wrought. Not only was there accord arising out of the common background of the Pietist and Evangelical movements, but numbers [sic] of the societies had similar polities and doctrines.[3]

Pietism in the broadest sense was not confined to Protestantism or the nineteenth century. Analogous impulses were to be found in the friars who had been in China during the Yüan dynasty and again in the Ming and Ch'ing periods, not to speak of the Roman Church outside China. In the nineteenth century, however, it may be defined as expressing 'the revival within the Reformed, Lutheran, and Anglican state churches of the sectarian, spiritualist, and mystical motifs of the medieval and Reformation periods'.[4] (One may add that it spread from those churches, and had a noticeable impact even on parts of the Roman Catholic Church; nevertheless it was mainly a Protestant phenomenon during the period in question.)

Pietism meant the doctrine of the 'inner light' without which all else was meaningless, the doctrine of individual 'conversion' as a traumatic and (hopefully) permanent transformation of the human personality, personal and private devotion and asceticism – resting usually on a single authoritative determinant of the proper principles of human conduct, the Bible.[5] The Bible was conceived of as needing no interpretation or explanation. It was not the erudition of Calvin, the balance of Thomas Hooker, or the thirst for knowledge of Newton or Leibniz which animated the Protestant mission movement, but pietism. Pietism within the Protestant Churches was not new. It could be found in the English Puritanism of the seventeenth century, Halle 'pietism' (whence came the modern term) following Spener from 1694, the latter's direct offshoot, the Moravian brethren, from 1722, John Wesley from his 'conversion' in 1738 and Methodism from the 1780's. For a long time it had existed within established denominations, side by side with rationalist emphases. Orthodox positions, retaining both respect for human intelligence and consciousness of its limitations, might incorporate elements of both pietism and rationalism. In the late eighteenth century, as orthodoxy lay comfortably inert, pietism and rationalism tended to diverge; the latter approached 'natural religion' and then deism, the former produced the evangelical revival.

Methodism and Baptism (though it was originally an offshoot of Anabaptism, only the late eighteenth-century revival brought it into prominence in England) were the chief products. The evangelical movement made for the poor, the uneducated, and the unchurched. Socially, the evangelicals deserve credit for discovering 'the forgotten man'. The results for foreign missions, and particularly for China, were, however, unfortunate and perhaps even disastrous. The missionaries came from institutions which were just in the stage of losing a sizeable share of their intellectuals to deism and the Enlightenment and of turning their attention away from the upper classes and the educated. The sequence of events could scarcely have been less propitious for the beginning of a new cultural confrontation between China and the West.

The result was a story filled with heroism and self-sacrifice. Robert Morrison suffered twenty-seven years of loneliness in order to baptize a total of ten Chinese. After him came other unlettered soldiers of the gospel, preaching to puzzled crowds, distributing Bibles and tracts, and making few or no converts. The faith in the Bible was such as to lead some missionary groups to dump water-tight crates of Bibles in Chinese translation into the ocean near the China coast, hoping they would float ashore, be opened and read, and produce conversions.[6]

There were, for decades, practically no conversions. However, in the 1850's the pietists had had a success so great and undreamed of that to this day many historians have evaded coming to grips with its meaning. Among the downtrodden of China there erupted the largest-scale rebellion of the whole Ch'ing period, the causes of which had little if anything to do with the work of the missionaries; the amazing fact, however, was that the rebellion adopted as its ideology a Chinese version of pietist Protestantism. The missionaries were fascinated, thrilled, appalled; and at least many of them were relieved when the T'ai-p'ings were crushed and they had no longer the responsibility of deciding whether or how to acknowledge their own handiwork. Nothing like it was to happen again, and the missionaries returned to their foredoomed efforts to achieve 'conversions'.

Several gifted men did come to perceive that the same methods that might 'save' the beggars of London could only amuse or repel the Chinese of any social level. Pietism indeed 'ran counter' to Chinese culture; in its purer forms it runs counter to any high culture of East or West. A few Protestant missionaries drew their own conclusions, and tried their best to restructure mission strategy. In the last years of the century it looked as if they might succeed, and the debt of the 'Hundred Days' of 1898 to them seemed for a fleeting moment to promise victory – both for their methods within the mission movement and for the reforms they advocated for China.

That moment, however, passed quickly. The missionaries who were seeking a new strategy to appeal to the mandarins were repudiated by their own colleagues; but at almost the same moment the stubborn pietist faith which had held for a century in the face of all evidence that it was inapplicable to Chinese conditions suddenly began to fade. Pietism yielded to modernism – first in Europe and America, then in China along with other mission fields. The change was so sweeping that the genuine learning of some of the evangelicals (or those who started as such) was renounced along with evangelicalism, so that what remained was not necessarily Protestantism (or indeed any kind of Christianity) at all, but almost wholly secularized doctrines of political and social reform and good works. Once again, as in the Rites Controversy, *mutatis mutandis*, the fate of Western thought in China was decided not in China, but in the West. The sparsely attended street chapels and the unread Bibles were replaced by YMCA gymnasiums and printed copies of Western constitutions. However, the Protestant modernists were to fail as their pietist predecessors had, and in a much shorter time.

MORRISON'S MISSION (1807-34)

The Dutch had the first Protestant missions in Chinese territory, in Formosa in the mid-seventeenth century, but Protestantism did not survive their expulsion. The first Protestant missionary to establish himself on the mainland was Robert Morrison in 1807. He was British, and the dominant element in Protestant missions in China was to be British until about the end of the century,[7] Americans coming to play the role of junior partner and a few Germans having to fit into the Anglo-Saxon framework as best they could.

The direction of mission efforts toward China owed much to the earliest Sino-British diplomacy and the extension eastward of the interests of the East India Company, but it was scarcely prompted by British admiration for China. A reviewer of the account of the Macartney embassy in 1792 by the earl's secretary wrote bluntly in 1805 that the Chinese 'are a mean and semi-barbarous race, distinguished by fewer virtues or accomplishments than most of their neighbors, and remarkable only for their numbers, and their patience and dexterity in the practice of certain mechanical professions.'[8] There was from the first a minority opinion, however, represented by Sir George Thomas Staunton (1781–1859). At the age of eleven the boy accompanied his father, a former administrator in India, with the same Macartney embassy and before and during the voyage launched into the study of Chinese with two Chinese graduates of Fr Matteo Ripa's college in Naples *en route* back to their homeland.[9] The boy was thus the only member of the embassy to be able to converse with the emperor. In 1798 he was sent by the East India Company to Canton, and soon became recognized as the first British Sinologist. In 1810 he translated a legal code which was the first Chinese book translated into English;[10] in 1823 he co-founded the Royal Asiatic Society; and he remained a friend of China.[11]

In 1798 a certain dissenting minister of Northamptonshire named William Mosely wrote a circular[12] urging establishment of a society to translate the Bible into Chinese; he saw this as the chief prerequisite for Protestants to convert the Chinese where the Jesuits had failed – because of their mistakes, not of 'insurmountable local difficulties'. On being told by a director of the East India Company that such translation was a 'practical impossibility', he set out to prove the contrary. He was overjoyed to discover in the British Museum a manuscript in Chinese labeled *Quatuor Evangelia Sinice*, which proved to be a translation not only of the four Gospels but also the Acts and Epistles, copied in 1737 in Canton, obviously by some Roman Catholic or student thereof. Mosely was able to establish that much by the help of Sir George Staunton, then the only man in England who knew Chinese. Soon thereafter Mosely met Robert Morrison, and evidently persuaded him to choose China as a mission field.

The young Morrison[13] had been born in 1782 in Northumberland, the son of a Scottish maker of shoe lasts and trees. At sixteen he joined the Presbyterian church; the following year he came upon some magazines devoted to foreign missions, and his interest was permanently aroused. As he acknowledged 'conversion', he became the dignified and serious – some might say gloomy and humorless – person he remained. His youthful diary is filled with torments about his own sinfulness, real or imagined – if real, then the sins must have been venial indeed.[14] Mosely put him in touch with a young Chinese who had just arrived from Canton to study English. Morrison, working with him, proceeded to copy the whole manuscript Mosely had found as well as a manuscript Latin–Chinese dictionary lent by the Royal Society, and began to learn Chinese. Thus Protestant missions in China were launched with the aid of early Roman Catholic scholarship, and it was to be some time before the Protestants caught up with its level of achievement.

In 1807 Morrison embarked for China, a few days after he had been ordained. Since the East India Company refused to carry any missionaries, he had to go by way of the United States. On arriving in Canton he adopted local dress and customs and ate Chinese food, but he soon found all this too difficult and resumed a European style of life. He saw as his chief task to translate the whole Bible into Chinese, as Mosely had desired, and he under-took to do so, reworking the partial New Testament manuscript from London and doing the rest of the translation himself. He then discovered that a mis-sionary named Marshman in Serampore, India, was doing the same thing, assisted by an Armenian born in Macau whose Chinese was probably not of the best. Both worked over fifteen years, each worrying about the other, finally completing the task about the same time (1822 and 1823). Morrison came in second; there were charges of plagiarism on both sides, and such charges also dogged the grammars and dictionaries that the two men wrote independently. Some of Morrison's partisans argued that it made little sense for a missionary in India to be working on a translation into Chinese. Reading Morrison's chronicles of lonely misery, however, one wonders if he could not as well or better have done his work in London. Neither translator proved himself competent, and Morrison was blamed for mistakes which reviewers thought he ought to have avoided with the help of Chinese scholars.[15] Unfortunately he seems not to have known any.

Having finally obtained an assistant, Dr William Milne, in 1813, Morrison lost him at once when the Roman Catholics forced him to leave Macau. Milne had an assistant named Liang A-fa whom he baptized in Malacca in 1816. Milne died in 1822, not long after burying his wife and two children. Morrison ordained Liang to the 'office of evangelist'[16] in 1823. But his own work had been largely fruitless. After he had been in China five years, he had written of one result of a tract he had published in Chinese: 'I have been informed that a person in the city of Canton, to which I have not access, was reformed in his conduct by means of the perusal of this tract. He was a Chinese Roman Catholic, of a vicious life.'[17] The 1828 Report of the Religious Tract Society first reported the work of Liang A-fa who was said to have prepared nine tracts and distributed them in a tour of 250 miles, accompanied by 'his friend Agony' (a Chinese).[18] After Morrison's first real reinforcement in the person of the American, Elijah Bridgman, arrived, the two wrote a report (1832) on the first twenty-five years of Protestant work in China. There was very little to say.

Morrison did his best to create institutions that would survive him.[19] He founded a Language Institution while on home leave in London in 1825, which collapsed within months of his return to China. He and Milne founded an Anglo-Chinese College at Malacca with Samuel Kidd as principal; it later moved to Hong Kong, and there failed. He established a clinic in Canton, which closed in 1832. A Morrison Educational Society, founded after his death, dissolved in the 1840's. He died in 1834. Seldom has great human effort led to so little.

China did not respond to Morrison, and he did not respond to her. The Chinese, he told Milne soon after the latter arrived, have 'all the cunning, deceit, and intrigue of the French, without any of their good qualities'. Milne's reactions were similar; Chinese temples, he wrote, 'are similar to Romish cathedrals'. 'China is a land full of idols; a land of darkness and spiritual death!'[20] It is clear that the evangelicals started with a bitter hatred of Roman Catholicism and transferred part of it ('...intrigue of the French', '...Romish cathedrals') to Chinese culture. Milne's own passions on this issue went so far as to lead him to oppose Catholic Emancipation in England and to abominate the Oxford Movement, an Anglican attempt to rebuild on the foundations of patristic learning, as a reflection of Catholic influence: 'there is just as much need for an exposure of the [Greek and Latin Church] Fathers in England, as for the refutation of Confucius in China'.[21] The narrow dogmatism of the pietist movement could scarcely be better illustrated. And yet if the evangelicals' intellects were meager and ill-trained, their characters must earn our admiration. James Legge wrote of Morrison, 'far inferior to Ricci in scholarly training, he was not inferior to him in indomitable perseverance...'[22] He labored unremittingly for his faith despite what seemed to be utter failure on every hand. As things turned out, even Morrison accomplished something, posthumously, as will appear below in the discussion of the T'ai-p'ing rebellion.

LEGGE AND THE TERM CONTROVERSY

The few Protestants in the China mission field after Morrison's death anticipated new opportunities following the West's first power confrontation with China in the Opium War and the treaty which followed it in 1842. One of the new arrivals, James Legge, who reached the new British colony of Hong Kong in 1843, was to show great intellectual power in grasping Chinese culture, but had little impact on the Chinese.

Legge was born in Huntly, Aberdeenshire (Scotland) in 1814, and his earliest religious inspiration came from the dissenting pastor, Dr Cowie – whose daughter was to become the wife of Morrison's assistant, Milne. At Highbury Theological College as a divinity student Legge displayed the photographic memory that served him well in China. Acknowledging a call to the Orient, he sailed in 1839, rejoicing to be nearing 'the seat where Satan has enthroned his power...'[23] He went first to the Dutch East Indies, Singapore, and Malacca, in 1840 becoming principal of Morrison's college there, where already he became convinced that only Chinese could succeed in mission work. He wished to go to Peking or Nanking, but the London Missionary Society decided on Hong Kong for him after it was ceded. In 1843 he – and the college – were transferred to the new colony. In 1849 he became pastor of an English congregation in Hong Kong. Apparently a decisive experience was seeing in 1858 the hall in Canton where the imperial examinations were conducted. He thereupon resolved to devote his life to Chinese literature. The result was his pioneer but still as a whole unsurpassed translation of *The Chinese Classics*, published in five volumes 1861–72 by subsidy of the wealthy businessmen Jardine. He visited the interior in 1861 at great risk – he did not lack courage – but his gifts were those of the mind rather than personality. In 1873 he left China for good and returned to Britain. In 1876 he became Oxford University's first Professor of Chinese. Except for short trips he remained at Oxford, teaching and producing nine more volumes of translation (six in Max Muller's *Sacred Books of the East*) as well as many shorter works until he died in 1897. His great merit was his contribution to Western knowledge of China; but also, as his views of China and Chinese culture changed, he endeavored to influence the conceptions of his fellow missionaries, and did have strong influence on one Chinese who became an important figure.

The issue that he wrestled with came out of a meeting held in 1843, soon after he reached Hong Kong, of fifteen missionaries to consider the problem of translation of the Bible into Chinese.[24] Evangelicals regarded this task as fundamental to the whole missionary enterprise; they had to recognize (by delicate silence) that Morrison and Marshman had failed, and the translation by W. E. Medhurst and Karl Gützlaff also was not satisfactory. The question at once arose of how to translate the word 'God'; it became known as the 'term question', as it had been called by the Jesuits long before.[25] There was disagreement between supporters of *shen* (spirit) and *Shang-ti*.[26] Both Morrison and Marshman had used *shen*, Medhurst and Gützlaff, *Shang-ti*. The question was referred to a subcommittee consisting of Medhurst and Legge. Legge supported *shen*, following his teacher (1838–9) in London, Samuel Kidd. The subcommittee thus was divided. In 1847 the committee reconvened and decided, incredibly, to leave blanks in the translation for the word *theos* so that everyone could insert his own preference, though Medhurst offered to support *T'ien-chu*, pointing out that the Roman Catholics had started with *shen* and later adopted the phrase.[27] Legge was at that time in England. However, he continued to study the question on his return in 1848; in 1850 he announced that he had changed his mind and that he believed that *Shang-ti* was the best solution.[28] It is possible he discussed the question with Sir George Staunton, who joined the fray in 1849 by declaring that *T'ien-chu* was unobjectionable, but 'it is an innovation, while Shang-Tee is ancient and classical'. Christians ought not to be in the position of seeming to introduce a strange new idol of their own, he continued, especially since the government tried to inculcate precisely that idea in the people. Medhurst is right, Staunton declared, because he knows the Chinese better than others[29] (evidently Staunton was unaware of Medhurst's concession regarding *T'ien-chu*).

The 'term controversy' continued for decades, and developed an aspect it had not had among the earlier Roman Catholics. They had debated how to translate the name of God into Chinese, but the converse question had not been agitated because they had not engaged in any such enterprise as Legge's translation of the Chinese classics into a Western language. Legge wished to render 'God' as *Shang-ti* in the Chinese Bible; he proceeded to render *Shang-ti* as 'God' in translating the classics. In 1877, at the first national

Missionary Conference in Shanghai, he held that Confucianism was 'defective rather than antagonistic' to Christianity; repeated his view, set forth in 1861 in his version of *The Book of Mencius*, that Mencius maintains the goodness of human nature in the same way as Bishop Butler[30] does in his *Sermons*; argued that many Confucian texts show that there is no man who does not sin; contended that Confucius, like Moses, neither teaches nor denies immortality, and that Confucius has not only the usually accepted 'negative' Golden Rule but also a positive version in Chapter 13 of *Doctrine of the Mean*; and reiterated his 'well-known conviction' that *Shang-ti* in the classics refers to God. He concluded:

Let no one think any labour too great to make himself familiar with the Confucian books. So shall missionaries in China come fully to understand the work they have to do; and the more they avoid driving their carriages rudely over the Master's grave, the more likely are they soon to see Jesus enthroned in His room in the hearts of the people.[31]

Legge's paper was read for him, since he was in Oxford. It gave such thorough offence that the Conference voted to exclude the paper from its printed record, 'in deference to the wishes of those who regarded it as taking one side' in the term controversy. One writer called this decision a blot on the conference, especially since several American papers touched the term question (presumably opposing *Shang-ti*); the horror of Confucianism shown at the conference 'fell little short of madness'; no sooner was the doctrine mentioned than someone, usually an American, rose to denounce it.[32]

A certain Rev. Andrew P. Happer continued the attack.[33] Legge's opinion about *Shang-ti* had been known since 1852, he stormed, and yet the number of Protestant missionaries who agreed with him could be counted on the 'fingers of one hand'.[34] Happer returned to the Rites Controversy, recapitulating it in some detail, sided resolutely with Clement XI's 'decree of 1704' forbidding the use of *Shang-ti* and *T'ien* to mean God, and declared that all Christian missions accepted this until Legge's pamphlet of 1852 in which Legge agreed with Ricci.[35] The term controversy continued a while longer; it was never clearly decided.[36] The term *shen* faded from the scene, and its supporters turned to *T'ien-chu*, which was given a kind of official sanction by being used in the memorial prepared by the Missionary Conference of 1890 for the emperor. Nevertheless one computation shows that 90% of the Protestant books printed in 1892 employed Shang-ti,[37] which may simply have meant that those among the missionaries who wrote books followed Legge but were greatly outnumbered by their less scholarly colleagues.

The 'term controversy' no doubt occupied more of the Protestant missionaries' time than it might if they had had more than a very few converts to instruct and churches to help organize. However, it was no empty debate about the meaning of words; it involved the whole question of whether the ancient Chinese had been monotheistic and the related question of whether Chinese culture had elements Christians ought to respect or whether it should simply be attacked and destroyed. Legge left no doubt of his conversion to the belief that classical Confucianism had been monotheistic, and demonstrated it by removing his shoes on entering the Altar of Heaven in Peking and declaring, 'This is holy ground', to the horror of his fellow evangelicals.[38] He did not accept the argument that the God of the Chinese was not 'the same being' as the God of the Christians;[39] there was but one God. He was the sort of man who would not have been impressed by the apocryphal contention that the poems of Homer were not written by Homer, but by another poet of the same name.

In fact Legge had by his own route recapitulated the path of Ricci and his followers in the Rites Controversy, as he himself recognized: 'About the terms I entirely agree with his [Ricci's] opinion, nor do I altogether differ with him about the ritual practices.'[40] The Rites Controversy, it will be recalled, had three contentious aspects, dealing with the rites for Confucius, the ancestral rites, and the term for God. For the Protestants, oriented above all to the Bible, the last of the three aspects was bound to be in the foreground, and since the overwhelming majority of the missionaries knew little of Chinese culture but knew what they didn't like, which was almost everything in it, the question of the rites was not even up for discussion – until the last decades of the century, when as will be mentioned two or three brave men fought to have it considered too. Legge was primarily a scholar, and though his opinion was similar to Ricci on the rites (as well as terms), he did not crusade for it.

He knew his fellow-missionary audience was mostly in another intellectual world from his; he noted that 'the scholars of Confucianism had received a higher intellectual training than those who came to teach them...'[41] He warned, 'the idea that a man need spend no time in studying the native religions, but has only, as the phrase is, to "preach the gospel", is one which can only make missionaries and mission work contemptible and inefficient'.[42] But he was not heeded. The strong anti-intellectual coloration of evangelicalism, which recoiled from any attempt to influence the intellectual elite even if the missionaries had had the education needed to do so, prompted Legge's opponents to hoot down his arguments; that tendency was so strong that its exponents were willing to resort to using even the edicts of abhorred 'popery' as sticks to beat the position of the foremost scholar among them.

The missionaries of the early nineteenth century had no impact whatever on the main body of Chinese literati, and sought to have none, but their appeal to the lower depths of society had unexpected results in the T'ai-p'ing rebellion. Legge himself had a fateful encounter with the movement. About 1854 a Swedish missionary brought Hung Jen-kan, one of its leaders, to Hong Kong where he came to know Legge. Legge liked and respected him, but told him to stay away from the T'ai-p'ings, many of whose tenets he disapproved. When Legge sailed on home leave, Hung Jen-kan returned to Nanking despite Legge's advice, though he left his brother as chief servant in the Legge household. Legge, though a critic of the T'ai-p'ings, nevertheless later had good words to say for them. If there had been willingness to negotiate with them in 1860 or 1861, he wrote in 1862, 'we should have found that their calling as "foreign brethren" had a real good substantial meaning in it; in any event, why should we have fought them? What *casus belli* did we have? Why could we not have respected them as belligerents?'[43] By that time, the fate of the rebellion had been decided.

PROTESTANTISM AND T'AI-P'ING CHRISTIANITY

Robert Morrison had arrived in China during the reign of the Chia-ch'ing emperor (1796–1820), successor to the Ch'ien-lung emperor (during whose reign the Society of Jesus had been dissolved for the time being). In the Tao-kuang reign (1821–50) the Chinese Empire had had to cede Hong Kong to the British and admit the West to the treaty ports. In the last year of the reign there erupted the greatest internal convulsion China had experienced for centuries, the T'ai-p'ing rebellion, which lasted during the entire reign of the Hsien-feng emperor (1851–61) and into the following T'ung-chih (1862–74) period.

The causes of the rebellion must be sought in China's political, economic, and social fabric as a whole. They included growing pressure of population on tillable land, economic dislocation resulting from the new Western trade and opium smuggling, increase in banditry and unrest organized by secret societies, the mounting financial troubles and political weaknesses of the central government, whose ruling house seemed to be approaching the end of what Chinese recognized as the 'dynastic cycle',[44] and ethnic issues involving the relations between non-Chinese minorities and the Chinese and the feelings of many Chinese toward the ruling Manchus. What concerns us here is not the real causes, course, and effects of the great rebellion but the way in which the doctrines of its leaders reflected Western thought.

In 1836 a Hakka farmer boy, twenty-two, named Hung Hsiu-ch'üan was taking the state examinations in Canton. He was handed a series of nine tracts by Morrison and Milne's convert, Liang A-fa, entitled *Good Works to Admonish the Age* (*Ch'üan-shih liang-yen*), which were based on Morrison's translation of the Bible.[45] Accounts seem to agree that he scarcely glanced at the tracts at the time, although to a psychologist what followed might suggest that important parts of it lodged themselves somewhere in the recesses of his mind.[46] In 1837, having failed the examinations a second time, Hung suffered a mental illness in which he had visions of ascending to heaven. The Heavenly Father informed him that devils were found to be at work in heaven, and traced their activity to Confucius. The Father charged Confucius with confusing people 'so that they do not even recognize me, and your name has become greater than mine'.[47] Though Confucius tried to escape, he was caught and flogged for his crimes. Hung himself, who proved to be the Heavenly

Father's son next younger to Jesus, the Heavenly Elder Brother, then drove all the devils out of heaven and into hell. The Heavenly Mother, wife of the Father, and Hung's sisters then brought him 'candies and fruits', and the Father commanded him to return to earth and drive out devils there.

For the following six years Hung taught as before in the schools of his village near Canton. In 1843, the year in which Hung failed the examinations for the third and final time, a cousin borrowed the tracts by Liang and when returning them urged Hung to study them carefully. Only now did Hung appear to recognize that God and Jesus as he dreamt about them and as they were depicted in the tracts were the same. At this moment Hung underwent a conversion of approximately the sort for which the missionaries who dumped Bibles in the sea must have hoped and which they ought to have feared; Hung proceeded to try to reconstruct Christianity by himself, using the tracts as his source. He and his cousin baptized each other. Hung began to preach the new doctrine and converted relatives and friends. He threw out ancestral tablets and conducted forays to break idols. Thereupon he was dismissed from his teaching position.

With another young man who had failed the examinations, Feng Yün-shan, Hung made his way north into Kwangsi province to preach for a time, returning to his village in 1845–6. Having heard of a foreigner preaching a doctrine like his in Canton, in 1847 he reached the city to find an American Southern Baptist missionary, Issachar J. Roberts, and for two months received instruction from him. Apparently Hung's money gave out, and he returned to the area in southern Kwangsi where Feng had organized a group among the Hakkas called Society of Worshippers of God (Pai Shang-ti Hui), numbering over 3,000. Partly to flee oppressive officialdom and extensive bandit activity in the area, many more came over to the group for protection. By 1850 about 10,000 members of the sect, now organized and armed, were at Chin-t'ien. Late in that year an imperial army attacked them and was repulsed. The rebellion had begun.

In January 1851 Hung proclaimed himself Heavenly King (T'ien Wang) of the new Heavenly Kingdom of Great Peace (T'ai-p'ing T'ien-Kuo). In December he named a number of subordinate 'kings' who also acted as generals, with Yang Hsiu-ch'ing, the Eastern King, as a sort of chief of staff. Moving slowly at first, the rebels crossed Hunan, capturing Changsha in September 1852, then followed the Yangtze to Nanking, which they seized in March 1853. Here they established their capital and main base for expeditions north and west. In October they were in the suburbs of Tientsin and the emperor was preparing to leave Peking. But the rebels could not take the capital, and fell back. The northern expedition was a failure, and the western expedition was only partially successful. The leaders faltered not only militarily but politically. In Nanking by the end of 1853 the Heavenly King had become a figurehead, the real power resting with the Eastern King, Yang.[48] He was, however, unable to maintain the momentum of the movement, and rivalry among the leaders increased. In September 1856 Yang was assassinated and perhaps 20,000 of his partisans massacred. For a time (November 1856–May 1857) it appeared as if the Assistant King, Shih Ta-k'ai, evidently a man of some ability, might become an effective leader, but he was forced to flee. For the two and a half years from the assassination of Yang to April 1859, the rebel movement was on the defensive.[49] At that time there appeared in Nanking a new leader, the Heavenly King's cousin Hung Jen-kan, who had also failed the imperial examinations but showed a level of ideological sophistication Hung Hsiu-ch'üan never had. He was given the post of chief of staff and the title of Shield King (Kan Wang). Hung Jen-kan was fresh from a period in Hong Kong and nearby points (1855–8) during which he had known or studied with the missionaries James Legge, Joseph Edkins, Alexander Wylie, and Issachar Roberts.[50] He tried to rationalize T'ai-p'ing ideology and to persuade the Heavenly King to cooperate with foreign governments and introduce reforms based on Western models. He was clearly the most sophisticated, if not certainly the most intelligent, of the T'ai-p'ing leaders. By this time, however, their generals had become used to operating without clear central directives and had become increasingly indifferent to the ideology of the movement. The Shield King strove for two years to put the T'ai-p'ing house in order, but in February 1861 he was demoted and from then on things went from bad to worse.

The Shield King's warnings about Westerners were amply confirmed when in 1860 England and France decided to take part in defending Shanghai and environs, and the so-called 'Ever Victorious Army' was formed under the command of the American Frederick T. Ward and later the British Captain Charles George ('Chinese') Gordon – who was to die dramatically at Khartoum. Though it experienced its defeats, the Ever Victorious Army contributed powerfully to the overthrow of T'ai-p'ing power. In the meantime the Hunan armies of the most potent imperial general, Tseng Kuo-fan, which had besieged Nanking in 1858, 1860, and 1862, finally captured the T'ai-p'ing capital. They entered the city on 19 July 1864. The Heavenly King had died several weeks before. Tseng reported the massacre of 100,000 men; none of the T'ai-p'ing troops surrendered. This was the decisive blow. It took until February 1866 to wipe out the rebels south of the Yangtze, and a group of them which joined the Nien rebels fought on until 1868. However, the T'ai-p'ing cause was lost when its capital was occupied.

Why did the T'ai-p'ings, having come so close to success, fail? Franz Michael, author of the most recent study, emphasizes the role of the scholar-gentry who rallied to the defense of the Chinese tradition, rather than that of the dynasty itself. The rebels, declared Tseng Kuo-fan, had 'stolen the ways of the foreign barbarians', forced the scholars to give up the Confucian classics and to read instead Christian works, destroyed Confucian temples (as well as Buddhist and Taoist temples and idols, which offended the common people rather than the scholars), making 'Confucius and Mencius weep bitterly in the underworld'.[51] Since the Confucianists stood by the Ch'ing dynasty, the rebels' only hope was popular – that is, peasant – support; and in Michael's opinion that was denied to them by the T'ai-p'ing notion of the 'sacred treasury' – a version of primitive communism – as well as the rebels' increasingly harsh treatment of the rural population.[52] We may sum up by saying that the rebels needed either the scholars or the peasants to win. Their only chance of gaining the support of either group, Michael clearly implies, was by following the program of Hung Jen-kan, which was one of state promotion of private property, 'rule by law' which would be achieved by the educated, and Western-inspired reform generally.

Such a program might have attracted the support of Western powers or at least secured Western neutrality, especially since the whole T'ai-p'ing ideology was at least ostensibly founded on the Christian religion. In fact, it seemed to have a chance of doing so at least twice, in 1853–4 and 1859–60. Just after the establishment of the rebel capital at Nanking, T. T. Meadows, Charles Taylor, Elijah Bridgman, and other missionaries visited the leaders. The shock of recognition was great, even overwhelming; the rumors were correct, the rebels professed what was obviously a form of Christianity. One writer noted with approval that the T'ai-p'ing's new version of the *Trimetrical Classic* (the traditional Chinese primer) had a style 'remarkably similar to the early Anglo-Saxon poetical versions of scriptural and theological subjects'.[53] A missionary saw in one of their camps tables with offerings, one with three bowls of tea, one for each Person of the Trinity.[54] Meadows ecstatically contemplated the rebels' plan to substitute the Bible for the Confucian classics as the basis of state examinations:

[in a] population of 360 millions of heathens, all the males who have the means, and are not too old to learn...will be assiduously engaged in getting the Bible off by heart, from beginning to end. Should the thing take place, it will form a revolution...unparalleled in the world for rapidity, completeness, and extent...[55]

Augustus F. Lindley wrote: 'Errors, and some very grave, undoubtedly existed; but...the great truth that the Ti-pings [*sic*] admitted and recognized the principal points of the Christian faith, remained.'[56] Meadows, Lindley, and others were frank apologists for not only the religious beliefs but the political cause of the rebels, being 'politically desirous for their success',[57] and seeking to promote support for them or at least to prevent Western intervention on behalf of the Manchus. James Legge later noted that the missionaries as a whole expressed their approval of the T'ai-p'ings in 1853,[58] and then drew back from that position.

The missionaries' support (though there were some with reservations, even in 1853) did not, however, lead to Western assistance or even benevolent neutrality toward the rebels. Partly the reason was the diplomats' and traders' distrust of the evangelicals because of their propensity for emotionalism and getting into trouble, partly the preference of the former for dealing with the known established authorities rather than unknown quantities which might prove even more intractable.

The T'ai-p'ing rebellion certainly exhibited the influence of Western thought; but the character of that influence requires careful appraisal. The question may be examined in two parts: the significance of traditional Chinese, non-Christian elements in the rebel ideology, and the extent and nature of its Christian elements. The T'ai-p'ing ideology has been called a 'composition' (that is, a synthesis) of Christian, Confucian, Buddhist and Taoist influences and ideas and practices of old Chinese secret societies.[59] It is true that Confucian virtues are defended in some T'ai-p'ing literature, Buddhist and Taoist traces may be observed in some of their ceremonies, and such devices characteristic of the older secret societies as riddles were employed. Such facts do not at all prove the T'ai-p'ing ideology to have been an amalgam of religions, any more than the Jesuits' use of the Chinese tradition proves that they were not orthodox Christians. It is a question of essence against accident, the outward dress versus the inward character.

The significant facts are as follows. The rebels were far less tolerant of Confucianism than Ricci (or James Legge), and ideologically opposed to it in a way Ricci (and Legge) were not. The way Confucius figured in Hung's visions as master-mind of the devils and Hung's destruction of tablets have already been mentioned. The rebels 'strictly enforced the proscription of the Confucian classics' and burned them wholesale,[60] and they destroyed many Confucian shrines. Whether or not, as Vincent Shih suggests, the leaders 'blamed these Confucian classics for barring them from a life of which they aspired' – since several of them failed at the state examinations – there was no doubt that they 'attacked Confucius and his ideas with a great fury'.[61] As for the Buddhists and Taoists, they looked on them 'merely as two sects of idol-worshipers' which preached 'false doctrines'.[62] As for secret societies, William Stanton points out that the T'ai-p'ings would receive into their ranks only those members of the Triad society who would agree to give up their affiliation and accept the new doctrines.[63]

As Michael puts it, 'what Hung propagated was not a traditional rebellion but a religious movement that broke with tradition'.[64] The rebels sought not to establish a new dynasty of the old type – they even refused to use the old title 'emperor' – but to overthrow the social order based on the Confucian gentry and to establish a new one, which could only be based on a new ideology.[65] The T'ai-p'ing ideology based itself on the Bible and the writings of the rebel leaders who purported to develop and interpret it, and not at all on any non-Christian works or doctrines taken from the Chinese tradition.[66] The T'ai-p'ing doctrine was not syncretist.

The second question to be explored is that of the influence on T'ai-p'ing ideology of Christianity. It is curious that not a single work that I have encountered makes the distinction indispensable to the successful exploration of this question; not one specifies that it is the particular type of Christianity to

which Hung and his followers were exposed, Protestant pietism (or fundamentalism), that must be studied, and its influence assessed. Investigators
have postulated a Christianity as it were outside of time and space, and attempted to compare it to the teachings of the T'ai-p'ings.[67] The historical
question can scarcely be resolved in such a manner.

Eugene P. Boardman has examined the question of the rebels' doctrines
and Christianity at length under the headings, 'What the Taipings Took' and
'What the Taipings Failed to Take'. He points out that in theology they 'took'
monotheism, the idea of the fatherhood of God and his universality, the
concept of the Holy Spirit, the notion of sin (but without any idea of an
'original sin' common to all mankind), the idea of Christ as savior sent by
God the Father to all men, the need to make sacrifices to God but not to have
images of Him, and the concept of a Devil and Hell; in religious practice,
they took baptism, the keeping of the Sabbath, and the Ten Commandments.
To Boardman's list we may add: community of goods; prohibition of tobacco,
opium, alcohol, and sex (adultery, including lust, being the worst sin of all);[68]
equal rights for women; the identification of religion with morality (or, better,
reduction of religion to morality); the use of a style of writing accessible to the
common people for religious propaganda.[69]

What Boardman says the T'ai-p'ings 'failed to take' included the doctrine of
love (that is, *agape*), the sacrament of the eucharist, and the 'social gospel'.
Meadows and many others have pointed out that they also had no priesthood.
Boardman concludes that despite the circumstances attending the particular
form in which the Protestant missionaries presented it, 'the Taiping religion
still was not Christianity'.[70] Vincent Shih, while terming this a 'sound conclusion', still cogently declares that Boardman 'seems to set the standard too
high...'[71] Boardman faults the T'ai-p'ings, for example, for failing 'to take' the
doctrines of love and humility, but as Shih points out the rebel writings
abound in them.

If the T'ai-p'ing religion is carefully examined, it proves to have reproduced with remarkable fidelity most of the main features of Protestant fundamentalism, the only version of Christianity known to Hung and his followers.
The missionaries were honest enough to recognize T'ai-p'ing indebtedness
to their work, though perhaps some shrank from contemplating some of their
own uglier features as reflected in the Chinese mirror that the rebels provided.
In a number of cases, for the T'ai-p'ings the actions of the missionaries spoke
so loud that their words could not be heard. Thus many Protestants (although
Anglicans and Lutherans came from state Churches) insisted on the separation
of Church and state, but many of the missionaries acted as diplomats or in
other ways directly assisted their home governments (none of them served the
Chinese government in any capacity until the end of the century); the
T'ai-p'ings' 'divinely' inspired leaders also assumed governmental functions.
The Chinese were told that the Ten Commandments were the important
prohibitions, and T'ai-p'ing leaders reproduced them, but in fact the mis-

sionaries inveighed as strongly against smoking and drinking as against any sin enumerated by Moses, and against illicit sex or even merely 'having a lustful heart' most of all. The rebels emulated them in exacting puritanical behavior of their followers, though some of the leaders conspicuously exempted themselves from such demands. Protestants might identify two (out of the original seven) sacraments, baptism and the Eucharist, but the one to which the fundamentalists attached chief importance was baptism, signifying 'conversion' in their special sense; the T'ai-p'ings did likewise. The missionaries of course did not teach that Hung Hsiu-ch'üan was some kind of special assistant ('younger brother') to Jesus,[72] but they said that anyone could under divine guidance interpret the Bible for himself; this left Hung free to interpret every use of the character *ch'üan* (meaning simply 'all, complete') in the Chinese versions of the Bible as referring to himself. This was, to be sure, irrational behavior, but extracting Biblical quotations out of any reasonable context was not unique to China; use of the Bible for cabalistic purposes and what can only be called divination was prevalent among Western pietists, and in his 'Biblical mysticism' Hung has been compared to a Western contemporary who was a formidable enemy of his movement, Charles George Gordon.[73] The missionaries did not all, or at least openly, say that Confucianism and other Chinese doctrines should be uprooted by force, their monuments destroyed, and their books burned; but the evangelicals spoke and acted as if those doctrines ought to be wholly repugnant to a Christian, and the T'ai-p'ings put such attitudes vigorously into practice. If *agape* was not very prominent in T'ai-p'ing behavior, neither was it in that of missionaries who preached a religion in which salvation would descend like a thunderbolt onto a single lone soul and make him live thenceforward an abstemious life of private rectitude. If there was no organized T'ai-p'ing Church, neither was there as yet any Protestant Church in China. There were only missionary societies in Europe and America concerned with China, and in China itself stern preachers, colporteurs of scripture, and prohibitors of 'ungodly' behavior on the part of that tiny handful of Chinese who had undergone 'conversion' at missionary hands. If the T'ai-p'ings had a religion heavily dependent on the Old Testament and the attributes of the Hebrew Jehovah, a religion of fear, taboos, and wrath, so did the missionaries.

So much can be said for the strange doctrine preached by Hung Hsiu-ch'üan and practiced by many of his followers. However, there was even among the T'ai-p'ings a more reasonable and purer current of Christian thought, as examplified by Hung Jen-kan, the Shield King, in the period 1859–61, when he was the Heavenly King's chief of staff. He attempted nothing less than a complete overhaul of T'ai-p'ing doctrine and revision of the rebels' political and economic program. In his religious teaching he showed understanding of the doctrines of original sin, redemption, and forgiveness. Instead of destroying the Confucian classics, he intended that, in a revised form, they be used in education along with the Bible and the writings of the T'ai-p'ing leaders. He wished to create a Christian gentry, recruited on the basis of genuine merit, building from the ethics of Confucianism into the cosmology and theology of Christianity. With such religious and cultural perspectives, he combined the concept of the rule of law, the idea of China as one among a family of nations which stood on an equal footing, and the desire to introduce railroads, steam power, and other technical improvements from the West. For a time the Heavenly King seemed favorably inclined toward his cousin's program, and Hung Jen-kan did his best to present the face of reformed T'ai-p'ingism to Western visitors. However, despite his temporarily exalted position, he failed to achieve adoption of his major ideas.[74]

Where did Hung Jen-kan acquire such an outlook, quite different from the anti-intellectualism and morose thundering of the fundamentalists? He brought it direct from Hong Kong; he did not work out its major features in Nanking, for he had such views on his arrival. Who among Protestant missionaries preached, by the middle 1850's, the compatibility of much of the original Confucian ethic with Christianity and respected the classics as a means of leading the Chinese to God? James Legge, out of whose household Hung came direct to Nanking. We cannot document the influence; but the circumstantial evidence is overwhelming. There were, to be sure, other learned and gentle missionaries; Legge was not entirely unique. Joseph Edkins and Alexander Wylie, whom Hung had known in the treaty ports – and Edkins later visited him in Soochow, in 1860 – were two. However, Legge had worked out his ideas more clearly than any of his contemporaries on the basis of a learning that surpassed theirs, and he doubtless deserves a large share of the credit for the Shield King's reform program.

Hung Hsiu-ch'üan was, despite the undoubted fact that he was mentally ill, capable of working out a doctrine and a program, along with others, that had some cohesion and certainly influenced thousands or even millions of people to some degree. It was a program full of weaknesses, a program that was in part accurate reflection, in part ignorant caricature of the teachings and behaviour of the Protestant evangelical missionaries. To the extent it was ignorant, it may be said in Hung's defense that the missionaries of the sort he knew never had insisted on the necessity of patient and exhaustive study in order to make sense of the Christian religion; what was necessary was the Bible and a pure heart, and that was all. Hung Hsiu-ch'üan reflected, even if he also distorted, the Protestantism of Morrison, through whose lone Chinese disciple Hung learned the basis of the religion he preached. In the next generation there was, however, a different tendency appearing in the missionary milieu, the Protestantism of Legge; Hung Jen-kan reflected, with little or no distortion, that tendency. The Shield King was, as far as we know, in a tiny minority, perhaps a minority of one; if Legge was not quite that isolated, he remained all his life, in China and England, a deviant with almost no followers, so that his paper finding good in Confucianism was hooted down and banned in 1877, as noted above, years after the remnants of the T'ai-p'ings were wiped up and their doctrines exterminated in China.

Having tried to deal with the question of the influence of the particular kind of Christianity, Protestant fundamentalism, to which the T'ai-p'ings were exposed, on their ideology, which is the chief historical question, we may now briefly examine the theological question which lies behind Boardman's conclusion that 'the Taiping religion...was not Christianity'. The question is, was T'ai-p'ing doctrine orthodox or heretical? Two methods may be employed, comparative and canon-legal. For comparative investigation the context must be not the history of China but the history of Christian sects in all countries. In fact the rebels' doctrines and politico-social system have many parallels in that history. In some respects T'ai-p'ing teaching is reminiscent of Gnosticism, the earliest Christian heresy, in which some features of pre-Christian religious and philosophical systems were retained by those professing Christian belief. In its armed crusade to build a Kingdom of Heaven (t'ien-kuo meant exactly that) on earth, the movement recalls the Waldensians of the thirteenth century, the Anabaptists who founded a New Jerusalem at Münster in 1532–5, the Puritans who undertook to make England into a 'godly' commonwealth in the seventeenth century. T. T. Meadows called the T'ai-p'ing doctrine a 'Chinese Swedenborgian Christianity'.[75] Emanuel Swedenborg was a Swedish mystic whose followers founded a Church of the New Jerusalem. He had a number of visions, including one of the Last Judgment (which, having occurred in Swedenborg's presence in 1757, was therefore not to be expected in the future). He seemed to anticipate that his own revelations would lead to a church related to Christianity somewhat as the latter had been to Judaism. Despite the obvious parallels, however, Meadows's reference must be regarded as one simply to a particularly eccentric person within the pietist tradition from which the Protestant evangelicals came.

Looking further in the lineage of pietism, we encounter in the United States in the T'ai-p'ings' own time a sect with many features in common with theirs. In 1820, stimulated by the then feverish revivalistic atmosphere of Palmyra, New York, one Joseph Smith had the first of a series of visions which led eventually to the founding of what others called Mormonism and what he and his followers termed the Church of Jesus Christ of Latter-Day Saints. The Bible was basic, but in the nineteenth century there was vouchsafed a new revelation, the first since Biblical times. The result was written on gold plates, with a special pair of glasses supernaturally provided for reading them, since they were in an unknown language. This Book of Mormon was to supplement the Bible, and further divine guidance was anticipated in 'continued revelation'. The Mormons did not try to overthrow the government, but they founded a theocratic community in Utah in which religious and political authority lay in the same hands. There they had their own prophets and apostles who owed nothing to Christianity since the time of Christ. They practiced communalism and some of them entered into plural marriage; they banned alcohol and tobacco. The Mormons acknowledged only personal sins, or transgressions of mediated divine commands, and had no notion of 'original sin'. They held that the United States held a special providential position in the world, and had their own pseudo-history; their account of early America is much less satisfying to scholars than the T'ai-p'ings' account of the beginnings of Chinese history. In all the respects enumerated and others, the Mormons were similar to the T'ai-p'ings.[76] They still exist, while the T'ai-p'ings disappeared a century ago; but during the time when both existed, there were many parallels.[77]

The T'ai-p'ing movement thus appears to belong to the history of Christian heresy and schism,[78] in many of its doctrinal as well as political and social manifestations. In the T'ai-p'ings' own time Catholics from the first disavowed their teaching and most Protestants slowly and reluctantly came to do so. Somewhat unexpectedly, it appears that a strong argument can be made, even from the presumably most rigorous position in canon law, that of the Roman Catholics, that the T'ai-p'ings were neither heretical nor schismatic. Lawlor writes, 'St Augustine held that those who have not fathered the error but received it from others, who do not cling to it pertinaciously but seek the truth, "are by no means to be reckoned among the heretics".'[79] There at once springs to mind Hung Hsiu-ch'üan, leaving his Kwangsi sect for Canton to seek baptism (although he and his cousin Li had baptized each other already) from Issachar J. Roberts, who refused to give it to him. Indispensable to heresy, in the Roman Catholic definition, is 'the stubborn inflexible will, once the falsity of the doctrine in question...has been made clear to the erring Christian, to persist...' It is doubtful that anyone tried, whether or not successfully, to make clear to Hung Hsiu-ch'üan that he held any 'false doctrines'. It thus seems probable that a canon lawyer might have a substantial basis for exculpating Hung Hsiu-ch'üan of heresy. As for schism, the T'ai-p'ings did not at all 'break away from fraternal love'; on the contrary, they acknowledged their 'barbarian brethren' with both surprise and *agape*.[80] Even if the Rev. Mr Roberts had not driven Hung Hsiu-ch'üan away, there was no Chinese Church for Hung to join, let alone one to separate from. It appears difficult even to sustain the charge of schism.

It may of course be contended that the T'ai-p'ings by derivation shared in the offense of heresy which Roman Catholics allege in all the Protestant Reformers, arguing that although the latter expressed differing views on various theological points, 'they were in agreement in demanding that the Bible be the sole source of faith to the rejection or neglect of tradition'.[81] At the root of the T'ai-p'ings' misconceptions and distortions of Christianity was the missionaries' own uncompromising belief that the Bible, utterly unadorned and unexplained, was enough to make a man a Christian. Of course in practice Protestants, even the most unyielding fundamentalists, always explained to 'converts' their understanding of what the Bible meant. But in the case of the T'ai-p'ings there was no chance to do so; the rebel leaders were on their own –

and the literal meaning of the basic Protestant position thus was given a naked implementation almost unique in the history of Christianity.[82] But to say that the T'ai-p'ings were, from the Roman Catholic standpoint, heretical in the same sense all Protestants were, when the only question is their relation to Protestantism, is not to say anything significant.

Altogether the remarkable thing was the degree to which the T'ai-p'ing leaders reflected the motives, emphases, and spirit of the Protestant fundamentalists even when they carried them further than the missionaries intended or approved of. T'ai-p'ing Christianity, as the doctrine deserves to be called, was in a way a justification of the evangelical belief that the Chinese Bible, without written notes or even the oral explanations of the missionary, would of itself change a man's life or even millions of lives. Of course the evangelicals did not foresee the form that the change might take. In 1853 their joy outweighed their misgivings; by 1859–60 the latter had come to prevail, accompanied by emotions ranging from embarrassment to horror. The diplomats and traders were uneasy about the rebels from the first; with the missionaries neutralized, the Western powers could take measures in support of the Ch'ing *status quo* they preferred to the T'ai-p'ing crusade. It need not be argued here that Tseng Kuo-fan and the other gentry leaders were not chiefly responsible for suppressing the rebellion; it may be suggested that if more Western aid than they actually received had been required, it might well have been forthcoming.

The failure of the rebellion, as Stelle has pointed out, meant the failure of T'ai-p'ing Christianity.[83] The failure of the rebel religion in turn might have meant a heavy blow for the chances of further Protestant mission activity if it had not been for the fact that the Western powers, by the new treaties of 1858–60, extorted from the Ch'ing government further privileges for the missionaries. Protestantism had been the basis of the professed ideology of the greatest rebellion in Chinese history; this fact alone, by the way, effectively disproves the often-repeated assertion that in recent times (perhaps in contrast with the early modern period) Christianity held no attraction for the Chinese. However, as things turned out, during the 1860's Protestantism emerged as the religion of the Western intruders and their governments in almost precisely the manner the Yung-cheng emperor had feared over a century before.[84]

If Hung Jen-kan had mustered sufficient support to be able to establish control of the rebel movement, the fate of Protestant-derived T'ai-p'ing Christianity in China might have been quite different; such Christianity, under the leadership of men like the Shield King, open to the Western improvements that China needed, drawing on the best in Chinese tradition and willing to use it in reforming China, might have produced a regime quite different from the weak and vacillating one of the Ch'ings during their last fifty years. In this light the demotion of Hung Jen-kan and the final defeat of the rebels mark the loss of an opportunity for a viable Chinese Protestant

Christianity comparable to the loss of an opportunity for a viable Chinese Catholic Christianity caused by the papal decision of the Rites Controversy. If Westerners were chiefly responsible for the ending of the latter, they must also bear a heavy responsibility for the ending of the former.

The Protestantism of Morrison was too indifferent to Chinese culture, too arrogant about its own peculiar features, too ignorant of the fundamental aspects of the cultural confrontation of China with the West, to provide Hung Hsiu-ch'üan with an ideological basis whereby he could in the long run make good his challenge to authority; the Protestantism of Legge remained an unpopular view of a tiny minority among the missionaries, and the single Hung Jen-kan which it produced was not enough. The non-missionary, secular Westerners had their share in defeating the rebels, but regardless of the importance which ought to be attached to their military intervention, it may be said that they recognized the grave weaknesses of the rebel movement and acted on them. Of all the Westerners concerned, it was not Ward and Gordon who were chiefly responsible for the disaster of Chinese Protestantism, but the evangelicals who laid on T'ai-p'ing shoulders a sectarian burden too heavy for them to carry to victory. The enlightened views of James Legge were too isolated in the missionary milieu and propagated, by Hung Jen-kan, too late, too gently, and with too little response from the T'ai-p'ing environment to lighten that burden materially.

TIMOTHY RICHARD AND THE REFORM MOVEMENT

From the decisive defeat of the T'ai-p'ings in 1864 to the end of the nineteenth century and well into the twentieth the evangelicals plodded on in their old paths. Medical missions, inaugurated by Peter Parker in 1834,[85] aroused gratitude in a populace without hospitals or any medical care except that of dispensers of herbal medicines and acupuncture. Poor and uneducated patients seldom, however, were able to respond to the preaching that attended their treatment, even if they tried to please their benefactors. A certain Dr Maxwell reported that 'it is certainly discouraging, after 14 days work, to be told that the Name of the Son of God is "Satan" '.[86]

The best thing to do, it seemed, was to keep a stiff upper lip about the meager results attained. A report for 1870 stated, 'the field is peculiarly hard, labourers few and in the comparative infancy of mission work in China analogy and experience teach us that it is yet early to expect great results'.[87] A report of 1898 stated bravely, 'we sow where others reap and we rejoice with them'.[88] In 1907 it was the same: 'There is a certain amount of selfishness in seeking for big results to put on paper and send to friends, and we have to remind ourselves that faithful work done should be dearer to us than prominent statistics.'[89] That is to say, the conversions produced by medical missions were almost nil.

The ordinary missionaries did try, after the securing of toleration to Christianity by the treaties of 1858–60,[90] to exploit the new situation and apply new methods. A certain Hudson Taylor, after a youthful visit in 1853, returned to China in 1866 to stay. At this point there were not quite 100 Protestant missionaries in China, almost all of them on the coast and in the treaty ports. Taylor launched the China Inland Mission, which provided several innovations: missionaries were to penetrate the interior; they were to be selected irrespective of denomination (but must have 'soundness in the faith in all fundamental truths', which guaranteed fundamentalism); they were to wear Chinese dress, eat Chinese food, and follow Chinese customs as far as possible. Within a decade the CIM boasted fifty-four missionaries and had become the largest single non-Catholic missionary group in China.[91] However, there was no requirement that the missionaries know anything about China or Chinese culture, and if the CIM workers gave less offense than others, they had scarcely any more positive impact.

Good people of minimal education racked their brains to think of ways to be effective. Members of the Bible Christian Methodist Mission reported from Yünnan: 'Friends who want to institute something which appeals to all Chinese will find a harvest festival...just the thing they need...We have made a beginning with an Easter Festival, but that has not caught on.'[92] A poignant story is told by the chronicler of a certain Baptist mission:

Shou-yang is on the road from Taiyuanfu to Hwailu [in Shansi]. It is a clean town, nestling in the bosom of clean hills. The people are hardy and industrious. They are well-to-do, and like most hill folk are of an obstinate disposition. They are hard to convince, but once influenced they become firm and steadfast disciples.

The mission was established there in 1892. Eight years later eleven adult missionaries and two children were massacred during the Boxer Rebellion. The report is not clear but it appears that two missionaries and a total of nine Chinese converts remained in the autumn of 1900.[93] That is to say, before the massacre the missionaries outnumbered the converts. Only slightly less pitiable examples could easily be multiplied.

The tragedy of Protestantism in China was at root the fact that although it failed ever to influence the intellectual elite substantially, in either its fundamentalist or modernist phase, it always had the potential for doing so. A respect for learning was never entirely lacking in the Protestants. Had not virtually the first act of the Reformers been the translation of the Bible into the German vernacular, which required a knowledge of at least two or three languages? Even poor Morrison had regarded his first task as a scholarly one – translation of the Bible into Chinese. As has been noted, however, only James Legge and very few others went beyond the indispensable rudiments of learning – Western or Chinese – in their missionary work. The fundamentalists did not suffer pangs of conscience or concern for their devotion to the unexplained text of the Bible; at worst, they gloried in their myopia. Marshall

Broomhall, a chronicler of evangelicalism, proudly reports that a correspondent had sent him an advertisement displayed in his city: 'The Gospel for suffers [sic] from tooth-ache.' Broomhall commented, 'such things are a strong proof of Bible influence. The people are beginning to think in Bible terms.'[94]

The old evangelical tradition persisted unchanged in the later nineteenth century. At the first nationwide missionary conferences held in Shanghai in 1877 and 1890 the continued prevalence of the half-educated and ignorant among the missionaries was demonstrated. At the 1877 conference Legge's views were simply suppressed. At the 1890 conference, the main resolution urged that 'in view of its paramount importance the evangelistic work be pushed forward with increased vigor and earnestness in order, if possible, to save the present generation'.[95] Considering that at this moment (1893), after eighty-odd years of Protestant mission work, there were an estimated 37,000 Protestant communicants in the whole of the Chinese Empire,[96] such determination may be regarded as either admirably courageous or as incredibly disoriented to the real world. Already evidence was at hand that China was in the initial stages at least of extensive reception of Western thought. To most of the missionaries, the alternatives open to the Chinese remained either continuing their current road to eternal damnation or the single new road of 'conversion' to evangelical Protestantism. In fact there were several other alternatives even within the framework of Westernization, some of them perhaps as repellent to the missionaries as that of remaining 'heathen'.

In the 1870's there appeared in China a Protestant missionary who perceived a range of alternatives good and bad. Timothy Richard was born in Wales in 1845. Having been converted when fifteen or sixteen, he was accepted for China by the Baptist Missionary Society in 1869. At that time he knew nothing of China. No one in Europe, his biographer asserts, had ever read the whole of the Confucianist, Taoist, and Buddhist classics (perhaps wrongly, for by now qualified Orientalists were professors in the major European universities); he laments, 'altogether...we all began at the wrong end. Instead of going to convey an alien religion to China, should we not first have gone to find out whether already it had not a better one than our own?'[97] It was a question that had occurred in approximately the same form to James Legge, but to no one else of whom we have record among the Protestant missionaries.

Richard found his way to that question, and some answers to it, slowly and painfully. The story begins with a missionary sermon he heard delivered by Edward Irving on the text of Matthew 10.11 in the King James version: 'And into whatsoever city or town ye shall enter, enquire who in it is worthy; and there abide till ye go thence.' The conclusion drawn by Irving and accepted by Richard was that a missionary should always seek the 'worthy', meaning the men of highest character. But Richard soon came to extend the meaning of the word to include the educated class of China. Irving had warned against missionaries' showing any 'preference of rank', lest they be 'like the Jesuits to

lay their artful toils around the high and noble and princely of the Nation . . .'98
Whatever Richard thought of Irving's caution, in practice he came to ignore it.

Richard reached Shanghai in 1870 and settled in Chefoo alone. He was soon joined by a colleague, who in 1874 departed for New Zealand, leaving him alone again. In an important sense he remained alone all his life. He had friends and admirers among the other missionaries, and he had a devoted wife (married in 1878), who shared his views completely and collaborated in his work. For the rest he was constantly in the position of attempting to convince some other person of something he was reluctant to accept – either persuading Chinese to become Christians, or fellow missionaries to abandon narrow evangelicalism. In 1874 or 1875 he moved to Ch'ingchou. Deciding to don Chinese scholars' garb, shave his head, and wear an artificial queue, he instantly found it easier to be received by his neighbors. In the first five years he made three converts, in the year after his adoption of Chinese dress he made fifteen. But individual conversions were not to be his chief concern. He was already aiming his efforts at the scholars. His first step was characteristic:

At this period the greatest opponents to Christianity were the scholar classes, and in order to convince them of the value of Christianity by practice rather than by theory, I decided to make a grant of a dollar each to all the Sui-ts'ais [*hsiu-ts'ai*, holders of the first degree in the imperial examination system] of Ch'ang Lo.99

Thus began Richard's apostolate to the scholar-gentry. His intellectual limitations may be suggested by the quotation, but it also evidences his ingenuity, determination, and concern for the Chinese as they were rather than as evangelicalism demanded they become. His contact with geomancy (*feng-shui*) led him to conclude the way to end such beliefs was to teach the natural sciences. 'I maintain', he wrote, 'that the study of science ought to be held in as much reverence as religion, for it deals with the laws of God.'100 And he promptly drafted a scheme for a series of scientific textbooks. He was to draft many comparable or still more far-reaching schemes for the use of the Chinese or his fellow missionaries during the next decades.

At Ch'ingchou he soon acquired a new Westerner colleague and a Chinese named Ch'ing. Ch'ing had acted as a secretary to the T'ai-p'ing rebels; Richard reported that he was 'one of the finest Christians ever found in China, and as a colleague was equal to any two or three average foreign missionaries'. Ch'ing deepened Richard's determination to have the Chinese Christians take as much initiative as possible, and he endeavored to set their congregations on a self-supporting and self-managing basis at the earliest possible moment. He was understandably annoyed when a certain Dr Nevius, having been struck by Richard's success in having the Chinese take the lead, wrote a pamphlet entitled *Dr Nevius' Missionary Method*, a copy of which was mailed to Richard by his own missionary society.101

In 1877 he went to Shansi, then the scene of one of the greatest famines of

Chinese history, in order to begin an energetic relief effort. He could do little to alleviate the starvation that may have led to fifteen or twenty million deaths, but he collected funds from both Westerners and Chinese and his unremitting efforts won him much Chinese respect. Convinced that Chinese officials were inept at relieving famine and that Western efficiency could greatly have reduced the casualties, he still made friends with several successive governors of Shansi and the great viceroys. In 1880 he talked with Li Hung-chang, and was impressed by Li's statement that there were no Christians among the educated Chinese. Returning to Shansi, for the next three years he delivered monthly lectures on the sciences to a group of officials and scholars in Taiyuan. Some of his Baptist colleagues were 'rather shocked that he did not think human nature altogether bad, and that he believed that Darwin knew more of science than Moses'.[102]

As he continued his Chinese studies, his respect for the traditional culture increased. He had been working on Confucianism through Legge's translations for some time, and continued to do so as he applied himself to reading and writing Chinese. Viceroy Tso Tsung-t'ang had caught his attention by remarking that there was no real antagonism between Confucianism and Christianity. The leading scholar of Shansi, he found, admired Ricci's *The True Doctrine of the Lord of Heaven* and had views similar to Tso's. On Taoism he wrote a pamphlet to show what was 'true' in its teachings and where he thought Christianity had gone beyond it. He became interested in Buddhism to the extent of coming to believe that what he called the 'Higher Buddhism' of Japan and originally of China had its origin in Nestorian Christianity.[103] Of course his fellow missionaries considered 'acknowledgment of any good in the native religion[s]' to be 'rank heresy'.[104]

In 1885 he took home leave and presented to the missionary societies his proposals to reform Protestant missions in China. He suggested that a 'high-class' mission college be established in each provincial capital, beginning with the maritime provinces, to influence the leaders to accept Christianity; he urged that each new missionary learn the Chinese language, study the indigenous religions, and employ more Chinese assistants; he proposed the establishment of seminaries for Chinese ministers who would receive instruction not only in theology but the usual Western university subjects. The silence of his colleagues was deafening. 'After this,' he wrote, 'I began to realize that God would have me bear my cross alone...'[105]

Richard established good relations not only with many Chinese officials and scholars but also with Roman Catholics. As early as 1878 he sent for some Roman Catholic books in Chinese, since at that time very few Protestant books 'suitable for presenting to intelligent Chinese' had been translated.[106] The books he ordered were those written by the Jesuits of two centuries before; with a few omissions he found that they would serve his purposes admirably. So far had he departed from his predecessors who tried to convert Chinese by floating Bibles ashore that Mrs Richard wrote to her ardently evangelical brother, 'the Bible is the last thing my husband gives a convert, the Old Testament last of all'.[107]

By this time Richard's critics were charging that he 'taught a mixture of science, popery, and heathenism for the Gospel of Christ. . .'[108] The science he certainly taught, with whatever books and apparatus he could lay hands on. As for 'popery', he acknowledged common Christian foundations with Catholics, treated them as friends and co-religionists, and in practice refused to accept the Protestant doctrine that the Bible was a sufficient basis for Christianity – at least in China. Concerning the papacy, he wrote in 1884, 'Popology wrecked the Romanists in China once and the infallibility dogma [promulgated in 1870] now makes it utterly impossible for any thinking people who know anything of history to adopt their system.'[109] Many distinguished Catholics also deprecated – if not openly – papal action in the Rites Controversy and the promulgation of the new dogma, not merely those who left Rome to become 'Old Catholics' as a result of the Vatican Council of 1870. Thus it was true that he was not entirely hostile to Roman Catholicism. As for 'heathenism', he valued the truth, as he saw it, to be found in Confucianism, Taoism, and Buddhism. 'Christ came to fulfil the aspirations of the Jewish prophets', he wrote. 'Christianity comes in like manner to fulfil the aspirations of the sages of China, India, and Arabia.'[110]

His use of science, the writings of Roman Catholics, and the portions of the Chinese tradition compatible with Christianity in order to influence the educated class infuriated his colleagues as the somewhat similar views of James Legge (though he seems to have had less concern with science than Richard) had done in the previous generation. Perhaps Richard offended them even more, for he was indefatigable in urging his projects on his fellow evangelicals, and blunt in his criticism of their failings. 'There can be no doubt', he wrote, 'that one reason why many Confucianists do not adopt Christianity is the poverty of Christian literature as compared with Confucian literature.'[111] In 1886, after most of the early mission colleges had been founded, he said that in all of China there was not one example of 'what the *Chinese* call a high class institution' run by Protestants.[112] The missionaries themselves were poorly educated. In some countries, he declared, the missionaries 'are far superior to the chiefs. In China we are often *inferior*.'[113] And he perceived the storm that lay ahead: 'If Christianity does not convert by the million perhaps some other religion may yet do so.' If the 'knowledge and science of the West' were not to be introduced through the Christian Church, he predicted that it would be supplied by anti-Christian agencies.[114] He was quite right.

After the Baptists rejected his plan for a first-rate Christian college, he thought of leaving the mission. But circumstances then opened the way to permit him to undertake much of what he thought most important. In 1890 Dr Alexander Williamson,[115] founder of the Society for the Diffusion of Christian and General Knowledge for the Chinese, died. Richard's Baptist superiors, probably glad to be rid of his importunities, consented to let him accept an offer to replace Williamson. In 1891 Richard went to Shanghai, and was able to launch a massive effort to reach scholars through the printing press. Soon he attracted the support of officials, notably Viceroy Chang Chih-tung, who told him that if he could, through his books, 'bring forty of the highest officials to see eye to eye, then the rest of the mandarins would follow their lead'.[116] Richard himself translated Mackenzie's *History of the Nineteenth Century*. It was completed just as the Sino-Japanese War was ending and at once gained a large readership. Though relatively few copies were sold through regular channels, Richard estimated that there were a million pirated copies in circulation.

In 1895 came Richard's chance to discover how many scholars had been reading his books and to advocate his ideas in person. The occasion was the triennial examination in Peking for the *chin-shih* (third and highest degree). Gilbert Reid, who had many acquaintances among the literati, and Richard hired rooms and invited candidates to attend lectures and discussions and have tea there.[117] A memorial was drawn up, protesting the Treaty of Shimonoseki and demanding certain reforms. K'ang Yu-wei,[118] soon to become the best-known scholar of the day, was chosen to draft the memorial; it was signed by over 1,200 *chü-jen* (holders of the second degree, and aspirants to the third), but did not reach the emperor. Richard wrote his wife that in the memorial he 'was astounded to find almost all the various suggestions I have made boiled down and condensed into a marvelously small compass. No wonder he [K'ang] came to call upon me when we had so much in common.'[119] It is difficult to follow the chronology at this point. Goddard writes that after the memorial failed, Richard hired Liang Ch'i-ch'ao as his secretary and for three months the meetings continued in his and Reid's rooms. A Society for the Study of Self-Strengthening (Ch'iang Hsüeh Hui) was organized from among those in attendance.[120] However, since K'ang called on Richard only in October 1895, this means that either K'ang had taken part in the Richard–Reid meetings only incognito or unrecognized by the missionaries, which seems unlikely, or that he had not attended and had been informed about the discussions by Liang or others. It seems most unlikely that the main features of the memorial and Richard's proposals coincided by chance, and Richard's graceful refusal to press the point need not confuse anyone. Richard had been tirelessly drafting various detailed reform proposals and discussing them with Li Hung-chang, Chang Chih-tung, Tseng Chi-tse (who had been minister to England, France, and Russia), and others, and it would have been easy for some of them to come to K'ang's attention quite aside from the sessions in Richard's and Reid's rooms.

For a time the Ch'iang Hsüeh Hui of Peking issued a newspaper, *The Globe Magazine* (*Wan-kuo Kung-pao*); it consisted mainly of reprintings from Young J. Allen's newspaper of the same name, to which Richard had been a prominent contributor and which he edited during Allen's absence in 1898.

Sun Chia-nai told Richard that he had been reading Richard's translation of the Mackenzie *History* to the emperor every day for months. Richard was offered the presidency of the Imperial University of Peking, but refused. In 1896 Liang published a new edition of *New Tracts for the Times (Shih-shih Hsin-lun)*. The first edition of this publication had been in 120 volumes in 1826; it was reissued in a sharply anti-foreign and anti-Christian version in 1889. Liang's edition had many essays by foreigners and Christians. It was in 20 volumes and had 580 essays and documents. Of these 160 were anonymous, the remaining 420 by 135 different writers but most by 6: Liang had 44, K'ang 38, Richard 31, and three Chinese officials had 28, 25, and 18 each.[121]

During most of 1897 Richard was absent from China. Almost immediately on his return there occurred a kind of *coup* in which the young Kuang-hsü emperor (1875–1908) seized the reins of power from the Empress Dowager, named K'ang Yu-wei secretary of the Tsungli-yamen (foreign office), and issued a series of reform edicts. Richard was invited to become adviser to the emperor himself. At the very hour Richard had an appointment to see him, he was seized by the Empress Dowager, and the so-called Hundred Days of Reform came to an end.[122]

Although the Reform movement of 1898 proved abortive, the failure of the Boxer Rebellion in 1900 convinced the Empress Dowager that reforms were after all unavoidable. Imperial edicts soon expressed disapproval of foot-binding, inaugurated educational reform, took steps to prepare for a constitutional system, and broadened (and in 1905 abolished) the imperial examination system. All of these reforms except abolition of the examinations owed much to Richard's literary enterprise. In 1907 he wrote, 'one of the best proofs that our literature has done good is that some of our books are now out-of-date, because the reforms they advocated have been carried out. We claim a humble share in the awakening of China.'[123] In his memoirs he went further to assert that 'the effect of this propaganda [of the SDK] had produced the Reform Movement...'[124] Teng Ssu-yü writes that Richard, 'a far-sighted missionary of long experience who had intimate contacts with higher officials, helped the reform movement a great deal...'[125]

Richard's work was without doubt a decisive factor in suggesting to K'ang, Liang, and others certain courses of action. They perceived China's weakness in the face of foreign encroachment by both the West and Japan, but needed help in charting a path for reforms. Richard's detailed and oft-reworked proposals came to hand at an opportune moment. The only thing lacking was a full appreciation of the way the Manchu court operated and of the weapons available to the anti-reform party. The side of Richard that was all impatient energy and rationalism may indeed have contributed to the precipitateness and lack of caution that led to the Reformers' downfall within a few months. Perhaps a bit of blame ought to accompany the credit that was rightfully his.

After the Empress Dowager resumed full power, Richard did not fall into despair. He warned of the coming Boxer danger, though he was not heeded either in England or the United States – where he was when news of the massacres began to arrive. Returning to China, he sought no vengeance; he did propose that Shansi pay an indemnity, not one to Westerners but one which would be used to establish a provincial university 'to remove the ignorance and superstition that had been the main cause of the massacre of the foreigners'.[126] The proposal was adopted. Richard was to be in charge of the Western studies department for ten years; all students were to be either *hsiuts'ai* or *chü-jen* from Shansi, and all teaching was to be in the Chinese language. William E. Soothill became principal and worked closely with Richard. Richard relinquished his control to the Chinese several months early, in November 1910. An imperial plan to duplicate the university in all other provinces never was implemented, and the Revolution of 1911 effectively put an end to the institution, though the buildings were not damaged. Nevertheless hundreds of young men had been educated and sent out as teachers, and Soothill reports that when Sir John Jordan visited Shansi in 1920, he found it the 'most advanced and best governed province in the country'; the Anglo-American Commission appointed to study Chinese education confirmed its educational pre-eminence; and in 1922 it was reported that 50% of the villages in the province had primary schools.[127]

Richard's last years were not so unequivocally inspiring. He had won a place in the estimation of high Chinese officials and the emperor himself which no Westerner had had since Verbiest; his knowledge of China had given him access to high places in Europe and America. It all seems to have gone to his head, not in the sense of making him conceited, but of persuading him that great things were easy. His wife's restraining hand was gone; she died in 1903.[128] (The second Mrs Richard was a different sort of woman.) Christian literature had led to the Reform movement in China, he believed; in 1900 he suggested to a missionary conference in New York that it might lead also to the 'nucleus of a parliament of man and a federation of the world'.[129] He had already sent a circular to all the rulers of Christendom 'in order to prepare their minds for the coming federation of the world.'[130] After noncommittal but friendly statements had been made to him on the subject by Prince Ch'ing and Marquis Saionji in 1904, he announced at the Peace Congress in Lucerne in 1905 that China and Japan might be willing to join a federation of nations.[131] Resigning his secretaryship of the Christian Literature Society in 1915, he returned to England, his health failing, and died in April 1919.

Richard's impact on China was great, his merits noteworthy. His devoted admirer Soothill writes:

He sought to clothe Christian ideas in Chinese dress. Apart from their names, there are strong resemblances, natural and not acquired, between Timothy Richard and Matthew Ricci. Both endeavored to appeal to the Chinese from the authority of truth nationally acknowledged rather than from an external authority which was not recognized.[132]

Richard was indeed like Ricci in seeking to create a Chinese civilization that would be Christian without abandoning its ancient wisdom and refined arts, by means of establishing in high places an atmosphere favorable to the propagation of Christianity. 'I am after the Leaders,' he said; 'if you get the Leaders you get all the rest.'[133] In 1902 he told the Shanghai Missionary Association that China was ruled by 'about 2,000 civil mandarins', and that they were the proper missionary objective.[134] He also was concerned for the poor and hungry, did much to aid them directly, and worked hard to assure that Chinese Christians of all social classes should have their own churches and minister to each other in their own language. But his aim of 'conversion by the million' could not be achieved, he knew, by the evangelicals' kind of individual conversions.

His objectives, however, outran his capacities. He was always handicapped by his lack of solid early education. Soothill acknowledges, 'for a man who could work so hard, so long and persistently, his reasoning at times had perplexing gaps. He was not built, for instance, for the patient, meticulous work of translation.'[135] His feverish eagerness for results led him to underestimate the difficulties in transplanting not only Western technology and science but also Western political systems to China. Richard's aim of basing his efforts on 'Christian literature' depended on a kind of philosophical and literary sophistication which he did not quite possess. As a result, he came to place ever-increasing emphasis on purely secular reform – educational, social, and political. In these areas he had, indeed, his maximum impact; but the conversion of mandarins to Protestantism did not accompany the favorable reaction and even occasional implementation that followed his submission of proposals to one high official after another.

The reasons for Richard's failure lie probably less in his personal weaknesses than in the fact that, in contrast to Ricci, he remained virtually alone in his perception of the missionary task. His literary and cultural preoccupations never penetrated the spirit of Protestant missionaries in China. In the 1901–14 period, as before, much of Christian literature remained 'in inferior literary style, not enough was of the kind to bring conviction to the new student class, and an insufficient number of foreigners and Christian Chinese of ability were devoting their time to its production'.[136] By that time it was too late.

Soothill reports an unidentified person's writing 'some years' before 1924, when his book was published, that 'to this day it is no uncommon thing to be stopped by strangers in different parts of the province [Shantung] who remember Li T'i-mo-t'ai [Richard's Chinese name], and want to know where he is and whether he will ever come back'.[137] It is understandable that those who knew him and understood him could never forget him.

CONCLUSION

Richard's tireless efforts won him the sympathy of a few fellow missionaries.

Even those who were not caught by his vision were impressed by some of his arguments.[138] Following Richard's strategy, Gilbert Reid in 1894 founded a 'Mission Among the Higher Classes of China'.[139] W. A. P. Martin, who was to become president of the Imperial University of Peking (founded 1897) on Li Hung-chang's nomination, adopted Richard's position on the rites, and valiantly defended it. At the missionary conference of 1890 he made a plea for toleration of the Confucian and ancestral rites by Christians, which was almost unanimously voted down in a scene reminiscent of the 1877 conference's suppression of James Legge's comparable paper.[140] The evangelicals had no more use for Richard than they had for Legge, or for the Chinese tradition; as Latourette writes, 'Protestant missionaries, with few exceptions, still viewed with entire disapproval the religious systems of China...'[141]

Curiously, the relation of Roman Catholic missions during the nineteenth century to Chinese culture was quite similar to that of the Protestant ones. The religious impulse that produced the latter also stirred the former. In 1822 a pious laywoman, Pauline Jaricot of Lyon, founded an Association for the Propagation of the Faith, and not long afterward a widespread revival of Catholic missions was under way. The Lazarists had maintained in Peking their feeble outpost, inherited from the Jesuits when the order was dissolved in 1773. Thus when the restored Society of Jesus returned to China in the 1840's, its missionaries went not to Peking but to the Shanghai area, making Zikawei (Hsü-chia-hui) their base for central China. The Missions Étrangères, Franciscans, and others took other regions. What they could do in any region was another matter. The papal decision in the Rites Controversy prevented them from thinking of work with the educated class. Since Catholics could not pay ritual respect to their ancestors or Confucius, they could not take the imperial examinations or aim at state office, and therefore they 'could have no standing in the political or intellectual life of the country'.[142] Catholics were restricted almost entirely to work with the poor and ignorant. It must be said that many desired to do so, for pietist and evangelical impulses affected the Roman Church as well as Protestant denominations. As a result, writes Cary-Elwes:

Apparently no new methods were tried, no heart-searchings made. The Chinese clergy were still kept down to the lower ranks of the hierarchy: the main concentration of energy was still [in 1900-10] directed to evangelization. Unlike the Protestants...the vast possibilities of education were not greatly exploited by the Catholics, partly from lack of funds, partly from the conviction that the essential purpose was to preach Christ.[143]

Despite lack of funds – the salary of the ordinary Catholic missionary for a year might be less than that of the ordinary Protestant for a month[144] – the Catholics made many more converts than the Protestants. They were not hesitant to live in the interior or adopt the Chinese way of life, and not reluctant to baptize infants or possibly impure adults,[145] believing that if the first generation of converts was apt to be defective in its Catholicism the second generation was not. As a result, by 1900 the number of Roman Catholics in China may have been from 10 to 20 times as great as that of Protestants.[146] But though Catholic missionaries had many advantages, in the nineteenth century they had few in relation to the problem of adaptation to the Chinese tradition, which Catholic converts had to renounce almost as thoroughly as those of the Protestants.

Westerners other than missionaries – diplomats, traders, and the few who had taken service with the Chinese government – took a more conciliatory line. Sir Robert Hart, the wise head (from 1863 to 1907) of the Chinese Customs, was able to appraise fairly and judiciously the Chinese predicament in confronting different religious, economic, and political pressures and counsels put forward by Westerners, and offered the missionaries this advice:

Christianize but do not Westernize, is in fact what each missionary should aim at, lest he lade men with grievous burdens and hinder them that are entering: if people's hearts can be won for the Church, whatever else is befitting or deserving of praise will in due time follow. . .[147]

In similar vein, the Chinese chargé d'affaires in Paris had not long before promised: 'As for all these magnificent discoveries of your sciences, we shall introduce them into our national practice, but one by one, without shock and without brutal alteration of our customs and our habits.'[148] Alas, neither he nor anyone else could keep such a promise. And even while speaking optimistically about the post-Boxer prospects, Hart must have remembered with concern what he had been told decades earlier by Wen Hsiang, a celebrated official of the T'ung-chih period:

You are all to anxious to awake us and start us on a new road, and you will do it, but you will all regret it, for, once awaking and started, we shall go fast and far – farther than you think – much farther than you want![149]

By the time the Boxer Rebellion had been put down, there was no longer any question about whether China was going to undertake technical, social, and political reform on Western lines; but there was a serious question about what China's cultural basis and system of values would be like in the era ahead. The Christian community was a tiny fraction of the population, but that was not its chief weakness. The decisive element in the failure of the Protestant evangelicals who then dominated the mission field was the same as that in the failure of the Roman Catholic missionaries of the nineteenth century.[150] Neither group had perceptibly touched the scholar-gentry (Richard's '2,000 civil mandarins'). The right 2,000 (or 5,000 or 10,000) converts would have been enough to influence or even determine the future of Chinese culture; Christians had perhaps 820,000, almost none of them the right ones for the purpose – to be sure, a purpose which most evangelicals did not want to have and one which Roman Catholics under papal authority had for almost two centuries been denied the possibility of having.

Protestant evangelicalism in China was, considering the sums of money expended and the lives sacrificed to the enterprise, an almost total failure. To be sure, it had its moments of glory and its isolated great men. Its most conspicuous if fleeting success came in the formation of T'ai-p'ing Christianity, whose defenders almost overthrew the Ch'ing dynasty and some of whose leaders wished to change the whole imperial system. Its most distinguished representatives were James Legge, who did so much to bring Chinese culture to the West but achieved so little in the field of missions in China, and Timothy Richard, who was nowhere near the scholar Legge was but had the gift of influencing men as Legge did not. What happened to Richard was that, failing to gain the support he required for an apostolate to the learned elite, he turned increasingly to the cause of secular reform for which the strength and prosperity of the Western powers were all the evidence needed to make converts. He did not become a theological 'liberal' or 'modernist' as the generation of missionaries after 1900 became; he retained his Protestant theology and tried to adapt the methods of its propagation to the Chinese culture from which his intended converts came. In retrospect it may be suggested that the task he, like Legge, undertook was too great. The evangelicals' suspicion of learning went too deep, their hostility to 'heathen' culture was too strong, their sectarian pride and sense of self-sufficiency were too much a part of their identity to be diminished or eradicated. What Legge and Richard and their few supporters were asking of the overwhelming majority of evangelicals was that they cease to be what they were.

There never was any substantial 'Christian literature' of the kind of which Richard dreamed; the kind of literature he circulated which had an impact on the officials and reformers of his day was mainly about the scientific and political achievements of the West.[151] Richard indeed pioneered this kind of literature and can claim an important share in its impact, but his fellow evangelicals remained indifferent to it. They played some part in social reform: the unequal position of women, the evils of footbinding, the scourge of opium, the denial of education to the lower classes, the lack of medical care – these and many other social ills yielded gradually to the patient toil of the evangelicals in the provinces before imperial reform edicts took up the cudgels against them. But the scientific knowledge and political reform which became the watchwords of the early twentieth century owed little to the evangelicals with very few honorable exceptions, notably Richard himself. It must be said that even Richard was unable to work out clearly the relation of political liberalism to Protestant Christianity. Indeed it appears that he never really conceived it to be a problem, and thus only unwittingly bequeathed it to his successors.

Richard had turned away from the intractable problems of China to those of world federalism and world peace – which at least seemed to him soluble – during his last years in China. It was in fact well before he departed for England that the stubborn self-confidence of the pietist evangelicals gave way.

Curiously so did the self-assurance of the bearers of the Chinese tradition, the scholar-gentry, and then the very foundation of the class was destroyed by the abolition of the examination system. The problem of the best Christian missionaries from Ricci to Richard, how to make the scholar-gentry look on Christianity with favor, thus disappeared in a short space of time. The scene changed, and a new cast of characters appeared. The Protestant 'modernists' confronted the new university youth. The evangelicals' few Chinese converts were swallowed up by history, leaving on the surface of the clashing and mingling tides of Western innovation and Chinese tradition scarcely a visible trace.

3

CHRISTIAN MODERNISM: SUN YAT-SEN (1895–1925)

> I remember when we were all reading Adam Smith. There is a book, now. I took in all the new ideas at one time – human perfectibility, now. But some say history moves in circles, and that may be very well argued; I have argued it myself. The fact is, human reason may carry you a little too far – over the hedge, in fact. It carried me a good way at one time, but I saw it would not do. I pulled up; I pulled up in time. But not too hard. I have always been in favour of a little theory; we must have thought, else we shall be landed back in the Dark Ages.
>
> Mr Brooke, in George Eliot, *Middlemarch*

INTRODUCTION

During the three centuries of more or less continuous contact with the West that China had experienced up to 1900, the dominant nationality of the Westerners who influenced China had changed several times. In the early seventeenth century Italians and Portuguese had been most prominent; Frenchmen had become more numerous in the late seventeenth and early eighteenth centuries; in the nineteenth century the most influential had been Britishers; by the early twentieth century Americans were taking the limelight. These changes reflected the shifting weight of world power. In the Renaissance the Mediterranean trading cities and states had explored the East; in the period 1660–1715 Louis XIV had made a bid for continental and colonial supremacy; after 1815 Britain ruled the waves and most of the land they touched; by the beginning of the twentieth century the United States had expanded westward to the Pacific and, with its immensely increased national strength, across it.

One might have expected the changing picture of dominant nationality in China to make a considerable difference. Actually it seems to have made little. What was more important than the nationality of the dominant Westerners in China was the prevailing current of thought in the West as a whole, or at any rate of that segment of Westerners who could think of traveling to the East. There were historical reasons why Christian humanists who were Italian Catholics rather than German Protestants, Christian pietists who were English rather than Hungarians, Christian modernists who were Americans rather than Frenchmen, came to China – but though it might have made some difference in each case if others had come instead (and in each case some others did come), it was their intellectual commitments rather than their nationality which affected the Chinese from the cultural standpoint.

70

Around 1900 one of these nationality shifts occurred – from Britishers to Americans. A second change was of great moment on the educational and cultural scene: the shift from passivity toward Western cultural influence to active pursuit of it. Many more Chinese sought out Western institutions in China in which they might enroll; many more went abroad, to Japan and to the West, as students. Those who went to the West, for a time at least, were likely to experience Christian modernism; those who went to Japan were apt to be introduced to the new currents of Western secular thought, often through Japanese mediation. A third change was, then, the simultaneous appearance for the first time of more than one alternative in Western cultural influence; and therefore three chapters are necessary to deal with the period from about 1890 to the 1920's.

As evangelicalism weakened and died in China, both Christian modernism – in China and in the West – and secular liberalism – to a slight extent in China, substantially in Japan and in the West – attracted the Chinese who looked abroad for enlightenment. The difference in their appeal was not only intellectual, but social. Since the pietist evangelicals had resolutely refused to point their efforts in the direction of the educated classes, the modernists, as they moved into the ascendant among the missionaries, would have had to make a marked change in strategy if they were to influence the intellectuals. They did not, partly restrained by American democratic ideology in its populist phase, partly handicapped by their own paucity of learning. As a result Christian modernism made an impact not to any extent on the intellectual elite, but on the less schooled Chinese – those who were as impatient with the need for systematic intellectual preparation as their Western mentors. The result was the Christian modernist impact on the early Kuomintang and Sun Yat-sen.

THE RISE OF MODERNISM IN THE WEST

'Some time about 1890,' writes Nichols, there took place 'a radical break in continuity in the theological leadership of the chief denominations which effectively dismissed the theological traditions central [from the Evangelical Awakening at the opening of the century until about 1890]...in American Protestantism.'[1] The chief factors in the change were probably the challenge of new scientific ideas and discoveries, especially the evolutionary theory of Darwin, the findings of the new Biblical archeology, the development of higher criticism and Biblical exegesis notably by Julius Wellhausen and Heinrich Holtzmann; the rise of pragmatism in philosophy, owing much to Friedrich Schleiermacher's theory of experience as the heart of religion and Rudolf Eucken's philosophy of activism, culminating in the work of William James;[2] and the growth of modern nationalism as a doctrine partly dependent on the everywhere newly strengthened powers of the nation-state after the 1860's. One element in the change was the reassertion of reason's part in religion after a century in which emotion had held sway; but the emphasis on the need for action and effectiveness, the practical as against the theoretical, did much to offset such reassertion. Christianity's invocation of the Kingdom of Heaven was given a ring of immediacy and materiality.

The 'self-assurance of modern man' at the turn of the twentieth century was given perhaps its most powerful statement in the theology of Albrecht Ritschl (1822-89), 'the ferocious opponent of Pietism...and the opponent of all metaphysics in theology', who taught that 'the quintessence of the task imposed upon man, which at the same time is his highest good and his own final aim, is the kingdom of God, in which the love of one's neighbour is activated'.[3] Ritschl, writes Nichols, dwelt on

God as revealed in concrete historical fact. In this recommendation he made his great appeal to a realistic fact-minded generation...He denied the doctrine of original sin and held, rather, that men have a tendency to good. Their cultural achievements, consequently, he esteemed optimistically, in terms of progress... The work of Jesus Christ, in bringing the believer to God, meant bringing him into a Kingdom of moral ends. This Kingdom seemed little more than a stage in the moral progress and unification of the race...Ritschlianism became thus the theological framework for much of the liberal social gospel, as a program for the mastery of life for which God's support was available.[4]

Ritschl's influence may be seen in Adolf Harnack, the eminent scholar who wrote the still unsuperseded *History of Dogma* (1885-9), Ernst Troeltsch in *The Social Teaching of the Christian Churches* (original published in 1912) and, even if partly by way of challenge to Ritschl, in Albert Schweitzer in *The Quest of the Historical Jesus* (1906). George Herron and Walter Rauschenbusch in America and R. J. Campbell, who supported Keir Hardie as he prepared to help found a Labor party, in Britain, moved in similar directions. Such men and the ministers who followed what they were understood to be saying had a great effect in reorienting Protestantism. Meanwhile in France Alfred Loisy, in England Friedrich von Hügel (German-Scottish by birth), and in Italy Antonio Fogazzaro attempted to introduce the same sorts of ideas into Roman Catholicism, but the papal encyclical *Pascendi* (1907) curbed their efforts.

It has been argued that 'America's most unique contribution to the great ongoing stream of Christianity is the "social gospel" ',[5] but the statement is an exaggeration. What replaced evangelicalism around 1900 in America was 'a liberal theology derived from German philosophical idealism', or more accurately that wing of German idealism, led by Ritschl, which was chiefly ethical and social in emphasis.[6] Horace Bushnell, the pioneer of the American social gospel, drew heavily on Schleiermacher's theory of experience; Washington Gladden, who followed him, was attracted by the idea of a religion 'that laid hold upon life with both hands, and proposed, first and foremost, to realize the Kingdom of God in this world',[7] as Ritschl taught. A few who were not ministers, such as Henry George, 'proclaimed a militant

Christianity that would crusade against economic injustice' and 'held that the social question was at the bottom a religious question'.[8] George in turn was the chief early influence on Walter Rauschenbusch, the 'greatest prophet of the social gospel'; and George D. Herron, chief modernist preacher of the 1890's, for some time supported George's single tax as the basis for his ideal society of the future. In 1896 Charles Monroe Sheldon wrote *In His Steps*, a novel to popularize the 'social gospel', which sold 23,000,000 copies in English alone (it also appeared in 21 other languages) up to 1933 and became one of the best-sellers of all time.[9] After Herron was divorced by one wife in 1901 and took another in a non-religious ceremony, his leadership of the social-gospel movement collapsed and soon passed to Rauschenbusch, author of *Christianity and the Social Crisis* (1907), *The Social Principles of Jesus* (1916), and *A Theology for the Social Gospel* (1917) – in the last title avowing that for him ethics came first and theology second, as indeed it did for the whole movement. He went further than Herron in developing a 'Christian Socialism', and helped to move like-minded people into the Socialist party and toward, as the chief periodical of this trend put it, 'loyalty to the International Socialist Movement as the means of realizing the social ideal of Jesus...'[10] Scott Nearing, Harry F. Ward, and some other active propagators of the social gospel at this stage ended, as did Sun Yat-sen, as at least partial sympathizers with Russian Communism.

Naturally the rise of Protestant modernism and of its American variant, the social gospel, had an impact on foreign missions. In 1895, at the conference of the newly organized Open and Institutional Church League, its secretary called for unity among the denominations so that 'they can work out the problems of Christian service in city, country, and abroad without the present waste of forces'.[11] The very formation of the Federal Council of the Churches of Christ in America in 1908, which for the first time brought the various denominations into a common organization, reflected the growth of social-gospel thought and its determination to be influential abroad as well as at home.

The pietist evangelicals, having abjured any learning divorced from the Bible,[12] found themselves ill-equipped to meet the modernist challenge. The modernists discussed economic theories, social conditions, political forces, as well as the new biology and other scientific developments. The fundamentalists chose to tackle the new ideas head-on, without adequate preparation, and were repeatedly worsted. The most dramatic American instance came late – when in 1925 the deeply religious old fundamentalist William Jennings Bryan took part in the Scopes trial and the atheist Clarence Darrow made a complete fool of him.[13] Long before that time, fundamentalism had been for the most part silenced and superseded by modernism among the missionaries of China.

MODERNISM SUPERSEDES FUNDAMENTALISM IN CHINA

The Roman Catholics

It has been noted that Roman Catholic fundamentalism was an important phenomenon during most of the nineteenth century, and that Roman Catholic modernism was a development of some importance in Europe. Perhaps because Catholics in the United States during this period were found mainly among the poor and uneducated, Catholic modernism showed little strength in either the United States or the China mission field, where Americans became prominent or even dominant during the early twentieth century. Catholic evangelicals continued to work among the Chinese rural poor during that period. Beginnings were made in education: the Aurora University was effectively founded in 1905 in Shanghai by the Jesuits, Fu-jen University was established in Peking, and in 1922 a Higher Studies Institute was created in Tientsin. By 1900 there were three or four printing presses at work.

The most significant new developments in China Catholic missions rejected fundamentalism, but not in the name of theological modernism. They were, surprisingly, based on the revival of the Ricci strategy. Around 1900 individual voices had begun to be raised in China in support of re-examining the whole problem. A. T. Piry wrote from Peking that if the Dominicans had not interfered with the Jesuits out of jealousy and aroused the Holy See, 'China would have rapidly become Christian in the seventeenth century, for the government favored the missions and would have lent a hand'. The literati remained at root not an obstacle to reform but its most likely vehicle, and yet Catholic converts in that class were non-existent. The remedy, Piry believed, was simply to permit the rites to ancestors and Confucius and permit the marriage of Christians with pagans.[14]

One man seems to have been chiefly responsible for leading the Roman Church back to a belated acceptance of the Ricci position; he was Father Vincent Lebbe.[15] Lebbe, of mixed Flemish and English descent, joined the Lazarists at eighteen. While the bishop of Peking was in Rome in 1900 Lebbe happened to meet him; the result was that Lebbe decided to go to China. He soon proved himself a trouble-maker. He refused the protection of the French consuls, which Catholic missionaries of that time all too readily sought; the action of the Tientsin consul taken in a certain land case Lebbe condemned as amounting to theft, and as a result he was banished to a small mission near Ningpo. From there in 1917 he wrote a powerful letter to his bishop, which impressed the dignitary so much that he sent it on to Rome. In the letter Lebbe demanded that the missionaries take as their point of departure the aspirations of non-Christians among whom they worked, attempt to discern all that was 'legitimate and true' in such aspirations, and proceed from there to build indigenous churches. By that time Lebbe had virtually single-handedly charted new methods for Catholic missions. He had conducted public lectures for intellectuals in Tientsin, formed Catholic lay associations, and established the first Chinese Catholic newspapers: a weekly, *Public Benefit Record* (*Kuang-i Lu*) in 1912 and a daily, *People's Welfare* (*I-shih Pao*) in 1916. They rapidly were imitated in other parts of China.

Two popes found Lebbe's arguments persuasive. The result was Benedict XV's encyclical *Maximum illud* (1919) on missionary methods and the establishment of an Apostolic Delegation to China (1922), superseding the French protectorate of Roman Catholicism in China which had existed since 1860, by Pius XI. In 1924 the first plenary council of the church in China was convened, and in 1926 the first Chinese bishops since Gregorio Lopez were created. Pius XI called Lebbe to Rome for a time, but since he had become a naturalized Chinese citizen[16] he returned to China in 1927. He was active during the Sino-Japanese war, and died in 1940 after being severely wounded in the fighting. He thus lived to see the Rites decision reversed in 1939 by Rome,[17] though not to see created the conditions in which the methods of Ricci could be successfully resumed in China.

The direction in which Lebbe was working partook of the methods of Protestant modernism: the lectures, comparable to those of what will be called the modernist evangelists; the lay associations, comparable to the YMCA; the popular press. They were adopted at about the same time the Protestants were taking them up, and probably were at least partly inspired by the Protestant example. However, Lebbe like Ricci appears not to have been interested in exploring the margins of heresy or in substituting socialism for Christian theology. What he was fighting was the Western-centered orientation of the Catholics in China which had, since the Rites Controversy, not merely forbidden Chinese rites and the Chinese traditional doctrines but had also prevented a Chinese clergy and a Chinese Church from taking form.

The paradox of Lebbe's apostolate (and the reason for the limited extent of its success) was that it was based on a respect for Chinese culture that the Chinese intellectuals themselves were already rapidly losing. In 1913 an observer in China wrote:

It is a bewildering phenomenon that just when China was ceasing to appear grotesque to Western eyes she began to appear grotesque to the eyes of many of her own sons; that just when we Europeans were realising with amazement the high value of China's social and political philosophy, her ethics, her art and literature, the Chinese themselves were learning to treat those great products of her own civilisation with impatient contempt. We long tried our best to persuade them that their philosophy was absurd, their art puerile, their religion satanic, their poetry uninspired, their ethics barbarous, their conventions upside down; and now, when we are more than half conscious of our own errors of judgment, they are putting us to confusion by insisting that we were almost wholly right.[18]

Fundamentalists, Catholic and Protestant, had contributed powerfully to the change Johnston outlines. When the fundamentalists passed from the scene, the positive effects of their work were seen to be negligible; but the negative effects, which Johnston mentions, lingered; the consequences were to doom the Ricci strategy as revived by Lebbe among the Catholics,[19] but apparently to facilitate the task of the modernists among the Protestants, and to give them a victory that was for a time regarded as unequivocal and decisive – a President of a Chinese Republic who was a Christian; however, it was a victory that proved in time hollow and abortive.

The Protestants

Shortly after the Shanghai Missionary Conference of 1890, a critic of missions wrote:

Their aims they consider settled beyond controversy, their methods they assume to be consecrated by the example and precept of their Founder; and with these axiomatic truths as a basis, they are in the habit of summing up their success by the arithmetical formula by which sportsmen count their game; so many missionaries in the field, so many baptisms.[20]

At their conferences, Michie declared, they were preoccupied with themselves, their doctrines, their organizations, their methods, their piety, their humility; but the state of the Chinese mind was virtually ignored.[21] As for W. A. P. Martin's paper at the 1890 conference entitled 'A Plea for Toleration', Michie wrote, 'the title of his paper is one that cannot be discussed by any Protestant body'.[22] What Martin advocated tolerating was certain aspects of Confucian and other traditional Chinese doctrines; but the fundamentalists were still unwilling to tolerate or even study them. At a London meeting in 1905 the chairman remarked that there was now a subject called comparative religion; but 'I do not think that we who hold to the Christian faith need in the slightest degree be concerned with such a study as that'.[23] No one challenged his remark.

   Some fundamentalists retained their old methods decades longer, applying them in some of the new schools the missionary societies were founding. The first of these was St John's College in Shanghai (1879); during the 1880's there followed Tengchow College in Shantung, Canton Christian College, and the (Methodist) Universities of Peking and Nanking. For the first two decades they all were more secondary schools than colleges or universities, but they had no competition in training young Chinese who desired either Western learning or the opportunities that Western learning might bring them. In such respects, however, they might fall short of expectations. The catalogue of one school for 1912, though declaring openness to 'different opinions', announced: 'the spirit of obedience must accompany true study of the Bible. . . [our aim is] to encourage to as holy a life as it is possible for a pardoned sinner to live'.[24] Another institution's report for 1915 stated that in all three of its colleges, 'on Sundays the older students go out singly or in bands for evangelistic work. . .'[25]

In the early years of the century Chiang Monlin enrolled in a Christian school in Hankow in an active search for Western ideas, but was disappointed in finding the teacher to be a missionary who 'taught nothing but the Bible' and so was assumed to know nothing else.[26] Those who reached America under Christian sponsorship to study in universities sometimes still found fundamentalism surrounding them in the social circles toward which they were directed. To a Chinese student who had studied Darwin, Huxley, Mill, and Spencer, lamented one, 'an old, good landlady's doctrines of hell and heaven, punishment and judgment, offer no attraction'.[27] A cultured American who went to church, the student continued, made a great impression; but only one in fifty Chinese students, she contended, ever encountered any such person. Neither in America nor in China was fundamentalism apt to be associated with culture.

It would be too much to say that modernism was usually associated with culture, but it did have its literature – even literature that was acceptable to those who had had a whiff, at first- or second-hand, of Darwin and Spencer – and its spellbinding preachers or lecturers. In the early years of the twentieth century both appeared in China, and modernism began to displace fundamentalism in missionary circles.[28] The chief instrumentalities were the Young Men's and Young Women's Christian Association and what we might term the modernist evangelists (to distinguish them from the pietist evangelicals, who individually might seldom address a crowd or even not wish to do so – as an 'evangelist' must).

The YMCA was operating in China from 1885, the YWCA from 1900; the YMCA in China had its first national convention in 1901.[29] Its first steps were halting; Soothill mildly reports that Timothy Richard in the beginning stages of YMCA work 'looked upon its literature as its weakest feature', and then tries to be charitable by noting that 'young men do not generally care for profound lectures out of school!'[30]

Within a few years, however, the extent of YMCA activity increased, and more serious attention was given to the literature that ought to be recommended to the Chinese student. At a conference held in July 1911 in the Western Hills (near Peking), the most prominent items on the suggested reading list for teachers who were to organize classes there were Rauschenbusch's *Christianity and the Social Crisis*, Shailer Mathews's *The Social Gospel* (1910), Francis G. Peabody's *Jesus Christ and the Social Question* (1900), and William DeWitt Hyde's *Outlines of Social Theology* (1895).[31] In an appendix to the conference report John Stewart Burgess recommended to his readers the Chinese translations of Rauschenbusch, Peabody, and Matthews as giving the 'underlying social message' of Jesus. There were a number of such conferences. Doubtless many of their organizers were hazy about the theological origins of the views they were disseminating, but some of the modernists knew them and some of their critics recognized them. In 1910 one demonstrated the growing popularity among missionaries in China of Ritschl and his school by inveighing against its purported errors, singling out for particular reprobation its pragmatist contention that 'no ideas are legitimate which do not verify themselves in experience...'[32]

The YMCA not only held conferences but also provided a framework in which the modernist evangelists could operate. One of the first of them was John R. Mott, himself one of the prime movers of YMCA activity outside the United States. In 1907 Mott conducted a series of meetings for the students at government schools. In 1911 and then again in 1913 (with Mott), one of the most effective American speakers, George Sherwood Eddy, conducted numerous meetings attended by thousands; in Mukden in 1913, 4,000 on a single evening. Eddy repeated his performance in 1914 and 1915. Eddy's early years in New York, he reports,

gradually opened my eyes to see the *system*, economic and political, which was essentially, inherently and inevitably evil, as slavery and feudalism had been before it. All three were economic systems of privilege which exploited the workers in the interests of the owners, who possessed the means which control practically the whole of life...The capitalist economics which I had studied under...Hadley at Yale did not seem to work or satisfy.

He begged his readers, 'do not think that I went [to Asia] as a narrow evangelist of dogmatic orthodoxy to force an alien creed down the throats of resisting people, or merely to change the label of their religion without changing individual or social institutions...We went to build a complete new social order in the East, as now we are attempting to do in the West.' What precisely did that mean? It meant that 'nothing short of a revolution which would be at once intellectual, social and spiritual could now save China...I, for one, did not want to see China follow the example of the West, but she could not escape revolution in her own way'.[33] Eddy converted high officials in Hangchow, Foochow, and other cities as well as students. In Canton President Sun Yat-sen, he reported, was his invited guest at one meeting where he lectured.[34]

By 1915 Eddy's modernist revival meetings were drawing 3,000–4,000 students a night in thirteen Chinese cities.[35] The evidence suggests, however, that what drew the young people in such numbers to hear the Westerners was not the Christianity of the Christian modernists, but their modernism – which taught that the prevailing capitalist system, in Eddy's words, was 'inherently and inevitably evil', that it must be swept away to make room for a 'complete new social order', and prophesied that 'by violence or non-violence, *it will surely come*'.[36]

The message of Christian modernism was out with the old, in with the new, in China as in America and elsewhere. Such men as Eddy might protest their admiration for 'the priceless elements of abiding value in both the ancient cultures and the religions of the Orient';[37] they were all in favor of relativism among religions,[38] and had none of the hostility of the fundamentalists toward

Confucianism, Buddhism, or Taoism; but they plainly thought that China's religions had nothing to say to modern man, while Christian socialism did. As for their Chinese audiences, they gathered that the modernist evangelists favored revolution, before the 1911 events which ended the Empire and after they had brought into being an abortive, corrupt, and helpless Republic. If Jesus Christ's teachings amounted to this, instead of what the pietists had long said they were, they deserved a hearing.

If modernism began to affect Protestantism in China in the first decade of the twentieth century, by the third decade it had swept the field. At the National Christian Conference held in Shanghai in May 1922, a delegate reported, harmony prevailed despite a small group of fundamentalists who sought to sow dissension. 'One can feel only pity', he wrote, 'for these "ancientists".' In one week he had encountered more 'talk of theological discussion' and animosity than for the last twenty years.[39] The modernists thus did not try to take up any particular theological position; any 'theological discussion' among the Protestants was apt to be confined to 'ancientists'; what the modernists wished to talk about and did was social and political change.

Some Chinese accepted conversion at the hands of the modernist evangelists in China. Others, including Sun Yat-sen, had achieved their intellectual formation earlier, almost wholly in missionary institutions in China and abroad, at a time when modernism was displacing fundamentalism – or, more accurately, when beneath a Christian exterior and profession of faith was developing a corpus of ideas at radical variance with Christianity, in the shape of unlimited faith in progress and man's ability to create new institutions with reference almost entirely to reason and almost not at all to tradition – Western, Chinese, or other. Out of such boldness was developed the mind of the mature Sun Yat-sen and a minority of his fellows. This minority, however, was of great importance, for they shaped the beginning of the Republic and then, when the Republic proved stillborn, the remolding of the Kuomintang, from which the near reunification of China in 1928 stemmed.

SUN YAT-SEN AND THE EARLY KUOMINTANG

Sun's career

Sun Yat-sen had many traits which were peculiar to himself, and others that reflected the Chinese culture from which he came; but his debt to the Christian modernism of the West was great, indeed fundamental. What was intellectually slipshod in his grasp of the new science and politics of the West or cavalier and superficial in his treatment of Chinese tradition, what was foreign to the traditions of the literati in Sun's work, has been of considerable embarrassment to his followers and has provoked derision and even contempt in his critics, contemporary and posthumous. When his intellectual formation is properly understood, however, he may have to bear less weight of personal blame for his deficiencies. Christian modernism has not yet had many serious historians, and its influence on China is one of the topics in most need of study. Sun more than once thought of himself as another Hung Hsiu-ch'üan, and it appears that indeed Protestant modernism was as faithfully reflected in his thought as Protestant fundamentalism was in Hung's.

Sun Yat-sen[40] was perhaps the first Chinese in history to receive a foreign education without receiving more than the barest beginnings of a Chinese education first.[41] He was born near Canton. Before leaving the area at the age of twelve, he apparently became literate in Chinese, having at least been through the Three Classics in the village school. He was to spend a total of about twenty-eight years abroad before becoming President of the Republic of China at the age of forty-five.[42] His brother arranged to bring Sun to Honolulu, where he was laying the foundations of a prosperous business, and enrolled the boy in the British, Anglican, and monarchist Bishop's School (Iolani) there. Sun rapidly learned English and certain tenets of evangelicalism – he loved the hymns, became a regular reader of the Bible and discussed Christian doctrine at length,[43] and committed himself to the fight against 'superstition' – which apparently meant to him at least idol-worship and at most any non-Protestant religious beliefs.

When his father learned of Sun's involvement with Christianity, he summoned his son home. Sun was now sixteen. Returned to his village, he met another boy, Lu Hao-tung, who had also learned English and Christianity, in Shanghai rather than Honolulu. Together they were able to apply what they had learned to enthusiasm for the memory of the T'ai-p'ing leaders and emulation of them, for Sun proceeded to mutilate idols in a temple, as Hung Hsiu-ch'üan had done, and like Hung was consequently compelled to leave his village.

Sun went to Hong Kong and entered Queen's College. A young American missionary named Charles R. Hager, who had been only a few months in China, met him and baptized him in 1883 as a Congregationalist.[44] What little formal education he had in Chinese subjects was almost entirely acquired at Queen's, because of the institution's requirements, along with his Western studies. While there he paid his respects to filial piety sufficiently to undertake a marriage with a girl chosen by his parents, but she remained in their household while he made his career. He accompanied Hager on one evangelistic tour, and his success was such as to persuade Hager that he would have made a great evangelist. In a sense, of course, he did become a great evangelist.

After another journey to Honolulu he was sent back by the Congregationalists of Hawaii to Hong Kong to become a minister. Since, however, there was no adequate seminary in the vicinity, after a few months he began to study medicine instead with a Presbyterian medical missionary, Dr John G. Kerr, and soon entered the new British Medical College. Graduating in 1892, he began to practice medicine in Macau, but soon was compelled by regulations to leave. With his friend Lu Hao-tung he went north to try to see Li Hung-chang; his aim was to present a comprehensive letter about China's needs and to try to obtain a post in a new medical school in Tientsin. He failed, though his letter was published by Young J. Allen's periodical, *The Globe Magazine* (*Wan-kuo Kung-pao*) in Shanghai. By the time it was in print Sun was back in Honolulu again, where in November 1894 he began to organize his first revolutionary society, the Society for the Revival of China (Hsing Chung Hui). The oath the members took was administered on the Bible, after Sun himself had first sworn to it.

A Hong Kong section of the new society was formed from a group of Sun's friends of whom several had studied in mission schools or had become Christians: Yang Ch'ü-yün, Hsieh Tsuan-t'ai (Tse Tsan-tai), born in Australia and baptized at seven, who called himself a 'Christian' in his old age; and Huang Yung-shang (Wong Wing-sheung), whose family had 'Christian orientations'.[45] Sun and most of the Hsing Chung Hui leaders thus belonged to the category of 'graduates of missionary schools who had come from poor families of uncertain social status and who had been partially foreignized and in some cases actually converted to Christianity'.[46] After organizing an abortive plot in Canton in which 'most of the leading plotters were Protestants... [who] had turned a chapel into one of their main hideouts',[47] Sun went to England via America.

In London he underwent a romantic though dangerous experience by being abducted and held in the Chinese Legation. During his confinement he prayed fervently and regularly. He told the English servant assigned to him that he was a Christian and that the emperor wanted to kill Chinese Christians just as the Turkish sultan wanted to kill Armenians because they were Christians.[48] The servant smuggled out word of what had happened to Sun, and his English host and former mentor from Hong Kong's Medical College, Dr James Cantlie, managed to raise a furor in the press which caused his release. The Manchus' efforts to punish him for his revolutionary activities made him an international figure. On his release he wrote a Chinese Christian friend in Hong Kong:

I am like the prodigal son and the lost sheep: I owe everything to the great favor of God. Through the Way of God I hope to enter the Political Way. I hope you will not cease to write to me about the Way of God.[49]

Herron and Rauschenbusch would have understood him very well.

Sun spent several months in England,[50] reading furiously in a variety of books ranging in theme from politics to agriculture, being impressed particularly by Karl Marx and Henry George, and observing that there were revolutionaries in Europe as well as China. In 1897 he returned to Asia and settled in Yokohama's foreign quarter. This he made his base for organizing Chinese revolutionaries. At first the Japanese supported and encouraged him, but as Japan's power grew and the Manchus seemed ready to consider reform, Japanese enthusiasm for Sun's movement waned.

Nevertheless Sun was able to organize in Tokyo a kind of military school for self-supporting Chinese students, exacting an oath from cadets to which 'equalization of land rights' (*p'ing-chün ti ch'üan*) was added to the three aims of the Hsing Chung Hui oath.[51] However, the school did not prosper, and Sun again visited Hawaii, the United States, and Europe to drum up support and funds. In July 1905 he returned to Japan, where new and surprising success awaited him. The next month the T'ung-meng Hui was formed, drawn in large part from the student community; by 1906 Sun had almost a thousand recruits.

For several years Sun's plebeian, Westernized or Christian revolutionary cohorts had competed unsuccessfully with the constitutional-monarchist and syncretist intellectuals who followed K'ang Yu-wei and Liang Ch'i-ch'ao, and had often been snubbed by them. The shift of the Chinese students in Japan to Sun's banner reflected a new mood of impatience for action; they 'chose a leader who fit their mood'[52] on the basis of his renown as a revolutionary leader. But they did not necessarily accept Sun's ideology or pay serious attention to it.

The T'ung-meng Hui program repeated the four-part oath of the military school; the Three People's principles were formulated a few months later. They were *min-tsu*, *min-ch'üan*, and *min-sheng*, later translated as 'nationalism, democracy, and people's livelihood'.[53] In his Canton lectures of 1924, Sun claimed that the Three Principles were his translation into Chinese of Lincoln's phrase 'of the people, by the people, and for the people'. For the time being, however, he made no serious effort to give the slogan any coherent substance. Outside of overthrowing the Manchus, only one idea had firmly lodged itself in his mind: the single tax of Henry George, which lay behind his demand for equalization of land rights.[54]

During the next six years the T'ung-meng Hui attempted ten revolutionary *coups*, all failures. Sun became *persona non grata* to an increasing number of countries near China. By 1910 he had to find asylum in Europe or the United States. In 1906 he had acquired one life-long disciple in Judge Paul Linebarger, an American in Manila who owed his first meeting with Sun to his Chinese cook. Resigning his judgeship, Linebarger left the Philippines and devoted the rest of his life to propagandizing on behalf of Sun's cause. Probably it was in 1910 that the American amateur warrior and eccentric hunchback, Homer Lea, offered to 'throw in my lot with you'.[55] Although Lea was apparently slated to become Sun's chief military adviser, he was to fall ill almost immediately on arriving in China with Sun, and returned home to die without ever fulfilling Sun's hopes of having found in him a 'Lafayette'.

The Revolution of 1911 found Sun in the United States. A Denver newspaper brought him the news of the revolutionary seizure of Wuchang beginning 10 October; a St Louis newspaper informed him that he was to be the first President of the Republic of China. A cable to London requested his return home, and he arrived in Shanghai 24 December. Elected Provisional President five days later, he was inaugurated in Nanking on 1 January. He proclaimed the adoption of the Western calendar and religious toleration, which he interpreted precisely as most missionaries did: protection for Christianity combined with an assault on 'superstition'. Orders for the destruction of idols and temples followed, and many temples were converted into schools.

Sun's moment of triumph was short-lived. Yüan Shih-k'ai still controlled the north, and Sun, in an act of self-sacrifice, abdicated the presidency to him on 12 February. The only institution successfully modernized in China at that point was part of the army, which Yüan controlled. China's politics refused to turn into American politics at the touch of Sun's wand. A struggle between Yüan and the new Kuomintang, formed in August 1912 by Sung Chiao-jen and amalgamating the T'ung-meng Hui with other groups, became focused on the issue of a foreign loan. The upshot was a 'Second Revolution' by the Kuomintang in the summer of 1913. It was defeated, and in August Sun fled to Japan. The Republic soon became a farce. Yüan, abetted by his own American adviser, Professor F. J. Goodnow of Johns Hopkins University, moved in the direction of restoration of the empire with himself as emperor, was unsuccessful, and in June 1916 died suddenly. In July 1917 there was a second abortive effort by the monarchists, in which K'ang Yu-wei briefly reappeared on the scene, which was directed at restoring the boy emperor of 1911, P'u-i. The Republic was now re-established in name, but in fact it became the tool of Yüan's generals and their colleagues for the next decade.

Sun, desperately casting about for support, during this period drew closer to the Japanese than at any other time in his career. In early 1914 he may have accepted, in return for the promise of Japanese aid, conditions not far from the Twenty-One Demands of 1915.[56] But after the Demands themselves evoked rage in Chinese public opinion there could be no further thought on Sun's part of such a course. In the meantime he put away his first wife and took a second, Soong (Sung) Ch'ing-ling, beautiful, cosmopolitan, American-educated liberal, and the embodiment of his hopes for the Chinese people. Miss Soong had become Sun's secretary, replacing her sister when she married a wealthy man then serving as YMCA secretary in Tokyo named H. H. Kung (K'ung Hsiang-hsi). In 1914 Sun reorganized the Kuomintang as the Ke-ming-tang (Revolutionary Party) under his own direct command (it was to resume the name Kuomintang in 1919).[57]

In 1917 Sun returned to Canton and during the next few years sought three times to establish a power base there. In January 1923, a month before he was to return to Canton with final success in establishing a base for the reconquest of China, he was visited by a Soviet representative, Adolf Yoffe, in Shanghai. Thus began a swift rapprochement with the USSR under the terms of the first Soviet united-front strategy. Apparently one last unsuccessful effort was made to obtain United States aid instead, in an interview with US Minister Jacob Gould Schurman in the spring. Thereafter for Sun there was no turning back. In the summer Chiang K'ai-shek (Chiang Chieh-shih) was sent to the USSR; in October Michael Borodin arrived in Canton. Sun had found his Lafayette, but he was Russian.

In 1924 Sun delivered the lectures that became the *San Min Chu I* (commonly translated as *The Three People's Principles* though doubtless more accurately as *Triple Demism*). The twelve lectures on *min-tsu* and *min-ch'üan* were delivered from January through April; the four (the series was never completed) on *min-sheng* were given in August. Sun was already a sick man. In November he went to Peking at the invitation of the 'Christian general', Feng Yü-hsiang, and the new President whom Feng had installed, Tuan Ch'i-jui. Sun was hospitalized on arrival, was operated upon in January, and died of cancer on 12 March 1925, at the age of 58. His family, against leftist opposition, gave him a Christian funeral.

Sun's doctrines

The apotheosis of Sun began at almost the moment of his death, with the delivery of his 'Will' (with whose authorship rumor credited Wang Ching-wei) to the public. Soon afterward he became the object of a cult. Under the Kuomintang regime thereafter, under the Communists when they took over the mainland, it became impossible for individuals to evaluate his work without governmental interference. Books about him by Westerners who knew him are heavily colored by their impression of his charismatic personality. His critics, being confronted with an idol, often succumbed to the temptation to try to smash it,[58] but iconoclasm is in itself no more scholarly an enterprise than the manufacture of idols.

Three questions merit discussion: What was Sun's debt to specific Western thinkers? To what extent did he owe his intellectual inspiration to the West and to what extent to China? How may his general intellectual formation be characterized?

The problem of Sun's indebtedness to individual thinkers of the West has been widely discussed. He was heavily influenced by what he knew of Darwin, and the *San Min Chu I* is studded with references to the theory of evolution. He derived the proposals he set forth for the realization of *min-sheng* from Henry George's notions of land rent and the single tax. He accepted much of Karl Marx's interpretation of history and political views, though perhaps Marxism's effect on him was as much negative – by leading him to leave out of account what Marx left out – as by instilling in him the fundamental Marxian commitments. He was apparently some kind of revisionist as early as he was some kind of Marxist, but there is no doubt that in his late *rapprochement* with the Communists he was drawn in an orthodox Marxist direction, only to be checked by his encounter with Maurice William's book.[59]

The story of William's book is a curious one indeed. William was an obscure Brooklyn dentist and socialist who in December 1918 undertook to write a justification of orthodox Marxism and ended with a book challenging both the fundamentals of Marx's teaching and the claims of the Russian Communists. The book made a remarkable if fleeting impression on a number of distinguished men of the time. John Dewey in attacking 'the forcing of production apart from consumption' acknowledged his debt to it.[60] Oswald Spengler wrote a preface to a German translation in 1924.[61] James T. Shotwell wrote that Sun's reading of William's book 'may yet turn out to have been one of the most important single incidents in the history of Modern Asia... [William furnished the text in which Sun] shaped his own individual thinking and so set the course of the new China definitely away from communism'.[62] Dr William, nearly bowled over by what such luminaries regarded as his book's effect on his renowned Chinese reader, thereupon assembled sets of parallel passages which show that Sun's position on Marx and the USSR as set forth in the spring lectures was substantially different from the one given in the August lectures, and which strongly indicate that his own formulations account for Sun's on these subjects in the lectures on *min-sheng*.[63] There seems no doubt that William's book at least provided assistance to Sun in any impulse he may have had to draw back from the last degree of intimacy in the Canton–Moscow *entente*, and since the *min-sheng* lectures were his last extensive utterances, those seeking to break the connection with the USSR doubtless found it easier in consequence to do so while appearing to adhere to Sun's doctrinal legacy. Sun also quoted Rousseau (mainly in order to argue with him on the basis of what he conceived to be the implications of Darwin), Mill,[64] and others.

The second problem requiring examination is the extent of Sun's intellectual indebtedness to the West as contrasted to the Chinese tradition. The problem has not been very carefully handled by Sun's commentators. Paul Myron Anthony Linebarger, in his detailed examination of the *San Min Chu I*, is at great pains to deal with the difficulty that arises, he says, when one's object is 'to transpose certain parts of the traditional Chinese ideology, as they were, and as Sun Yat-sen reshaped them, into one frame of reference provided by the ideology of twentieth-century America'.[65] He goes on to argue that Sun was 'much less influenced by Western thought than is commonly supposed to be the case, and in applying Western doctrines to Chinese affairs was apt to look upon this as a fortunate coincidence, instead of assuming the universal exactness of recent Western social and political thought'.[66] The meaning of the sentence depends on the antecedent of 'this'; it appears to be: 'the monumental fact that China is in only a few respects comparable to the West, and that the ideas and methods of the West lose the greater part of their relevance when applied to the Chinese milieu'. In other words, Linebarger's sentence contends that in applying Western doctrines to China Sun was glad that they were mostly inapplicable – which is scarcely plausible. But there is no doubt that Linebarger is persuaded that Sun was the heir of ancient Chinese thought. In fact, he begins his study of Sun with a long discussion of Confucianism, for the most part assuming rather than demonstrating that it is related to the *San Min Chu I*. He does try to cite some evidence: for example, he notes that one of Sun's 'favorite expressions' was *t'ien hsia wei kung*.[67] The phrase is indeed cited once in the *San Min Chu I*; it is also used in the abdication manifesto of the Manchus. The latter source does not prove that the Manchus were democrats any more than the former proves that Sun was a Confucianist, in whole or part.

Similarly, Leng and Palmer argue that Sun was 'deeply rooted in Chinese culture and never advocated wholesale Westernization'.[68] With much justice they note that 'both his admirers and critics agree that he had an unshakable faith in China's traditional culture and derived many of his ideas from Confucianism', referring to Tai Chi-t'ao, Sun Ching-ya, Richard Wilhelm, and Judge Linebarger as admirers and M. N. Roy as critic. The difficulty, however, is that these conclusions do not necessarily follow from the evidence. An examination of Sun's works is required.

Sun's major works include the following:[69]

(1) *Chien-kuo Fang-lüeh* (*Program of National Reconstruction*), consisting of three rather disparate works.
   (a) *Sun Wen Hsüeh-shuo* (*The Philosophy of Sun Wen*), 1919. An English version is Dr Sun Yat-sen, *The Cult of Dr Sun* (trans. Wei Yung, Shanghai, 1931). Ch. VIII is the 'Autobiography' (*Tzu Chuan*).
   (b) *Min-ch'üan Ch'u-pu* (*The Primer of Democracy*), 1917. A text on parliamentary rules, thus far untranslated.
   (c) *Shih-yeh Chi-hua*, 1922. It was written in both English and Chinese; an English version is Sun Yat-sen, *The International Development of China* (New York and London, 1929).
Alternate titles of the three parts are *The Program of Psychological/Social/Material Reconstruction*.
(2) *Chien-kuo Ta-kang* (*Fundamentals of National Reconstruction*), April 1924. English versions in Min-ch'ien T. Z. Tyau (ed.), *Two Years of Nationalist China* (Shanghai, 1930), Appendix 1 and pp. 29–33; and Hsü, *Sun*, 85–9.
(3) *San Min Chu I* (*The Three People's Principles*), 1924. The best translation is Pascal M. D'Élia SJ (ed. and trans.), *Le Triple Démisme de Suen Wen* (2nd ed., Shanghai, 1930), of which an English translation was published in Wuchang, 1931. See also Dr Sun Yat-sen, *San-Min Chu I: The Three Principles of the People* (trans. Frank W. Price, ed. L. T. Chen; Changsha, 1938 [first printed in 1927], and Hsü, *Sun*, Parts V, VI, and VII.
(4) *Wu-ch'üan Hsien-fa* (*The Five-Power Constitution*), July 1921. Translation is in Hsü, *Sun*, 90–115.
(5) Manifesto of the I Congress of the Kuomintang, January 1924. Drafted not by Sun but by Wang Ching-wei, after consultation with Borodin. English versions are Appendix II of Tyau, and Hsü, 120–41.

Of the preceding, 1b, 1c, 2, and 5 need not detain us long. The *Min-ch'üan Ch'u-pu* deals with an entirely Western subject, parliamentary rules. *The International Development of China* consists of a series of detailed suggestions for development of China's industry and communications, with a short conclusion implying that Darwin's discoveries about evolution made Adam Smith's views about competition obsolete, and holding that in turn 'it has been discovered by post-Darwin philosophers [he may have had Kropotkin in mind] that the primary force of human evolution is cooperation and not struggle as that of the animal world . . .'[70] The *Chien-kuo Ta-kang* is a brief 25-point program recapitulating the Three People's Principles and the Five-Power Constitution, adding nothing to 3 and 4. The Manifesto of the I Congress of the Kuomintang sets forth the Three People's Principles again, following a discussion of the situation in China at the time. In none of these is there any trace of the influence of Confucian or other varieties of Chinese thought.

This leaves 1a, 3, and 4. The *Sun Wen Hsüeh-shuo* is wholly intended to set forth and defend Sun's 'delighted' discovery that 'the precept bequeathed by the ancients and to this day believed by our people is seemingly right but really wrong'; that is, that the aphorism, 'to understand is easy and to do is difficult', is the reverse of the truth, and instead 'to understand is not easy and to do is not difficult'.[71] He also attacks Wang Yang-ming's doctrine: 'To know and to act should be combined.'[72] He criticizes the concentration on literature exhibited by Chinese scholars over the centuries, blames it partly 'for the decline of the national grandeur and the lack of scientific and material progress', and holds that Chinese literature contained no theory of logic or grammar until 'these subjects were imported from abroad'.[73] The *Sun Wen Hsüeh-shuo* is not merely a non-Confucianist book, it is an aggressively anti-Confucianist book. Its burden is that if the Chinese will only abandon their foolish notion that doing is difficult, and come to believe (as John Dewey told Sun Westerners believe), that doing is easy,[74] all will be well. It need not necessarily be concluded that Sun was a follower of Dewey. The liberal missionary ethos was one of eternally 'doing', and there was a strong pragmatic streak in Protestant modernism.[75] The sagacity of the book's message need not be evaluated; its Western origin, however, seems clear.

The *Wu-ch'üan Hsien-fa* deals with Sun's scheme of China's future government. In addition to the three powers expounded by Montesquieu, executive, legislative, and judicial,[76] Sun proposed two more: censoring and examination. The examination (*k'ao shih*) power might appear to be taken from the Chinese institutional pattern, but Sun legitimizes it by reference to the system of selection used in the British and American civil service (although he believes the latter to have in turn been borrowed from China). Indeed his account of the examination system as used in Chinese history would clearly suggest that it disappeared in early imperial times.[77] It is inconceivable that he did not know better; doubtless his wording may be explained by his desire not to appear to adopt a system the Manchus used – and kept until six years before the Revolution. Twice in his lecture he refers to a book which is evidently John W. Burgess's *The Reconciliation of Government with Liberty*, both times for the purpose of gaining Western sanction for his censorate or censoring power (*chien-ch'a*).[78] It is characteristic that in perceiving the advantages of the Chinese censorate and examination systems, Sun feels the necessity to justify them by reference to the West. In attempting to use these ancient institutions in the entirely new context of a Chinese democratic polity, Sun can be credited with originality, though his account in the lecture of how they were to function stops with the comparison of them to machinery – he assumes that machines work and thus so must his 'five-power constitution', which 'can accomplish wonders like the modern motor car, the aeroplane, and the submarine'.

Finally the *San Min Chu I* itself may be scrutinized. The discussion of *min-tsu* begins with Sun's argument that cosmopolitanism was the old Chinese doctrine, and that it was pernicious in its effect.[79] What matters, says Sun, is whether ideas are useful or not; if they are useful, they are good, if not, they are bad; and cosmopolitanism is useless and bad. What must be done is to take the Chinese family and clan feeling and convert it into loyalty to the nation. Hence came the very phrase Sun used for nationalism: *min-tsu*, meaning, 'the clanification of the people', that is, the transmutation of the whole people into a single clan with respect to feeling. But the idea he has in mind has in the six lectures on *min-tsu* been given the substance of the idea of modern nationalism, child of the West in the era following the French Revolution. The idea is not very consistently developed in a positive sense, but negatively his message is clear enough: opposition to imperialism. It should be remembered that these lectures come from the period when his attraction to Marxism and the USSR was at its height, and Lenin (although at least partly at second- or third-hand) must receive much of the credit for the way the argument is developed.

The means of arousing Chinese nationalism, he holds, are three: return to ancient Chinese morality, return to ancient Chinese learning, and the study of Western science. When examined, these methods prove misleading. Under the heading of morality, he enumerates what he regards as traditional Chinese virtues, among them the 'charity toward all' of Mo Tzu which he says is 'the same thing' as the teaching of Jesus.[80] And that is all; the virtues remain enumerated, but not otherwise used in his argument. He turns to traditional Chinese learning, and quotes with approval the *Ta Hsüeh* (*The Great Learning*)'s admonition to better oneself first and then one's family, state, and world.[81] He then proceeds immediately to indict the Chinese for their lack of Western manners, as demonstrated by the unacceptability to Westerners of the behavior of certain Chinese he tells about, and demands that they learn to brush their teeth and not to break wind. His next argument is the real one: Chinese nationalism can be advanced by learning from Western science. Note that this argument does not show Sun's *intellectual* debt to the West; he merely says, surely with accuracy, that Chinese have the capacity to adopt Western technology. The intellectual debt in his discussion of *min-tsu* is to the many theorists of nationalism, Wilson, and Lenin.[82] The rest is consideration of ways to implement the idea.

In his discussion of *min-ch'üan* he points to the Confucian maxim *t'ien hsia wei kung*,[83] but he does not pretend that it is a democratic maxim or that Confucius was a democrat. He rightly traces democracy back to ancient Greece. He confronts the dilemma all democratic thinkers have had to face in reconciling equality and liberty and resolves it by opting for the former: 'The individual must not enjoy too much liberty, but the nation must have complete liberty.'[84] There shall be a government by the people, in the sense that they shall have, in order to implement the 'five-power constitution', the four rights enjoyed by 'some of the northwestern states' of the USA: the suffrage, recall, initiative, and referendum.[85] But governing for the people evidently requires more. In this respect Sun avoids Lenin's naive formulations from *The State and Revolution* to the effect that anyone with a little elementary education can govern, and opts for a government of experts, people who have *neng* or know-how, responsible to the whole people's exercise of the *ch'üan* in *min-ch'üan*, the people's power, which is his phrase for democracy.

The third of the People's Principles is *min-sheng*, which he preferred to translate as 'people's livelihood'. It came to mean socialism to him; William's revision of Marx was one carried out by a socialist in the name of righting wrongs done to socialism by Marxists and the Third International, and he accepted it within that intellectual framework.[86] His whole discussion of *min-sheng* is taken directly from the Western socialist storehouse: Marx, as corrected by William; Henry George; Darwin, as used by socialists and as corrected by such people as Kropotkin.

Summing up, in none of Sun's major works, including the *San Min Chu I*, can there be distinguished any idea significant to his argument that comes from the Chinese tradition. In intellectual inspiration Sun was almost wholly indebted to the modern West, and in particular to the American scene where he found, directly or indirectly, most of the ideas that influenced him.

But to enumerate the Westerners on whose ideas he drew does not solve the problem of Sun's intellectual formation. Neither historically nor descriptively can his cast of mind be said to be merely a function of the particular grab-bag of ideas he assembled over the years. The substance of Sun's outlook was to a large extent derivative, but in the way he handled Western ideas and in the ideas he selected he was much less like a Western secular thinker than like the Protestant missionaries and theological liberals who so profoundly influenced his youth and with whom he kept in contact over the years. He was intellectually cradled in the Protestant missionary milieu of the post-1890 phase. Not so much for his ideas as for his cast of mind, he owed a great deal to his association with the Englishmen who were his teachers in Iolani and such missionaries as Charles R. Hager, Dr John G. Kerr, and Sir James Cantlie; Japanese Protestant clergy and laymen,[87] already following the shift from fundamentalism to modernism that their Western mentors had undergone, helped him and sympathized with him; and he kept in touch with liberal Protestants through the Chinese YMCA, Christian colleges, and other channels right up to his death.[88] Many of the theological liberals, having cast away the anchor of Scripture and never having had any in Tradition, were floating freely in an atmosphere in which they competed feverishly with one another to out-modernize the modernizers and to show that they were not 'old-fashioned'. No idea seemed too outlandish to be denied a hearing, few ideas seemed worthy of the exhaustive analysis which might divert them from catching other new ones as they came along. No ancient institution seemed sacrosanct, nothing new seemed impossible of creation. To accept a fragment of a new idea and to defy the traditionalist to prove it to be unrealizable in the future was the hallmark of this sort of mentality. Resigning the Presidency in a gesture of self-sacrifice in order to hurl himself on the plan of building 75,000 miles of railroad in China in five years[89] – a third of the mileage then possessed by the United States, more than the USSR or the whole of South America has today – was an action which not only harmonized with the new liberal missionary mentality, but evoked their plaudits the world round.

As the fundamentalist missionaries had applauded the T'ai-p'ings for coming close to being their kind of Christian, so did the liberal missionaries applaud Sun for *being* their kind. Not a biographer or student of Sun's neglects to mention his training in Protestant schools and hospitals and his various Christian statements and associations throughout his life; but scarcely any have recognized to what an extent his intellectual formation was not only the result of mission training, but came to be that of the liberal Western Protestant. To be sure, he caricatured the mental processes of liberal Protestants in many of his speeches and writings and indeed his actions, as the T'ai-p'ings had caricatured the fundamentalists.

However, there was a difference. The T'ai-p'ings had had little contact with the Protestants, Sun had much. That difference partly reflected the divergent approaches of the fundamentalists and the modernists, each dominant in the period in question. The T'ai-p'ings had to work out things for themselves by way of a few tracts and casual contacts with missionaries, as indeed the fundamentalists who dumped Bibles in the sea intended, with whatever misgivings they might regard the results. Sun had the advantage of having been educated almost from the start in the schools and hospitals on which the modernists, priding themselves on being practical, placed their reliance. Hung Hsiu-ch'üan had had a classical education; Sun, wrote Cantlie approvingly, 'whilst yet a boy, saw and understood the uselessness and senselessness of education in Chinese schools, and knew full well that an intimate acquaintance with the Chinese classics led to nothing'.[90] Take an intelligent, curious Chinese boy, unencumbered by tradition, give him a mission school education, and there was nothing particularly surprising to the missionaries about the fact that he should end up as President of China. If then something should go wrong, it was doubtless the result of Yüan Shih-k'ai's or someone else's reactionary treachery ('Judas' was the term that sprang to the mind of old Judge Linebarger).[91] It could not be the outcome of the intellectual shallowness, the superficiality of analysis, the gaily optimistic spirit in which a 2,000-year-old political system was to be shattered – as the young Sun, fresh from Honolulu, had shattered his village idols – before any sane plan could be set in motion for what was to take its place, of the belief that, with the help of God and his twentieth-century modernist prophets alone, anything whatever could be done, or of any other similar qualities in the teachers or in their obviously capable, dynamic, charismatically effective pupil.[92]

Sun's debt to Protestant modernism

In what sense was Sun a Christian? There is no doubt that he thought himself as a Christian, at least from time to time, throughout his life, and that he never rejected Christianity as he understood it. In an autobiographical sketch prepared at the request of H. A. Giles and published in 1898, he wrote: 'As for my religion, I worship Jesus.'[93] The descendant of Confucius of Sun's generation has reported that Sun whispered on his deathbed to him: 'I want it to be known that I die a Christian.'[94] Many students have simply ignored these remarks as if they had nothing to do with Sun's career but only dealt, as the liberals say, with a 'private matter'. Others have sought to explain them away, perhaps in the wish to defend Sun from the allegation that he was a Christian. Thus one, arguing that Sun 'did not take Christianity... seriously', adduces such evidence as that Sun did not go to church often or observe Christian holidays, and that 'un-Christian actions' of his included participation in 'un-Christian' ceremonies in joining the Hung organization in Hawaii.[95] These points need not detain us; it is more puzzling why the same writer believes that Sun's false claim that his father was a Christian is evidence *against* Sun's Christianity. For our purposes the validity of Sun's title to be considered a Christian need not be adjudicated; there is ample evidence that the modernist missionaries so considered him,[96] and there is much that he so considered himself. We need go no farther. We are seeking only to elucidate Sun's intellectual formation.

A clue is given us by Judge Linebarger, who left his judgeship in the Philippines to become Sun's disciple[97] for the rest of Sun's life. Linebarger was himself the son of a Methodist minister; he had been destined from infancy for the ministry, but during a stay in Europe in his youth seems to have lost his faith and changed his vocational aims. Nevertheless, as his son declares, 'the intensity of conviction, the reliance upon faith, the trust in a benevolent fate were never to escape him'.[98] There are perhaps few more curious associations than that of the ex-Christian American Linebarger with the Christian Chinese Sun. As a secular evangelical himself, Linebarger well perceives Sun's debt to the missionaries and acknowledges it in numerous addresses he made on Sun's behalf: The Chinese laborer works too hard; 'this pain of labor is wrong. Dr Sun preaches that this pain and anguish and suffering on the part of the masses must disappear.' 'The West has sent thousands of missionaries to China. China has sent only one to the West... [The former] have preached the Gospel of a life after death. Dr Sun, as a missionary to the Western man, is preaching the gospel of a life before death.' In speaking of Sun's 'methods of getting converts', Linebarger declared, 'Dr Sun never makes the mistake of trying to obtain a convert in the same manner a missionary obtains his convert to Christianity. The missionary appeals to a man's heart. Dr Sun has more success than any missionary has ever had because, he not only appeals to his heart but to his reason as well.'[99]

Linebarger saw Sun as a missionary for secular ends, a missionary from China to the West; he was doubtless right. Moving endlessly around on slim financial resources, always successful in knowing how to get an audience of Chinese or Americans assembled for him on the shortest notice, holding his audience spellbound for hours with speeches containing many of the features of effective sermons, Sun showed that he had mastered many missionary skills. As for the problem of heart and head, Judge Linebarger's remarks were more pertinent to the passing fundamentalist missionary type than to the newer liberal missionary. The modernist was apt to be embarrassed about too direct an appeal to the heart, and was prepared with a heterogeneous array of new ideas to appeal to the head[100] – perhaps not very coherently or profoundly, and perhaps not on the basis of specifically Christian ideas.

Sun Yat-sen was very much like that. His was, as Linebarger said, an earthly gospel – like Ritschl's and that of the whole 'social gospel' movement. It was a gospel full of the new science and technology, however clearly understood; Cantlie observed that Confucianism no more hinders a Chinese from being a Christian 'than does a belief in Darwinism prohibit an Englishman from being a devout Churchman'.[101] It was a gospel full of zeal for social and political reform and even revolution. Bishop Restarick writes:

It will have been noted that Dr Sun, and some of the men associated with him, were Christians. This led to the opinion that the foreign religion made men rebellious. The opinion was based on fact, for wherever Christianity has been preached it has made men dissatisfied with wrong and tyranny... the religion of Jesus teaches the worth of the individual and this leads to the turning upside down of many old customs. While the social structure of China had many excellent points, there was so much cruelty and oppression in the political life of the nation that young Chinese who had been educated in mission schools developed a burning hatred toward the whole system.[102]

What he said was true, except that it was not applicable to 'wherever Christianity has been preached' (the Protestant missionaries were apt to be weak on church history and indeed history generally), but only to certain regions and periods – among them Protestant China missions since about the turn of the century. The fundamentalists had tended to despise Chinese culture and customs, but though many temporarily supported the T'ai-p'ings' attempt to overthrow the government and the old culture by revolutionary means, they did not directly preach or advocate any kind of political or social change.

Their modernist successors had little use for Chinese culture or customs, and were prepared to recognize all kinds of political action including revolution as legitimate methods of sweeping them away. Not long before the Revolution of 1911 Sun told a San Francisco audience:

> Our greatest hope is to make the Bible and Christian education, as we have come to know it in America, the means of conveying to our countrymen what blessings may be in the way of just laws. We intend to try by every means in our power to seize the country and create a government without bloodshed.[103]

It was through Christianity 'as we have come to know it in America' that Sun derived the basis of his vision of the future.

His contacts had come to be with Protestant modernists in the United States and to a lesser extent Europe (especially England, where because of his knowledge of the language he was more at home). From Protestant missionaries generally – fundamentalists and modernists alike – he had acquired the outlook which integrated his hatred for 'superstition' – idol worship and the Chinese religions in general (not necessarily including Confucian 'philosophy', as many missionaries were coming justifiably to regard it), footbinding, opium-smoking, arranged marriages, the barring of women from public life, the toleration of dirt, personal habits unpleasant to Western fastidiousness, and many other customs then prevalent in China.[104] According to Judge Linebarger, 'Sun Yat-sen was most apt to talk in terms of morality and morale by preference. The fact that Sun Yat-sen came from a Chinese Confucian background into a Western Christian one cannot be ignored.'[105]

From the modernists, Sun acquired a rationale for an earthly, social gospel, one in which the fight against evils, including oppression and tyranny, acquired absolute sanction and into which he went with unflinching faith. It was not faith in a doctrinal system, such as that the Communists possessed; with Sun the faith came first, then a weak slogan or two, and years afterward he got around to trying to infuse some content into the slogans. He is reported to have said: 'God sent me to China to free her from bondage and oppression, and I have not been disobedient to the Heavenly mission.'[106] This is not to say that he thought constantly about his supposed divine mandate; many of the modernists did not think very much about religion either, except in times of crisis. On the day before Sun died, he said, 'I am a Christian; God sent me to fight evil for my people. Jesus was a revolutionist; so am I.'[107] It is a statement inconceivable for a Chinese Christian to have made thirty years earlier, before modernism changed the face of Protestantism everywhere.

Sun came from a social and cultural level which gave him easy access, once he had obtained a modicum of mission-school education, to Chinese, Japanese, and Western Protestant clergy and laymen wherever they were, to the merchants and tradesmen who made up the bulk of the overseas Chinese he visited in many different countries, and to the relatively few Chinese students in Japan[108] and America who were attracted to YMCA's and other Christian groups of various kinds. Bishop Restarick is doubtless largely correct when he suggests that Sun's circle of friends over a period of years molded or even warped his image of the Chinese people:

From boyhood he had associated with Chinese who had been in contact with western men and women, and he took them to represent the whole of the people of China. In Honolulu, in Hongkong, and in his travels about the world, his friends were those who had lived under foreign governments and had been educated abroad; and they, in a measure, appreciated his ideas and understood something of democracy. He appeared to think that the mass of people in China were as ready as his intimate friends to understand and value constitutional government.[109]

If Sun did not necessarily assume that all Chinese were like himself and his Westernized and missionary-influenced friends, at least he had great confidence that the group he represented would be able to lead the rest in the directions he believed to be right. He showed little concern lest the ancient culture and age-old social and political institutions of China offer serious impediments to the kind of wholesale Westernization he envisaged,[110] except for his temporary conviction, expressed in the *Sun Wen Hsüeh-shuo*, that the old aphorism that 'action is difficult' was somehow delaying China's march to Utopia. But then, there is not much evidence that he was a profound student of either Chinese culture or institutions.

The group to which Sun did not have easy access was the intellectual elite – either the old literati or the new university student group which became important after the abolition of the examination system in 1905. In 1925 Wu Chih-hui confessed, 'I suspected that he [Sun] was illiterate. It was only after I met him [in 1908 in London] that I realized that he was the sort who always had a book in his hand.'[111] Chu Ho-chung, having read the text of an oath drafted by Sun for revolutionaries when they met in Brussels in 1904, told him, 'K'ang and Liang say that you don't know your ABC's. Having seen that the text of your oath is so tersely and skillfully written, I know that what they say is in error.' Sun replied proudly, 'I also have worn out the bindings of a great many books.'[112] But Wu and Chu's change of attitude was not typical of the young Chinese intellectuals; what remained characteristic of the group was the two men's original expectation of Sun. The literati and the students looked down on Sun all his life and after his death. Cantlie, probably reflecting the attitude of many missionaries, wrote,

it seemed impossible to develop a master-mind in China fitted for the great task of reform from amongst the rich, the powerful, the families of ancient lineage, or the philosophic *Literati*; so Providence selected a man from the humbler classes, a man endowed with gifts which money cannot buy, nor all the learning of East or West produce...these gifts...may be summed in the words, Faith, Hope and Charity...a living expression of the Sermon on the Mount.[113]

Later, Cantlie reflects on how many Western subjects Sun had dipped into, and on enumerating them becomes carried away: 'Sun Yat Sen is without doubt the man possessed of the widest and most liberal education in China to-day. Learning is the one quality that the Chinese respect above all others, and Sun's position to-day is due as much perhaps to his learning as to his unselfish patriotism and untiring efforts for his country's good.'[114]

But it will not do. Sun's Chinese learning, much of it acquired sporadically in his spare time, however far it finally went, did not take; and his Western learning amounted to about what a Protestant missionary aware of the short-comings of his seminary training who decided to learn all about the world could learn in *his* spare time. It is true, as Wu and Chu noted, that he read a lot of books. They were largely Western books; they did not harmonize; and Sun was incapable of applying rigorous critical methods to the task of deciding what was wheat and what was chaff. But that did not slow him down in his determination to throw out the Manchus, put into action his hodgepodge of slogans derived from the West, and turn Chinese civilization upside down.

Lyon Sharman accurately writes that Sun 'himself was a Westernized Chinese, thinking in terms of the West more than in Eastern terms'.[115] She concludes:

Sun Yat-sen is typical of the impact of Western ideas upon China. If we do not admire the result of our influence, we must at least recognize it as our handi-work...Sun Yat-sen was typical also of the half assimilation of Western ideas which has been an inevitable but an unlovely phase of the transition...[He wanted] the 'modernization' of China – meaning the introduction of Western science, Western institutions of government and Western methods in industry ...At China's present problem, the small working-shop and handicraft industry, he does not even take a glance...[He] is also typical of his period in his faith in reforms by rationalization; of this faith the program is the solidified ex-pression...he assumed too readily that China's progress must be along the specific progress-paths of other lands – of Japan, of the United States of America, of Russia...China must not stop at Sun Yat-sen's level of political intelligence.[116]

Sharman comes to the very edge of pointing out Sun's intellectual debt to Protestant modernism, and then stops. She speaks of the mistakes which the West, through 'our traders, our governments and our missionaries',[117] has made. No doubt it has made many, through the groups enumerated and others. But in the nineteenth and early twentieth centuries it was not the Western diplomats who believed China ought to be turned upside down on a given Monday morning. They tried, however wisely, to bolster the Manchus against the T'ai-p'ings, restored them after they had been in effect overthrown by the armies punishing the Boxers, and kept hoping against hope for reform, not revolution, to save the Ch'ing regime from its own short-sightedness and corruption. (A few missionaries, such as Timothy Richard, also tried to aid the Ch'ing officialdom and the K'ang-Liang variety of constitutional monarch-ists to carry out reform; but they were rare.) It was not the traders, who were apt to regard Chinese contracts as trustworthy, Chinese governments as untrustworthy, and usually didn't care what the Chinese did as long as they didn't bother their Western-style enclaves of commercial offices and gracious living. It was not, for the most part, Roman Catholics; Father D'Élia did seek praiseworthy elements in 'triple demism', but only after Sun died and the Nationalists had succeeded in more or less unifying China for a period. It was not fundamentalist Protestants, who abstained from working out projects for the overnight social and political transformation of the Middle Kingdom, although many of them helped generate a root-and-branch kind of nihilism toward the Chinese tradition which revealed itself in T'ai-p'ing times and later played its part. Who was it? In September 1912, to an enormous Protestant audience, Sun himself asked,

where did the idea of revolution come from? It came because from my youth I have had intercourse with foreign missionaries. Those from Europe and America with whom I associated put the ideals of freedom and liberty into my heart.[118]

The Protestant modernists (and the secular liberals who came after them)[119] have surely earned no Westerner's criticism by their defense of 'the ideals of freedom and liberty'. They may, however, have been a trifle rash in their tacit assumption that those ideals were universally exportable without serious institutional impediment, that what mainly needed correction was the social and political institutions under which men lived, that if one had faith and was prepared to act on it old evils would crumble readily enough, that neither knowledge nor action was so very difficult if one began with a Protestant modernist outlook – all of which they communicated to a few Chinese, outside China in Sun's youth and in China via mission schools a little later.

CONCLUSION

The fundamentalists knew what the Bible (in their preferred translation) said, though many of them did not have any very clear idea of what the best scholars held that it meant; very few had any thorough grounding in systematic theology or church history or comparative religion,[120] in modern science, or in Chinese culture; almost none had any use for the intellectual elite of China. The modernists were sometimes hazy about what the Bible said or meant; their systematic religious or scientific education was usually no better than that of the fundamentalists; they willingly accepted relativism among religions but seldom followed their ostensible 'acceptance' of Chinese culture by any serious study of it, and therefore they could show no concrete or convincing kind of respect for it; they were quite as baffled by the literati, and in many ways as distrustful of them, as the fundamentalists. They were convinced that Christianity was 'not a static set of doctrines, but a dynamic experience'[121] – one which ought to include sweeping aside the ills of the past and establishing a new social order by some kind of revolution, in America, China, and everywhere else. Since salvation for the individual had apparently failed in China, why not salvation for Chinese society all at once?

Before the 1920's, many of the theological liberals confined their social and political speculations about China largely to the problem of how China might become like the United States or perhaps Western Europe. When during the 1920's Sun discovered the merits of the Soviet system, many Protestant modernists in the West, China, and elsewhere were also finding kinship between Communism and Christianity, and continued to suggest that the West needed radical social and political change into the 1930's and later, long after Sun was dead. By that time the Kuomintang had worked out its own relationship to Communism as a doctrine and as a system, largely cut off from the further evolution of advanced Protestant political theology. To be sure, the Kuomintang retained at least some ritual reminders of the intellectual formation of its leader. The ceremonial known as the 'Monday service', conducted in all schools and governmental offices in memory of Dr Sun, is 'distinctly reminiscent of Protestant forms of worship, especially when ·a rousing hymn of revolution and an exhortation were added to the ceremonial'.[122] Chiang K'ai-shek and his wife are Protestants to this day, though no doubt not of the most advanced kind. But Kuomintang ideology has developed and been altered, whether or not successfully or consistently, since the death of Dr Sun Yat-sen.

Sun took China into the stage of being a Republic; when the Republic proved abortive, he initiated another effort to make it work which had some success after his death. But he never took the Chinese intellectuals fully or wholeheartedly with him into his world-view or his particular doctrines. Morrison had in a curious way reached the Hung Hsiu-ch'üans, taking along with him the fundamentalists, but failed because he could not touch the Tseng Kuo-fans; Richard had reached the Chang Chih-tungs and the K'ang Yu-weis, but failed because he could not take along with him the fundamentalists of his day; people like John Mott and Sherwood Eddy reached people like Sun Yat-sen, taking along with them the modernists, but could not reach the Liang Ch'i-ch'aos, the Hu Shihs, or the Ch'en Tu-hsius. In that last stage of serious Protestant influence on China, a great Chinese leader of Protestant modernism seemed to succeed (in 1911-12), seemed to fail, seemed to succeed again (in his last months and even more after his death, in 1925-8 and later), and still finally failed.

The Communists have his widow and claim his heritage; the Nationalists in Taiwan have his party and what they can preserve of his vision. The Chinese intellectuals, wherever they are located, may acknowledge his personal gifts and his political services to their country, but they never accepted his leadership in the cultural field which they regard as fundamental. The Chinese intellectuals were to choose among aggressively secular teachings of the West or a syncretic combination of them with Chinese traditional doctrines, without any substantial debt to missionaries, Christianity, or crypto-Christianity, except in so far as some secular Western doctrines have their own complex debt to pay to the once-dominant religion of the West.

4

SYNCRETISM: K'ANG YU-WEI, T'AN SSU-T'UNG, AND LIANG CH'I-CH'AO (1890–1929)

> Our nation has a great responsibility...to enrich our culture with Western culture, and to enrich Western culture with our culture, so that they may fuse into a new culture...
>
> Liang Ch'i-ch'ao, *Impressions from My European Journey* (1919)

INTRODUCTION

Throughout the nineteenth century the major foreign intellectual influence on China, for good or ill, had been the missionaries and the thought of the West which they brought with them, in however truncated or distorted a form. We have traced the change which overtook Protestantism in the West in the last years of the century and subsequently in China and examined to what extent the post-1890 trend of Protestant modernism was reflected in the teachings of Sun Yat-sen and the Kuomintang. At about the same moment two other currents of thought took form that owed more than a little to Western influence. One was secular liberalism, which antedated the rise of Protestant modernism in the West and partly produced it there; in China it was represented by Yen Fu, Ts'ai Yüan-p'ei, and the students of Peking University who created the May Fourth Movement. The other arose among the literati and was designed to revive and renovate the Chinese tradition, but by intention or not it incorporated important elements of Western thought, and thus it is here termed syncretism.

The chief syncretists were K'ang Yu-wei, Liang Ch'i-ch'ao, and T'an Ssu-t'ung. K'ang's reinterpretation of Confucianism was the starting point of the syncretists, but they also drew on Buddhism and even Taoism. To such Chinese or Sinicized doctrines they added formal and substantive elements borrowed from Western Christianity, secular liberalism, and socialism. Politically the movement passed from constitutional monarchism to moderate republicanism in the person of Liang Ch'i-ch'ao. The reconstruction of the Kuomintang and the victory of Chiang K'ai-shek raised the views of Sun Yat-sen to a high position and relegated the views of Liang to the dustbin of history, even though Chiang and Liang were by no means fundamentally opposed to each other in their political views. With the death of Liang a syncretic school can be said to have ceased to exist, though a few later writers,

99

such as Liang Sou-ming[1] and for a time Fung Yu-lan, later continued some of its themes and objectives.

The syncretists began at a moment when intellectual Westernization was widely assumed to mean, at least initially and fundamentally, adoption of Christianity. This in itself is powerful evidence of the missionary impact in China, even on those who despised and detested Christianity and Christian missions. Such a perspective on the West is suggested by none other than the empress dowager, Tz'u-hsi, who is reported to have said in 1903 or thereabouts that the Chinese 'look back at the oldest teachings and compare them with the new. People seem to like the latter the best. I mean that the new idea is to be Christians, to chop up their Ancestral Tablets and burn them.'[2] It was assumed that 'new [Western] ideas' (as contrasted with Western techniques, for example) began with Christianity. Even a generation earlier than 1903, there had been a great change; few if any Chinese assumed that intellectual Westernization meant Christianization. The change resulted partly from the growing secularization of the West itself, partly from the shift in the kind of Western influences to which China was being exposed – a shift for which both Chinese and Westerners were responsible. The course of the syncretist movement, as it is here described, reflected this change. K'ang Yu-wei began as a 'religionist', as Liang Ch'i-ch'ao put it; Liang ended as a philosopher for whom strictly religious issues were secondary or of only partial significance. Both were also much interested in political change, as was Sun Yat-sen. Unfortunately K'ang's and Liang's efforts to relate thought and action to the actual political events in China were nearly complete failures, despite what seemed fleetingly to be victories for what they stood for. Of course Sun also experienced repeated political failure, until in his last years the formation of the Canton–Moscow axis led to revival and victory for the Kuomintang.

THE REVOLUTION IN CHINESE EDUCATION

Neither interest in the West nor knowledge of it was lacking among Chinese intellectuals before the 1890's. Leaving aside the Chinese influenced by the Jesuits[3] and the T'ai-p'ing leaders, numerous scholar-officials of the middle and later nineteenth century were thoroughly conscious of the need to learn from the West. In the 1840's Wei Yüan advised learning Western technology in order to hold the Western powers at bay. About 1860 Feng Kuei-fen expounded China's need for 'self-strengthening' (*tzu-ch'iang*, a phrase from the *Book of Changes*) in the governmental, military, and educational fields.[4] Tseng Kuo-fan, the great governor-general whom Feng assisted, wrote in 1862 of the need to 'learn their [Westerners'] superior techniques'.[5] He was one of several officials who during the T'ung-chih 'restoration' promoted the introduction of Western technology in military and naval affairs and communications. Wang T'ao, who began as a traditional scholar but was suspected of close relations with the T'ai-p'ings, fled to Hong Kong to spend several years helping James Legge with his translations of the Chinese classics; he also acted as a journalist, advocating not only technological but also institutional (though not cultural) borrowings.6

The educational side of 'self-strengthening' led to the establishment of foreign-language schools (T'ung-wen Kuan) in Peking, Shanghai, and Canton. From 1862 European and American missionaries were among the instructors, including W. A. P. Martin at Peking and Young J. Allen at Shanghai. Missionaries were also important in the decision to send Chinese students abroad to study. The first to go abroad was Yung Wing (Jung Hung), who began at the age of four to study in Mrs Karl Gützlaff's school in Macau and entered the Morrison Society School in 1841; he finished Yale in 1854, and was thus also the first Chinese student to be graduated from an American university. In turn he persuaded the emperor, through the support of Tseng Kuo-fan and Li Hung-chang, to send a group of Chinese students to the United States in 1871.7 The first Chinese students went to Europe in 1875, mainly to Germany. As a result of Sir Robert Hart's persuasion, the government also sent the first envoys to foreign courts. In 1878 the first minister to England, Kuo Sung-t'ao, returned, declaring: 'Confucius and Mencius have deceived us.' His attitude did not endear him to his fellow officials, and he found it necessary to retire to his home province. If Chinese might return home contaminated with dangerous Western ideas, they might alternatively become expatriates, as did Yung Wing, who became a United States citizen and died in Hartford. However, the shrewdest officials knew such risks had to be taken.

In 1898 Chang Chih-tung expressed the view prevalent, though not unchallenged, in high places in his celebrated work, *Exhortation to Learning* (*Ch'üan-hsüeh p'ien*), which was subsequently translated. It was intended as an alternative to the policy of the Hundred Days, advocating gradual educational reform on the basis of 'Chinese learning for the cultural foundation, Western learning for practical needs'.8

Soon the flow of Chinese students abroad became steady and sizeable. China's new envoy to Japan, Yü-keng, took with him the first Chinese to study in that country. The number increased rapidly: there were 1,300 in 1904, 2,400 in January 1905, 15,000 in September 1906,9 though before long Chinese students began to lose interest in studying in Japan. The remission of the Boxer indemnity in favor of scholarships for Chinese led to a great increase in the number studying in the United States. Y. C. Wang estimates that a total of just under 35,000 Chinese finally studied in Japan (1900–37); just over 20,000 studied in the United States (1854–1953).10 It is difficult to ascertain how many studied in the various European countries, but doubtless the total for all of them together was substantially below that for either Japan or the United States.

Thus by the end of the century it was becoming more and more common for Chinese students to learn Western languages and study Western subjects, either in governmental or missionary schools[11] in China or in the universities of Japan, the United States, and Europe. The intention of such officials as Chang Chih-tung was that the students retain their traditional values and concentrate on learning the useful arts of the West. In fact many students also came to reject the Chinese tradition, though such rejection did not become widespread or visible until the second decade of the twentieth century. A more important line of demarcation at the end of the nineteenth century, which became clear only during the reform movement of 1898, was between such officials as Weng T'ung-ho, tutor to the emperor, who desired to 'borrow Western methods without affecting China's moral tradition', and the literati who followed K'ang Yu-wei, wishing to 'amputate the imperial system'.[12] In other words, there remained (at any rate after the defeat of the Boxers) no serious question about whether to borrow Western methods; they had to be borrowed. The question remained whether the Chinese tradition, in particular 'imperial Confucianism', was to be retained as the foundation of Chinese values, or whether substantial borrowings from Western thought were necessary to secure the survival of part of the Chinese cultural tradition. In terms of the slogan of Chang Chih-tung's *Exhortation to Learning*, the question was no longer about *yung* (techniques) but only about the character of *t'i* (the foundation): would the latter be traditionally Chinese only or would it be syncretist? K'ang, T'an, and Liang offered a syncretist answer. It was ultimately rejected by the Chinese intelligentsia and never was accepted by any of the regimes in power: neither that of the Ch'ings in their last years, nor the military men who held the reins during the first two decades of the Republic, nor the Kuomintang after 1928. Nevertheless, it was an answer that deserves investigation on its own merits, and one that proves to have a more ancient lineage than superficially appears, for in their belief that the Chinese cultural tradition could and should survive if reinterpreted and modified by borrowings from the West K'ang and Liang were in agreement with Matteo Ricci and Paul Hsü, James Legge and Hung Jen-kan, and Timothy Richard. What was new in K'ang-Liang syncretism was the fact it was Chinese literati who undertook for the first time to work out its basis with little Western tutelage.

In the modern world, not only in China in 1900, no serious possibility of rejecting Western thought *in toto* appears open to any non-Western country; the possibility of retaining to a significant extent indigenous cultural values, along with intellectual borrowings from the West, has been and is the serious one. In this respect the work of K'ang and Liang is of more than merely historical interest and of interest to more countries than China.

K'ANG YU-WEI

His life

K'ang Yu-wei came from a scholar-gentry family in the vicinity of Canton.

Born in 1858, he received thorough training in neo-Confucianism from his grandfather, so that his schoolmates rewarded him with the sobriquet 'Sage Yu-wei' for his habit of constantly beginning statements with the words, 'Confucius said'. His father died in 1868. In 1876 he embarked on intensive studies with Chu Chiu-chiang as this teacher. The same year he was married to a girl three years older than he, with whom he never spent much time – he took two concubines later – but to whom he remained devoted until she died in 1922.

His first inkling of the West came from his reading in 1874 of Hsü Chi-yü's geographical treatise, *Ying-huan chih-lüeh* (1850),[13] and one or two other books. He underwent some variety of religious experience in 1878, when he was twenty, at which he ceased his Confucian studies with Chu and busied himself with Buddhist and Taoist literature. In 1879 he visited Hong Kong, 'saw the elegance of the Westerners' houses and the good order of the streets, and for the first time realized that the governments of the Westerners had laws'.[14] In 1882 he saw Shanghai *en route* back from one of his several attempts to pass the imperial examination in Peking for the *chin-shih* or third degree, and his interest in the West was thereby intensified. Its first practical result came in 1883 when he refused to permit his first daughter's feet to be bound and urged others to follow his example. In the same year he subscribed to Young J. Allen's *The Globe Magazine*[15] and temporarily abandoned preparation for the examinations in favor of Western studies, though in 1889 he took them again and passed with high marks.

In 1890 Liang Ch'i-ch'ao and his friend Ch'en T'ung-p'u came to study with him in Canton. They assisted him in completing his first major work, *A Study of the Forged Classics of Hsin Learning* (*Hsin-hsüeh wei-ching k'ao*), in 1891. Taking as his point of departure the *Kung-yang* commentary on the *Spring and Autumn Annals*, he held that the so-called Old Texts of the Confucian classics were forgeries by Liu Hsin (?46 BC–AD 23) and thus challenged the dominant Old Text views of the day with a New Text view. In doing so he followed the path which led from Tung Chung-shu (176?–104? BC) to Chuang Tsun-yü (1719–88) and his grandson Liu Feng-lu (1776–1829), a line of thought which criticized despotism and discussed the problems of checks on the ruler. He went farther than any of them, however, in branding the scriptural documents of the competing Old Text school as forgeries. Next came the task of reinterpreting the New Texts. In 1896 he finished his *Confucius as a Reformer* (*K'ung-tzu kai-chih k'ao*), four years in the writing, in which he depicted the Master as an original thinker and prophet[16] who recorded not China's past but his philosophy for the future, one who projected a development toward benevolent constitutional monarchy and eventually democracy (*min-chu chih t'ai-p'ing*).

In 1898, the year of publication of *Confucius as a Reformer*, K'ang's opportunity to act as a reformer himself seemed to have arrived.[17] The apparent radicalism of his new book, which alarmed and angered conservatives among the officials, was scarcely carried over into action. The reform decrees of the Hundred Days, which were chiefly inspired by K'ang's ideas, envisaged nothing more than revision of the examination system, establishment of new educational institutions, and economic reform. It is true that he sought to set up an independent bureau from which real administrative organization might emanate, in vain because of the speed of the empress dowager's counter-*coup*, but even that measure looked no farther ahead than the establishment of a constitutional monarchy.

K'ang escaped to Japan and thence to Canada, where he founded a constitutional-monarchist party, the Society for Protecting the Emperor (*Pao Huang Hui*). With a single exception this group abstained from Sun Yat-sen's method of attempting violent action, which was recognized to carry little chance of immediate success, and K'ang devoted most of his remaining years to working out his views concerning the future of Chinese culture and politics. He re-emerged briefly into the arena of public affairs in the summer of 1917 to support Chang Hsün's brief and abortive restoration of P'u-i, the last Ch'ing ruler, as emperor, but he returned at once to retirement in Kwangtung. His last years were devoted to speculation of various kinds; he wrote in 1923 in a colophon to a letter to Timothy Richard of 1898: 'I, an old man who ...has rendered no useful service to the country and found no place on earth to bury his sorrows, manage now only to make excursions into the heavens.'[18] Less than a month after a stirring celebration of his seventieth birthday, in 1927, he died.

Of K'ang's thought in general might be said what Carsun Chang partly says and partly implies about K'ang's most important work, the *Book of the Great Community* (*Ta T'ung Shu*): it was Confucian in inspiration, Buddhist in mode of exposition, and Western in its view of the political future.[19] Hsiao Kung-ch'üan has termed K'ang 'a Confucian revisionist';[20] Hsiao has also held that 'in addition to making the last significant contribution to Confucianism, he prepared the ground for the reappraisal of traditional culture...'[21] K'ang sought radically to revise Confucianism and consciously attempted to combine elements in it with elements drawn from Buddhism and the West. Here the question requiring examination is his debt to the West.

Confucianism on the Protestant model

According to Fung Yu-lan, K'ang in his youth was led by events to ask himself two questions:

(1) Why is it that Westerners belong to organized Churches, whereas the Chinese do not? Why, in other words, does not China have an institutionalized state religion?
(2) China, despite her size and population, is subject to all kinds of pressures from the West. Does this not point to the need for self reform on her part?[22]

The answers he gave were that China must have an organized Church and political reform. Fung suggests that anyone wishing to introduce such changes in China 'was still obliged to express them within the context of this Classical Learning', that is, through medium of the New Text school. This bit of the doctrine of historical necessity is not very convincing, as Yen Fu during the same period found it possible to express his reformist views through commentaries on translations of Western literature. The evidence indicates that K'ang, to be sure, wished to reform China; but that he also was convinced that the 'three doctrines' (*san chiao*) of the Chinese tradition contained substantial elements that were true and useful to mankind.

Like many other Chinese of his day, K'ang lamented that in confronting the West his cultural tradition was represented by a weak and corrupt government, and he wished to alter the institutional terms of the confrontation. Like very few of his contemporaries, he believed that not merely technical but also cultural borrowings from the West were essential if those terms were to be successfully altered. Like Sun Yat-sen, he preferred to think in terms not of borrowing but of choosing ideas and institutional concepts on the basis of their validity and not of their national or cultural origin. He did not argue that each people had its own cultural heritage, one that should and could not be replaced by another, but he took it for granted; in this respect he differed from the radical wing, at least, of the new university students, who by the 1900's were attacking their own traditions. In sum, he shared with the reactionary officialdom an attachment to Chinese tradition, while he shared belief in the necessity of cultural borrowing from the West with the radicals and revolutionaries. Endeavoring to find a syncretist solution, he found himself misunderstood and damned from all sides and increasingly isolated in his views.

Up to the Revolution of 1911 at least, K'ang sought to establish an organized Church in China[23] and to make its government into a constitutional monarchy. In undertaking to create a Church, he did not consider the possibility of adopting Christianity, or if he did we have no record of it. It is true that Der Ling reports that the empress dowager told her that 'K'ang Yu-wei . . . tried to make the Emperor believe that [i.e., the Christian] religion. No one shall believe [it] as long as I live.'[24] But nowhere is there to be found any evidence that K'ang was secretly a Christian or ever attempted to convert anyone, let alone the emperor, to Christianity. Perhaps K'ang tried to talk to the emperor about his ideas regarding the need for a state Church in China in relation to the influence of the Christian Churches and either the emperor or the empress dowager when she heard of the conversation misunderstood what he was saying.

Nevertheless the debt of K'ang Yu-wei, as well as Liang Ch'i-ch'ao and T'an Ssu-t'ung, to the Protestant missionaries (or, more precisely, to such syncretist deviants within pietist ranks as Timothy Richard and Young J. Allen) is a problem of major significance that has so far not been adequately considered and that we cannot solve here.[25] Chi-yun Chen has pointed out that a number of K'ang's methods in the school he ran for Liang Ch'i-ch'ao and others in the 1890's in Canton were obviously drawn from missionary practice: K'ang reported that he told Ch'en T'ung-p'u a series of enumerated truths about the world, noting that after hearing each one Ch'en 'immediately believed and bore witness to [*cheng*, a term 'often used to translate the "testimonies" made by Protestant converts'] it'. After K'ang went to Peking in 1894, in missionary fashion he used to shout 'China is doomed!' to astonished passers-by, to the horror of his fellow gentry. After the end of the Hundred Days, in Hong Kong he told the editor of the *China Mail* that 'he owed his conversion to reform chiefly to the writings of two missionaries, the Rev. Timothy Richard and Dr Young J. Allen'. There seems no doubt that in the 1890's his interests centered in religion. In 1896 Liang wrote to him: 'Our mission is a religious one. Whether the nation is safe or ruined has nothing to do with religion. Perhaps we had better take no concern for it [the nation], and concentrate on our study [of religion]. When we succeed [in our study], we will then go out to preach [*ch'uan-chiao*, 'a term used specifically to translate missionary preaching'].'[26]

K'ang sought to Christianize and more specifically to Protestantize Confucianism. He divided the task into three parts: first, he sought to restore the purity of the original Confucian doctrines based on the New Texts, casting out the 'forged classics', as Luther had done to Christianity. In the first interview with him granted to Liang, fresh from three years' study of Han Learning in the Canton school founded by Juan Yüan, K'ang produced trauma in a twelve-hour tirade: 'item by item, he completely shattered and rejected the scholarship I had hitherto so greatly cherished'.[27] Second, K'ang wished to drive out 'heterodox' and 'superstitious' practices, by which he clearly did not mean Christianity. In his July/August 1898 memorial, he argued that such practices were disgraceful because they were considered barbarous by visiting Europeans and Americans. Third, he wished to give Confucianism the exterior forms of Protestant Christianity. In two memorials of May 1895 and July or August 1898, he argued that China's morality was debased because religion was lacking, and urged that Confucianism be proclaimed the national religion, that the calendar years be counted from the birth of Confucius 'just as the Western calendar was counted from the birth of Jesus Christ', that the Western practice of worshipping the one true God be taken as the model, and that churches be established to preach the Confucian classics ('Bibles') and to institute observance of the Sabbath (*sic*).[28]

Liang Ch'i-ch'ao later wrote, 'since K'ang mistakenly considered Christian worship in Europe as the basis of good government and state power, he frequently attempted to equate Confucius with Christ...'[29] Confucius, he maintained, was sent by Heaven; basing himself on a passage from Han apocrypha, K'ang wrote:

Heaven, having pity for the many afflictions suffered by the men who live on this great earth, (caused) the Black Emperor to send down his semen so as to create a being who would rescue the people from their troubles...[30]

Compare John 3.16 (Revised Standard Version):

For God so loved the world, that he gave His only begotten Son, that whosoever believeth on him should not perish, but have eternal life.

Since the apocryphal passage recounted that Confucius was conceived as the result of a meeting between his mother and the Black Emperor in a dream, K'ang was even able to provide Confucius with a virgin birth.

Confucius was to serve in the place of Christ, but he also was to do something more. In the Book of Rites (*Li Chi*), K'ang found mention of two stages of development, Great Community (*Ta T'ung*) and Small Tranquillity (*Hsiao K'ang*). He reversed the order and equated these two stages with the last two of three stages mentioned in the *Kung-yang* commentary: the three are Disorder (*Luan Shih*), Approaching Peace (*Sheng-p'ing Shih*), and Universal Peace (*T'ai-p'ing Shih*). His own ideas for constitutional monarchy he identified with Confucius's ideas about the institutions proper for the age of Approaching Peace; Democracy, Universal Peace, and the Great Community would follow in the distant future. This was the burden of *Confucius as a Reformer*. Carsun Chang concludes: 'Confucius was, in other words, the Jesus Christ of China, but in addition to this he had progressive ideals.'[31] Or, one might put it, Confucius emerged as a Chinese Jesus with the political views of a Timothy Richard.

It was during this period that K'ang met Timothy Richard, for a time saw much of him, and to some extent worked with him. His effort to remake Confucianism in his image of Protestant Christianity and to use it as a basis for 'saving China', though doubtless many of the gentry who supported him at that stage did not clearly understand his drift, was an important part of the reform movement of the 1890's. The rebuff of 1898, however, sent him off in a somewhat different direction – but without his erstwhile pupil Liang Ch'i-ch'ao, who found a path of his own.

The 'Book of the Great Community'

K'ang's best-known work, the Book of the Great Community (*Ta T'ung Shu*) was completed in 1902, although the first draft dated back to 1884-5. It was not published even in part until 1913 and not in its entirety until 1935. In it K'ang discussed what Confucius had only mentioned, the future Age of the Great Community. In the view of Hsiao Kung-ch'üan, the book provides in embryo the three ideas that soon would inspire the new students: hedonism, humanitarianism, and egalitarianism, as advocated by K'ang, would become 'science', 'socialism', and 'democracy'.[32] They were, to be sure, projected far into the future – in two or three centuries, perhaps, they might be implemented.[33] There would be swept away the obstacles within the nine spheres of relationships within the universe, and heaven on earth would be attained. The method of argumentation and even some of the terminology is Buddhist; in the end, Confucianism, Christianity, and Islam would be swept away; those of inferior understanding would devote themselves to Taoism; those of superior understanding would study Buddhism and actually 'roam in Heaven'.

The nine classes of obstacles to be removed in order to achieve the Great Community would be boundaries of nation, class, race, sex, family, occupations, administrative organization, species, and suffering. The result would indeed be, as in the case of so many utopias, a 'Great Sameness' (the basic meaning of *t'ung* is 'same'). Non-state institutions of every kind would disappear, including the family and private property, for the state would operate all nurseries, schools, hospitals, homes for the aged, apartment houses in which the citizenry would live, and the gigantic dining halls in which they would take their meals. The means of moving toward this kind of society would be a series of disarmament conferences.[34]

A good deal of discussion has centered on the question of whether K'ang borrowed features of Western utopias or, if not, whether there are common characteristics. In referring to Western utopian writers he was apt to make mistakes; for example, he spoke of 'the Englishman, Mr Fu', when he doubtless meant the Frenchman Fourier.[35] Hsiao points out the close similarity of Étienne Cabet's *Icarie* to K'ang's utopia, although it is doubtful that K'ang was acquainted with Cabet at all.[36] The assumption that changes in institutions would restore mankind to a condition of pristine perfection was very much in the air in the contemporary West, as it had been intermittently since the time of Rousseau – an assumption that did not at all seem to exclude the concomitant notion that the state must take stern measures against backward persons who persisted in obstructing the realization of a great society. Thus K'ang declared that the (not-quite) perfect society must still prohibit laziness, the idolizing of individuals, competition, and abortion.

There was some basis for utopianism in Mencius's notion of fundamental human goodness and in scattered mentions of ideal states, whether in the past or by implication in the future, in the Chinese classics, and scant basis in the Chinese tradition for the defense of individual liberty against imposed uniformity. Full-fledged utopian socialism or Communism is, however, a specific product of the mid-nineteenth century West, and the Great Community is a work inconceivable for a Chinese to have written without some exposure to the thought of the West. Derk Bodde writes that the book

combines idealism, radicalism, and keen prophetic insight, with a curiously naive confidence in technological progress as the key to human happiness, which in this respect makes it quite un-Chinese and typical of Western nineteenth century optimism.[37]

Hsiao, noting K'ang's debt to both Chinese and Western sources, convincingly argues that although 'borrowing freely and widely from others, he [K'ang] attained a utopian wisdom (or extravagance) that is characteristically his own'.[38]

The positive side of *The Great Community* is the free rein it gives to K'ang's fertile mind and the indication it contains of the room that existed for development in the thought of traditional China. If we do not take too seriously K'ang's contention that the classics meant what he says, nevertheless some of his ideas may still be compatible with what the classics said. On the negative side may be reckoned his refusal to tolerate diversity among human beings and his willingness to envisage, as the proper means of ensuring the greatest happiness, the extinction of all freedom in the name of a 'Great Sameness'. It is doubtful that Confucius envisaged any such thing, and certain that some contemporary Westerners did. Despite the errors in the Soviet historian Tikhvinsky's treatment of K'ang Yu-wei,[39] there is some justification for his identification of K'ang as an exemplar of the stage of 'Utopian socialism' in the development of Chinese thought. Such justification lies not in Tikhvinsky's distorted notions of 'feudalism' in China or in his view that K'ang's doctrines reflected 'the wish of the Chinese peasant'. Moreover, there was an important difference between the Great Community of K'ang and Western Utopian socialist visions: the latter concentrated on small units (model communities, phalansteries) which would spread to include the nation and the world, the former started with a world state. In the sense, however, of paralleling the stage of Western thought in which socialists contented themselves with postulating ideal future commonwealths without resorting to revolutionary action to realize them (as the state socialists would shortly do), K'ang's work is noteworthy.

The Great Community was more than that, to be sure; it drew on elements of the Chinese tradition in a revolutionary way but by no means in a manner completely unrelated to the tradition. In his own life K'ang was a moderate reformer (only in an age when the flood of new thought was tearing all familiar guideposts from their moorings could he have been thought for a moment to be reactionary, which he emphatically was not), but in his thought he was partly a revolutionary prophet. One is reminded of Plato, for whom the *Republic* set forth his utopian ideals, but for whom the *Laws* and a long life of teaching embodied his sense of present obligations and the practical requirements of the day. The unique feature of K'ang as shown in the *Book of the Great Community* is that he was a revolutionary (in the realm of prophecy) in two traditions, Chinese and Western. He was a prophet, in the sense not of having foreseen a society ever likely to come about, but of foreshadowing the combination of authoritarian elements in the Chinese institutional past with authoritarian strands of Western thought which would occur in Chinese Communism.

'On National Salvation through Effort in the Material Realm'

The *Book of the Great Community* was completed in Darjeeling in April 1903. Just at that moment the death of his most dangerous enemy at the Peking court persuaded K'ang that he might safely emerge from his seclusion, and he set forth to travel through southeast Asia to America and Europe. The result was his *On National Salvation through Effort in the Material Realm* (*Wu-chih chiu-kuo lun*), completed in 1905. It was written under the influence of K'ang's double concern about the rising strength of the Chinese revolutionary movement and about the possibility that Chinese concentration on moderniza-tion in education had contributed to the growth of revolutionism, which added nothing at least to the present strength of China. In the essay he sug-gested an alternative path, that of industrialization, on the basis of his world travels and particularly of his experiences in America. He identified the 'root of China's weakness' as its deficiencies in 'science and technology' (*wu-chih chih hsüeh*),[40] and declared, 'that which enabled the Europeans to occupy a position of power on earth is not their philosophy, nor their [doctrines of] popular sovereignty and liberty; it is the power of science and technology...'[41] This marked a shift away from K'ang's earlier preoccupation with religion and the humanities, including political philosophy, and thereby he moved toward emphasizing problems in which he himself was no specialist. For a man who had earlier suggested, in his commentary on the *Doctrine of the Mean* (*Chung Yung*), that he himself was the great sage predicted by Confucius himself to follow in a hundred generations' time, the following statement is astonishingly modest: 'although I have a measure of earnestness and possess some know-ledge, I am most useless concerning the work of national salvation – because I know nothing about the practical enterprise: industry'.[42] However, he did not therefore suggest the abandonment of the great Chinese humanistic tradition; he warned against 'empty words' – especially those coming in a steady stream from the West into China, but also those based on Confucian themes without any relevance to the world of the day. He expressed himself in a contradictory manner on the question of whether the morality of the West was superior or inferior, but he did not equivocate on the need for China to industrialize. His observations of Europe and America had led him to respect private enterprise as a means of achieving rapid economic growth, but his ideological presup-positions remained opposed to preserving it in the long run. As far as his constitutional-monarchist views were concerned, they remained applicable, for he saw the importance of political stability as a prerequisite to sound economic change.

'Lectures on the Heavens'

With growing discouragement K'ang witnessed the Revolution of 1911, the convulsions of the unsuccessful young Republic, and the attempt of Yüan Shih-k'ai to restore the monarchy. After his participation in the abortive attempt to restore P'u-i in 1917, he withdrew to retirement by the West Lake in Hangchow. The final vision of the Great Community had been of a kind of post-Utopia in which those of superior wisdom would 'roam the heavens';

and given all the intermediate stages through which mankind would have to pass before reaching that one, he chose to undertake it alone. He even called his house the Hall of Roaming the Heavens (T'ien-yu T'ang). With a dozen or two disciples, he developed his Buddhist-inspired doctrines of freeing oneself from the miseries of the universe by mystical exercises.

The book *Lectures on the Heavens* (*Chu-t'ien chiang*), however, is not a handbook of Buddhist meditation, but a serious attempt at discussing astronomical problems supplemented by speculative and reflective remarks on the character of the universe. He begins by brushing aside the Chinese astronomical tradition as worthless, and coming down firmly on the side of Western empirical methods in the science of astronomy.[43] Most of twelve out of the fifteen chapters of the book deal with Western astronomical findings and his own observations on them. He speculates about a number of unprovable matters, such as the existence of human beings on Mars and elsewhere outside of the planet Earth, which is no more than otherwise reputable astronomers have been doing for a long time and continue to do; there is not an iota of evidence to support such hypotheses, but since they deal with the material rather than spiritual realm, they are apt to be treated as lying in the realm of 'science' by the public of our day. K'ang then proceeds to deal with the '240 heavens', which he regards (unlike Buddhist speculations on the same subject) also as dealing with the real and material universe, and whose existence he believes to prove that the universe is infinite. There is no obvious reason to take these remarks any less seriously than such observations as Arthur C. Clarke's on 'the existence of a billion life-bearing worlds in our single galaxy...'[44] There is no evidence to support either. In W. H. Auden's words: 'Yes, it may be so. Is it likely? No.'

In Chapter 11 of the *Lectures* K'ang raised the question of the existence of God and, relying on what he was able to make out of the philosophy of Kant and Bergson, categorically affirmed that God exists. In doing so he followed Kant in refusing to rely on rational proofs but instead arguing from moral necessity.[45] His own position thus was stated finally as being close to Bergson's in adhering to a sort of pantheism as a result of rejecting monotheism. At this point reliance on social and political reform, constitutional-monarchism, and the establishment of Confucianism as a religion have yielded to a fundamentally religious outlook which owes much in its formulation to Western thought and brings him close to the kind of vague religiosity of Eddington and Jeans, for whom science – a science that they understood and practiced, not 'science' as an unanalyzed dogma – provided an only partially satisfying account of the universe.

K'ang's effort at syncretism thus was not wholly successful, since he himself in his final phase turned his attention increasingly away from the Chinese tradition and in the direction of Western science and philosophy. Even though he did not advocate doing so, that does not change the fact of what he did. But although he turned increasingly toward the West for inspiration, it was not to its liberal and socialist political thought that was sweeping over the new students; it was rather to Western science, which he understood only partially, and philosophy, much of whose underpinnings thus remained obscure to him. The non-political direction he took in his last years, coupled with his pride and even arrogance in personal relations, help to account for the manner in which he became isolated from his contemporaries. When his old students gathered to celebrate his seventieth birthday, they did so in the spirit rather of honoring an old monument than of celebrating a thinker who remained influential. That was not his students' fault; he had been forgotten or scorned by the young radicals. As the leader of the reform movement of 1898 and a serious seeker after a way of combining Chinese and Western intellectual traditions, he deserves neither scorn nor neglect.

T'AN SSU-T'UNG

K'ang's younger contemporary, T'an Ssu-t'ung, also sought inspiration in both the Chinese and Western traditions. He was born in Hunan in 1865. His father, the governor of Hupeh, was a man who was baffled by his son, and his mother died before he was twelve. From the unhappiness of his home life, T'an sought refuge in study, and rapidly read many translations of Western works, especially those dealing with science. In 1893 he visited Shanghai and there met John Fryer and other missionaries.[46] Hearing in 1895 of the organization of the Society for the Study of Self-strengthening, T'an went to Peking to learn more about it. K'ang had left the capital, but T'an made friends with Liang Ch'i-ch'ao and became interested in K'ang and Liang's reformist aims as well as in K'ang's researches into the classics.[47] During official service in 1896 in Nanking he studied Buddhism. In 1897 he returned to Hunan, which was becoming the center of the reform movement in South China – a remarkable development Timothy Richard credited to the publications of the Christian Literature Society. T'an was a leader in the Southern Study Society (Nan Hsüeh Hui) and edited the first newspaper in Hunan, which began 22 April 1897.[48] As assistant to the governor of Hunan, T'an contributed to the carrying out of significant reforms in administration and communications. During the Hundred Days' reform of 1898 he was summoned to Peking and after an audience with the emperor was given a responsible position in which to prepare reform decrees. The *coup d'état* of the empress dowager came only sixteen days later. Refusing to flee in full expectation of a martyrdom that he thought would serve the cause of reform better than anything else he could do, T'an was arrested and executed.

T'an's chief work was *A Study of Benevolence* (*Jen-hsüeh*), written in 1896–8, an attempt at religious and philosophical syncretism. He drew on Confucian, Christian, and Buddhist teachings[49] in combination with what he had managed to learn about Western science. The combination produced some fantastic results; for example, he filled a page with a set of pseudo-algebraical equations about 'benevolence' (*jen*).[50] He contended that 'benevolence' was merely the functioning of 'ether' (*i-t'ai*), which was the 'element of elements' (*yüan-chih chih yüan-chih*), and could be neither created nor destroyed. Taking forms that seem different but are yet basically identical in the 're-ligions' of Confucianism, Christianity, and Buddhism, 'benevolence' would lead in the direction of change, a change that would end in the same Great Community (*Ta T'ung*) as K'ang Yu-wei foresaw. In T'an's view such change would be founded on the very nature of things, and it was thus inconceivable that the triumph of the Great Community could be avoided. With such faith he faced and accepted martyrdom.

His letters cast light on his view, comparable to K'ang's, that the essential elements in the great religions were similar or identical. In Peking, he wrote Ou-yang Pan-chiang, 'I have the acquaintance of some Christians. Our views are more or less in harmony. It is interesting that the minds of people from all parts of the world are alike as if they came out of the same mold...'[51] T'an commented on a book of Alexander Williamson's that it explained the major religions and the different schools of each. He continued,

As for the teachings of these religions, some are profound and subtle; others are nonsensical and incomprehensible. However, no matter what kind of religion one is speaking of, every one believes in (1) mercy, what our Confucianists call 'benevolence' and (2) the soul, which is referred to in the Book of Changes thus: 'The spirit forms the substance, and the wandering soul causes the changes.' If one talks about mercy and does not mention the soul, he can convert only sages and wise men, but cannot enlighten the ignorant.[52]

Confucianism, in a word, has been confined to the elite:

the authorities never thought of propagating it as a religion among the common people. After the Eastern Han, Buddhism arose; and recently, Christianity is replacing it. The Christian priests and ministers said, 'China does not teach its own people, therefore she cannot forbid us to teach them for her'. They argue that all men are ethically equal, and we have no basis for denying their argument. Hence the gentlemen of the Society for the Study of Self-strengthening are deeply concerned about the decay of the Confucian teaching and wish to establish a Confucian church. We should imitate the way Westerners preach their religion to spread Confucianism among the common people.

However, the Chinese courts, at the behest of officials, banned the Society, which was trying to propagate Confucianism, while leaving under official protection the missionaries who were trying to spread Christianity. T'an suggested the solution: 'I think for the time being it is better to put Confucianism aside, and borrow the name of Jesus Christ; ask Mr Chia Li-shih [C. T. Gardner?] the British consul-general in Hankow, to be the chairman, and establish a Society for the Study of Self-strengthening in Hunan.[53]

In such vein T'an showed himself like K'ang Yu-wei in his desire to imitate Christianity in order to compete successfully with it and also in his willingness to be influenced by it – for example, its teaching that men are ethically equal and its concern for the common people. In *A Study of Benevolence* he often mentions 'Confucius and Jesus' and 'Confucian scholars and Christian clergy' together, displaying his respect for Christianity and his belief that it and Confucianism share common features.[54] In a lecture before the Southern Study Society he criticized the literati's prejudices against foreigners and specifically Christians: their ethical teachings in some respects were superior to those of the Chinese, and as for anti-Christian polemics, 'if we slander their Jesus, they may be justified in slandering our Confucius'. Obviously T'an's colleagues followed him in such views. In the organ of the Southern Study Society, a certain Lo T'ang wrote that there was nothing evil about Biblical teaching that one should love God and one's fellow man, though 'when it comes to explaining the supernatural character of the Savior, they strain one's credulity'.[55]

T'an read the works written or published by Timothy Richard, quoted extensively from him, and was influenced by him. Richard worked in preparing Buddhist texts with T'an's Buddhist teacher, Yang Wen-hui (1837–1911).[56] and Richard's contacts with T'an are evidenced by the portrait of the latter, with hands in the Buddhist posture of adoration, that appears in Richard's *Conversion by the Million*.[57] T'an's contention that the three religions of Confucianism, Christianity, and Buddhism were basically similar' (note, not the traditional *san chiao*, which were Confucianism, Taoism, and Buddhism) may partly reflect Richard's ideas. T'an never considered, as far as is known, converting to Christianity.

T'an Ssu-t'ung's book and his ideas were much less noticed than his martyr's death, but they are of interest as reflecting that fleeting moment when it seemed that part of the Chinese tradition might be preserved along with the new Western ideas in a modernized China. In his belief that intellectual confrontation with the West had to begin with facing up to the religious issue, he was much like K'ang Yu-wei. In his interest in Western social institutions and their relation to the free development of the individual, he was perhaps closer to Liang Ch'i-ch'ao. His great talent and learning no doubt would have led him to broaden and deepen his thought and move, as K'ang and Liang did, in new directions.[58] As with others in history who were martyred young, we can only speculate, but it is certain that early twentieth-century China needed every T'an Ssu-t'ung it had and could ill afford his loss.

LIANG CH'I-CH'AO

His life

Liang Ch'i-ch'ao was born in 1873, son of a Kwangtung farm family which boasted a number of educated men. Under the tutelage of his grandfather, who was a holder of the first degree, Liang learned the Four Books and two of the Five Classics before he was six; he thus started much like John Stuart Mill, many of whose ideas he came to share. At the age of twelve he took the first degree, and at sixteen the second, two years later marrying the examiner's sister. In 1890 he received his first setback; he failed in his first attempt, in Peking, to take the third degree. On his way home he seems to have made his first contact with Western literature in Shanghai, and in September through a friend met K'ang Yu-wei in Canton.

As already mentioned, the effect of the interview was immediate and deep. He 'abandoned the old learning' (ch'u chiu hsüeh)[59] and plunged into Western studies. For three years he and his friend, Ch'en T'ung-p'u, studied in a school they persuaded K'ang to establish called the Hall of Ten Thousand Plants (Wan mu-ts'ao T'ang), in which both Western and Chinese learning were taught in K'ang's own curious mixture. In 1895 the school was closed; K'ang and he went to Peking to take the chin shih examination, and both failed. There K'ang and he discussed the condition of China following the war with Japan, and they organized the great reform memorial whose immediate object was to prevent ratification of the Treaty of Shimonoseki. It was at about this time that Liang was employed, for a few months, by Timothy Richard as his secretary. In July 1895 K'ang founded the Society for the Study of Self-strengthening, of which Liang became secretary, and he read many Western books before the society was banned three months later.

In the spring of 1896 Liang went to Shanghai to become editor of the newspaper The Times (Shih-wu pao). There he was patronized by men of the 'Western-expert' variety in the Kiangnan Arsenal and other such concerns. In the newspaper's columns and outside it he agitated for such reforms as women's rights and the abolition of footbinding. In the fall of 1897 he went to Hunan to join in the local reform movement, in which T'an Ssu-t'ung was active.

The Hundred Days found him in Shanghai recovering from an illness. At K'ang's summons he went to Peking, and was named by the emperor as head of a new translation bureau. When the empress dowager's coup occurred, he fled to Japan; he had parted company with K'ang Yu-wei for good. He remained in Japan except for three brief trips, until 1912. After a year or so there, he wrote that 'my mind has as a result changed, my thinking and words have become so different from before as to appear to be those of another person'.[60] He read and wrote endlessly, successfully editing the newspapers Public Opinion (Ch'ing-i pao) and The New People (Hsin-min Ts'ung-pao).

He visited Canada and the United States in 1903, and his observations paradoxically seem to have led him to turn away from previous republican leanings toward constitutional monarchism once again. Therefore he co-operated with the Manchus when they undertook to introduce a constitution and organized a political party to support the cause, but it was banned in 1908. In 1910 he made an effort to rally the constitutional monarchists by starting another newspaper, but it was then too late.

When the Revolution overthrew the dynasty and the empire, he came to terms with it. In November 1912 he returned to China a famous and popular man. In May 1913 he established the Chin-pu Tang or Progressive Party, and tried to work with Yüan Shih-k'ai, the leader of the Peiyang military faction who had emerged as President of the Republic. In September he was taken into the cabinet as minister of justice, and worked to establish an independent judiciary – but his efforts were in vain, and he resigned in March 1914. He was invited to head the Bureau of Currency instead in April, but again resigned in February 1915 on realizing his impotence. He now became convinced that Yüan must go, and by December was deeply involved in the southern agitation which compelled Yüan in March 1916 to renounce the imperial title that he had conspired to resume the previous December. In June Yüan died unexpectedly.

The end of Yüan Shih-k'ai did not secure conditions in which republican institutions could become a reality, but Liang continued to do what he could to make them such. President Li Yüan-hung asked Liang to head the Presidential Secretariat; he refused, but he helped reorganize the old Chin-pu Tang as the so-called Research Clique, and returned to Peking in January 1917. During the spring crisis over whether to declare war on Germany Liang tried to mediate between forces supporting the real power in the government, Tuan Ch'i-jui, and those opposing him. For a brief moment the Ch'ing dynasty in the person of the last emperor, P'u-i, was proclaimed restored by Chang Hsün, assisted by K'ang Yu-wei. This restoration lasted only two weeks, and Tuan entered Peking to reinstitute the Republic, backed by Liang among others. Several Research Clique people entered the cabinet, Liang this time as minister of finance. In August the government courted popularity in some quarters by declaring war on Germany, but by November Liang was again disillusioned, and resigned his ministry. A brief civil war at the end of 1917 and beginning of 1918 ended in Tuan's resuming effective power, but Liang remained aloof. He sailed for Europe in December 1918, where he spent a year. From 1920 he lectured, wrote, and in general concentrated on the problems of Chinese culture rather than those of the politics of the Republic until his death, which came in 1929.

His thought

Liang Ch'i-ch'ao became 'the foremost intellectual figure of the first two decades of twentieth-century China'.[61] Despite the fact that he served twice as cabinet minister, organized political factions, lectured, and wrote serious scholarly works, Pascal D'Élia is probably right when he asserts that journalism was Liang's real calling.[62] He had, in Hu Shih's words, 'one of the most powerful pens ever wielded by man'.[63] His vernacular style assured him a large readership. He, like K'ang Yu-wei and T'an Ssu-t'ung, was able to exploit an unprecedented situation which had two aspects: distinguished scholars who were not officials undertook to address themselves to the public, and they did so in a written language which was easier than the classical and therefore open to large numbers and to new social groups. In the past high officials and distinguished scholars had often – though not always – been one and the same: Lin Tse-hsü, Tseng Kuo-fan, Chang Chih-tung had been nineteenth-century examples. With the disappearance of the examination system in 1906, traditional scholarship was no longer the way to officialdom. The officials were more rarely scholars, and fewer scholars were appointed to official posts. The students of the new universities in China or those newly attending the universities of Japan or the West were, before 1911 and after, discontented with the government and ready to read the writings of such reformers as Liang. Liang's personal gifts in explaining and criticizing both the Chinese tradition and new Western (or Meiji Japanese) thought were great, and accounted for much of the popularity he enjoyed from about 1898 to his death, although during his last decade he no longer commanded as much attention as he previously had. In an important sense Liang was thus a figure of the intellectual transition from the literati who were both scholars and officials to the parting of ways between the new officials who were not tradi-tional scholars and not often drawn from the new students and the new students, educated in an atmosphere quite different from that of the tradi-tional scholarship. By the time of Liang's death the literati were fast dis-appearing; what he demonstrated was their ability to adapt to the new situa-tion. However, the abolition of the examination system (instead of its reform and retention, advocated by a number of Chinese and Westerners) was the death warrant of the literati as a class, and it was only a question of waiting for them to disappear.

As befits a figure of transition, Liang underwent several changes in outlook. Three main phases of his thought may be distinguished after he met K'ang Yu-wei in 1890 and decided to abandon the old learning. In the first phase, from 1890 to 1898, he followed the lead of K'ang in providing a religious reinterpretation of Confucianism.[64] Even at that stage, however, he seems to have had more concern with political matters than K'ang. During most of the 1890's Liang found kinship between *min-ch'üan* ('the people's power') and Western parliamentarism. He advocated the separation of the executive from the legislative power (of course not a feature of British or in his time French parliamentarism, but rather a principle of Montesquieu's and the American system), the creation of a representative assembly, and eventual abolition of the monarchy.[65] In this phase he read many Western books in translation; in the catalogues he compiled for the use of others, no books on Western political theory appear, the nearest thing to it being Timothy Richard's translation of Mackenzie's *Nineteenth Century*.[66] However, his emphasis at this point lay not on immediate political changes but rather on educational reform. Modern schools must be established and the examination system modified; that was the burden of his essay *On Reform* (*Pien-fa t'ung-i*), published in *The Times* from August 1896 to October 1897).[67] Since this was also the thrust of Timothy Richard's reform proposals at this stage, the fact that Liang offered to act as

Richard's secretary and did so for several months at the end of 1895 and the beginning of 1896[68] argues that Richard's personal and oral influence was as important as any of the Western books he read in forming Liang's early liberal stance.

Liang's arrival in Japan in 1898 inaugurated the second phase of his thought. His generalized political and educational liberalism now yielded to a strongly individualist kind of Social Darwinism. Though Yen Fu's translations first introduced him to Darwin, it was the Darwinian viewpoint of Katō Hiroyuki, as well as Fukuzawa Yūkichi and Nakamura Masanao, which fully registered with Liang. The right of the strongest and the survival of the fittest were ideas that attracted him at this stage. Applying them to the individual, he stressed above all liberty (*tzu-yu*). Echoes of Western liberal anti-clericalism may be found in his repudiation of K'ang's efforts to establish a Confucian state religion: 'I love Confucius, but I love truth more...' His Darwinian categories also included the nation. Identifying England as his ideal of a nation which was both free and powerful, he was willing to explain and even justify English and other Western imperialism in the Orient on this basis.

For a time he was also influenced by Japanese Pan-Asianism, which was having a vogue, but in the course of translating (by 1900) the curious but immensely popular novel of Shiba Shirō called *Strange Encounters of Elegant Females* into Chinese, which in leisurely fashion developed a Pan-Asian message, he came to reject it. China could not look to Japan in achieving its place in the sun, but must instead develop its own national consciousness (*kuo-chia ssu-hsiang*) and forget the delusion that it was identical with the universe (*t'ien-hsia*, 'all under heaven'). This was the burden of his essay, 'The Theory of the New Citizen' ('Hsin-min shuo').[69]

Liang had after a time broken with K'ang's effort to make Confucianism into a religion and rejected K'ang's Great Community on the grounds that it excluded competition; he also dissociated himself from K'ang's constitutional monarchism. Only a few months after arriving in Japan he joined with eleven others at a meeting in Enoshima to pledge themselves to the cause of revolution. In theory this opened up the possibility of an alliance between Liang's followers and Sun Yat-sen's revolutionary group; it seemed that one might have been effected very briefly on the occasion of T'ang Ts'ai-ch'ang's revolt in 1900, but it came to nothing. The social and intellectual gulf between the literati and the 'mission school students'[70] was too great, and Liang never again made a serious move to cross it.

In 1903 Liang's visit to the United States brought him into the third phase of his thought. Curiously, his observations of the disorder in San Francisco's Chinatown seem to have been the decisive factor in provoking this change.

If we tried to carry out an election among such people [as the Chinese of San Francisco], can we really succeed?... The people of the Chinese mainland are no better than those of San Francisco. In fact, their level of development is actually far below those in San Francisco... To sum things up in one sentence, the Chinese people today can only suffer strong rule and cannot enjoy liberty.[71]

As a result he suddenly began to find Bluntschli and Bornhak much more interesting than Rousseau, Mill, and Fukuzawa. Republican revolution would lead to chaos and authoritarianism, not freedom. He wrote, 'alas, republicanism...I love you but I love my country more...I love freedom more...' Reform from within the Manchu regime was the answer. Sun Yat-sen and his followers, Liang charged in 1906, did not even know the difference between social reform and social revolution, and thus unwittingly drew on both incompatible Western tendencies.[72] Like his Russian contemporaries in and near the Octobrist party, however, Liang found he could not cooperate with the imperial government for a simple reason: the government would not cooperate with him. The period in which he hoped for a reformed empire lasted only eight years, terminating with the empire itself.

His disillusionment with republicanism, however, was not so deep that he found it impossible to come to terms with the republic. Indeed, the problem of trying to persuade Yüan Shih-k'ai, Tuan Ch'i-jui, and other such men to undertake reform was not very different from that of trying to persuade the Manchus to liberalize; the institutions of the militarist Republic were not very different, and the failure of reform under the Republic was not very different, from the situation under the Empire. For six years he kept trying to do what he could; in 1918 he gave up and sailed for Europe.

Once again it was travel, and observation of the West or a Westernizing country, which led him to enter his fourth and final period of thought. In Europe he noted the reaction against Darwinism, against scientism, and against the assumption that Western culture was superior. Liang now returned to the Kung-yang strand of Confucian thought. As Philip Huang points out, when Liang wrote that Chu Hsi immersed himself in Buddhism only to return to Confucian texts, he clearly implied that he did the same with Western thought as Chu Hsi had done with Buddhism.[73] However, he by no means returned to his position of the 1890's. After 1903, Liang wrote, he 'never again spoke of the "forged classics", nor did he [Liang] refer very often to "institutional reforms" '.[74] He meant, of course, the position he had previously adopted under the tutelage of K'ang Yu-wei. He was right. In the post-1918 period he again pondered Kung-yang ideas, but treated them not as the real ideas of Confucius but as 'only a tool intended to serve as a bridge for transformation in thought'.[75]

He now sought a middle way. He strove to reconcile the claims of the individual and the community, emphasizing cooperation as a means of doing so; he endeavored to defend the value of the family, the nation, and private property (which K'ang's Great Community sacrificed); he attempted to mediate the 1923 controversy on metaphysics and science by declaring both sides wrong and suggesting that the two must be harmonized. In Huang's view, he tried to wed Confucianism to liberalism. In doing so, Liang 'assumed that there was a greater whole in which Chinese and Western civilizations could be in a harmonious relationship, and he drew ideas as freely from the West as he did from his own heritage'.[76]

The author of the most recent published biography of Liang alleges, in particular reference to the 1890's, that China 'still had its many live thinkers of traditional ideas, but the ideas were none the less dead'.[77] In the view of some critics such judgments mean that the book 'can hardly be taken as a work of objective, historical scholarship'.[78] Whether or not such a harsh evaluation of the book is warranted, Levenson appears to possess a kind of knowledge of whether an idea is alive ('not simply when somebody thinks it, but when it has real reference to an objective situation') unhappily denied to many others. It seems of little use to lecture Liang posthumously about the difficulty of separating what was permanently true and good in the Chinese classics from what was of only transient and local significance.

Liang strove not to create a system of thought but to work out methods of handling problems – philosophical and political – that would not be limited in their application to Chinese culture but would still serve the needs of his country. Like K'ang Yu-wei and T'an Ssu-t'ung, he sought to transcend the bounds of nations and cultures in his thought; he consciously adopted positions not because they were based either on Western or Chinese ideas, but because they were, in his view, sound in themselves and had a firm relation to reality. He tried to practice the ideal of a free man, rejecting the outworn, admitting the possibility that evidence might throw in doubt the validity of tenets the Chinese had cherished for millennia or his own current pet idea, whether based on foreign or indigenous models, constantly seeking to re-evaluate his positions, engaging in self-criticism. Thus he successively decided that K'ang was right in holding that Confucius had been misinterpreted ever since Hsün-tzu, and that true Confucianism meant constitutional monarchism; that only revolutionary republicanism could save China; that revolutionary republicanism would lead only to chaos; that the Republic created by the Revolution was the best available vehicle for reform; that there was no immediate hope for significant political progress, and only patient work on cultural fundamentals could contribute to a better future. And yet throughout these apparently sharp changes of position he held to the idea of the value of the individual and the need for unflagging pursuit of the ideals of truth and justice. Whether a republic or a monarchy would best serve China he judged in terms of what he thought would be the result under existing conditions, given China's historical experience and the character of the Chinese people at the moment, for the values that he regarded as permanently important.

The ideals Liang cherished owed much to the West, from the moment he encountered K'ang Yu-wei and then Timothy Richard and other missionaries and began to read Western books, in China and in Japan. Moreover, certain important changes in his thought were powerfully influenced by his image of the West and what the current fashions in Western thought were. His successive attachments to Darwin and Mill, Bluntschli and Bornhak, Kropotkin and Spengler were key ones in his thinking. He always tried to keep Confucian, and also Buddhist values and insights before him, never accepting changing trends in Western ideas as necessarily decisive for what Chinese ought to think. From first to last he tried to seek a double ground in both Western and Chinese (regarding Buddhism as having been indigenized in China) culture.

To be sure, he looked at the Chinese cultural tradition through the eyes of one who had some acquaintanceship with the West and could understand Western perspectives on it. For the Buddhist, he wrote, 'from the start until he achieves Buddhahood, his constant effort is to convert superstition into understanding'. Buddhism was a faith 'which contributed wisdom and not superstition'.[79] Without challenging his contentions about Buddhism, one may suggest that he sometimes tried to defend it in the terms a contemporary Westerner would use. In life, he valued Buddhism as egalitarian and as relating to this world; as for immortality, he ended by holding that our individuality dies, while our collectivity persists; but he suggested that at least the individual reputation of a man may live on in a more than commonplace sense. As for Confucius, he 'is a man, a great sage, a great teacher, but he is not God, he is not a supernatural being, he is not a spirit'.[80] It is a statement to which neither Confucianists nor others need take exception, but it would be made only by one who had Jesus in mind as a point of comparison (and indeed the sentence follows just such a comparison in Liang's work quoted) and had been made by a number of Christian missionaries including Richard. Liang was no enemy of Christianity, and sometimes defended it against unfair detractors; thus he replied to those who asked why Buddhism did not prevent the ruin of India and virtually perished there, that Christianity had not prevented the ruin of Palestine and had virtually perished there, but that this was no argument against Christianity.[81] But he repeatedly pointed out that in several centuries Christianity had made little headway in China and 'the people of the upper classes who have become converts have been rare'[82] (a favorite theme of Richard's, though he deprecated the fact and was trying to change it); the conclusion he drew was that China was not very susceptible to Christianity, and moreover, since it had been undermined in the West in recent times,[83] the fear of Christianity that led K'ang to try to erect a new Confucian cult as a barrier against it was unjustified. K'ang had in the 1880's been reacting against a power that Christianity may have had then but by the turn of the century was losing, in Liang's view. Both K'ang and Liang saw their tasks in regard to Chinese culture as partly determined by developments in the West, in the realm of both institutions and ideas; but Liang was perhaps more sensitive to the implications of developments abroad than K'ang, and at any rate reflected more nearly the impact of a generation later than K'ang's.

In D'Élia's words, Liang wished the end of education to be that, regardless of his nation or culture, 'every man receives a truly humane education and can enjoy his own rights, that he should not be a puppet in the hands of another, but that he should be endowed with initiative, that he should be master of himself and not the slave of another, that he should know how to govern himself, that he should be a man of his time and his country'.[84] This was not only his educational doctrine, but his hope for mankind. He believed that both Chinese philosophical and religious tradition and the most recent developments in Western thought justified such a hope. If he was responsive to changes in Western thinking, he responded to them only if he felt that Chinese reality and Chinese culture justified such response. His syncretist solution to the problems of China was unfashionable by the time he died, as even more K'ang's was (T'an's never had become well enough known to be fashionable). Liang Sou-ming, Carsun Chang, and a few others tried to continue K'ang's and Liang's syncretism, and to prevent the Chinese cultural tradition from dying. However, in general, Confucianism went into an intellectual coma in the 1920's at about the same time as Christianity in China, speaking in terms of what came to be the dominant currents among the intellectual classes. It is too early to say that neither will ever revive, despite the abandonment of the examination system (1906) and the destruction of Christian schools (after 1949) which were the institutional bases for their existence on a meaningful or large scale. However, in the decade of the 1910's the Chinese intellectual scene, having so long seemed to be mainly attached to the Confucian tradition and only slightly responsive to foreign teachings, abruptly saw the entrance of radical and principled anti-traditionalism and all-out Westernization in the field of thought. Both Christianity and syncretism were at least for a considerable period and perhaps permanently overwhelmed.

5

LIBERALISM: TOWARD THE MAY FOURTH INCIDENT (1898–1923)

And society welcomed [the flood of Western ideas into China after 1900]; like people who for a long time had lived amid want, who found it sweet to eat with gusto the roots of grasses and the bark of trees, the meat of frozen sparrows and putrid rats, they did not ask whether they would be able to digest it all or even whether it would make them ill, or whether indeed sanitary and wholesome food might be found in its stead.

Liang Ch'i-ch'ao, <i>Ch'ing-tai hsüeh-shu kai-lun</i>

INTRODUCTION

In February 1913 the former empress dowager, Lung-yü, died at the age of forty-six. The government of the Republic lowered flags to half-mast and appropriated $1 million (presumably Chinese dollars) for the funeral. Her coffin was loaded on the train for transportation to the cemetery to the tune of Chopin's funeral march.[1] The opening years of the twentieth century in China's intellectual life were somewhat like that – the old and new in Chinese culture and Western innovation were mixed in all conceivable proportions and combinations, producing effects often grotesque or simply mystifying to the foreign observer.

The Christian modernism present in the thought of Sun Yat-sen and the syncretism of K'ang, T'an, and Liang both failed to win the allegiance of the major portion of the new intellectual class, whose center came to be the new universities of China (though the universities of Japan and the West were also important recruiting grounds for the new group). Syncretism was compromised, perhaps fatally, by having one foot planted in the Chinese past; moreover, K'ang was compromised by his unwillingness ever to renounce constitutional monarchism clearly in favor of some other political stance, Liang by his association with successive leaders of the *tuchun* Republic. Triple Demism started as a series of slogans for revolutionary action rather than a coherent ideology, and when it finally advanced pretensions to be such, had difficulty in winning acceptance from the intellectuals. It may be an overstatement to say that 'the doom of the Kuomintang was sealed from the time when Dr Sun failed to convince the scholars of Peita [National Peking University] that his *Three People's Principles* could give them intellectual leadership',[2] but there seems little doubt that the Kuomintang would have done better not to demand that Triple Demism function as an official ideology to which intellectuals must subscribe. If they had not had at least to feign public adherence to it, they might more willingly have tolerated the government that purported to stand for it. They might support the Kuomintang against the Peiyang militarists, from the mid-1920's until the partial reunification of China in 1928 and even be willing to accept Kuomintang rule for years or decades after that, but Dr Sun's thought was to many of them quite a different matter.

The third competitor for popularity among the new intellectuals was liberalism, often with socialist overtones, as had twentieth-century liberalism in the West, but still to be distinguished from the organized state socialism of the Second and (after 1919) Third Internationals. Its first Chinese prophet was Yen Fu; its chief spawning ground Peking University, under Ts'ai Yüan-p'ei; its mature spokesman Hu Shih; its moment of triumph the May Fourth Movement (1919). During this period the Marxists also made their appearance, especially in the persons of Ch'en Tu-hsiu and Li Ta-chao, and the Russian Communists assisted the Chinese Communists to attain an apparently strategic position in the coalition that carried the Kuomintang close to victory and enabled it to go on alone to win. But the break-up of the Canton–Moscow *entente* by Chiang K'ai-shek showed the shallowness of Communist strength at that stage. Liberalism remained closer to the position of being the received doctrine of the new intellectuals until the end of the 20's, when its popularity was receding rapidly.

During these years China was beset by a plethora of different issues, social, economic, political, and cultural, deeply entangled with one another. The political issue was, curiously, not in the foreground. There was widespread dissatisfaction with the Republic, but no very clear political alternative to it in view – at least until the October Revolution in Russia. A number of social problems seemed to yield quite easily, after the preparation that went back some distance into the pre-1911 period. On footbinding, opium-smoking, the seclusion of women, and arranged marriages there was little debate and widespread change of habits, especially among the urban population. In the realm of the economy, private enterprise learned to adapt a variety of modern methods from the West, grafting such new branches with some success on to the very old tree of Chinese handicraft and merchandising.

The cultural issues started easy and wound up difficult to solve. The missionaries had first used the vernacular as the printed word – though Hu Shih and others soon found much older antecedents in the Chinese novel and drama. Chinese students in Japan very early discovered, even if they were using mainly Japanese translations, that the literature of the West was written in the vernacular, and it was still easier to learn that fact in Western universities. The vernacular (*pai hua*) movement was the result. The vernacular could be used to transmit any kind of idea; there was no necessary connection between the language used and the ideas it conveyed. Yen Fu, the earliest great translator and ardent Westernizer, preferred *wen yen* (the classical language) to *pai hua*; Hu Shih wrote his earliest tracts preaching the use of the vernacular in *wen yen*. Chinese familiarized themselves with Western art and music, and yet such cultural importations did not decide the problem of the relation of China's culture to the West in the future; it is possible, for example, for Westerners to enjoy Chinese opera or cuisine without abandoning their own, and it was possible for Chinese to learn to enjoy the foreigners' arts without imperiling their cultural roots.

The issue soon came to be, therefore, what function the cultural innovations were going to serve. Were they to be weapons for an attack on the traditional culture whose objective was to destroy it, or were they to be ends in themselves, accepted if found good, rejected if found bad? Were they to enrich the tradition and expand its horizon, or were they to shatter it? Western liberalism had a series of thoroughgoing changes to propose for Western culture and Western institutions, but despite the occasional excesses of its advocates – Diderot declared he would not rest until the last king had been strangled in the entrails of the last priest – in the West the liberals came as much to fulfill as to destroy. In China liberalism could, it appeared, be enthroned only by uprooting the tradition in a sweeping manner. Lu Hsün in his writing provided some literary flags which those who drew that conclusion might hoist.

Before the twentieth century what Westernization occurred in China was the result mainly of Christian missionaries. Liberalism in China, like Triple Demism and syncretism, was the result not so much of Western initiatives as of Chinese efforts to work out cultural solutions. That did not exclude inviting in secular missionaries from America and Europe to preach the liberal gospel; several made triumphant progresses through intellectual China during the period, notably Bertrand Russell and John Dewey. After all, the source of liberalism – like that of Triple Demism and T'ai-p'ing Christianity – was not in doubt; it was the contemporary West.

YEN FU

The prophet of Chinese liberalism was born in a village of Fukien in 1853 in a family of scholar-gentry. He had an intensive traditional education, though it terminated after his father's death, when he was fourteen. He was then sent off to Foochow Shipyard School, enrolling in a course where English was the language of instruction, and was graduated in 1871. After some time at sea, he was sent to England in 1877 and there discussed the sources of England's greatness with the first Chinese envoy, Kuo Sung-t'ao.[3] The answer both gave at this stage was that her greatness rested on her court system. In 1879 Yen returned to China, taking service in the Foochow Arsenal School and then the Peiyang Naval Academy in Tientsin.

It was in 1881 that he read his first influential English book, Spencer's *Study of Sociology*. He was above all impressed by the thought that true knowledge lay in the Western science that had been the basis of his own education, and that the problem was to apply its methods to the study of society. In 1895 he set forth in a series of essays his belief that the West's power came ultimately from 'an entirely different vision of reality'[4] from that which the Chinese had; Chinese cyclical ideas were contrasted with Western notions of progress, to be attained through struggle and the survival of the fittest – and thus he demonstrated the hold Darwinism through Spencer had gained on him. Spencer, however, preached individual liberty and found nationalism abhorrent, while Yen Fu was interested in England's 'public virtue' through which individual energies had been released and yet at the same time consolidated in the service of the state.[5]

Yen Fu's belief that Western science must be the basis for knowledge in the world of the 1890's, reiterated in essays he wrote during the decade,[6] led him to his first translation of a Western book, Huxley's Romanes Lectures, published in 1893, *Evolution and Ethics*. The translation (paraphrase would be as good a term) was entitled simply *On Evolution* (*T'ien-yen lun*), and was published in 1898. Schwartz terms it the 'first serious attempt since the Jesuits to present contemporary Western thought to the literati, and to demonstrate the high seriousness of this thought...'[7] Yen Fu's choice was curious, since Huxley was challenging Social Darwinism in the name of human ethical values, and thus translator polemizes with author in the commentary.

The Huxley translation, which swept the Chinese educated world, was the first of several. Yen Fu produced Adam Smith's *Wealth of Nations* in 1900, to show the background of contemporary English political economy; in the disappointing aftermath of the Hundred Days, he translated John Stuart Mill's *On Liberty* – the manuscript was lost as he fled the Boxer Rebellion, miraculously recovered, and issued in 1903. In Montesquieu's *Spirit of the Laws* (1909) he sees the end of the evolution of mankind as democracy and the rule of law; Edward Jenks's *History of Politics* (1904), the first half of Mill's *Logic* (1905), and W. S. Jevons's *Logic* (1909) completed his major efforts at translation. He accepted Mill's radical inductionism, but rejected his positivism, and clung (as he had throughout) to the notion of the unknowable. He might have based this on Kant, but the grounds he adduced were those of Buddhism and Taoism, especially the latter. In 1903 he published his only major work on Chinese culture, a series of commentaries on a new edition of the *Tao Te Ching* prepared by Hsiung Chi-lien. In it he used Taoism as a means of challenging Confucianism, though he also criticizes Lao Tzu's rejection of high culture.

During these years Yen Fu became a towering figure in the world of Chinese literature and thought, but he never attained any other kind of power or prominence. Fleeing to Shanghai in 1900, he soon returned to the Tientsin-Peking area; he acted as agent for a mining concern, headed a translation bureau at Peking University, was superintendent of a school in Anhwei. In 1910 he was named member of the new Legislative Council, Rear Admiral, and in 1911 member of the Naval General Staff. For a few months in 1912 he headed the College of Letters at Peking University, for about a year he was adviser to President Yüan Shih-k'ai. After his name was used (apparently without authorization) in connection with Yüan's attempt to restore the empire, he withdrew from public life, spending most of his remaining years in Peking. He died shortly after returning to his native village in 1921.

Benjamin Schwartz questions Chou Chen-fu's interpretation of Yen Fu as gradually reverting from Westernizer to traditionalist.[8] Indeed he never did deserve the name traditionalist. From the time he first read Herbert Spencer to his dying days he contended that his own version of Western liberalism was compatible with Taoism, and to that extent might be considered a syncretist. However, although he was not an unqualified crusader against the Chinese tradition, as were his successors in the Chinese liberal camp, the thrust of his intention and of his work was always to introduce the most up-to-date Western secular and scientific knowledge into China and especially to show how the secret of the West (in particular England) rested on an intellectual tradition whose maturest fruits lay in national-liberal Social Darwinism, liberating the individual for efforts on behalf of the nation. The world moved too fast for him, and in his last years he mourned old friends who, 'while they were all equipped with new knowledge, were at home in the old tradition'.[9] But he never wavered in his belief that the new, Western knowledge and doctrines were essential to the restoration of Chinese wealth and power.

If the doctrine of the absolute value of the individual was alien to him, so that his liberalism is more nationalist than individualist, he could not be said to have distorted very far the reality of Western institutions and the operative side of English liberalism of his day. World War I brought disillusionment and even despair to him as it did to many in the West and to Liang Ch'i-ch'ao and others in China who counted on the indefinite prolongation of the period of relative peace and economic growth that lasted from 1815 to 1914 in Europe. It sent him back to meditate anew on Chuang Tzu and his other Taoist texts, but it did not lead him to redirect his thought or to repent a lifetime of liberal prophecy.

The thought of Yen Fu seems to have had little effect on his contemporaries; but his translations contributed enormously to the popularity of liberalism among the rising group of the new students in Japan and elsewhere. In 1906 it was reported that chief among the books influencing the Chinese studying in Japan was 'an attractive translation of Huxley's *Evolution and Ethics*'[10] – obviously Yen Fu's. In 1911 a YMCA secretary published the results of a questionnaire to a considerable number of Chinese educators and a few foreigners in a position to answer it intelligently inquiring what Chinese students were reading. Most replying thought Huxley's *Evolution and Ethics* and Spencer's *Principles of Sociology* were the two books most influential among students. Also prominently mentioned were Darwin's *Origin of Species*, Mill, Rousseau, Jenks, and Kidd (*Social Evolution*). Burgess in reporting the results suggested another list of books which 'ought to help the Chinese to pass beyond Spencer, Huxley, Mill, and Adam Smith'.[11] In 1915 Burgess complained that most Chinese students, starting with Confucian agnosticism (if one does not know men, how can one know heaven?), added to that a 'superficial reading' of Darwin, Spencer, and Huxley in excellent Chinese translations.[12] During the next few years, the Chinese students did 'pass beyond' the British liberal writers Burgess enumerated, though not to the writers he hoped, but instead to later socialist and Communist works. However, the attachment to Social Darwinism that was so pronounced among Chinese students, especially those in Japan, during the opening decades of the twentieth century, owed much to the works Yen Fu chose to translate or paraphrase.

LU HSÜN AND THE REJECTION OF THE CHINESE TRADITION

In the Chinese reception of Western liberalism the beginnings made by a translator, Yen Fu, were followed by the great impact of a writer of belles-lettres (and also essays), Lu Hsün. Chou Shu-jen, who was to take the pen name Lu Hsün, was born in 1881 in Chekiang province.[13] At the age of seventeen he left his native city for Nanking, where he enrolled successively in the Naval Academy and the Railways and Mines Academy. In the latter he was first exposed to the varieties of Western thought through a radically Westernizing principal who assigned papers on such subjects as 'On Washington'. When Yen Fu's translation of Huxley's *Evolution and Ethics* appeared, he devoured it eagerly, and in subsequent years read many of the other translations by Yen Fu and by Lin Shu, who produced Chinese versions of Western belles-lettres.[14]

In 1902 Lu Hsün joined the Chinese student community in Tokyo and there spent the next seven years. He first undertook to study medicine. 'What precisely is the ideal kind of human nature? What is the greatest deficiency in the nature of the Chinese people? What is the root of the illness of his nature?'[15] The answer, he concluded, lay in the spirit, not the body. When he saw a film of the Russo-Japanese War in which a Chinese spy for the Russians was executed and a crowd of Chinese stood impassively watching the execution, his conclusion was reinforced and led to action: he abandoned medicine for literature, as the best method of curing the ills of the spirit.[16]

As a student in Tokyo Lu Hsün plunged deeply into the study of the West. He learned some German, though for the rest he had to depend on Japanese and Chinese translations. East European belletristic writers held a special fascination for him. His brother Chou Tso-jen lists those whom he admired as particularly the Russian (or, better, Russianized Ukrainian) Nicholas Gogol, and the Pole, Henryk Sienkiewicz, but also such Russians as Andreev, Garshin, Michael Lermontov, Anton Chekhov, and Vladimir Korolenko, the Hungarian Sandor Petöfi, and certain Czech and Finnish writers.

Lu Hsün's growing hostility to traditional Chinese culture seemed to make him especially receptive to new Western writers who themselves were challenging ideas prevalent in the preceding years: Nietzsche, Ibsen, Kierkegaard, and Schopenhauer. Lu Hsün heaped scorn on those returned students who used Western slogans without understanding their implications, who adhered to the doctrines of materialism and majority rule without perceiving that these doctrines had themselves been superseded by positivism and individualism in the West.[17] But though he returned to the same theme in praise of poets he regarded as romantic individualists, such as Byron, Pushkin, Lermontov, and Mickiewicz,[18] this line of argument was not pursued. He fluctuated between individualism and socialism, materialism and idealism, science and art, in his writing over his whole creative period. In one opinion, however, he became ever firmer and more single-minded: it was necessary to borrow from the West in order to save China, and saving present-day China meant burying the Chinese tradition of the past.

From 1915 on the chief publishing vehicle of the young Chinese who shared these perspectives was the journal *New Youth* (*Hsin Ch'ing-nien*), edited by Ch'en Tu-hsiu, who was to become dean of arts at National Peking University and later to found the Chinese Communist Party, and supported by Hu Shih.[19] One of Ch'en's and Hu's chief associates and a close friend of Lu Hsün's, Ch'ien Hsüan-t'ung, approached Lu in 1918 in order to persuade him to contribute to the journal. Lu responded as follows:

Supposing there is an iron chamber which has absolutely no window or door and is impossible to break down. Supposing there are many people fast asleep in it who are gradually being suffocated to death. Since they will pass from sleep to death, they will not experience the fear and agony of approaching death. But you people start shouting; you rouse the few who are not asleep, only to make them suffer the agony of death. Do you think you are doing them a kindness?[20]

But this ironic response was followed by his agreement to contribute something.

The result appeared in *New Youth* in May 1918: it was a short story entitled 'The Diary of a Madman' ('K'uang-jen jih-chi'). The story was later republished as the beginning piece in the first volume of Lu Hsün's short stories, *The Outcry* (*Na han*). As C. T. Hsia points out, it was 'the very first story composed in the Western manner...(both the title and form are indebted to a story by Gogol)' in China.[21] One of those who have translated the story, Wang Chi-chen, declares that it 'may be regarded as the overture and finale of all his writings'.[22]

The story itself ostensibly consists of thirteen entries in a diary by a man who succumbs to delusions that those around him are cannibals plotting to eat him. Twenty years ago, the madman writes, 'I trampled the daily account book of Mr Hoary Tradition under my feet, a deed which he greatly resented' – this was a reference to the whole canon of the Confucian classics, which had been compared in value to mankind with businessmen's account books – and he thinks this may explain why people are looking at him strangely. Consulting a history, in which 'benevolence' and 'righteousness' (*jen* and *i*, the two chief Confucian virtues) appeared on every page, the madman finds written between the lines the words, 'Eat human beings!' Recalling instances of cannibalism from Chinese history, he concludes that although 'I have a tradition of four thousand years of man-eating', there may be some children who have not as yet tasted human flesh. The last line, which any educated Chinese today readily recognizes, is: 'Save, save the children.'[23]

The theme of the story was widely repeated by the men who had persuaded Lu Hsün to write it.[24] The epithet *ch'ih jen* (man-eating), came to be often used in connection with any reference to Chinese society or culture by the young radicals of the literary revolution, especially during the period following the May Fourth Movement of 1919.

Lu Hsün took the title of his story from Nicholas Gogol's 'Notes of a Madman' (*Zapiski sumasshedshego*, usually translated as 'The Diary of a Madman'). Lu's brother Chou Tso-jen, compared him with Gogol,[25] and Lu Hsün obviously thought he was following in Gogol's footsteps, though he declared without excessive modesty that his story's 'sense of outrage was deeper and broader' than that of Gogol's 'Diary'.[26] In this respect he and his brother seriously misinterpreted Gogol, but in so doing they were only following a host of Russian and foreign critics or, more often, simply popularizers who wrongly considered Gogol a social and revolutionary writer instead of one who projected his own fancies in literary guise.[27]

Lu Hsün imitated the form of Gogol's story. His message, however, owed little or nothing to Gogol, even to his misconception of what Gogol was doing. It cannot be credited to any single Western writer or thinker, but it was entirely Western in essence. Without mentioning any Western ideas, Lu Hsün addressed himself to the heart of the Chinese cultural tradition, Confucianism; he said plainly that it must be destroyed root and branch, in such a fashion that there could be no hope of doing the job effectively with any living adults, so that only children who had not begun the traditional education or become compromised by participation in the traditional cultural patterns could escape the evil legacy of the past. If in a man-eating society the tiny minority that perceives its wickedness is thought mad, the task of destroying the evil culture and the evil society will be monumental, but nonetheless unavoidable. He looked at the Chinese tradition and found it deserving of extermination and replacement by the thought of the West.

He was perhaps the first Chinese to do so, the first absolute Westernizer in China. Sun Yat-sen had himself owed nothing of great significance to the Chinese tradition, but he sought to salvage aspects of it by finding them compatible with Triple Demism and reinterpreting parts of it to suit his purposes, and never called for an uncompromising assault against it. Yen Fu acknowledged the thought of the West as superior, and did much to popularize it, but sought to soften his anti-traditionalist stance by finding merit in Taoism, if precious little in Confucianism. But Lu Hsün looked at the Chinese past, proclaimed it to be wholly evil, and raised in China the unembellished banner of *Ex occidente lux*.

His choice concerning what to substitute for the Chinese tradition is a good deal less clear than his desire to smash it. Lu Hsün was exposed to many varieties of recent Western thought. To take one example out of dozens that might be culled not merely from his work but from other literature of the period, in a single essay in the volume *Graves (Fen)*, Lu Hsün managed in the course of eleven Chinese pages to mention eighteen different figures from the history of Western thought whose names required Romanization in parentheses to be intelligible even to the Chinese reader – from Thales and Copernicus to Geoffroy St Hilaire and T. H. Huxley, giants and pygmies, ancient Greeks and modern Englishmen thrown in together.[28]

That did not mean that Lu Hsün, or many of his contemporaries feverishly eager to profit from modern Western learning, lacked understanding that Western thought had developed through various phases or that he ignored the problem of choosing among or reconciling diverse Western tendencies in his search for the proper models for Chinese youth. As early as 1907 he criticized some of his fellows who would shortly be active in the Revolution of 1911, inquiring: 'Of what use is it to clutch the branches and pick up the leaves of the tree, meanwhile simply repeating "arms manufacture", "parliament", "constitution"?'[29] It was necessary to go back to the trunk of the tree, to its root, before one could make sense of Western civilization. In the essay in question Lu Hsün got no farther back than the French Revolution and the Industrial Revolution, with a side glance at the Reformation. However, he perceived the difficulty. His warning is one that the followers of Sun Yat-sen would have done well to take seriously. China might indeed manufacture modern arms with little preparation, but could it set up a republic without the cultural prerequisites that the West had brought to the establishment of its republican governments? It was an argument that could be turned either way: since China could not do so, either it must abandon the attempt to imitate Western politics (as some conservatives were saying) or it must go on to imitate Western culture as well. Lu Hsün argued the latter. He never found himself at home in politics,[30] or for that matter managed to adopt a firm position in the realm of culture. He was chiefly a writer rather than a thinker. But his influence on his generation, though a generalized one, was great. He sounded the first trumpet of the May Fourth Movement and uttered one of the most resounding battle cries of Chinese liberalism.

THE CIRCLE OF 'THE NEW YOUTH': CH'EN TU-HSIU AND HU SHIH

In 1915 a journal was begun that became the organ of advanced Chinese liberalism and radicalism. There had been serials in Chinese as early as 1815, when the missionary William Milne started a monthly in Malacca; in Chinese in China from 1833, when another missionary, Karl Gützlaff, published a monthly in Canton; in Chinese in China and owned and published by Chinese since 1873, when a group headed by Wang T'ao issued a newspaper in Hankow.[31] However, *The New Youth* rapidly won among the Chinese students a kind of popularity that has never been equaled before (or perhaps since) by any single serial publication in China. The editor, Ch'en Tu-hsiu, and several contributors, notably Hu Shih, Li Ta-chao, and Wu Chih-hui, made up a distinguished array of personalities.

Ch'en Tu-hsiu was born in Anhwei province in 1879.[32] As a child he studied the classics with his grandfather (his father died when he was a baby), who beat him to encourage diligence. At seventeen he took and passed the examination for the first degree, and the next year he went to Nanking intending to take the second. The sight of the examination cells had impressed James Legge sufficiently to make him undertake a lifetime of work in translating the Chinese classics; but the same sight appalled Ch'en Tu-hsiu, and on the spot he decided not to take the examination. He had already reacted negatively to his grandfather's brutality and he felt that much of what he had had to do by way of preparation for the examinations was senseless, but up to that point he had intended to satisfy his mother's wish that he take them. In 1897, however, he once and for all turned in a different direction.

For a time he became interested in the ideas of K'ang Yu-wei and Liang Ch'i-ch'ao. He moved about a good deal. In 1900 he went to Tokyo; in 1907 to France; in 1910 he came back to China; he fled from Yüan Shih-k'ai's regime to spend time again in Japan. In 1915 he returned to China and started a new magazine. On 15 September in Shanghai appeared the first issue of *The New Youth*[33] under his editorship. In the first issue he called for adoption of a Western, positive evaluation of youth instead of the traditionally negative Chinese one; he expressed the hope that the Chinese youth 'will achieve self-awareness, and begin to struggle...to exert one's intellect, discard resolutely the old and the rotten...'[34]

Ch'en also told the Chinese students that through democracy (*jen-ch'üan*, lit.: human rights) and science they could build a modernized China.[35] The old order had to be swept away and the Chinese tradition overthrown to make way for 'modern civilization' – that is, the outlook of the West. At that stage France epitomized his ideals: it had given the world democracy, the idea of evolution (which he ascribed to Lamarck), and socialism.[36] In the fall of 1918 he posed a choice for China: either the 'enlightened path to republicanism, science, and atheism' or 'the obscurantist path of despotism, superstition, and theocracy'.[37] It was virtually the same formulation of alternatives that had been proclaimed by Arnold Ruge's Left Hegelian *Deutsche Jahrbücher* and echoed by Alexander Herzen in 1842. But Herzen at that time had not yet embraced socialism, while Ch'en Tu-hsiu seems to have been a cosmopolitan and democratic socialist from the time he first visited Japan to 1919. Only in 1920 did he decide he had to make another choice – one between democracy and socialism; he opted for Moscow's version of the latter.

In succeeding issues Wu Chih-hui (to be discussed later) summoned the youth to abandon their disdain for tools and their use in the real work of the world. Li Ta-chao, Kao I-han, Liu Pan-nung, Ch'ien Hsüan-t'ung, Fu Ssu-nien, and others soon to be recognized as leaders of the 'Chinese Renaissance' adorned the pages of the journal with essays on literary, political, historical, and other subjects – but whatever the subject, there was a didactic note in virtually every contribution.[38]

The first year or so of *The New Youth* was only prologue. In December 1916 a new chancellor of National Peking University was appointed. He was Ts'ai Yüan-p'ei, born in Chekiang in 1876. He had reached Hanlin status in the imperial bureaucracy, joined the T'ung-meng Hui, studied at Leipzig, served briefly in 1912 as minister in Sun Yat-sen's cabinet, revisited Germany and France, and now proceeded to reorganize Peking as a kind of university quite new in China. Ts'ai served notice that it would no longer function simply as a training-ground for officials, but would engage in research in such a manner as to meet Western standards and would conduct both instruction and scholarship under conditions of academic freedom. The new chancellor made some startling appointments. Ch'en Tu-hsiu became dean of the School of Arts (there were three others: Science, Law, and Engineering). New teachers soon were to include Ch'ien Hsüan-t'ung, Shen Yin-mo, Chou Tso-jen, Wu Yü, Kao I-han, and Hu Shih; the new librarian was Li Ta-chao. The staff of *The New Youth* virtually migrated to the arts faculty of Peking University. Much of China's future was being intellectually determined in that crucial period; to cite only one example, Mao Tse-tung was an assistant to Li Ta-chao and under his influence was beginning to study Marxism. Lu Hsün was close to the liberal professors, though he did not receive a faculty appointment until 1920.

Hu Shih joined the circle of *The New Youth* in 1917. Hu Shih's ancestral home, like Ch'en Tu-hsiu's, was in Anhwei, but Hu was born in Shanghai in 1891.[39] His father also died when he was very young. Returning to Anhwei with her son, the widow entered the boy in his uncle's school, though he knew almost a thousand characters by then. At the age of ten or eleven, he encountered a line of Ssu-ma Kuang, an eleventh-century scholar-statesman, which quoted an earlier writer describing the tortures of hell but ironically remarking that they were ineffective because nothing remained of the dead to suffer torture. It is sometimes said that the result was to make him an atheist; in any case it led him to reject the gloomy variety of Buddhism in which the women of the family who surrounded him believed.[40]

In 1904 his half-brother took him to Shanghai, where he spent the next six years, four of them in three different new schools. There he read widely; he was especially impressed by Yen Fu's translations and Liang Ch'i-ch'ao's essays. After reading Yen's version of Huxley's *Evolution and Ethics* he chose as pen name 'Shih' meaning 'fit', in the sense of the phrase 'survival of the fittest', as did many other young Chinese during the same period.[41] In 1910 he passed the second set of 'Boxer' examinations (that is, for scholarships financed by remission by the US of the Boxer indemnity), placing 55th out of 70, and left China.

He enrolled in the College of Agriculture at Cornell University, following the notion then current in China that one should learn a useful art. In early 1912, moved by events at home, he transferred to philosophy, receiving a BA in February 1914. Dissatisfied with Cornell Graduate School, he transferred in the autumn of 1915 to Columbia. With John Dewey as his mentor he wrote a thesis on 'The Development of the Logical Method in Ancient China', which he defended in May 1917. During his student years in the US he changed his mind about several things but neither then nor later about the need to study first and change the world afterward.

In July 1917 he reached Shanghai and joined the circle of *The New Youth*. Articles of his had already been published in the magazine; the most important, 'Tentative Proposals for the Improvement of Literature' (*Wen-hsüeh kai-liang ch'u-i*) came out in January 1917 and had been developed by Ch'en Tu-hsiu into a call for a 'literary revolution'. Hu Shih's successful advocacy of using the vernacular in writing, contained in these and other works, remained his chief claim to be an innovator and constituted his single most important contribution to Chinese life. He began with poetry, and he was doubtless influenced by Harriet Monroe and others who were seeking to use ordinary language in poetry from 1912 on in the United States.[42] Moreover, he was influenced by the whole intellectual atmosphere in the America of his college years, where the word 'Renaissance' was used as widely and loosely as 'revolution' was used in the 1960's, where everything was either new or had to masquerade as new. The immediate occasion of his espousal of the cause of the vernacular was an odd and amusing one. His Boxer stipend was mailed to him every month by a Chinese Christian secretary who enclosed slips of a characteristically American self-improvement or 'booster' variety, such as 'Do not marry before the age of twenty-five' or 'Plant more trees – trees are useful'. In early 1915 one of the slips urged support for Romanized Chinese script to promote popular education. Hu fired off a tart reply to one presumed not to be well enough educated to tamper with problems of language, then decided the question had merit after all and began to consider the short-comings of classical Chinese.[43] By the summer of 1915 he was discussing his ideas with his fellow students; only Chao Yuen-ren and a very few others agreed with him. But he was now prepared to argue that the vernacular literature was the best China had and that a 'Renaissance' of such writing was needed.

He soon was coupling his interests in the vernacular with a concern for the liberation of the individual from all oppressive restraints of the past – in which he drew on the ideas of Ibsen – and in particular the liberation of women. As professor of philosophy, which he became in the fall of 1917, in other capacities at Peking University up to 1926, and as a co-editor of *The*

New Youth, he greatly influenced the contemporary student generation. He frankly acknowledged his debt to America and in particular the pragmatism of his mentor John Dewey. However, he did not attack Confucianism as Lu Hsün did; rather he looked into China's past for attitudes similar to those of the modern West which he approved. He found them and analyzed them in serious scholarly fashion, far removed from Sun Yat-sen's habit of quoting Chinese precedents of dubious relevance to points he wished to make.[44] The great novels *were* in the vernacular; the scholars of Han Learning *were* men who employed painstaking critical methods in examining texts, even though Hu occasionally exaggerated in arguing similarities between aspects of the Chinese past and the modern West.[45] However, the thrust of his ideas came clearly from the latter: he wished to give Chinese youth a sound education based on Western scientific method and the principles of Deweyan pragmatism.[46]

Hu Shih believed that the China to which he had returned in 1917 was suffering from such serious political ills that the best thing he could do was to abstain from talking about politics for twenty years.[47] He violated his resolution a few times, but in general hewed to it to the end of his life both on the mainland and in Taiwan. First the educational foundation for a liberal polity had to be laid. Like many Western liberals of the 20's and 30's, he accepted part of socialism: he found much of the Marxist critique of Europe applicable, though he denied that it was as relevant to the United States, which exhibited the 'religion of Democracy' in action. Since liberty and equality had not been adequately secured by *laissez-faire* for many decades, socialist ideals had to be added, and on a visit in 1926 he found the Soviet system to have many positive features (as well as negative ones that would make it impossible for such men as he to live under it). Nevertheless, the ideals of socialism 'are merely supplementary' to democracy.[48]

Although he worked with Ch'en Tu-hsiu and Li Ta-chao after the latter two became Communists, Hu himself never flirted with Communism. He rejected dialectical materialism on the plausible ground that it was a metaphysical philosophy of pre-evolutionary times. In several articles he called the young Chinese to the study of problems, not of 'isms'; though it may be pointed out that he, like other pragmatists, was declaring that all 'isms' should be cast out except the one he espoused,[49] he would have no truck with readymade utopias of any kind. As a liberal he believed that science required him to abjure existing religious beliefs, though he talked a bit about a Religion of Immortality of his own fabrication.

In 1926 Hu left Peking to go abroad; he returned to Shanghai from 1927 to 1930 and then became Dean of Arts at Peking University, remaining in the city until 1937. When the Sino-Japanese War broke out he went abroad to plead the case of China and also (for the first time) the Nationalist government; he spent all but seven of his remaining twenty-five years away from China. He died as president of Academia Sinica on Taiwan in 1962. But his basic position was worked out in the late 1910's and early 1920's, and he had repeatedly to recognize that the time for his ideas had not come (if it would ever do so) in China.

In the winter of 1918 a group of students of the liberal professors organized a new journal called *New Tide* (*Hsin ch'ao*), which used also the English title *Renaissance*. It had been discussed the previous fall by Fu Ssu-nien, Ku Chieh-kang, and Hsü Yen-chih; the group was joined by Lo Chia-lun and others, and Hu Shih agreed to serve as their adviser.[50] Ch'en Tu-hsiu promised university support. The magazine first appeared 1 January 1919. Side by side with it there continued to appear *New Youth*. In January 1919 Ch'en Tu-hsiu conceded that critics of his magazine were correct when they accused it of trying to destroy Confucianism and a whole series of elements of traditional Chinese culture, but justified such aims because they were entailed by the editors' commitment to support 'Mr Democracy' (*te-mo-k'e-la-hsi hsien-sheng*) and 'Mr Science' (*sai-yin-ssu hsien-sheng*).[51] In the same month, in *New Tide*, Lo Chia-lun defined the meaning of the name of the journal: the new tide meant the October Revolution in Russia and its ramifications.[52]

Later Lo, Fu Ssu-nien, and others of the 'New Tide' group became uncompromisingly anti-communist, and this represented a movement to the right on their part. Nevertheless neither they nor any sizeable number could at that time be described as Bolsheviks or even Marxists. They envisaged, in Lo's phrasing, revolutions in which democracy would defeat monarchism, plain people would defeat warlords, and laborers would defeat capitalists; but there was no espousal of the particular Marxian doctrine of historical materialism or of the cause of the proletariat as the single predestined vehicle of progress. The 'New Tide' leaders were in early 1919 mainly a kind of social democrat which was not necessarily Marxist, and closer to Louis Blanc than to the Second International – let alone the Third.[53]

Probably a few months before the May Fourth incident, a Marxist Research Society was organized in Peking. Li Ta-chao was the prime mover, and he was certainly moving in the direction of Marxism.[54] However, it was 1920 before both Li and Ch'en Tu-hsiu can be more or less clearly identified as having accepted conversion to Marxism. In the early months of 1919, the Peking students, with some support among those in other cities, had reached a position of militant democracy in politics with strong social overtones, coupled with a commitment to science (or, as D. W. Y. Kwok puts it, 'scientism').[55] In an important sense the work of Yen Fu, Lu Hsün, Hu Shih, Wu Chih-hui, Ch'en Tu-hsiu, and others (with only vaguely perceived assistance from Christian modernism and its practitioners in China) had prepared the tinder lighted on 4 May 1919. It was the greatest moment of Chinese liberalism thus far, and liberalism in China was never to equal the popularity it enjoyed at that moment and during the aftermath.

THE MAY FOURTH INCIDENT

In late April word reached Peking that the Peace Conference under way in Paris would award Japan Germany's former privileges in Shantung province. A meeting was planned by the New Tide group and others for 7 May, the anniversary of Japan's Twenty-One Demands on China in 1915. However, student reaction was too sharp and spread too swiftly to wait for that date, and on the evening of 3 May it was decided to meet the next day. A meeting on the morning of 4 May heard speeches, and a demonstration took place which ended in some violence later in the day. The ministry of education vacillated. Over a thousand students were jailed, and then released, as merchants, workers, and businessmen indicated their support of the student movement. Even the Western envoys in Peking showed their sympathy.[56] It was a moment of seeming national awakening, founded in protest against the injury to China's dignity which her allies evidently were not hesitant to inflict at Paris, and yet more broadly based in the feeling that China had been some-how held back, partly through the status as a semi-colony of the West into which she had fallen since 1842, partly through voluntary subjection to out-worn customs and values, and must take sweeping or even revolutionary steps to enter the modern world. John Dewey, who by chance had arrived in Shanghai on 1 May and witnessed the entire movement, wrote:

To say that life in China is exciting is to put it fairly. We are witnessing the birth of a nation, and birth always comes hard... To think of kids in our country from fourteen on, taking the lead in starting a big cleanup reform politics movement and shaming merchants and professional men into joining them. This is sure some country.[57]

Such moments of unity do not often last long, and 4 May was no exception. On 20 July appeared Hu Shih's article, 'More Study of Problems, Less Talk of "Isms" ', which called for piecemeal attack on China's problems. Li Ta-chao at once replied, denying the need to choose either 'problems' or 'isms' to the exclusion of the other, and from his own growing Marxist convictions asserted that a change in the economic basis was a prerequisite to successful solution of individual problems. John Dewey in lectures at National Peking University and elsewhere provided impressive authority for Hu's liberal-pragmatist position. He discussed democracy and possible ways to realize it in China. Distinguishing political, social, and economic aspects of democracy as well as 'democracy in people's rights', Dewey still ended with an assertion especially welcome to the socialists: 'economic life is the foundation of all social life'.[58] Ch'en Tu-hsiu in *New Youth* repeated this assertion and reinforced it. While faithfully echoing Dewey's call for grass-roots preparation for democracy on a nation-wide basis, to take the form of local self-government and trade unions, Ch'en's basic lack of faith in political institutions remained. As he had expressed it a few months earlier: 'What is politics after all? Everybody must eat – that is important.'

What Dewey meant to say and what the young Chinese heard him say were therefore not necessarily identical. This was also true of Bertrand Russell, who visited China in the fall of 1920 and remained for several months. Russell did insist on the need for China to establish effective government, and he advocated that such a government be parliamentary and constitutional in form, though he doubted that democracy was practicable for some time to come. Somehow, however, this part of his message did not receive much attention. What the Chinese heard was his attack on imperialism and his advice that China should try state socialism. In effect, he argued, the proper model was Russian Communism: he was reported as saying that he hoped 'every civilized country in the world should experiment with this excellent new doctrine'.[59] The Soviet model was not suited for Western Europe, Russell contended, but he regarded it as the best one for increasing production, and that was China's most urgent need. State socialism, he wrote, was best for a country such as China that was 'economically but not culturally backward . . .'[60]

Russell had a substantial impact on the young Chinese; they also left a deep impression on him. 'There is, among the young', he wrote, 'a passionate desire to acquire Western knowledge, together with a vivid realization of Western vices. They wish to be scientific but not mechanical, industrial but not capitalistic. To a man they are socialists, as are most of the best among their Chinese teachers.[61] His description, if applied to the Peking students and their fellows in a few other cities, was quite accurate. It is not clear, however, whether he fully realized that in recording their values he was also describing his own values with some precision, and in so doing unwittingly explaining where they had obtained just those values – from men like himself, Western liberals of the preceding and current generation. He was ostensibly an admirer of at least certain aspects of the traditional Chinese virtues (though not explicitly of Chinese traditional culture):

China may be regarded as an artist nation, with the virtues and vices to be expected of the artist: virtues chiefly useful to others, and vices chiefly harmful to oneself. . . The Chinese have a civilization and a national temperament in many ways superior to those of white men. A few Europeans ultimately discover this, but Americans never do. They remain always missionaries – not of Christianity, though they often think that is what they are preaching, but of Americanism. What is Americanism? 'Clean living, clean thinking, and pep', I think an American would reply. This means, in practice, the substitution of tidiness for art, cleanliness for beauty, moralizing for philosophy, prostitutes for concubines (as being easier to conceal), and a general air of being fearfully busy for the leisurely calm of the traditional Chinese.[62]

The new students, however, were not much concerned with the untidy beauty that Russell purported to like among the Chinese people; moreover, it is doubtful that they absorbed much of such remarks except possibly the contempt for the 'muscular Christianity' of the YMCA. Though Russell verbally declared that the Chinese, if 'let alone...will, in the end, find a solution suitable to their character, which we should certainly not do', he nevertheless made it quite clear that he had a solution in mind for not only China but all other countries as well: 'even peace alone can never be secure until international socialism is established throughout the world'.63 From Russell, many of the new students learned that advanced liberals in the West had become socialists.

But though Russell vigorously attacked imperialism, he placed indigenous private capitalism next to state socialism in terms of desirability as a means of achieving economic development,64 and in 1921 the Progressive Party (Chin-putang) organ, *Reconstruction (Kai-tsao)*65 published a number of articles by Chang Tung-sun and others in which it was argued that capitalism might as well be permitted to develop its productive powers fully before being replaced by socialism.66 Others criticized the 'guild socialists' of the Progressive camp and took an unequivocal stand in favor of socialism.

As for liberalism, its political side was stillborn. The increasingly open corruption and malfeasance of the warlord governments in Peking led to dis-illusionment and frustration on the part of the would-be political liberals. In May 1922 a manifesto drafted by Hu Shih though initiated by Liang Sou-ming and Li Ta-chao suggested 'good government' as an immediate objective for all Westernized political factions ranging from democratic to anarchist.67 All signers were not liberals, but the content and tone of the declaration were unmistakably liberal. By 1923 the ruling warlords had given their answer, in effect: Ts'ao K'un was elected the new president by whole-sale purchase of votes in parliament.

In 1921 the magazine *New Youth* had already come to an end. There was a dispute between liberals, many of whom were then trying to avoid overt political commitment, and Communists; it was complicated by the fact that Ch'en Tu-hsiu had gone to Shanghai in the fall of 1919 and in December 1920 moved on south to Canton. In January 1921 the unresolved debates were cut off by suppression of the magazine by the French Concession in Shanghai. About the end of 1920 *New Tide* also closed.

CONCLUSION

The May Fourth Movement had run itself out, and political liberalism in China had had its day – or as much of a day as it has ever had up to this moment. The currents of thought here analyzed under the heading of 'liberal-ism', however, were far from exhausted. The literary revolution was vic-torious. The vernacular was introduced in the schools by order of the Ministry of Education in 1920; it was firmly established as a language (soon, the only language) suitable for any kind of writing. The socialism that Dewey had treated with respect and that Russell had advocated was widely accepted among the intellectuals. The pragmatism that Hu Shih had taken over from

Dewey became widespread in Chinese educational circles. In September 1921 Paul Monroe of Columbia University came to China to survey her schools; Professor Twiss of Ohio State examined her scientific teaching, Professor McCall of Teachers' College, Columbia, investigated her testing systems, all at the invitation of the Ministry of Education. In November 1922 the ministry adopted a new statement of aims: education should promote democracy, individuality, and the needs of life.[68] Chinese educators, many of whom were graduates of Teachers' College, Columbia, continued for decades to be animated by such Deweyan objectives.

Chow Tse-tsung sums up his interpretation of the May Fourth Movement by saying:

Essentially, it was an intellectual revolution in the broad sense, intellectual because it was based on the assumption that intellectual changes were a prerequisite for such a task of [as?] modernization, because it precipitated a mainly intellectual awakening and transformation, and because it was led by intellectuals.[69]

Chow is quite right; it was an intellectual movement, and it was also a liberal movement. Like Western liberalism, it had anti-militarist and anti-clerical overtones; it was democratic and even plebeian in its espousal of the vernacular and its concern for the life of the common man; it was constitutional and parliamentary in its political aspirations; it was wedded to 'modern science', though the precise implications of this liaison might remain obscure; it was willing to envisage socialism in the sense of creation or maintenance of a state sector of the economy, but unwilling to espouse a proletarian revolution or other forms of violence which would destroy a private sector. It was not Western liberalism of the Adam Smith stripe which it espoused, to be sure; but no one ought to be surprised at that, since no significant Western liberal group in the early twentieth century still clung to Smith's ideas either, and from the time John Stuart Mill had admitted that something might be said for socialism liberalism had increasingly ceased to mean devotion to *laissez-faire*.

However, the liberalism of Hu Shih proved no more politically effective or viable a force than had the Christian modernism of Sun Yat-sen. The Republic could not flourish on either basis. Chiang Monlin, a distinguished liberal, confesses, 'for China to follow the constitutional pattern of the West without its background was to hitch China's wagon to the Western star';[70] or, he might have simply said, for China to follow the constitutional pattern of the West without its background proved impossible. The institutional prerequisites were lacking, and the liberal societies were unable to build them in the face of warlord regimes in Peking. The liberals did not give up hope; the problem was to make China like the West, and if it should take longer than anticipated to do so, that could not be helped. Chiang Monlin wrote:

The greater our capacity to absorb Western ideas, the more our civilization will be enriched. Poverty and disease, twin curses of Chinese national life, will gradually disappear in proportion to the extent and thoroughness of China's modernization. To me, in this respect, modernization and westernization seem inseparable, if not identical, since the process of modernization began in the West and has gone forward without interruption. So China cannot get one without getting the other.[71]

To be sure, it was not any old Western ideas Chiang had in mind, but the ideas of liberalism: in words Russell could have used and almost the same ones he did use, Chiang declared: 'modern science, with special reference to inventions and industry, will fuse with China's rich treasures of art and sound morals. A new civilization is in the making...'[72]

One of the characteristic features of Western liberalism at least in the past has been optimism, and in this respect Chiang shared the attitude of his fellow liberals in the West. Lord Russell wrote in 1962, two generations after his visit to China: 'I believe that if we are all, permitted to survive by politicians, the qualities in Chinese civilisation which have contributed so much will re-emerge and soften the present regime.'[73] All the historian can say is that, though Russell's prophecy may prove correct, events have thus far done little to justify the specific kind of optimism of the liberals in China.

6

SOCIALISM: ANARCHISM (1907–1922)
AND MARXISM–LENINISM (1920–1949)

Socialism is not a science, a sociology in miniature: it is a cry of pain...
Emile Durkheim, *Le Socialisme* (1928)

INTRODUCTION

The intellectual ferment that led to the May Fourth demonstration of 1919 thereafter receded, but it did not disappear; as it continued in smaller circles, unity yielded to diversity and even hostility. A quite rapid differentiation between liberalism and socialism occurred. The anarchist variant of the latter, which appeared to have a good start among Chinese students abroad, was speedily submerged by a new set of ideas: Marxism–Leninism. Those who were unsympathetic to the New Culture movement organized in opposition. In a short time, largely under the impetus of the interest in Russia generated by the October Revolution of 1917, a Chinese Communist Party was established.

Before 1900 there had been some challengers to the dominant neo-Confucian orthodoxy, most of them engaged in reviving other and ostensibly older strains in the Chinese tradition of thought. Some of the dissidents experienced Western influences brought them by the Jesuits in late Ming and early Ch'ing times, the Protestants in the nineteenth century. By the early twentieth century a kind of pluralism seemed to be emerging in which Chinese with varying debts to Western Christianity, liberalism, and socialism contended with one another in the philosophical, literary, and political arenas, some of them seeking to combine elements from Western and Chinese traditions.

It was only after the May Fourth incident, however, that the search for new cultural footings led to 'debates' that caught the interest of the whole Chinese intellectual class. The few Confucian conservatives fought New Culture, the dwindling band of Christian modernists resisted the anti-religious movement, and the embattled liberals felt themselves hard pressed by the rising tide of Marxism–Leninism. The anarchists were bested – as they had been in Russia in 1917 – and disappeared as an intellectual force, leaving Marxism–Leninism as the chief beneficiary of the popularity of socialism. The Christians proved unable to compete intellectually, and gradually retreated into the background. In the 1923 debate between 'science and metaphysics', liberals appeared as victors over a congeries of Confucianists, syncretists, and those influenced by Western philosophical idealism. The Marxist–Leninists took little part in that debate, but dominated the controversy on Chinese social history. By the 1930's the syncretists were no longer influential. The ideologists of the Kuomintang, having the at least temporary advantage of the political upper hand, seemed to have an opportunity to challenge Marxism–Leninism, but they were unequal to the challenge. 'Scientific socialism' had managed rather decisively to sweep the field before the Chinese Communist armies achieved nation-wide military victory.

THE ANARCHISTS IN PARIS AND TOKYO

It may be something of an exaggeration to say that anarchism 'preceded Marxism in Northeast Asia as the predominant radical expression of the Westernized intellectual',[1] if only because anarchism was less significant in China than among Chinese students abroad. The statement may be more applicable to Japan than China, and indeed it was from Japanese influenced by anarchism that some Chinese learned about it for the first time. The first mention of anarchism in Chinese seems to have been in a translation of writings by Shimada Saburō that was published in 1903.[2] France, however, was still more important in inspiring the formation of Chinese anarchist circles.

The acknowledged leader of the Paris anarchists who began to publish a weekly in 1907 was Wu Chih-hui. Born in 1865 in Kiangsu, he took the *chü-jen* degree in 1891 – partly by cheating. He subsequently taught at schools in Peking, Tientsin, and Shanghai, and while doing so became an anti-Manchu revolutionary. In 1901–2 he found it prudent to spend some time in Japan, and in 1903 he had to flee China for London, where he joined Sun Yat-sen's T'ung-meng Hui in 1905. In 1906 he moved to France and embraced anarchism in a circle that included Li Shih-tseng, Chang Ching-chiang and others. They were inspired above all by Bakunin and Kropotkin,[3] but also by the contemporary Elisée Reclus and the group around *Les Temps Nouveaux*, an anarchist organ edited by Jean Grave which was published from 1895 to 1914. The weekly the Chinese group started in 1907 was called *The New Century (Hsin Shih-chi)*, but its Esperanto title – several Chinese radical publications had titles in that artificial language – was *La Tempoj Novaj*, after the French journal. Condemning religion, the family, militarism, nationalism, all government, and of course the Confucian tradition, *The New Century* took up a cherished anarchist theme by condemning revolutions of elites and espousing revolutions of the masses. The Paris journal lasted until 1910.

Wu Chih-hui, like the other Paris anarchists, had had a good classical education, but came to scorn the Confucian classics uncompromisingly and condescendingly: 'the harmless gossip of the ancient farmers and their rustic philosophers sitting on their faggot piles and sunning themselves in the wintry sun...became the authoritative codes of morals and of government'.[4] Though

Wu had earned distinction as a philologist, he advocated education in 'the physical, chemical, and mechanical sciences and industries'[5] and in nothing else. The materialism he adopted from the West was of a gaily naive variety:

Spirit is but a by-product of the formation of matter. With 110 pounds of pure water, 60 pounds of colloidal solution, 4 pounds 3 ounces of protein, 4 pounds 5 ounces of cellulose, and 12 ounces of otein in a suitable combination, the result is an 147-pound 'I'.[6]

In his politics, however, Wu showed himself heir of centuries of literati skilled in the art of compromise. Not only was he, like a number of other anarchists, willing to join the T'ung-meng Hui; till his death he kept on good terms with Sun Yat-sen. When the Republic was proclaimed Wu was summoned to preside over a board which created a new phonetic alphabet, and he later held numerous official posts in the Kuomintang government. But he was also ready to cooperate with non-anarchists on the magazine *The New Youth*,[7] most of whom had little use for Sun Yat-sen's changing political organizations.

The Paris anarchist group had identified its position as that of 'socialism', and the Tokyo group did likewise. In Tokyo the anarchists were also for the most part men from scholar-gentry families: they included Chang Chi, Liu Shih-p'ei, and Ho Chen (Liu's wife, and one of the earliest women of some significance in their own right in the history of modern Chinese thought). They were all influenced by such Japanese anarchists as Kōtoku Shūsui and Ōsugi Sakae. In August 1907 Liu and Chang established a Society for the Study of Socialism. At the founding meeting Liu argued that both Confucianism and Taoism had disposed Chinese to distrust governmental interference or even government as such, and made clear that by 'socialism' he meant anarchism. He expressed willingness to cooperate with 'anti-Manchuism' (as some of the circle had done by joining the T'ung-meng Hui) for the sake of revolution, but declared anarchism superior because it was not nationalist and sought power not for its own advocates but for the masses.[8] Ho Chen cited Russian anarchism and terrorism as a model, and in fact several present were later tried and some executed (including Kōtoku) for the crime of assassination. Liu and his wife followed the Russian model in one respect, that of the terrorist's becoming entangled with the profession of police informer, and they both were forced to leave the group and Japan. Chang Chi went to Paris and was associated with the anarchist circle there from 1908 to 1911, after which he returned to China and joined the Kuomintang.

Before 1911 there were only a few anarchists in China – one example was Liu Ssu-fu, or Shih Fu, who after a short time in Japan returned to engage in terrorist activity, spending nearly three years in prison. On the eve of the Revolution he was planning to assassinate Tsai-li, the Prince Regent. He turned from political murder to puritanism; in 1913 he founded the Heart

Society (Hsin She) in Canton, which renounced meat, liquor, tobacco, marriage, family names (therefore 'Shih-fu'), religion, and political office. After the Revolution most of the Paris anarchists returned, and in early 1912 there was founded a Society to Advance Morality (*Chin-te Hui*), which included Wu Chih-hui, Li Shih-tseng, Chang Chi, and Wang Ching-wei. Chang Chi was soon attacked by the puritan group in Canton for accepting the presidency of parliament in 1913.

A united anarchist political force – in any case perhaps a contradiction in terms – never emerged. Wu Chih-hui and others interested themselves in the new (1912) Society for Frugal Study in France (*Liu-Fa Chien-hsüeh Hui*), which sent nearly one hundred students there, and in a similar society formed for Great Britain. In 1915 the Chinese anarchists remaining in Paris founded a new Society for Diligent Work and Frugal Study (*Ch'in-kung Chien-hsüeh Hui*), and the so-called 'work-study' program for Chinese in France continued after the end of World War I. By 1922, however, the chief work-study organization was controlled by Communists.

In China, a certain Ou Sheng-pai challenged Ch'en Tu-hsiu, who was by now a Communist, from the anarchist position. Ch'en declared that mass movements alone led nowhere and with engaging frankness identified Communism with authority and elites that alone could secure progress. One of the points that Ch'en intended to be most damning was his denial that the anarchism that 'has been very widespread among Chinese youth of late' was truly Western anarchism; it was, he said, rather an indolent, undisciplined kind of thinking derived from Chinese sources, especially Taoism.[9] Ou found himself with few supporters. By 1922 anarchism had declined to the level of a scarcely perceptible force in Chinese intellectual life. It had never managed to become a very powerful one; it had served as a school of radicalism for a few able Chinese students abroad, and that was about all. Anarchism yielded to Marxism–Leninism, though it is noteworthy that few prominent anarchists seem to have converted to Communism.[10]

THE ANTI-RELIGIOUS MOVEMENT

If the anarchists unequivocally opposed religion as 'unscientific', the liberal attitude, as expressed in China as elsewhere, tended to be one of detachment and tolerance. In 1916 and later the slogan of 'freedom of religion' became a popular one among the *New Youth* circle and its sympathizers. In 1920 Ch'en Tu-hsiu even wrote an article, later published in translation by a missionary journal, entitled 'Christianity and the Chinese', in which he declared, 'we should try to cultivate the lofty and majestic character of Jesus'.[11] Of course he made it clear that he valued Jesus not as a prophet or the Son of God but as a man who was also a reformer – a view not greatly at variance with much modernist Protestant thought, and one no Christian needed to regard as betokening hostility.

Soon afterward, however, a quite different attitude began to take shape. In September 1920 certain members of the Young China Association who were students in Paris proposed to the Peking executive committee that believers be barred: no persons who had religious beliefs should be admitted as new members, and old members who had such beliefs should resign. The Peking committee passed a resolution to that effect. T'ien Han, a member of the Association who was studying in Japan, protested; he declared that freedom of religious belief was protected by the Chinese Constitution and that the study of Jesus might have value even for the non-religious liberal – of which he himself was an example. In July 1921 the resolution was repealed.

The Paris students, however, had not finished. A group led by Li Huang wrote to several Sorbonne professors asking them whether man was necessarily religious, whether religion would survive in the modern world, and whether China needed a religion. Marcel Granet, Célestin Bouglé, and Henri Barbusse replied. Barbusse, a Marxist and later an adulatory biographer of Stalin, declared that Christianity 'is not worthy to be an agent of spreading new Western thought, nor to be a medium for the spread of morals'.[12] Dewey's and Russell's lectures provided more fuel for the fires of the opponents of religion.

In early 1922 a special number of the YMCA's journal called *Association Progress* announced a forthcoming conference of the World Student Christian Federation in Peking. According to C. S. Chang's account, a group of 'Bolshevik' students in Shanghai read the announcement, dismissed the sole Christian member of their group, and composed a manifesto of a 'Non-Christian Student Federation' and a booklet entitled *Why We Oppose the World Student Christian Federation*. The movement spread to Peking, and in March a new Great Federation of Non-Religionists (Fei-tsung-chiao Ta-t'ung-meng) supplanted the Shanghai group. The leader was the anarchist Li Shih-tseng and Wu Chih-hui was a prominent member, along with the liberal Ts'ai Yüan-p'ei and the Communist Ch'en Tu-hsiu. Only a few intellectuals, such as Chou Tso-jen, counseled restraint. A careful study makes clear that the anti-religious (or 'anti-Christian') movement, from the time of the March 1922 manifesto of the Shanghai group, was begun by Communists, soon supported by various spokesmen of the New Culture movement, and from 1924 on accelerated by nationalist feelings.[13]

Thrown suddenly into an accustomed arena of debate, the Chinese Christian students replied as best they could. The usual tack was to justify Christianity in terms of beliefs shared by liberals and Christian modernists: religion was useful to man and compatible with science; socialism was merely 'the actual practice of the Christian principle of the sacredness of labor'.[14] In fact the Christian modernist organizations never knew what hit them. Just after the May Fourth incident, for example, a YMCA summer conference was held at Wo-fo-ssu near Peking; John Dewey was one of the speakers, and many games were played. A worthy minister recounting the event advised, 'the right use of games can start the best cure' for the ills of China.[15] While the Christians played games, and tried to argue that Christianity was a better kind of socialism than other kinds, some Chinese intellectuals responded with hostility, but most were indifferent. They understood very well that, as one author wrote a little later, 'the enlightened West has surrendered her faith in the Joshua sun-miracle, and in the Virgin birth of Jesus...'[16] The Sorbonne professors, Russell, and Dewey contributed a decisive element to the argument: regardless of the arguments for or against Christianity, it was a fact that the advanced intellectuals of the West had rejected it, and therefore so must the Chinese. By about 1927 the question could be regarded as settled among most Chinese intellectuals.

THE FORMATION OF THE CHINESE COMMUNIST PARTY

As far as is known, Marx's name was mentioned in Chinese first in 1902 by Liang Ch'i-ch'ao in an essay on Benjamin Kidd.[17] The first translation of Marx was of his ten measures for advanced countries appearing at the end of the *Communist Manifesto*; the work of Chu Chih-hsin, it appeared in *Min Pao* in Japan in 1905. In 1908 the first chapter of the *Manifesto* and Engels's introduction to the English edition of it appeared in the Tokyo anarchists' journal, *T'ien-i Pao*, as did the second chapter of Engels's *Origin of the Family*; in 1912 Engels's *Socialism, Utopian and Scientific* was translated in *Hsin Shih-chieh*, published in Shanghai. No more translations of Marx or Engels appeared until May–June 1919, when *Ch'en Pao* published a supplement containing Marx's *Wage Labor and Capital*.[18] In April 1920 appeared the first complete Chinese translation of the *Communist Manifesto*. The first of Lenin's writings was translated late in 1919.[19]

Pre-Leninist Marxism hardly existed in China; Chinese Marxism–Leninism was clearly the product of the October Revolution in Russia, and the Chinese Communist Party was clearly the organizational creation of Moscow agents and remained a constituent part of the Comintern as long as that organization lasted. It would, however, be a great mistake on such grounds to dismiss the intellectual roots of Marxism–Leninism in China (a mistake made by the Kuomintang leadership among others in both East and West). To be sure, the Chinese who became Marxists (and many who did not) were deeply impressed by the October Revolution, unlike Marxist groups in the West and Russia which took form before any state-socialist party had won power anywhere. But the Russian Communist victory occurred at a time when a small section of the Chinese intellectuals had totally rejected the Chinese tradition and were searching for an ideology. A number of them were proud, intelligent, and well-educated men, not subject to recruitment as mere hirelings of the Comintern or any other agency.

'China's first Marxist'[20] was Li Ta-chao, who was born in 1888 in Hopei. Although he came from a peasant–trader family, they had enough money to educate Li in the new schools, culminating in the Peiyang College of Law and Political Science in Tientsin, which followed Japanese models. He was graduated there in the summer of 1913. He had supported Yüan Shih-k'ai for a time, but the assassination of Sung Chiao-jen in March 1913 seems to have ended his hopes in the republican regime. Going to Waseda University in Tokyo to study, he developed a liking for philosophical idealism; Hegel, Emerson, and Bergson were among the writers who most influenced him.[21] He returned to China in April 1916. In January 1918 he joined the editorial board of *The New Youth*; the following month he became chief librarian of Peking University. It took him another year to reach the point of saying that for thousands of years Chinese life had been 'without a bit of significance, without a bit of interest, and without a bit of value'.[22]

By the last months of 1918 Li Ta-chao had organized a Marxist Research Society which was superseded in December 1919 by a Socialist Research Society, including anarchists and other non-Marxian socialists. The group soon split; Li and the Marxists formed their own Society for the Study of Marxist Theory (*Ma-k'e-ssu Hsüeh-shuo Yen-chiu Hui*) in March 1920. In 1920 both Li and Ch'en Tu-hsiu had become Marxist–Leninists – Li more gradually, Ch'en on the basis of a sharper shift away from Dewey-influenced grass-roots democratic attitudes to which he still clung through 1919, though by the time he left Peking for Shanghai at the end of 1920 he had taken his stand. They and a few other Chinese were ready to join the international movement of revolutionary Communism.

Partially aware of these developments, the Comintern's Far Eastern Secretariat in early 1920 dispatched agents to help channel the leftward movement of some Chinese intellectuals into organizational form. Gregory Voitinsky and a Chinese interpreter, Yang Ming-chai, reached Peking, and through the mediation of a professor of Russian at Peking University, Sergei Polevoi, met Li Ta-chao. Li sent Voitinsky on to Shanghai to meet Ch'en Tu-hsiu.[23] There a Chinese Communist Party was secretly formed in May 1920 and Ch'en was elected secretary. A Socialist Youth Corps and other subsidiary organizations soon were established. In September Li Ta-chao and others established a Peking branch of the party and the Corps, Mao Tse-tung founded a Changsha Society for the Study of Marxism, and other branches of the Chinese Communist organizations appeared in China and also France. In July 1921 the First Congress of the party was held in Shanghai.[24] The split between liberals and Communists widened and became irrevocable in 1920–1. One sort of casualty was the originally liberal magazines; *The New Youth* became Communist-dominated, and *New Tide* did not survive the split.

Li and Ch'en were increasingly drawn into Communist politics. Li published a book dealing with history (*Shih-hsüeh yao-lun*, Shanghai, 1924) and articles dealing with the peasant question, the role of secret societies, and other topics. However, his main efforts were devoted to the formation and development of the Communist–Kuomintang *entente*. In 1922 he helped persuade Sun Yat-sen to enter it, and Li was the first Communist to be admitted to the Kuomintang on the individual basis that had been agreed upon. He participated in both CCP and KMT activities, and did much to increase Communist influence in the Kuomintang Peking organization. In December 1926 Chang Tso-lin entered Peking in force, and Li fled to the Soviet embassy, where he was seized and, in April 1927, hanged. His place in the Chinese Communist pantheon has thus far been secure.25

Ch'en, however, as general secretary (1921–7) of the party, fell victim as a result of the complex strategic maneuverings taking place within it. In a decision announced to the Chinese comrades in August 1922 and publicly sealed by the Sun–Yoffe manifesto of January 1923, the Comintern had undertaken to cooperate with Sun Yat-sen and the Kuomintang. Reluctant at first, Ch'en seems after a time to have accepted the new line more or less faithfully until Sun died in March 1925 and the Kuomintang's right and left wings drifted farther apart. After Chiang K'ai-shek's purge of Communists in Canton in March 1926 and in Shanghai in April 1927, Ch'en protested and urged Communist withdrawal from the *entente*. Nevertheless he was blamed for the final break which followed the expulsion of the Communists in July 1927 from the Left KMT regime at Wuhan, and in August he was replaced as leader of the party by Ch'ü Ch'iu-pai. In 1929, after Trotsky had already been defeated by Stalin in the Soviet party dispute, Ch'en became attracted to Trotsky's notion of permanent revolution and associated closely with a group of Chinese returned students from the USSR who had adopted a Trotskyist position. In a resolution formally adopted in 1930, Ch'en was expelled from the Communist Party. He tried to organize a competing Trotskyist faction, which collapsed in a short time. In 1932 he was arrested by the Nationalists and imprisoned; in 1938 he was released, and died in 1942. In his last years he returned to his earlier support of democracy, denouncing Soviet dictatorship and Communist orthodoxy.26

By 1928 Li Ta-chao was dead and Ch'en Tu-hsiu had fallen from leadership. But during the next decade a substantial number of other Chinese intellectuals, despite the Kuomintang crackdown on the Communists, remained or became party members or sympathizers.

LITERARY DEBATES (1920–1936)

During the 1920's and 1930's the fundamental intellectual battles were fought outside the arena of political parties. Most Chinese intellectuals were not ready to submit voluntarily to party discipline of any sort. The main scene of struggle became the literary societies, where the varieties of Westernization might be experimented with.

At the end of 1920 and the beginning of 1921 the first literary society, the Society for Literary Research (*Wen-hsüeh Yen-chiu Hui*) was formed.27 Shen Yen-ping, later to win fame as Mao Tun, had been appointed the new editor of the magazine *Novel Monthly* (*Hsiao-shuo Yüeh-pao*), which had been published by the Commercial Press in Shanghai since 1909. Cheng Chen-to, Chou Tso-jen, and a group of others in cooperation with Shen decided to found a society to support the renovated journal and to convert it into an organ of the 'new literature'. Cheng Chen-to drafted the constitution, Chou Tso-jen wrote a manifesto for the group. Its aims were to be to introduce foreign literature, review old Chinese literature, and create a new Chinese literature.

The ideological orientation of the Society was toward humanitarianism of a rather social cast. The Society's critics attributed to it the slogan 'art for life's sake'. Chou Tso-jen wrote (of modern writers in general, but the remark was obviously intended to apply to the Society in particular), 'the humanitarian ideal is their faith, the will of mankind is their god'.[28] Chou himself was apt to emphasize the individual, Yeh Shao-chün the family, Mao Tun the social class – he declared that the petty bourgeoisie was being unfairly slighted by writers who thought they had to write about manual labor. In general the Society refrained from taking a clear positive ideological position. Mao Tun decried both the traditional notion that the task of literature was to inculcate the proper way to live (*tao*) and the contemporary slogans 'literature for literature's sake' or 'art for art's sake' (as attributed to the Creation Society, to be discussed below). In an article of 1921, he argued that literature was a 'kind of science' whose proper subject matter was the contemporary life of mankind. On one occasion he declared: 'I do not approve the extreme humanitarianism of Tolstoy, but I am certainly opposed to those purely esthetic Chinese works that are foreign to human life.'[29] For members of the Society 'life' meant generally the real feelings, experiences, and above all sufferings of humanity. Though they did not address themselves to political or social solutions, they raised problems for which they believed such solutions were needed.

The chief effect of the Society was in introducing translated works of West European belletristic writers to the Chinese reading public. Cheng Chen-to discussed the problems of translation, characteristically on the basis of the 'Essay on the Principles of Translation' written in 1790 by an obscure Scottish gentleman named Alexander Fraser Tytler.[30] Cheng's chief conclusions were that translation must be faithful in spirit and letter to the original, and that retranslation from a language not that of the original – a common practice at that time – was to be avoided. Such writers as Ibsen and Strindberg, Zola and Maupassant, and above all the pre-revolutionary Russians – Andreev, Artsybashev, Dostoevsky, Gogol, Tolstoy, and Turgenev – were the object of the Society's labors; that is, the authors selected for translation were chiefly the realist and naturalist prose writers (or writers so interpreted) of the nineteenth and early twentieth century.

The May 30 Incident of 1925, in which the police moved against strikers in Shanghai, seems to have caused a crisis in the Society for Literary Research; the lack of response by Cheng Chen-to (who had succeeded Mao Tun as editor) in *Novel Monthly* may have led certain contributors to lose interest. However, already the previous year there had been important defections. Chou Tso-jen left the Society in 1924 and began to publish a new magazine in November. At about the same time Chou along with his brother, Lu Hsün, and several other writers including Ch'ien Hsüan-t'ung, Liu Pan-nung, and Ku Chieh-kang, organized a new group called the Thread of Talk Society (*Yü-ssu She*), which lasted from 1924 to 1931.[31] Chou continued his generally non-political line which a number of others followed, but Lu Hsün sharply protested the police action in the May 30 Incident and in general took a more activist stance than his brother. Deprived of some of its chief stalwarts, the *Novel Monthly* creaked on until January 1932, when the Japanese bombed Shanghai, but the Society for Literary Research fell to pieces in 1930.

A competing but by no means necessarily opposed group was the Creation Society (*Ch'uang-tsao She*), organized in mid-1921. It consisted chiefly of Kuo Mo-jo, Yü Ta-fu, and Ch'eng Fang-wu; they were studying in Japan, but they traveled back and forth from China and published in Shanghai. Kuo Mo-jo (born Kuo K'ai-chen)'s maternal grandfather had been one of only ten men from his prefecture in Szechwan during the entire Ch'ing period to obtain the *chin-shih* degree, though his father was a businessman.[32] As a boy he took part in the first new-style examinations in the fall of 1905. After studying in Chengtu and Tientsin he went to Japan in 1914. Though he took a medical course, he spent much time on literature, and was especially struck by Goethe, Tagore, and Whitman – whose combination of romanticism and identification with the downtrodden fascinated him in 1919 and harmonized with the two sorts of commitments between which he was then torn. Kuo and his friends had a brief period of popularity in 1923 when a *Creation Quarterly*, *Creation Weekly*, and *Creation Daily* were appearing simultaneously. However, in 1924 Kuo began to translate the Japanese Marxist Kawakami Hajime's book of essays and soon accepted Marxism–Leninism. In the aftermath of the May 30 Incident (1925) the Society shifted rapidly to the left; the slogans 'revolutionary literature' and 'proletarian literature' successively witnessed to the change. In 1929 the Society was banned.

Meanwhile a non-ideological kind of liberalism close to the original impulses behind *The New Youth* found expression among writers in the Crescent Moon Society (*Hsin-yüeh She*). Its notables included Hu Shih, Hsü Chih-mo, Liang Shih-ch'iu, and Wen I-to. Though it existed from 1923 on, only after it was reorganized in 1928 did it have much impact on literature. It insisted on adherence to the rules of prosody and metre; its substantive criteria of 'health and dignity', it appears, were less influential. Yü Ta-fu, having broken with Kuo Mo-jo and the Creation Society, joined the Crescent Moon Society about the time it was reorganized, though he soon left it for a more leftist milieu. There were still other societies concerned with literature, such as the No-name Society (*Wu-ming She*, 1925–30), which continued the translation and popularization of Western authors.

By about 1930, however, the area of debate among Chinese writers was narrowing, and the liberals' voice was enfeebled or silenced. One writer declares that with the death of Hsü Chih-mo in an air accident in 1931, there 'died the spirit of Western liberalism in modern Chinese literature'.[33] It may be an overstatement, but it does not greatly exaggerate.

At this time three new literary groups were formed. One, founded in February 1930 and called the League for Liberty (*Tzu-yu Yün-tung Ta-t'ung-meng*), included writers committed to several varieties of socialism. Among them were Lu Hsün, Yü Ta-fu, and Ts'ai Yüan-p'ei, who was a supporter of the Kuomintang, a group of Trotskyists following Ch'en Tu-hsiu (who by then had been expelled from the Communist Party), and several anarchists. Prominent among the colorations represented was a faction which thought of itself as 'Menshevik' and read such Russian authors as Plekhanov, Bogdanov, and Andreev – none of whom had ever been a Menshevik except (briefly) Plekhanov, though all had at least differed with Lenin. The League was not merely a literary group, but included merchants, journalists, lawyers, and teachers as well. Seeking to differentiate itself from both the Kuomintang or Kuomintang-influenced writers and from the Marxist–Leninist left, still another group appeared calling itself the Literature of Third-Party Men (*Ti-san-chung-jen Wen-hsüeh*), which attacked Kuomintang literature as fatal to freedom of thought but stigmatized revolutionary literature as a set of 'revolutionary eight-legged essays' (*ke-ming pa-ku*) – that is, as consisting of a new scholasticism whose new content ought not to obscure the fact that it was as hostile to originality of thought as the essays written for the old examination system.[34]

In the early 1930's one organization overshadowed the others, and it was Marxist–Leninist. It was the League of Leftist Writers, founded in March 1930. The chief figure in it was Lu Hsün, who had become a fellow-traveler the previous year;[35] its secretary-general was Chou Yang, who was to be a sort of literary commissar for the Communists after 1937 in Yenan and after 1949 in the new government, though other Communist leaders such as Ch'ü Ch'iu-pai were more important than Chou in making policy. Other major writers in the group included Mao Tun and Ting Ling. Kuo Mo-jo and Ch'eng Fang-wu brought the remnants of the Creation Society into the new organization.[36] In 1931 Hu Ch'iu-yüan, an essayist who had been close to the leftists since Wuhan but maintained an independent position, was attacked by Ch'ü Ch'iu-pai, and the debate served to consolidate the League's position to a certain extent. During the debate Ch'ü opposed the use of not only the literary language (*wen-yen*) but also colloquial Mandarin (*pai-hua*) for writing, declaring that the latter was merely the language of old novels irrelevant to contemporary needs. He advocated instead the use of 'common language' (*p'u-t'ung hua*); as Tagore points out, however, no such thing existed outside of Ch'ü's imagination.[37]

In 1936 the adoption by the Communists of a 'united-front' with the

Kuomintang led to the end of the League. Chou Yang dissolved it and replaced it by a new Writers' Association, proclaiming the slogan of 'literature for national defense'. Lu Hsün, Hu Feng, and others retaliated by forming an opposing Chinese Literary Workers' Association and called for 'people's literature for the national revolutionary struggle'. In October 1936 Lu Hsün died, embittered and puzzled. (Subsequently the Communists dissected this episode in a curious way: Lu Hsün – never a party member – was posthumously recognized as the chief luminary in the leftist literary firmament, but in 1954–5 Hu Feng and others were attacked for a series of 'errors' going back to the 1936 'battle of slogans'. In 1955 Hu Feng was imprisoned, and his subsequent fate is unknown.)[38]

By 1936 the period of literary debate may be said to have passed; party politics and the issue of resisting Japan had overshadowed questions of the social content of literature.

PHILOSOPHICAL DEBATES (1923–1937)

During the 1920's two issues divided Chinese intellectuals as a whole and helped to polarize them. The first was that of 'science versus metaphysics', opened by Carsun Chang (Chang Chün-mai) in a speech of February 1923 in which he attacked the notion of a philosophy of life based entirely on science. In sounding such a note he repeated the theme with which Liang Ch'i-ch'ao had summed up his post-World War I impressions of the West – the 'bankruptcy' of science which he found Europeans discussing, though he himself denied that science was either bankrupt or omnipotent.[39] Moreover, in 1922 in an article entitled 'The Scientific Spirit and the Cultures of East and West', Liang had defended science and urged the Chinese to employ its methods. Nevertheless, the crusaders against science found material in Liang which they could use, as they did also in Liang Sou-ming. The latter, in his book *The Cultures of East and West and Their Philosophies* (*Tung-hsi wen-hua chi ch'i che-hsüeh*), had singled out three cultures as fundamentally different from each other. Indian culture sought to extinguish desire, Chinese culture to satisfy it through harmony, Western culture to satisfy it through struggle.[40] Chinese culture needed to be criticized and renovated, but in a 'cultural dialectic' it was nevertheless to overtake the then-ascendant Western culture and even dominate the epoch that lay just ahead. Science could be put to good use, but it must be 'cured of its utilitarianism and prevented from committing further crimes'.[41]

In his opening salvo Carsun Chang drew on the ideas of the German nineteenth-century idealists, upholding the world of the 'I' as against the 'non-I', and also the intuitionism of Bergson. On the basis of such arguments he declared that science 'can never solve the problems of the philosophy of life, which depends entirely on man himself and nothing more...'[42] This was a plausible statement, repeating the proposition that science cannot settle questions of value, with which many Western scientists would agree. However, Chang went on to describe traditional Chinese civilization as 'spiritual' as contrasted with recent Western civilization, characterized as 'materialistic' – at least a tactical error, for many of his hearers, if forced to make a choice in those terms, by that time did not hesitate to opt for the matter.

The counterattack of the Westernizing intellectuals was delivered by the geologist and polymath V. K. Ting (Ting Wen-chiang). He labeled Chang's position as 'metaphysics', and under this heading lumped intuition, esthetics, morality, religious feelings, and all else that might be termed 'spiritual'. Metaphysics, he wrote, was a 'shiftless ghost' that had deceived Europe for two thousand years and now was attempting to do the same in China through Chang. He compared Chang to his namesake, the mandarin Chang Chih-tung,[43] who had declared that Chinese culture should be the basis but that Western technique should be borrowed for practical use. Ting declared that Carsun Chang made metaphysics the basis in similar fashion, reserving science for the realm of application. Ting's most persuasive passages were perhaps to be found in his recounting of the personal satisfactions which scientific experiment and inquiry could yield.

Many others commented on the exchanges between Chang and Ting. Although Liang Ch'i-ch'ao declared his neutrality, he acknowledged paternity of some of Carsun Chang's ideas by coming to his aid in fact; others willing to lend some support were the philosophers Chang Tung-sun and Fan Shou-k'ang. Ting's supporters included Hu Shih, Ch'en Tu-hsiu, and Wu Chih-hui. Hu Shih declared that natural laws governed the universe, and left no basis for belief in God, immortality, or religion; he nevertheless felt constrained to identify as his idea 'to live for the sake of the whole species and posterity' and labeled that 'the highest religion'.[44] Kwok with some justice compares the whole debate to the 'quarrel between ancients and moderns' as described by Fontenelle in seventeenth-century France[45] (although Fontenelle's was an imaginary dialogue constructed by a partisan of one side). The 'ancients' who were accused of supporting 'metaphysics' were clearly worsted; the 'moderns' espousing 'science' were victorious. There were elements of syncretism in the positions of Chang and his supporters, though they were not brought out clearly, let alone systematized. It was taken for granted by all participants that 'science' was identified with the West, and the victory of the Ting group strengthened the view that further intellectual Westernization was China's only hope.

The second great debate of the 1920's centered on questions of historical interpretation. A kind of curtain-raiser was the debate over ancient history, in which the issue was the degree of confidence historians could place in existing sources dealing with Chinese antiquity. The chief writers expressing skepticism about such sources were Ku Chieh-kang, Ch'ien Hsüan-t'ung, and Hu Shih. Three collections of essays, published in 1926, 1930, and 1931, were edited by Ku.[46]

In 1928 began the 'controversy on China's social history' (*Chung-kuo she-hui-shih lun-chan*). It was an exclusively Marxist and almost exclusively Marxist–Leninist (though not necessarily Communist) affair.[47] The authorities recognized by virtually all participants were Morgan, Marx and Engels, Lenin, and certain Soviet writers.

Perhaps the chief antagonists were T'ao Hsi-sheng, professor, publisher, and Kuomintang stalwart, and Kuo Mo-jo, who had identified himself with the Communist cause. Beginning with several articles in *The New Life* (*Hsin Sheng-ming*) in the fall of 1928, T'ao argued that China was more or less in the capitalist stage, Kuo in *The Readers' Magazine* (*Tu-shu Tsa chih*) that it was more or less in the feudal stage. T'ao and his supporters pointed out that land had been alienable and saleable in China for two millennia, that many landlords were of merchant origin, that the domestic market was growing rapidly, and that the technology of capitalism was visible everywhere. Kuo, Chu Ch'i-hua, and Liu Meng-yüan invoked Marx as authority for the proposition that commodity production and money economy are in themselves not at all peculiar to capitalism but existed in the slave-owning and feudal modes of production; they argued that capitalist technology was not indigenous but a foreign importation, and they identified Chinese agricultural society with landlordism and peasant tillage as described by Marx under the rubric of feudalism.[48]

The debate on China's social history demonstrated how fully not only Marxism but Leninism in its Stalinist version had carried the day. Marx's category of the Asiatic mode of production was introduced only marginally by Li Chi (not to be confused with the great archeologist of the same name). The category had been suppressed in the USSR after the Leningrad discussion of 1931, and most participants either chose to accept Stalin's authority or were uncomfortable with any suggestion that China had followed a path (either alone or in common with certain other societies) different from Western Europe's. The acceptable alternatives were, with some qualifications, 'capitalism' and 'feudalism', and that was all. *The Readers' Magazine* went on publishing special issues on the social-history controversy from 1930 to 1934, when the debate may be said to have come to an end. A number of the participants were from the reform faction of the Kuomintang; several were Communist Party members; a number were independent Marxists or Marxist–Leninists; but what was common ground to all was a willingness to conduct the exchanges in terms of Marxist categories.

In the meantime Hu Shih and V. K. Ting, through the *Independent Critic* (*Tu-li P'ing-lun*), maintained their liberal and critical position, providing some counterweight to the Marxist–Leninists. However, on the question of Westernization they remained as uncompromising as the Marxists. In *Speeches and Essays about Total Westernization* (*Ch'üan-p'an hsi-hua yen-lun chi*; three collections, 1934–6), Ch'en Hsü-ching and others laid down a gauntlet similar to that hurled by the liberals almost two decades earlier. There were some efforts to challenge the 'total Westernizers', exemplified by the 1935 *Manifesto for Reconstruction of Culture Using China as a Basis* (*Chung-kuo pen-wei ti wen-hua chien-she hsüan-yen*), signed by ten professors including T'ao Hsi-sheng. They did not assume a categorically anti-Western position in regard to cultural reconstruction, but they insisted on making Chinese culture the starting point. They were no more able to win a hearing than syncretists in China had been at any time since the May Fourth incident.

By the outbreak of the Sino-Japanese War, the Westernizers were in virtually unchallenged command of public discussion among Chinese intellectuals, and Marxist–Leninists were widely recognized as having a position of decided popularity. Why did the Kuomintang undertake extermination campaigns against Communists and yet permit Marxist–Leninist publications to enjoy such currency? In Hankow, it was reported, less than 20 out of a total of 90 bookstores were selling 'proper' books and magazines. Serious propaganda could be prohibited; 'proletarian literature' was admittedly a more difficult problem; if censorship was too strict, the progress of culture would be halted, while if it was too lenient, the party and the nation might be endangered.[49] Such was evidently the reasoning of some authorities. In fact, the Kuomintang leaders were somewhat ambivalent about Westernization in general and socialism in particular.

THE NATIONALISTS' ECLECTICISM (1925–1949)

In the mid-1920's the intellectual battles were overshadowed by stirring events. The Kuomintang was reorganized under Soviet direction, and in partnership with the Soviets and Chinese Communists prepared to launch the Northern Expedition. Sun Yat-sen died and was replaced by Chiang K'ai-shek, whose forces headed north from Canton in June 1926. In April 1927 he suppressed the Communists in Shanghai and continued with a Party Purification Movement to get rid of them everywhere he could. Chiang's forces reached Peking in 1928, but the Kuomintang regime made Nanking its capital. For a time anti-imperialist, anti-Japanese, nationalist, reformist, and socialist slogans and impulses were widespread among the students and intellectuals with the encouragement of various elements of the Kuomintang leadership. However, by 1930 disenchantment with the Nationalists was becoming pronounced among the students.[50] As Kwok points out, the Nationalists had simply won a series of battles, which 'left the question of social doctrines unanswered, and this disappointed a number of the intelligentsia'.[51]

The old intellectual weaknesses of the Kuomintang, which dated to the difficulty Sun Yat-sen had in his youth in earning the respect of Chinese intellectuals, was not remedied by Chiang's partial military victory. After Sun's death his person was virtually canonized and his works became virtually scriptural in the eyes of the Kuomintang leadership. However, despite the lip service given to Sun's 'three principles' since then (and to this day in Taiwan) and the quasi-religious 'Monday service' in the schools commemorating him, Chiang K'ai-shek began also to move in other intellectual directions.

As commandment of the Whampoa Military Academy, to which he returned from a stay in the USSR, Chiang chose as a textbook Ts'ao O's selections from the writings of the scholar-statesmen, Tseng Kuo-fan, Hu Lin-i, and Tso Tsung-t'ang.[52] In so doing Chiang lent his support to the Confucianist conceptions of virtue held by such men, though he acknowledged that their opponents, the leaders of the T'ai-p'ing rebellion, were their equals in ability. The Tsengs had concerned themselves with problems of stabilization which certainly faced the new regime; however, Chiang himself also lectured at Whampoa on revolution. In the meantime the Kuomintang as a party was issuing manifestoes of a revolutionary and (at the II Congress in 1926) even Marxist character. In 1927 the National Government banned official Confucian rites and ordered that funds previously used for them be turned over to the purposes of public education.

By the time of the III Congress of the party in 1929, revolutionary themes had been muted. In November 1928 Chiang urged army officers to devote leisure time to the study of the Four Books, and the Confucianist textbook used at Whampoa was reproduced in many editions. Much emphasis was placed on the study of the ideals of Tseng and Hu and of the practice of the T'ung-chih restoration.

In February 1934 Chiang launched a so-called New Life movement designed to influence the conduct of the ordinary man but also evidently to appeal to the intellectual. 'The weakness of China', he declared, 'is due to the fact that we have completely forgotten our ancient virtues.'[53] Mass meetings were held in numerous cities to turn the people's attention to the value of rectitude, reason, justice, and honor. This attempt at a new 'Confucian puritanism',[54] however, had virtually no success in university circles and scant effect on the Chinese people as a whole.

In the same year the Kuomintang's chief ideologist, Ch'en Li-fu, published a series of lectures under the title *Vitalism* (*Wei-sheng lun*) which, borrowing from Bergson and Driesch, attempted to provide Triple Demism with some kind of serious philosophical foundations.[55] As Brière points out, if his aim was to refute materialism, it was not achieved, since his basic unit of reality, the monad, was common to the vegetable, mineral, and all branches of the animal kingdom. In any case Ch'en's doctrines evoked little enthusiasm then or later. By the 1940's, when Chiang as China's leader was deeply embroiled in a war with Japan which he could only wait grimly for the Allies to win for him, he seemed to return to unadorned Confucianism. His ghost-written volume, *China's Destiny*, contained this passage:

China had for a long time her own philosophy of life which, as propounded by Confucius, elaborated by Mencius, and commented upon by scholars of the Han Dynasty, forms a sublime system, in itself. In comparison with other systems of philosophy, it is equal, if not superior, to any one of them.[56]

Chiang and the Kuomintang tried their best to deal with problems of institutional reform, economic modernization, and the concrete needs of China. As 'the only political movement which ever had a chance of successfully competing with the Communists',[57] it needed a strong ideology if it was to use that chance. Various possible ingredients were at hand and were employed to try to construct one. Triple Demism was always verbally retained and made the basis of compulsory university courses; its ill-assorted Western political doctrines, amalgamated in a Christian modernist spirit, were provided with some uneasily-fitting glosses, such as those of Ch'en Li-fu, designed to be acceptable to trained minds. Though Communism was clearly repudiated by 1927, some Marxism–Leninism survived in the party from the time that Sun Yat-sen had given it partial sanction; notable Kuomintang theorists such as T'ao Hsi-sheng accepted its framework in certain respects. There was also a serious attempt to revive neo-Confucian ethics and make it a guide to the behavior of the whole people.

All this amounted not to a fruitful sort of cultural pluralism, in which the disciplined development of competing outlooks was encouraged; the punitive measures taken against critics of the regime who confined themselves to thought and resorted to no action preclude any such interpretation of Kuomintang cultural policy. It did not amount to syncretism; it was probably impossible to marry the culturally radical approach of Sun Yat-sen to neo-Confucianism (not to mention 'vitalism' or Marxism); at any rate no one seriously tried to do so. Even eclecticism, implying a combination of diverse elements of thought, is not an easy word to apply to Kuomintang ideology. The fact was that in practice the leaders seemed to insist now on Confucianism, now on Triple Demism, now on Marxism or vitalism or something else, without ever clearly explaining what the relation among these viewpoints was supposed to be. No self-respecting intellectual could possibly accept 'Kuomintang ideology', a bag into which yowling and biting cats and dogs were stuffed together, on philosophical grounds. Some intellectuals accepted the regime – as Hu Shih did in wartime – on the grounds that no alternative governing elite could be found at the moment. But even that kind of acceptance was rare among intellectuals. Despite the Kuomintang's achievements, the practical dimension scarcely made it more attractive than the ideology to the students; as Israel says, they could not stomach 'a potpourri of warlord politics, treaty-port economics, hybridized Western education, rural conservatism, neo-Confucian morality, and ossified Sun-Yat-senism'.[58]

In 1935 Liang Shih-ch'iu, a fine critic who was then a professor at Peking University, wrote that 'left wing ideals have captured the imagination of most of our younger men'.[59] The terrible disruptions of the war soon afterward scattered the new educational institutions. The disaffection of the intellectuals did not spur the regime to attend to their financial problems or physical well-being. Never having warmed to Kuomintang ethos or ideals, already having been deeply influenced by 'attractively packaged Marxist doctrines',[60] a large share of the intellectuals were driven to bitterness or despair by the nation's or their own wartime sufferings. Until 1945 patriotic opposition to the Japanese more or less postponed the day of reckoning; when, at the end of the war with Japan, the civil war posed the alternatives of the Nationalists or the Communists, many intellectuals chose to join or accept the latter.

THE RISE OF COMMUNISM

The pre-1949 literature of Chinese Communism was less impressive than the outpouring of Marxist or Marxist–Leninist works by persons not members of the party. By the late 20's the two chief intellectuals of the early years of the party had passed from the scene. Even Ch'en Tu-hsiu and Li Ta-chao had written only scattered and inconclusive essays on Marxism before they were swept up into the organizational arena; Li's life was ended prematurely in 1925, Ch'en was driven from the party in 1929. It remained for lesser figures to produce extended expositions of Communist doctrine.

Among such persons were Li Ta, Li Chi, and Ai Ssu-ch'i. After some time spent as a student in Japan, Li Ta (1890–1966) returned to China in 1918 and soon became a Communist.[61] His book of over 800 pages, *Outlines of Sociology* (*She-hui-hsüeh ta-kang*), recapitulated a great number of problems as hitherto treated by Marx and Marxists. Li Chi, who had returned from Germany to become a contributor to *The New Youth*, produced a three-volume *Biography of Marx* (*Ma-k'e-ssu chuan*) which was really an historical survey of Marxist doctrine. More important was Ai Ssu-ch'i (1905–66), who had studied in Japan and returned only in the early 1930's.[62] His chief work was *The Philosophy of the Masses* (*Ta-chung che-hsüeh*), written in 1934 and published in 1936 under the title *Talks on Philosophy* (*Che-hsüeh chiang-hua*). The book went through 32 editions in twelve years, and made Ai the chief popularizer of the doctrines of the pre-1949 party.

Ai Ssu-ch'i, along with Ch'en Po-ta and a few others, was enlisted to help Mao Tse-tung when in Yenan during the late 30's he sought to establish himself as a theoretician in the face of taunts or hints by some of those with greater intellectual dexterity or Soviet experience, or both – such as Wang Ming (Ch'en Shao-yü) – that his achievements in this sphere were meager. (In this respect he was faced with the same problem as Stalin in the mid-1920's; a major difference was that Stalin then was already one of the leaders of a regime that governed an entire country.)

Mao Tse-tung was born in 1893 in Hunan; his father was a merchant from a peasant family.[63] Among the early influences on him were the ideas of K'ang Yu-wei and Liang Ch'i-ch'ao; after 1915 he became an admirer of *New Youth*, and there survives a lone article he published in the magazine in April 1917 advocating physical culture. He was graduated from the Changsha Normal School in 1918, where his philosophy professor had helped him place his article in *The New Youth*. When he went to Peking that fall, the same professor, Yang Ch'ang-chi, gave him the introduction that yielded him the position of assistant librarian under Li Ta-chao at the university. Li was to serve as his mentor in radicalism and then Marxism–Leninism; like Li, the young Mao (under the influence of Professor Yang) was attracted to philosophical idealism. As Li welcomed the October Revolution first as 'the victory of the spirit of all mankind' and later discovered Marxism, so Mao started with commitment and then tried to do his arduous doctrinal homework. He was converted to Marxism–Leninism, as Li was, during 1920; he was also influenced by a talk he had with Ch'en Tu-hsiu in Shanghai. He took part in the founding of the Communist Party in 1921. He was soon plunged into the work of the new Communist–Kuomintang *entente*; at that time he was clearly filled with enthusiasm for the arrangement and probably was regarded as guilty of an 'underestimation of the revolutionary force of the peasantry'[64] (contrary to a fair amount of still current folklore on the point). Thus he continued to collaborate with Chiang K'ai-shek 'longer than any other communist equally in view',[65] until the fall of 1926, and only after the collaboration ceased did he turn to contemplate the possibility of peasant revolution in his much discussed Hunan Report, resulting from an investigation in his home province in early 1927.[66] The Report was in any event not a contribution to theory but chiefly an account of events. Mao had little time for theorizing. By 1929 he was in southern Kiangsi, where the Communists sought to save what they could from the wreck of the *entente* with the Kuomintang and prepare a base for new kinds of action. After the extermination campaigns and the Long March, Mao found himself in Yenan (captured at the end of 1936) in Shensi[67] as leader of the party but, as mentioned above, in dire need of acquiring standing as a theorist.

The term 'Maoism' has been extensively employed in the West, but in China the officially-approved term is not Maoism (*Mao-chu-i*) but 'the thought of Mao Tse-Tung' (*Mao Tse-tung ssu-hsiang*).[68] Like Stalin's writings, Mao's are difficult to take seriously either as prose of quality or as exposition of problems; indeed, Mao's writings cannot be properly evaluated without reference to Stalin's. Despite the need of both men to achieve recognition as theorists within their parties and their undoubted wish not merely to win but to deserve it, however, it ought to be pointed out that the purpose of most of their writings was an immediate one: to persuade, to provoke enthusiasm of spirit and resolute action, sometimes to intimidate, persons in and out of party ranks in terms of current needs as they saw them, not to break new ground in the history of human philosophy or even thought. In the writings of both a simplified, popularly accessible style is used to expound a substance replete with unexamined assumptions and breathtaking logical leaps, often coupled with such phrases as 'as is well known'.

Mao's writings on philosophy purport to begin with 1937; it is claimed that he delivered two lectures in Yenan that were only later (1950–2) revised, amplified, and published: *On Practice* (*Shih-chien lun*) and *On Contradiction*

(*Mao-tun lun*).[69] The theme of the former was the last of Marx's theses on Feuerbach, which was simply translated thus:[70]

What is regarded as the most important problem in Marxist thought does not lie in merely the understanding of the laws governing the objective world in order to explain it, but in using this knowledge of the objective laws to actively change the world.

On Contradiction, surely one of the most primitive essays ever to claim the status of Marxist–Leninist scripture,[71] divided all views of the world into two, 'metaphysical' and 'dialectical', discussed the place of 'contradiction' in the second view, and distinguished between 'antagonistic' and 'non-antagonistic' contradictions. Only one philosophical text of Mao's clearly pre-dated the establishment of the nationwide regime in 1949, and that was one of 1940, about which perhaps the less said the better.[72]

Mao's interpretation of Chinese history and of the tasks of the Chinese Communist Party which he headed from 1935[73] on is of greater interest than his philosophical writings. Here his substantive debt to Stalin is great. In *The New Democracy* (*Hsin min-chu-chu-i lun*, 1940) Mao sketched his Stalinist view of the stages of Chinese history – slave-owning, feudal, and semicolonial-semifeudal – and set forth the prospect of a bourgeois–democratic revolution which would be in fact neither bourgeois nor democratic but would establish the hegemony of the Communist Party – which was Lenin's as well as Stalin's prescription for China as it had been for Russia.

In the period 1942-4, when the war had thrown the Chinese Communists increasingly on their own resources, Mao undertook to conduct a large-scale thought-remolding and morale-building campaign which was given the name of *cheng feng* (combining *cheng tun*, to correct, and *tso feng*, style of activity). In the documents of the *cheng feng* movement, as Boyd Compton writes, there are to be found

no basically new concepts; instead, it [the movement] represented the wholesale adoption of ideas and methods that were not Chinese...The attack on dogmatism and the plea for a sinified theory [for use in China] were orthodox in every way. [Georgy] Dimitrov demanded them vigorously in 1935. But the development of a Party capable of actually formulating its own program and writing its own handbooks was something new in the Communist world.[74]

In 1949 Mao's *On the People's Democratic Dictatorship* (*Lun jen-min min-chu chuan-cheng*) offered an innovation: not only would the 'bloc of four classes' ('workers, peasants, petty bourgeoisie, and national bourgeoisie') be allied in the revolutionary struggle, then just ending with the assumption of nationwide power; it would last into the period of 'dictatorship'. Such a position for the 'national bourgeoisie' had no precedent in either Lenin or Stalin.[75] There was later some discussion between Moscow and Peking about the significance of such an innovation in theory; in practice it made little difference, as the 'national bourgeoisie' was tolerated only to the extent that it did not exhibit any bourgeois characteristics.

From the time of the Party Reform Movement the Chinese Communist Party, under the leadership of Mao with Liu Shao-ch'i as his chief lieutenant (until the Great Proletarian Cultural Revolution of the 1960's), emerged as a disciplined and ideological schooled force ready to seize its opportunity for establishing itself in power. Already in 1946 Mao was telling Anna Louise Strong that a new struggle had developed between American imperialism and the Communist world to replace the struggle between Japanese (and Nazi) fascism and what he had not long before called 'the three great democracies' of Britain, the United States, and the USSR. By 1947 the Chinese Civil War had broken out in full fury, and by the fall of 1949 Mao's armies were victorious. The problems of a party competing for power were replaced by those of a party wielding power – such power that not only was Marxism–Leninism prescribed as the only possible kind of thought but the most draconian measures – quite unprecedented in the USSR – were taken to make sure that every possible citizen learned by experience how to renounce the errors of his past beliefs aloud to his neighbors and to espouse Communist ideas actively and overtly.

CONCLUSION

By the time of the Communist victory, China's intellectuals (the so-called literati having passed from the scene) had to decide where to take their stand. Ai Ssu-ch'i, Li Ta, Kuo Mo-jo, and others were already committed to Communism and remained on the mainland. Some non-Communists took up pro-regime positions: Chang Tung-sun joined the Democratic League, one of the partner organizations in Mao's 'new democracy', and beginning in 1949 served for a time on the Central People's Government Council; but in 1952 he was forced into retirement. Fung Yu-lan repudiated his most recent philosophical views (he had undergone several changes of mind in the days when one can scarcely suspect him of yielding to compulsion) and proclaimed Marxism–Leninism to be the only acceptable philosophy of the day.[76] Liang Sou-ming, who had years before abandoned philosophy for the practical work of rural reconstruction, made his peace with the regime as best he could – though he did not escape severe criticism and the need to confess shortcomings in 1956.

Others refused to compromise with the Communists, undoubtedly rightly suspecting that the Communists would not compromise with them. Hu Shih and Lin Yutang after a time returned from abroad to Taiwan but did not identify themselves with the Kuomintang. Carsun Chang lived in the United States, where he died in 1969; Ch'ien Mu took refuge in Hong Kong. Many Chinese scholars and professional men found careers in America, Europe, and other parts of the world.

When dynasties had replaced each other in the past, somewhat similar dilemmas had been faced, but there was an important difference: few Chinese intellectuals had ever spiritually identified with the Kuomintang, even though many lived under it and might even have determined to render unto Caesar.

Doubtless many conversions to Communism or decisions to remain on the mainland, which entailed the eventual necessity of paying at least lip service to Communist precepts (party membership was of course a reward for the loyal, not an option for the lukewarm), were the result of prudential, careerist, or other far from exalted motives. Some decisions to cast one's lot with Peking were, as in the case of the *Smenovekhovtsy* and others in Russia, caused by nationalism – hope for China as a nation to become united, strong, or even happy under the ruthless, even totalitarian rule of the Communists. Some who had the intention of remaining with ample mental reservations ended, as a result of 'thought remolding' or 'brain-washing', possibly as intellectual and spiritual wrecks but certainly as loyal Communists.

And yet there were certainly conversions of a different order, comparable to that which awaited Kuo Mo-jo at the end of a tortured spiritual odyssey in 1924, and which he described in a letter he wrote to Ch'eng Fang-wu:

We have been born in a most meaningful age, the age of a great revolution in human cultural history! I have now become a thoroughgoing believer in Marxism. For this age in which we live Marxism provides the only solution. Matter is the mother of spirit. A high development and equal distribution of material civilization will be the placenta of a new spiritual civilization...Now I am wide awake, Fang-wu! Now I am wide awake...I feel that I have found the key to the contradictory problems which I was once unable to solve. Perhaps my poetry will die as a consequence of this, but [if so]...nothing can be done about it...[77]

The missionaries of Christianity and the Western advocates of liberalism or democratic socialism had hoped for such statements of commitment, and obtained some, but the Marxism–Leninism to which Kuo and many others since then pledged their hearts and minds was the only Western doctrine to capture the whole of China (except Taiwan).

A handful – if that many – uncompromising traditionalists survived somehow in exile. Syncretism seemed at least for the time being to have passed into the rubbish-bin of history. The West had won; Marxism, the victor among the competing Western currents, was indeed uncompromising. The Chinese Communist leadership proved not to be satisfied with anything less than a complete re-evaluation of the Chinese past, an outright war of extermination on the Chinese cultural tradition, and a wholesale rejection of the Christian, liberal, and non-Communist socialist heritage of the West to which some Chinese had for a time enthusiastically responded. The re-evaluation of the past and the war against tradition are not at an end; their course is not part of our story; their outcome is uncertain.

7

THE WEST AND THE CHINESE TRADITION

A shabby house should not be destroyed before a new house has been constructed, and a damaged boat should not be abandoned until a new boat has been built.

Ho Kai and Hu Li-yüan, 'Hsin-cheng
An-hsing', *Hsin-cheng chen-ch'üan*

Half a century ago Father Léon Wieger wrote, 'There is nothing more for us to take in the Chinese past. Since 1912, everything is changed beyond recall.'[1] He was at least partly right, as those were who made similar remarks in 1949. After the republican Revolution of 1911 there were two attempts at restoration – one with Yüan Shih-k'ai as monarch and the other with the last Manchu, P'u-i (Aisin Gioro), back on the throne. But both provoked instant and decisive reactions, though at least the second attempt envisaged not restoration of autocracy but the creation of a constitutional monarchy; there was a widespread fear of going back to the old days that manifested itself in refusal to accept their symbols. The conversion of P'u-i into a docile subject of the Communist government by the time of his death in 1967 indicates the truth in what Wieger said. The hope of restoration of the Republic to the mainland, voiced by the leaders in Taiwan, seems to have little greater substance than K'ang Yu-wei's post-1911 hope of restoring the Manchus as symbols.

The historian ought to be professionally immune to the naive claims of revolutionaries of past and present that they were inaugurating a completely *novus ordo seclorum*. However, he need not scruple to acknowledge that some events do mark decisive turns in human history. When the Chinese examination system came to an end in 1906, it was decided (failing a restoration of the system that would have had to come soon to be effective, and in fact never came) that after the lapse of some years a certain sort of human being would never walk the earth again. One of the last Jesuits in Peking inscribed on a monument in the Society's cemetery the following lines:

> Abi, viator, congratulare mortuis,
> Condole vivis, ora pro omnibus,
> Mirare et tace.

> Depart, traveler, congratulate the dead,
> Mourn for the living, pray for all,
> Marvel, and be silent.

The author of those lines knew that some earthly things pass away and never return.

Nevertheless it is possible even in the Chinese world of today to find traces of the long cultural confrontation between the West and China,[2] and it would be unwise to attempt any categorical assessment of the extent to which such traces survive even under the rule of the Communists. Moreover, aspects of that complex encounter may yield us glimpses of what may happen in the future. The past will not come again, but the past is our best clue to the possibilities that the present may hold.

The West reached out to China in the field of thought through four main groups of men: Roman Catholic missionaries, especially the Jesuits; Protestant missionaries, especially the evangelicals; secular intellectuals representing twentieth-century liberalism and socialism, including anarchism, in various shades and combinations; and Communist functionaries representing a party in power in Russia and sympathizers from other countries. As in the days when Buddhism swept much of China under the T'ang dynasty, barbarians made a substantial contribution, actively and passively, by their writings, utterances, and actions, to changing China.

Though they represented four different historical phases of the encounter between China and the West (despite the fact that each group remained on the scene after it yielded its dominant position to another), these four groups may also be compared analytically.

The Jesuits, led by Matteo Ricci and mostly following his lead, were the group that went furthest in the direction of accommodationism, with the result that the Western Jesuits and their Chinese converts constitute the most imposing single group of syncretists in our story. They envisaged the creation of a Chinese Christian culture, whether it might become the predominant form as in the Philippines or one of a sizeable minority as in Viet Nam, and on a small scale did indeed succeed in creating such a culture. Before 1610 Ricci laid the foundations for a symbiosis of a renovated Confucianism with the newly accepted Christian faith, the psychological grounds for which rested partly on the achievements of the Jesuits in the realm of technology and science, particularly in astronomy, and partly on the obvious uprightness and selflessness of character which distinguished the leaders of the China mission and many of its lesser luminaries. During the transition period of 1610–66 Adam Schall and others successfully maintained (after a crisis) their prestige in astronomy and weathered the change from the Ming to the Ch'ing dynasty. From 1666 to 1722 Ferdinand Verbiest (who died in 1688) and others led the Jesuits through the ordeal of the Rites Controversy, powerfully and tirelessly supported by the K'ang-hsi emperor and many distinguished Chinese Christians. It was during this period that the basic contradiction always potentially present in the Jesuit mission came to the fore: that between the fact that the order was committed to the pursuit of truth in a worldwide intellectual apostolate and the fact that the same order was bound to an especially demanding kind of discipline at the hands of the Holy See.

Such powerful testimony as that of Joseph Needham may be adduced to the effect that, in his conception of Chinese thought, 'to a large extent Ricci was right'; but even if problems involving interpretation of ideas can never be settled to everyone's satisfaction, it can still be said that the Jesuits' honest effort to interpret the central thread of Chinese culture as one compatible, after certain excisions, with the message of Christianity was frustrated by the contradiction just mentioned. The K'ang-hsi emperor never abandoned the Jesuits to the day of his death, but his successors had had a sufficient demonstration of the fact that the Jesuits were ultimately dependent on the West and that those intellectual ties might be followed by other more dangerous types of links. After the emperor died in 1722 the fate of the Jesuit mission was therefore sealed.

The Jesuits' scientific and technical prowess was never in question, and some of the most gifted artists and scientists among the Jesuits appeared in later reigns up to the dissolution of the order in 1773, but the successors of the K'ang-hsi emperor ceased to trust the Jesuits with functions other than utilitarian ones. The infant Chinese Christian culture was thereby throttled; Catholicism was doomed to become the religion of the poor and the unfortunate, not of any perceptible number of prominent intellectuals.

If we take 1722 as a convenient date for the wreck of the Jesuits' enterprise, over eighty years elapsed before a new group of Westerners came upon the scene. That is, no competing agencies in the realm of Western influence were present on the Chinese scene when the Protestant evangelicals arrived and no such agencies had been present for decades.

The evangelicals' general line was one of refusal to compromise with 'heathenism', that is to say, with any major aspect of Chinese culture. The result was that Robert Morrison, from 1807 until his death in 1834, achieved virtually no results at all. It may be regarded either as a fantastic and unexplainable accident, or instead as a striking demonstration of the readiness of the Chinese in the mid-nineteenth century to receive new Western teachings, that the single active Chinese convert of the Morrison mission, Liang A-fa, was responsible for the tracts that inspired Hung Hsiu-ch'üan after 1843 to develop the ideology of the T'ai-p'ing rebellion. The fact that out of the evangelical tradition could come a few men who were prepared not merely to say 'no' to the entire Chinese tradition is demonstrated first by James Legge, whose more sophisticated and gentler touch is reflected in Hung Jen-kan's attempt to broaden and deepen the T'ai-p'ing doctrine to appeal to Confucian scholars. But neither Legge nor Hung Jen-kan was strong enough to modify the rigorist pattern that evangelicalism had established. In consequence the final defeat of the rebels in 1864 also encompassed the permanent defeat of evangelicalism as a possible source of influence on the educated Chinese.

From 1850 Legge tried in the 'term controversy' to press some of the same issues that had earlier agitated the Roman Catholic mission movement in the 'rites controversy'; but the Jesuit position on the rites had been a position accepted both in broad circles of that movement and by the Chinese court itself, and was attacked by a minority that could not have won without papal intervention, while Legge's position on the terms challenged the widely accepted evangelical stance and never came near making that challenge good.

Beginning in the 1870's Timothy Richard by trial and error moved onto a slightly different track, that of acknowledging merit in the Chinese tradition, though he lacked the intellectual equipment necessary to try to reconcile Protestant Christianity and Confucianism. His sympathetic attitude toward China was sufficient for him to win a hearing and even achieve some implementation of his practical proposals for educational, social, and governmental reform. His contribution to the reform movement and the Hundred Days of 1898 was noteworthy, but the counter-*coup* of the Empress Dowager dashed many hopes and none of the remaining ones were realized. The 'Christian literature' on which he staked so much remained only a slogan, not a description of a body of effective written or printed matter. Richard lent what weight he could to the Legge position in the continuing 'term controversy', but like Legge he found only a few sympathizers, and made no greater headway than Legge had. Making their way back to the accommodationist position of Ricci, Legge and Richard found the majority of evangelicals as unyielding as Ricci's successors had found the papacy, and their defeat at the hands of their fellow Westerners was no less resounding than that which the Jesuits had suffered.

The papacy, of course, remained at the helm of Roman Catholicism after the decision on the rites; the evangelical predominance in the Protestant mission movement, however, rapidly disappeared at the turn of the twentieth century. The evangelicals lost their position of leadership at about the same moment that the Chinese scholars lost theirs with the abolition of the examination system. The 300-year old problem of whether the traditional Chinese intellectual class and traditional Confucianist thought could be reconciled with Christianity thereupon vanished from the docket of history.

Who would succeed the Confucian literati? At the turn of the century two alternative groups appeared, even before the end of the examination system: the mission-school students and the students of the new secular universities. The mission-school students often had chiefly or only Westerners as teachers, and thus tended rapidly to imbibe the draughts of new intellectual fashions as administered by their foreign mentors – more rapidly than those who had to learn of Western developments second-hand through translations or other means. Some such students went into the new revolutionary movement of the T'ung-meng Hui and its successors, the Nationalist Party (Kuomintang), notably the leader of both groups, Sun Yat-sen.

Sun began his education abroad, before evangelicalism petered out and Protestant modernism replaced it (about 1900–10) in China, but he kept in close touch with advanced Protestant theology. The new modernist movement and in particular the 'social gospel' of socialism and revolution made a great impression on Sun. His usual hosts in the West were not the atheist and socialist societies or labor party groups that might welcome other radical foreigners, but the churches and the YMCA's and YWCA's in which the social gospel was in full swing. Sun achieved such renown that he was chosen to be first President of the Chinese Republic in early 1912, though after a few weeks he abandoned the post and it was not until 1923 that, becoming established in Canton, he was ready for a second foray into national politics. This time he did so in cooperation with the Soviet regime and the Chinese Communist Party, reflecting in his willingness to make such an arrangement the continuing evolution of Protestant modernism in the West, whose advanced spokesmen were willing to acknowledge Communism as having at least some kinship with the socialism they had been discussing for several years and certainly recognized 1917 as a revolution with positive content, if not one of the exact sort they had had in mind. Until his death in 1925 Sun thought of himself as a Christian, but his religious mentors had become so politically oriented that they required no follower of theirs to talk much about religion, and so to this day Sun's intellectual formation has not been widely recognized as what it is: a hodgepodge of Western notions assembled in a Protestant modernist spirit, promising quick and easy earthly salvation. He has thus been blamed for an intellectual shoddiness which was only in part, and perhaps even small part, his own.

Sun was never acknowledged by the literati as one of them, and thus despite some tentative efforts by intermediaries at harmony the constitutional monarchist scholars following K'ang Yu-wei and Liang Ch'i-ch'ao held aloof from him and his party. K'ang and Liang reflected Western influences in part, but since they attempted to build on a revised version of the Confucian tradition, they may be called 'syncretists' – men who were seeking to identify truth whether it was to be found in China or the West (or Japan, where several of them began to learn about the West, and some of whose thinkers were themselves wrestling with the problem of what form Westernization should take in their country), and to combine the best of both intellectual worlds.

In the 1890's K'ang attempted to reinterpret Confucianism as a doctrine leading in the direction of reform, and in 1898 seemed to have won the chance to implement it in the way he thought best. That chance proved fleeting, but he continued to work on the need he saw to make Confucianism into a state religion, from which position it might acquire the dignity and influence Christianity had in the West (and had even gained in certain circles in China), and to bring about reform in the empire; and he undertook to mix Buddhism, Western science, and other ingredients into new philosophical perspectives. He died in 1927, disappointed and largely ignored by the younger generation. T'an Ssu-t'ung attempted a similar sort of combination of Confucianism, Buddhism, and Christianity, but he was martyred in 1898, and we can only speculate what influence he might have attained. Liang Ch'i-ch'ao started under the shadow of K'ang's Confucian revisionism, but soon took an independent road. After the failure of the Hundred Days' reform of 1898, he traveled ideological paths that led him to republicanism and back once again to constitutional monarchy, then to an effort at working within the framework of the warlord republic after Sun turned the presidency over to Yüan Shih-k'ai. In 1917 he gave up his attempt, and spent his last years, until his death in 1929, in pondering the questions of cultural syncretism. A few others tried to follow the syncretist path, such as Liang Sou-ming and Carsun Chang. However, it earned little support from a generation of intellectuals bent on Westernizing as fast as possible.

The variety of Westernization that for the first time seemed to capture a large section of Chinese intellectuals was liberalism, and the milieu that it found congenial was that of the new secular universities. The students of these institutions, or simply the 'youth', as they were apt to be called, initially worked, as the syncretists did, from translations and from instruction at Japanese, European, and American universities. The first and most popular of the translations were the work of Yen Fu, beginning in 1898; his versions of Huxley, Adam Smith, Mill, and other Western authors were eagerly devoured by the students of the early twentieth century. Yen Fu's own ideas of national liberalism were less important than his translations, which led contemporaries increasingly to look to the West for light. Lu Hsün, a writer of belles-lettres, powerfully supported such impulses by his rejection of the entire Confucian heritage, notably in the story, 'The Diary of a Madman' (1918). By that time the students at Peking and other universities had acquired a set of prophets of the new liberalism and several magazines through which the new ideas could be given currency. Ch'en Tu-hsiu, Hu Shih, and other returned students gathered at Peking University in particular and under the protection of a sympathetic administration helped to set the stage for more than individual expressions of opinion. On 4 May 1919, a demonstration against the Versailles Treaty voiced the determination of the not overly numerous, but widely spread and vociferous new 'youth' not to settle for the warlord republic, but to seek a new order in China based on Western liberal models.

It was difficult, however, to know how to go about such tasks. For a time the memory of the glorious moment of 4 May sustained energies, and on lecture tours in China John Dewey and Bertrand Russell fanned the enthusiasms of their young audiences. But nothing happened to the government, and the war-lords were willing to let the liberal fervor of the young wear itself out. A liberal manifesto of 1922 was ignored, and the momentum of 4 May exhausted itself. The literary revolution, introducing the vernacular into print on a large scale, the emancipation of women, and the restructuring of the family continued to have their effects. However, most of the advanced intellectuals soon passed beyond liberalism.

During the 1920's there were still traces of earlier ideas and passions in the air. A brief debate occurred between a bewildered and intellectually inept Christian minority and the militant secularists. The liberals tried to form some socially and even politically oriented literary societies, as did other groups with chiefly esthetic interests. All such societies yielded, however, before a trend of growing politicalization, fed by the Canton–Moscow *entente* and by no means slowed by its break-up. The League of Leftist Writers (1930) benefited from the trend. The philosophical debates of the 1920's and 1930's witnessed to the growing popularity of Marxism–Leninism, even some Kuomintang writers accepting its terms of reference.

The Kuomintang leadership that now more or less effectively ruled China sought to mix strands of the Confucian tradition with the Triple Demism of Sun Yat-sen and add other ill-assorted ingredients. Though the mixture doubtless had some salutary effects on the behavior of many people, as an elixir for the intellectuals it was an almost total failure. When the Kuomintang government was battered by the Japanese war and then assaulted by the Chinese Communist armies, few intellectuals had any store of loyalty to it on which the government could try to draw.

The result was the victory of Communism.

The educated Chinese had never for two millennia or more wholly accepted any single system of religious or ethical thought as sufficient guides to action in all spheres of human life. Even before the coming of the West brought in its intellectual complexities, Confucianism as interpreted by various schools existed side by side with Taoism or Buddhism or other sorts of ideas and values, Confucianism by no means always being in unquestioned ascendancy. After the arrival of Westerners Christianity, liberalism, and anarchism had their loyal followers or cautious admirers. Christianity, the only religion among the currents introduced from the West, had no clear implications for political and social life and permitted simultaneous commitments to one sort or another of institutional change as it (in the interpretation provided by the Jesuits and such Protestants as Legge and Richard) permitted or even encouraged continued respect for Confucianist tenets. Liberalism asked no unqualified commitment of its supporters, and anarchism had few supporters.

Marxism–Leninism, on the contrary, supplied a set of answers to all basic questions at once, as it demanded rejection of all the old and new positions mentioned in the preceding paragraph; it permits the invocation of precepts or examples from the Chinese tradition or from the Western past only when they are judged acceptable under Marxist–Leninist criteria (as has been the case with Communist governments in the USSR and elsewhere).[3] What could be more un-Chinese? How could six or seven hundred million Chinese have been converted to the latest Western pseudo-religion – or, more pertinently, how could even a few hundred thousand devotees have been recruited who would impose it on the masses?

Doubtless part of the explanation lies in perception of China's old ills and of the failure of officials under the Manchus or the warlord republic or the

Kuomintang regime to reduce such ills very much and to give China something like the wealth, power, efficiency, or welfare observed or wrongly
thought to exist elsewhere in the twentieth century. Doubtless the misery of
the burgeoning peasantry and of the growing working class, as perceived by
the intellectuals, was another factor, one steadily deepened by the growth of
population unaccompanied by any significant institutional reform.

The miseries and inhumanities of China, however, were very old, even
though their forms and intensity might change. What was new was the intellectual and spiritual dislocation of the twentieth century. The Chinese
tradition was pronounced dead, moribund, or unfit for survival on all sides –
by most Westerners, despite lip service or even genuine tribute to certain
aspects of Chinese culture, and with increasing sharpness by almost all
Chinese intellectuals. The corrosives of modern Western thought, splashed
about by enthusiastically iconoclastic young Chinese, left a void in the realm
of religious, philosophical, political, economic, and other ideas all at once. The
shocks of war undermined the political order, committed to various things new
but by the 1940's all too obviously aging, of the Kuomintang – to the extent it
ever managed to supplant the imperial system and the ineffective institutions
of the pre-1927, warlord Republic. The cultural abyss then yawned, and the
Communist faith beckoned. The 'shabby house' was demolished, and China
set about to erect a new one; the results have been such as to suggest that the
counsel of Ho Kai and Hu Li-yüan was wise.

Robert N. Bellah writes,

To the liberal Westerner or Asian, there is little doubt that a syncretic ideology,
stressing continuity with the best of the past and progress toward a better future,
preferably underpinned by a reformist religious position and a commitment
to liberal values, seems the best solution for Asians to follow.[4]

Leaving aside the tautology lurking here (to the liberal, liberal values seem
best), one may concur with Dr Bellah; not only to the liberal but to anyone,
Easterner or Westerner, syncretism may seem a solution preferable to principled rejection of the indigenous cultural tradition. Not only to Communists
but to many others, however, it did not seem preferable, and some students of
China would today conclude that as an alternative solution it belongs only to
the dead past.

If there is any validity in the comparison with the history of the USSR,
however, it may yield suspicions that the Chinese tradition and the potentiali-
ties of syncretism in China are not wholly dead. The Russian and other
national traditions seemed to die under Stalin and yet have seemed to revive
in the minds of sizeable minorities – intellectual and non-intellectual – since
his death. During the Hundred Flowers episode of 1957, for example, the
supposed unanimity among mainland Chinese intellectuals in support of
Communism was abruptly revealed as a myth. No one can be sure what has

happened since.[5] On earlier occasions in Chinese history, to be sure, a number of apparently successful burials of schools of thought proved highly premature.

In the *Tso Chuan* Mu Shu, an official of the state of Lu, is asked to explain what the ancient saying 'dead but immortal' means. Mu Shu replies, 'I have heard that the best course is to establish virtue, the next best is to establish achievement, and still the next best is to establish words. When these are not abandoned with time, it may be called immortality.' Judged in these terms, the Chinese tradition cannot yet be confidently pronounced dead.

CONCLUSION: THE WEST IN RUSSIA AND CHINA

Russia, like China, may be described as an artist nation: but unlike China it has been governed, since the time of Peter the Great, by men who wished to introduce all the good and evil of the West. In former days, I might have had no doubt that such men were in the right...I cannot now take this view.

Bertrand Russell, *The Problem of China* (1920)

Why did not Prospero see that I would use the Aryan tongue which he taught me as a means by which to curse him?

Ernest Renan, *Caliban* (1878)

THE SECULARIZATION OF THE WEST

Over the last five centuries we have distinguished a series of intellectual influences at work in Russia and China that derived from several variants of Christian thought and from the secular political 'isms' – liberalism, socialism, and Communism. Some constituted a rather precise system of beliefs, others covered a loose and shifting congeries of ideas. At one extreme is the view held within an organization whose leaders are recognized as having the authority to define the elements of faith, such as the Roman Catholic Church and the Communist Party; at any given moment (since the content of belief changes even in such organizations) it is possible to be specific about what members are bound to believe (even if any given individual may have strong reservations about some doctrine). At the other extreme is liberalism, which never had any organizational 'International'; even national political parties calling themselves 'liberal' differed from one another and among their members, and the current of thought called liberalism, broader and less homogeneous than the views of those who belong to 'liberal' political parties, is even less easy to generalize about. The pre-Communist socialists (as well as the post-1919 ones) did have their Internationals, and the Protestants, at the start, had their authoritative ecclesiastical bodies, but the strong individualist tendencies to be found in certain branches of Protestantism and non-Communist socialism (especially anarchism) prevented discipline from being enforced to any great extent among either group. Before the rise of the totalitarian state, in any case, organizational discipline explains very little about the beliefs of men in the modern West, since usually it was possible to escape the discipline of a given organization by leaving it. As for Russia and China, *mutatis mutandis*, men

long ago developed methods of coupling overt submission with covert devia-
tion, especially in the realm of thought.

The two general headings, Christianity and the secular political 'isms',
invite a comparison much more extended than can be made here. When
Christianity was the prevailing religion of the West, it permitted or generated
the development of systematic theology and certain kinds of philosophy and
political ideas, not to mention crucial innovations in the sciences and arts.
However, Christianity was not construed to require (moreover, it may be
argued, it does not permit) any systematic doctrine about history, politics, or
economics any more than it does about the natural world – which is, in the
Christian view, God's creation whatever it is found by scientists to be like.
Christianity has never meant a monism of any kind – even in its ontology,
which has always been dualist, counterposing matter and spirit. Though there
were efforts to link Christianity with monarchy, capitalism, or some other
transitory human institution, support of no such institution could ever be
shown to be entailed by Christian belief. Similarly, Christianity has never
been shown to be culture-bound. It emerged in the Near East and immediately
spread to certain areas of Europe, Asia, and Africa, later became identified
with Europe (a geographical expression which owes its meaning to its virtual
identity with the culture of Christendom in the High Middle Ages), and again
spread to extra-European areas. There were efforts to associate Christianity
with the West or even the culture of a given Western country at the given
moment, and many missionaries acted as if the one necessarily followed from
the other; but the best missionaries from St Paul to St Stephen of Perm to
Matteo Ricci to Timothy Richard (representatives of the undivided primitive
church, Eastern Orthodoxy, Roman Catholicism, and Protestantism respectively) never did so – in fact their doctrine, as they understood it, forbade
them to do so.

In the whole story of changes in Western thought, the decisive step came
with the emergence of the secular political 'isms' beginning with liberalism.
The problem of the not merely chronological but logical connections of such
'isms' with Christianity still requires extensive study. Atheism is a perfectly
possible position, but genuine atheism must actually repudiate all gods; if it
couples the overt murder of God with the effective deification of man or some
other entity or abstraction, it is a sham resting on philosophical confusion.
Atheism in fact is not one of the major categories in our story. Typically a
proclamation of atheist belief preceded or accompanied the proclamation of a
new earthly dispensation, a new secular gospel to be preached to all nations
and to become the foundation for a universal secular theocracy. In the foreword to his doctoral dissertation (1841), Marx delivered a verdict 'against all
gods heavenly and earthly who do not acknowledge human self-consciousness
as the supreme deity';[1] and this proved a crucial point for the whole socialist
movement.

Liberalism, which had its beginnings before socialism, typically refrained from raising theological or, within philosophy, the ultimate metaphysical issues. Voegelin may be in the strict sense right in saying that 'if liberalism is understood as the immanent salvation of man and society, communism certainly is its most radical expression; it is an evolution that was already anticipated by John Stuart Mill's faith in the ultimate advent of communism for mankind'.[2] Nevertheless liberalism may be found to fluctuate, in practice, between uncompromising and cautious positions: between a critique of the privileged classes and absolute biological egalitarianism, a critique of tradition and an unflinching rationalism that repudiates all previous human experience, a critique of clerical abuses and dogmatic atheism, a critique of militarism and pacifism under all circumstances, an optimism about man's ability to improve his own lot through changing the institutional environment and unquestioning faith in the perfectibility of man. No liberal International existed to require of its members recitation of formulated liberal credos, no single set of liberal texts acquired recognition as scripture. Liberalism was and is a group of currents running in several directions – here consistent *laissez-faire* economics (which somehow became transmuted into what many would call 'conservatism'), there a fixation on the single issue of civil liberties, somewhere else simply a kind of watered-down socialism. However, if liberalism might mean different things in relation to the domestic politics of Western countries and even criticize imperialism in foreign policy, none of its various currents had any developed notion of the diversity of human institutions or of human cultures. It was a product of the West, and it has not succeeded in universalizing its outlook.

In contrast, socialism held its ideas together better because its organizations were tighter. Most varieties of socialism came to insist on refusal to recognize theology as a discipline and on acceptance of basic doctrines in the fields of philosophy, politics, and economics. The Communists went much further than other socialists in such respects; in the USSR dogmas were proclaimed in the field of the arts and, under Stalin, even in the natural sciences. Socialism in its rigorist form is monist, and it has no more room for cultural pluralism than for social or political pluralism. (We are not considering 'socialism' as a label, either self-affixed or applied by enemies, for the beliefs of those who adduce empirical reasons for nationalizing medical care, fluoridating drinking water, or even taking under government ownership this or that industry or service.) During the past few years we have observed attempts to formulate types of 'national communism' in several countries; but religious features of the national heritage, which in every case (including Chinese, Korean, and Vietnamese) are of fundamental importance, are *a priori* inacceptable, and thus the traditional cultures cannot fully enter into the given rediscovery of 'national' traits. Socialism, like liberalism, is culture-bound.

Any doctrine that tries to replace religion by politics, God by deified man, as contrasted with political science as the systematic study of problems connected with the state, is apt to proclaim what has been called 'the prohibition of questioning',[3] the substitution of philodoxy for philosophy, the replacement of the love of wisdom by the love of unquestionable doctrines. (The prohibition of questioning has also at times been a prominent feature of the behavior of religious institutions including the Christian Church, but it cannot be shown to be implied in Christian doctrine.) In modern times the demand for such prohibition has been traced to Comte as well as Marx, and it is certainly not confined to the political left – as witness the extreme conservative movement following Ayn Rand that calls itself 'Objectivism', not to mention German National Socialism. But in the last third of the twentieth century no such doctrine is of an importance remotely comparable to socialism.

A great deal of conservative literature, from at least as early as the French Revolution, has lamented the fall from its formerly unchallenged position in Europe and among European-majority areas outside it of Christianity and the Christian Church in its Catholic or Protestant forms and attacked socialism or Communism as the work of Satan. Theologically this sort of argument may itself hover near the contention that God is dead, which Christians reject. Historically (our concern here), it explains nothing. The deification of man is of course a challenge to Christianity, a reaction to it, a repudiation of it; but its essential features are logically related to it nonetheless. 'Modern redivinization [of the world]', Voegelin plausibly contends, 'has its origins rather [than in neo-paganism] in Christianity itself, deriving from components that were suppressed as heretical by the universal church.'[4]

In several works Nicolas Berdiaev has contended that Communism was merely inverted Christianity and that moreover the inversion, occurring in Russia, somehow reflected the peculiarly Russian variant of religiosity. Gustav Wetter and others avoid the distortion committed by Berdiaev in interpreting the phenomenon as an exclusively or chiefly Russian one. They make comparisons of Communism and Christianity that are persuasive enough as far as they go.[5] However, such comparisons seem to lack the necessary historical depth and therefore risk seeming to isolate curious, amusing or frightening, coincidences rather than succeed in explaining historical phenomena.

No full account can be given here. Brief reference may be made, however, to the attempt at explanation given by Eric Voegelin in several works. He identifies the antecedents of Communism and also a variety of other fashionable intellectual movements in 'gnosticism'. Its roots lie, he argues, deep in human nature – in the continual temptation of man to attempt to murder God and replace Him. The 'central element' of gnosticism, he declares, is

the experience of the world as an alien place into which man has strayed and from which he must find his way back home to the other world of his origin. 'Who has cast me into the suffering of this world?' asks the 'Great Life' of the gnostic texts, which is also the 'first, alien Life from the worlds of light'. It is an alien in this world and this world is alien to it.[6]

From such alienation (Hegel and Marx) and feeling of having been 'cast' (Heidegger's *Geworfenheit*), rescue and salvation are found in the knowledge (*gnosis*) offered by the 'gnostics' from the followers of Valentinus, an Egyptian who taught in Rome in the second century AD (or, according to the Fathers, as early as Simon Magus the Samaritan as mentioned in Acts 8.9–24), to the various twentieth-century prophets who proclaim a new secular revelation.

Voegelin presents a skeletal analysis of the symbolism of 'gnostic' mass movements in roughly the following form:[7]

(1) symbols which are modifications of the Christian idea of perfection, which is both teleological and axiological
   (a) teleological only: progressivism in all its variants; Kant, Condorcet
   (b) axiological only: depiction of the state of perfection; Thomas More and others
   (c) both ('activist mysticism'): Comte and Marx
(2) symbols which derive from speculation on history, and which Voegelin traces to a twelfth-century thinker, Joachim of Floris (who in turn reacted against the historical vision of St Augustine which expected no particular future but the Apocalypse); Joachim identified three Ages, of Father, Son, and Holy Spirit, the last to begin in 1260
   (a) concept of a Third Realm: Biondo's 'ancient–medieval–modern' categories; Turgot and Comte's 'theological–metaphysical–positive' triad; Hegel's 'one is free, few are free, all are free'; Schelling's Petrine, Pauline, Johannine Christianity; Marx's and Engels's primitive communism–class society–communism; Hitler's Third Reich
   (b) leader establishing the third era (a position many urged St Francis for, in relation to Joachim's, and which he firmly renounced): Goethe's Faustian superman, used by both Marx and Nietzsche; Comte; Lenin
   (c) prophet who is precursor of the leader: Joachim himself, Comte, Marx
   (d) community of spiritually autonomous persons: for Joachim the community of monks; the twentieth-century totalitarian parties

The Joachite form of historical speculation, Voegelin argues, was prompted by the very success of Christianity during the High Middle Ages in Europe.[8] The notion of a Third Realm, we should note, appeared (in the form of a 'Third Rome') among the South Slavs and Muscovy not long after Joachim, and if it did not directly derive from Joachite notions it certainly came out of a common stock of trinitarian symbolism that inhered in Christianity. That symbol, however, did not generate a complete system of gnostic speculation or a gnostic organization, and as was earlier pointed out later Western writers have made more of the various 'Third Romes' than contemporaries ever did. Such systems of speculation and organization emerged only in the nineteenth century, both within the body of Christian thought (Schelling and Hegel) and outside it. However, the appearance of modern 'gnosticism', in fully developed form, in any other context than that of the Christian tradition is scarcely conceivable and has never taken place.

Voegelin's conclusion, and mine, would be that 'gnosticism' cannot ultimately succeed because it cannot alter the structure of reality; but that it can indeed succeed in the sense of influencing and regulating the lives of hundreds of people, producing worse consequences for mankind the more seriously its premises are taken, is all too apparent. Voegelin has a remedy: in his view a rediscovery of philosophy can occur and is occurring, one that has hope of breaking down the 'prohibition of questioning', turning back gnostic dogma, and restoring a perception of the real world in all its complexity and diversity. One may not entirely share his confidence and may yet insist that the central problem of mankind today is basically not military, not one of economic development, not one of political institutions, and that dealing with it through weapons or war, economic aid, and constitutions (though such instruments may be desirable or unavoidable for other, empirical reasons) is impossible.

'Modern gnosticism', Voegelin declares, 'has by far not spent its drive. On the contrary, in the variant of Marxism it is expanding its area of influence prodigiously in Asia, while other variants of gnosticism, such as progressivism, positivism, and scientism, are penetrating into other areas under the title of "Westernization" and development of backward countries.'9 The central problem is one of thought, and its locus as before lies not in the East but in the West itself; even if the Western mind is suffering from a paralysis ultimately residing in the spirit or the will, the problem remains to be worked out in the intellectual realm. Russia and China, and other countries outside the West, have always responded to the doctrinal innovation of the West, and may do so again.

A COMPARISON OF WESTERN INTELLECTUAL INFLUENCES IN RUSSIA AND CHINA

The inception of this study lay in the desire to compare the reception of successive Western intellectual currents in Russia and China, and at its completion the work of comparison may not yet be exhausted. In many ways the stories are different; this section explores the ways in which they are similar, or at any rate congruent, so that the impacts of the various currents studied in the two countries can be distinguished and contrasted.

Roman Catholic humanism10

Roman Catholic humanism brought to China the best Western learning of the day in the arts, sciences, and technology; a respect, which its adepts showed by intensive study and creative work, for Chinese culture; and a vision of a world joined in brotherhood by a single religion but a plurality of cultures as well as peoples, each developing its own genius and sharing it freely with other peoples. The Jesuit mission in China was a truly remarkable episode. It meant conversion to Christianity for a small minority, and some Chinese families preserve the effects of such conversion to this day; it also provided acquaintanceship with Western knowledge whose effects in China perhaps have not yet been fully traced by scholars. If the mission had not been stifled, it might have provided many learned Chinese of a later period with a permanent basis for evaluating successive Western influences and an additional ground of judgment of various strands of the Chinese tradition, whether or not those Chinese were Christian or sympathetic to the West or Western ideas of any kind.

Against this background the Roman Catholic influence in Russia may be better understood. Partial conceptions of cultural intercourse on a plane of mutual respect between the West and Russia, as entertained by such men as Antonio Possevino, were submerged in Polish sixteenth-century expansionism – half imperialism, half crusade – and thereafter any open acknowledgment of indebtedness to Roman Catholic influence was much more difficult. Its substantial impact, during the seventeenth century, was consequently harder for later scholars to recognize. The tragedy of Juraj Križanić, who in his mission of reconciliation broke his head against a wall of Muscovite hostility, becomes more poignant when compared with the Jesuit successes in China.

The Jesuits had a period in the late eighteenth and early nineteenth century when the chance of important and lasting influence in Russia seemed to be offered to them. To be sure, they were not then really a mission to Russia but rather simply the sole surviving fragment of the international order which happened to find refuge there. However, some of them attempted conversions, operating through schools and tutoring directed mainly at the gentry; and one may ask why they never made a serious effort to study Russian culture or work out their relation to it. The answer seems to be that by this time the Russian elite was itself so alienated from Russian culture that no Jesuit thought of approaching it through any avenue other than the cosmopolitan culture of the European aristocracy into which those Russians were trying to gain full entrance and acceptance. The expulsion of the order cut short its efforts, and the Society again concentrated not on Russia but on re-establishing itself throughout the world. The Roman Catholic influence in Russia that had integral significance to later cultural developments was covert: it was embodied in the pro-Roman Ukrainian clerics of the seventeenth and the turn of the eighteenth century, chief of whom was Stefan Yavorsky. At that moment such men, together with others of quite different orientations, made a brief stand behind Alexis Petrovich on behalf of the Russian tradition. Russia had its closest equivalent to Ricci in the last moment of Roman influence.

Protestantism: scholastic, pietist, and modernist

Protestant scholasticism was thrust on Russia suddenly and almost by accident, since Peter the Great found the example of Protestant states useful in reducing the Orthodox Church to state control and the few pro-Protestant Ukrainian clerics he could find to help him had had scholastic training. (To be sure, exposure to Roman Catholic scholasticism and knowledge of the Latin language on the part of earlier Kievan clerics provided some preparation.) The reorientation of Russian education carried out by Peter and his successors in the Orthodox seminaries perpetuated such influences institutionally for some time. Weakened by subjection to secular authority, imposition of an alien educational system, and loss of many of the staunchest and most devoted laity to the Old Belief, the Orthodox Church limped uncertainly into the later eighteenth century.

Since the German scholastics had had a channel of influence opened for them into Russia, the German pietists found it easier to tread the same path. The rationalist emphasis in scholasticism helped pave the way for Voltairianism and the Freemasonry of the 1770's; the emotionalist and intuitivist emphasis in pietism led to the Freemasonry of the 1780's, and pietism was virtually established as a state religion in 1817–24. Both currents persisted into later periods.

China escaped the benefits and burdens of Protestant scholasticism. The Protestant missionaries were pietists and most of them, following the Morrison pattern, were frankly not learned and at worst aggressively antiintellectual. Nevertheless even the Morrisons had to attempt learned tasks, such as Biblical translation, and though the results were frightful, there was some room among the evangelicals for genuinely learned men such as James Legge. Like Matteo Ricci, he combined a high level of intellectual achievement with deep respect (to which he found his own way, unassisted by any of his fellow evangelicals or by any of the tenets of pietism) for the Chinese tradition. However, he remained a lonely voice within the missionary camp, despite the fact that, as has been suggested, his influence can be discerned in the Shield King's efforts to provide some intellectual and political sophistication to the leadership of the T'ai-p'ing rebellion. The T'ai-p'ing leaders cannot well be blamed any more severely for resisting the Shield King's ideas than the pietist missionaries can for resisting Legge's. In Russia no Protestantizing thinkers can be found who had any wish to develop the indigenous tradition or who regarded it with respect. In China there were, at least, Legge and a few (though very few) others who did so. In Russia, however, Protestant influences did give the ecclesiastical intellectuals more or less serious training in the philosophy of the West, in particular German idealism. In China no such thing occurred.

Protestant influences were dealt a staggering blow by the failure of the T'ai-p'ing rebellion. Timothy Richard attempted to revive such influences using new methods. He and his few co-workers did spread some knowledge of the West in the realm of science and politics, but very little Protestantism and virtually no philosophy. Richard made a considerable contribution to the Reform movement of 1898, but little to the main current in Chinese cultural development. Once again, as in the case of Legge, Richard could not succeed in influencing the bulk of his fellow missionaries. They pursued the narrow path of pietism to the end and perished without creating, after 1864, more than a ripple on the surface of Chinese thought.

Protestant modernism had one great Chinese adept and had some influence on one outstanding Russian thinker, but the difference between the two men was wide. Protestantism, seemingly defeated and crippled in China as Roman Catholicism had been earlier (in both cases chiefly as a result of Western confusion rather than Chinese resistance), had an interesting last chance in Sun Yat-sen. The social gospel and Christian socialism never had a more influential follower anywhere, though students of China have been slow to understand the fact. Much of the doctrinal shallowness and therefore the practical ineffectiveness of Sun's party, before and during the early days of the Republic, may be traced to the intellectual deficiencies of the Protestant modernist missionaries. When Sun finally turned, as many of the Protestant modernists in the West had done, to the USSR as a model, he began to achieve success, though he died before that could be seen. In Russia modernism had an exponent, in part, in Vladimir Soloviev. It was for him a phase rather than a lifelong commitment; in this respect, curiously, the seemingly mercurial Sun was more consistent than Soloviev. One must not push the parallel too far; Soloviev was a philosopher first and foremost, Sun was political to his bones, and few politicians have ever been good philosophers. The point to notice is simply that already by the 1890's Russia had had enough philosophical training and experience so that modernism, in Soloviev, appeared not as the whole of truth but one aspect of it; for Sun, it was everything, or nearly so.

If only the Protestants in China had been teaching some philosophy, as the pro-Protestants (as well as some outright Protestants, mainly Baltic Germans) in Russia had been doing, events might have had a different course. China had virtually forgotten its Roman Catholic humanist phase, had had no Protestant scholastic phase and had been exposed to little learning in its Protestant pietist phase. How different from Russia, which had never lost the Western intellectual connection and had gone on from generation to generation building on what – even if it was only bits and pieces – had come to it earlier. At this point the sheer geography of the problem is obvious; expensive, long, dangerous voyages were a prerequisite to bringing Western influence to China and to renewing it, while a book or a man could always slip across Russia's Western frontier even when such entrance was illegal. Added to the problem of distance was, of course, the fact that Russia started with a cultural basis which was after all Christian as that of the West was, and though that basis was shallow and lacked any kind of real philosophical development, it was more fertile ground onto which the scattered seeds fell.

And yet on the other hand there was the compensating fact that Western influences in Russia fell upon a Muscovite culture that was impoverished and rude by comparison with the richness and refinement of that of China. A Ricci could immediately converse with and have fruitful intellectual exchange with hundreds of Chinese, a Possevino'with only a tiny handful of Russians. If Chinese could have been persuaded that Christianity was compatible with the Confucian tradition, little needed to be subtracted from the latter for much of Western learning to enter China unimpeded and to contribute to a majestic cultural edifice already in existence. In Russia educational and cultural institutions had to be created almost from scratch.

One great difference between the phases of Christian impact in Russia and China was the fact that there was a large-scale, continued mission movement in China in both Protestant and Catholic guises, while in Russia there were the late-coming, short-lived Jesuit missions and, with a few other exceptions, that was virtually all. Russians (sometimes the monarch and sometimes others) voluntarily imported Western Christian influences; to China such influences came, at first, uninvited (one should remember, however, the unanswered pleas made by Kublai Khan and by the emperors during the period of Jesuit ascendancy for the sending of more Westerners) and were, in the nineteenth century, mostly unwanted. And yet in both cases the impact was significant, and its extent seemed to have little to do with who originally took initiative to bring it about.

Liberalism

Secular liberalism had an influence in both countries that was rather brief and inconclusive. Liberalism in the West was basically a political, economic, and social doctrine about how one ought to behave and things ought to be organized in an open (or many-centered) society; it contained no prescription about how a closed (or single-centered) society might be converted into an open one. There was some early liberalism in Russia; aspects of it may be found in free-trade ideas discussed in the reigns of Catherine II and Alexander I, and in the teachings of the Decembrists. A more or less continuous liberal current begins in the 1860's in zemstvo circles and among Westerners of the moderate stripe, such as Kavelin and Chicherin, and carries through to Miliukov and the Kadets in 1905 and after. The Kadets benefited by the fact that substantial institutional Westernization occurred in Russia from the eighteenth century on and especially as a result of the Great Reforms, and the creation of a Duma seemed to provide confirmation of their analysis of Russian life and a lever for them to carry their program into effect – despite the fact that they were, on the failure of discussions with officials in 1905–6, still excluded from the government. They still suffered, however, from lack of any clear notion of how to build – or complete the building of – an open society in Russia, and from a virtually complete alienation from the peasantry and the rest of the common people who retained an outlook based on Russian tradition.

In China liberalism as a more or less coherent doctrine was represented chiefly by one thinker, Hu Shih, for he never managed – or really tried – to weld like-minded people into a party. Like the Russian Kadets, he and his friends lacked any notion of how to build an open society in China; unlike the Kadets, they could not benefit from institutional Westernization, for there had been next to none before 1911 and after 1911 the fragility and even fraudulence of the pseudo-Western institutions that had been established helped, if anything, to discredit liberalism rather than to strengthen its appeal. Tribute should be paid to the pioneering work of Yen Fu and to the apparent triumph of liberalism in the May Fourth (1919) incident, as indications that there was more than one liberal in China. But May Fourth was a great moment of liberalism of the heart, and when Hu Shih and others tried thereafter to intellectualize it, they lost many enthusiasts of the spring of 1919. The two great missionaries of Western liberalism, Dewey and Russell, ultimately helped the liberal cause very little, for they had no idea, any more than Hu Shih, of how to create a society in China in which liberalism could have meaning and applicability. It seems, indeed, that they never even identified such a problem. In any event, Russell was quite ambivalent about liberalism, and his good words for socialism and even Bolshevism offered Chinese youth no reason to stand firm for Hu Shih's moderate position.

Socialism

In Russia socialism began with Herzen and Bakunin, in its anarchist version, and in the Petrashevtsy circle there was to be found both Utopian and Christian socialism. Only in the 1860's, however, did socialism begin an uninterrupted development through all kinds of circles and groups that have been called 'populist', profiting from the contemporary nihilist rejection of existing institutions and often growing out of it. In the 1870's Lavrov and other émigrés were working out applications of Western socialist ideas to Russia. Populism came to be the almost universal creed of the *raznochintsy* intelligentsia, though it had a whole range of shadings of activism and doctrinal rigor. Non-Communist socialism in Russia was sometimes willing to identify a certain area of common ground with liberals, as in the Party of People's Right (1894), the Liberation Movement of 1904–5, and again in 1917; it also acknowledged comradeship or identity of aims with Communists, in the Russian Social Democratic Labor Party from 1898 or 1903 onward and in the leadership of Soviets in 1905 and 1917. Of course the difference between Communists and other socialists was not clear in those days; not only was the word 'Communist' revived by Lenin for his party only in 1918, but his willingness to use any methods and forego any sort of democracy – even within the party – was not then widely understood. The Socialist Revolutionaries and Mensheviks led the Soviets for several months in 1917, doing so ineptly and ineffectually, and finally failed. Nevertheless, part of their failure was owing to the refusal of some of their leaders to pursue a single objective, blinding themselves to everything else, as Lenin was willing and able to do, and what they refused to blind themselves to included democracy, human dignity, and even liberty.

In China there was no real socialism that was divorced from Protestant modernism on the one hand and Communism on the other. The May Fourth movement had some non-Communist socialist elements – anarchist and guild socialist, for example – but it was with little chance of success that they could match their modest hopes for the future against the spectacular, already accomplished, victory of the Communists in Russia.

The Chinese intellectuals of the new universities, who had replaced the old scholar-gentry, were open to Western ideas almost from the start. The new universities were themselves institutions created on Western models, and their curriculum consisted largely of Western subdivisions of learning even when such subdivisions were partly applied or extended to China. It was, after many had studied the West in Japan and through the mediation of Japanese, in the decade of the 1910's that Westernization came in like a flood as the new universities got seriously under way. In the West itself there were debates between liberals, socialists, and Communists – while a few Christians, whose theological and philosophical education was fragmentary, tried to paint themselves pink or red in order to stay in the debate at all. Thus the advanced intellectuals of China, looking at the West, hesitating for a moment over the attractions of liberalism, soon chose the apparently most advanced, the newest set of ideas – which were Marxist and Leninist.

Communism

In 1847 Herzen sought out socialists in the West as unquestionable brothers in the faith and oracles of its chances of successful propagation. In emigration Russians became international socialists, but most of those who did had long ago rejected the national tradition anyway. In both Russia and China we find instances of humble submission of questions of faith and morals to Western oracles: Zasulich to Marx on the question of a Russian revolution, the Chinese students of 1922 to Sorbonne professors on the question of Christianity. When Roman Catholics submit similar questions to the papacy for adjudication they risk limitless scorn. (I hasten to add that I do not believe in submitting any question to a single authority for final adjudication; when Westerners submit questions to courts, for example, they expect to find out what the law is at the moment, not eternal truth.) It is a paradox that the single humble submission of a question to authority we find in our story, from Roman Catholics, was that of the Jesuits to the *Emperor of China* regarding the meaning of the rites – not to a Western authority, though the papacy did indeed proceed to adjudicate the question, wrongly.

Finally, we find an interesting phenomenon. Liberalism and non-Communist socialism brought few missionaries – although there were, as we have mentioned, a few who visited China, more or less by accident – to Russia and

China. But Communism did. In an important sense the exiles returning to Russia in 1917 came as missionaries of Western Marxism, and the religious aura is unmistakable that surrounded Lenin from his arrival at the Finland Station, at first only among a few, who for the moment doubted the holy man and regretted it, as did St Peter, ever afterward. In fact there are few more inspired missionary efforts in human history than Lenin's. Opposed initially by almost everyone else including other Bolsheviks, he succeeded in his attempt to overturn and subvert the democratic revolution of February 1917 in order to bring about his personal version of the earthly Kingdom of Heaven, and in only a few months. Of course many circumstances favored him – but others seemed to block his way so definitely that Kerensky and a number of his colleagues dismissed the possibility that Lenin could win.

To China Voitinsky, Yoffe, and later Borodin and others were dispatched by Moscow in order to help organize a Chinese Communist Party, and despite the formidable language barrier Li Ta-chao and Ch'en Tu-hsiu recognized their 'barbarian brothers' as instantly and unequivocally as the T'ai-p'ings recognized the Protestant Westerners from the coast in the 1850's, for tracts and scriptures had preceded the Russian Communists as they had the evangelicals, many decades earlier. The 'returned students' who came back from Moscow in the early 1930's provide another example. The Communist effort is always first and foremost a missionary effort. The masses may be influenced by propaganda up to a point, but conversion is an individual matter, in which thought is an essential even though (often unacknowledged and unconscious) feeling may be decisive.

Syncretism

Syncretism is not a phase of Western influence, but an indirect result of Western influence in thought. Using the term to mean a fusion of indigenous with Western ideas or cultural characteristics, we find it present in both Russia and China. In Russia one may identify a group of forerunners in the coalition of cultural forces around Alexis Petrovich in the early 1700's, though it resulted from a willingness of those oriented to the indigenous tradition to work with those sympathetic to certain Western views rather than a combination of such ideas in any one person's head. A kind of syncretism can be seen in the Slavophiles, though they moved uneasily from a Western basis to try to adopt a Russian and Orthodox one rather than espousing a mixture of the two. Dostoevsky and especially Soloviev developed the notion of a harmonious meeting of West and East, and Soloviev tried to work out a double ground for his ideas, followed by others. The artists of the Silver Age and some Orthodox clerics who live into our day – notably Father Georges Florovsky – consciously worked on both the indigenous tradition and the Western tradition, including its latest innovations. The *Signposts* group issued the fullest manifesto of syncretism and almost its last word before the Revolution.

In China the finest flower of syncretism is to be found at the beginning of the story. When Ricci came to China, he came as a Western missionary (in the broad and figurative sense we have just been employing as well as in the narrow sense) of Roman Catholic humanism, but as an immigrant to China who became Chinese in all important respects other than ethnic, he was a syncretist who wanted to preserve all that was great and valuable in Chinese culture and add to it the Christian religion and the most advanced Western learning of the day. Paul Hsü and his other distinguished converts were zealous syncretists. The possibility for Chinese Roman Catholics to be syncretists disappeared with the papal decision in the Rites controversy and revived only with the papal decision of 1939, too late to have any notable effect on Chinese culture. James Legge had a vision of the possibility of syncretism, but no Chinese – except for the potentially crucial, actually not very significant example of Hung Jen-kan – caught it and tried to translate it into reality. Timothy Richard also had such a vision, but had influential followers only in the political and not the cultural realm.

Some would trace syncretism to the substance-function (*t'i-yung*) dichotomy of Chang Chih-tung and other nineteenth-century officials. However, this seems to be a mistake. Such men had no intention of adopting any part of Western culture; the formula was intended precisely as a means of keeping Chinese culture intact at the price of borrowing Western technology. The one more or less clearly developed syncretist movement that is to be found in recent times is that of K'ang Yu-wei and Liang Ch'i-ch'ao, who were in some doubt as to which Chinese ideas and which Western ideas ought to be married to each other. K'ang tried to make Confucianism into a religion, then went on to Buddhism, and never took an unequivocal stand on the point, meanwhile tasting various Western dishes in the political, economic, and scientific realm without settling on firm choices. Liang seemed to be less concerned with a need to make such choices; he thought Confucianism and Buddhism could provide important contributions to China's future along with Western notions of nationalism and liberty, changing his emphasis several times during his career. The Kuomintang after the death of Sun Yat-sen was the sponsor of various attempts to provide a mixed ideological foundation for the new China, none of them explicitly syncretic, none of them notably successful on the mainland or on Taiwan.

We know that Chinese culture is not dead; the surest sign of it is the all-out assault on it in the Great Proletarian Cultural Revolution, almost twenty years after Communist take-over. Whether syncretism still has a future in China is uncertain.

After the death of Stalin, however, it has become unmistakably clear that syncretism is reviving in Russia, or, perhaps better, what we have called the post-syncretic current of reconciliation between certain Western and Russian ideas and cultural features. The most recent trends in Soviet literature and the arts and in religion in the USSR and a steady flow of accounts of the intellectual life of Moscow, Leningrad, and other cities which cannot be fully reported in the official press make it clear that the ferment of the 1920's, the Silver Age, and Russia's traditional culture reaching back to the civilizing of the Eastern Slavs are considerably more interesting to the young than the latest editorial in *Kommunist*.[11]

Faced with the West, the non-West has two alternatives: to accept Western doctrines that entail destruction of the native culture or such serious damage as to call its very survival into question, or to combine certain Western ideas with the substantial portions of the native culture that have demonstrated over a long period of time their harmony with the historically developed characteristics and genius of the people concerned. The question is today being settled, in many parts of the world, in favor of the former alternative.

A number of non-Westerners (as well as Westerners, to their eternal credit) have counseled against indiscriminate Westernization, trying to point out that the Western tradition was long and complex, and that it was unwise to pick a few of its latest fruits without examining it to the roots. A pair of comments may illustrate. Lu Hsün, in 1907, before he became an uncompromising Westernizer himself, wrote, 'Of what use is it to clutch the branches and pick up the leaves of the tree, meanwhile simply repeating "arms manufacture", "parliament", "constitution"?' Sergei Bulgakov, in 1909, used the identical metaphor in writing,

From the many-branched tree of Western civilization, with its roots that go deep into history, we chose only one branch, without knowing and without wanting to know all the others, fully confident that we were grafting onto ourselves the most authentic European civilization. But European civilization has not only a variety of fruits and a number of branches, but also roots which feed the tree and with their healthy sap render harmless, to some extent, the many poisonous fruits.[12]

At that point the time for reflection was growing short, and the habit of borrowing from the West to the detriment of the indigenous tradition had become deeply ingrained.

Ultimately, every people ought to decide its own fate; but that principle has been very roughly handled by history, and in fact the destiny of many peoples has been determined by a small group of persons – as this book clearly shows, a small group often much more sensitive to what they themselves acknowledge (whether or not justly) as the culturally more advanced West than to the needs and above all the values (which determined how those needs were to be met) of the mass of their own people. Shall we, like Russell, come to doubt that 'such men were in the right'?

TOTALITARIANISM

Though cultural Westernization has a record of success in Russia and China culminating in the Communist revolutions of 1917 and 1949, institutional

Westernization had limited effect in Russia, even less in China; and after the Communists came to power many of the institutional changes were violently reversed. Instead of a 'crossing of the institutional divide' leading from a single-centered to a many-centered society,[13] both Russia and China changed their institutional direction and a third social pattern was created, more like the former than the latter but still different from either. Not merely political power but economic, social, and cultural power is strictly concentrated in one center. Social classes independent of the state have been systematically eradicated. A single cultural pattern has become not merely dominant but all-pervasive, and continuous overt allegiance to it is compulsory for all. Property has become a word meaningless to the operation of the economy, despite personal possession of apartments, furniture, and savings accounts. The rule of law has been superseded. Doctrines supporting the value of the individual are relentlessly combatted.

The totalitarian pattern, for such it may be called, may be summarized under the following headings:[14]

(1) monopoly of all political, economic, social, and cultural power by the ruling party as the governing agency of the state
(2) destruction of all social groups not directly dependent on the state
(3) monopoly of all oral, written, and published discourse by a single doctrine, as interpreted by the party leaders at any given moment
(4) absence of significant property
(5) law reduced to the instrument of the ruling party in achieving its goals
(6) doctrine that the state is prior to the individual, who has no defense in institutions or in doctrine against state power.

The result is a much more efficient and much more brutal kind of society than one with which the two countries began. The outcome was foreseen by mid-nineteenth century observers, whose nightmare was 'Genghis Khan plus the telegraph' (Herzen), a formula oddly foreshadowing Lenin's 'socialism equals Soviet power plus electrification', a phrase close to van Leeuwen's 'Islam of the technocratic era'. It preaches a headlong march ahead on one of the West's roads, that of technology, and thus breaks through doors which caliphs could never hope to pry open even a crack; it uses much of the institutional machinery which first saw the light of day in Sumeria, and can thus stir the ancient psychological reflexes of descendants of millennia of Oriental officials; it has an undeniable relationship, however complex, with the humanitarian precepts first enunciated before Christ by Jews and Greeks and restated by the 'gnostics' of the mid-nineteenth century. It looks East and West, forward and backward; it can muster formidable military power, crush revolts against itself and foment revolts in other countries. It calls to inevitable victories in the future in extension of undoubted victories in the past.

Did the influence of the East simply overwhelm the West, adding Western technology to the arsenal of Genghis Khan, and hanging out reassuring signs designed to deceive Westerners and Westernized Easterners who took the slogans of modern civilization seriously? The answer cannot be that simple. Totalitarianism is not produced only in the East, as the Nazi example shows; the very term was coined to explain the common features of German Nazism and Russian Communism, though it is now widely recognized that the Nazis fell far short of what Communism has achieved in approaching total control from a single center. Moreover, culturally Communism is the child (whose degree of legitimacy may be duly debated) of the Christian tradition as developed in the West. It is unpleasant that the revolution devours its children, but it is also incumbent on the father of the cannibal to acknowledge his paternity.

THE PROSPECTS FOR CULTURAL PLURALISM

Over the last five centuries the West has offered the non-West Christianity and then Communism, with a liberal and non-Communist socialist interlude between. By the later nineteenth century, Joseph Schumpeter has said, preaching without teaching was no longer taken seriously; teaching without preaching would move no one to action; but preaching in the guise of teaching proved irresistible.[15] Such was the case both in the West and the world outside it.

Marx was a writer whose social analysis remains of value; he was also a prophet, few of whose prophecies were realized except the crucial one – the victory (in some countries) of the Communists. Nevertheless Marxism-as-prophecy, that is, as secular religion, has its merits. They include the recapture of a vision of the wholeness of man (though it corrupted the Christian vision), the comprehension of man's need for both knowledge and faith (though it confused the two with one another), the perception of man's willingness to surrender individual pride to something greater (though substitution of the party for the church and of History for God was not quite successful), the faith that the individual man (even though Communists undertook to compel alterations in man's nature that no human agency can produce) can be changed.[16] Such merits are well illustrated by the 1890's in Russia, when Marxism provided not merely or chiefly a new economic analysis but a bridge to philosophy and to the category of truth over which a significant group of Russian thinkers passed. It did not have the same role in China; rather, it provided an easy way for a leading group of Chinese intellectuals simultaneously to claim to understand China's problems and its place in the modern world, into which they were thrown with little preparation, and to follow the tacit but effective principle of *ex occidente lux*. But the Chinese of the 1920's borrowed Marxism in its Leninist version just then taking shape, which was much more a simplified and vulgarized dogmatic system than a method (even if a defective one) of investigating reality.

The crisis of Marxian socialism in the West has continued ever since the

1890's, when German socialists began to observe that Marx's forecasts of the way in which capitalism would develop were not being realized. When Marxists took power in the USSR many Western socialists rejoiced, and the post-World War II gains of Communism in China and Eastern Europe produced similar euphoria without leading to any satisfactory solutions of the economic, historical, and philosophical contradictions and dilemmas of Marxism. There were various efforts to patch up the tattered garment of Marxian thought, by going back to the writings of the young Marx, by political alliances with the revolutionary romanticism of the New Left, by gingerly attempts at a 'dialogue with Christianity', and in other ways. The confessions by Soviet leaders of the crimes of Stalin (the crimes themselves, known through other evidence decades earlier, had affected few Communists, though they comprise an honorable roster of distinguished individuals) severely damaged the Soviet claims to embody the Salvation of Man; China and Cuba probably have a career of several years or decades ahead of donning that fallen mantle with some success. Marxism-as-prophecy is continuing its march.

Marx himself showed considerable appreciation of the differences among the various parts of the world with respect to institutional heritage, even if cultural diversity played no part in his thought because culture itself was regarded as entirely derivative from changes in the mode of production. Today's Marxist–Leninists, in Moscow, Peking, or Havana, still follow Stalin's unilinear scheme of development: feudalism and capitalism are found to be the chief phases of history everywhere (no matter how grotesquely the evidence must be distorted in order to find them) in the past and present. This scheme has the advantage, however, of binding mankind together into a unity in the eyes of many intellectuals of non-Western countries and does not prevent them from using the tongue 'Prospero' taught 'Caliban' in order to curse the teacher to whom they owe everything – and wish to owe everything, since they repudiate their own cultural heritages with vehemence.

Liberalism, before the emergence of socialism and since, also was entirely Europe-centered; its central propositions presupposed the institutions produced by the history of the West and did not even raise the problem of whether those institutions, or liberal prescriptions for the way in which they should be changed, could be exported beyond the West. (That some leading liberals, in the course of their writings – such as Adam Smith and the Mills, James and John Stuart – made some perceptive comments about the non-West does not affect this point.)

It is a curious if not wholly surprising fact that present-day conservatism suffers from the same disability. Attacking liberalism, it accepted as central the problems liberalism posed. Since liberalism has been imprisoned in the institutional setting of the West, out of which it has utterly failed to break in theory or in practice, so conservatism has had nothing of significance to say to the non-West. Conservatism's habit of accepting things as they are has opened it to the liberals' and socialists' unceasing charges of 'defending dictators' (always understanding that the dictators in question are non-Communist ones); its espousal of the value of tradition has left it seeming to support the oppressive institutions of the non-Western past as much as the brilliant and diverse cultural heritages of the Orient.

Christianity itself has survived alongside the post-Christian doctrines that in our day offer mankind earthly salvation with such effect. But it has lost even a firm competitive position, let alone a leading one, among the doctrines acceptable among Western intellectuals; much of its academic and philosophical grounding has eroded; and serious commitment among many of its followers has vanished. Although Christianity is currently making gains in parts of Africa and Asia and enjoying a remarkable resurgence in European Communist countries and the USSR, it languishes among the opinion-makers of the West. The vision of a Ricci abroad or of a Leibniz at home is not to be found.

For five centuries the thought of the West proved ultimately too powerful for the non-West to resist. The non-West took whatever the West offered at the moment as its most powerful intellectual instrument. The West first offered Christianity and then recalled the model in order to issue several new ones culminating in Marxian socialism. Many other cultural, social, political, and even military efforts, some of them leading to battles, were going on simultaneously, but that was the effort that ultimately mattered most. It was an effort conducted in a narrow arena, involving small numbers of people. Nothing can be so misleading, in the area of intellectual history, as the statement that 'only' such-and-such a tiny percentage of people are involved in this or that new belief or movement. The few always ultimately decide questions of thought, while powerful, practical men scorn them and their efforts – until they themselves come to be dominated, expropriated, or crushed thereby.

The West started with an enterprise of conversion in mind. A conversion finally occurred in Russia and China – to Communism, which was the organization of the major religion of leading intellectuals in the West. To be sure, many of those intellectuals had no religion at all, which made it easier to perceive Marxism to be the major religion of others. The West converted Russia and China to its major religion, though the identity of that religion changed from 1450 to 1950. It is of very substantial importance that Christianity, properly understood and in the interpretation in fact given it by its best exponents, would have countenanced cultural pluralism and designated no dogma to be imposed as the unquestionable solution of institutional problems, while Communism took just the reverse position in both respects. In any case, a conversion not to Christianity but to Communism occurred.

Substantial religious conversions are not new in human history. In the early centuries of our era Christianity took over the Mediterranean basin and then the continent of Europe (and for a time much of the Near East and Central Asia). In the seventh century Islam replaced Christianity in much of that territory except for Europe and reached still further east, all the way to

Indonesia. During roughly the same period Buddhism spread from India to become entrenched in China for a time and to take over Japan. Christianity might have spread, as the West expanded from the fifteenth century on, either as Islam did – by force – or as Buddhism did – by persuasion. To a minor extent it followed a rather Islamic pattern, as in the Philippines and Goa, but mainly it spread as Buddhism did, if only because the metropolitan governments limited the scope of action of the missionaries as often as they supported them.

Under such circumstances much depended on the character of the missionary religion. No instrument like the Christian humanism of the sixteenth century had ever existed before; no comparable symbiosis of an intellectually developed Christianity and sophisticated science has ever arisen since. It is difficult to see how such a phenomenon could have been duplicated elsewhere. An intellectual achievement of the sort required complete individuation, and that could occur only in a many-centered society of the kind which Christianity helped to develop in Europe and in which in turn it matured. At this point the question of the survival of other cultures was clearly posed. It has been argued here that the real choice they faced was destruction or syncretism; no uncompromising nativism, no xenophobic exclusion of importations in the field of thought could possibly have succeeded.

A final paradox is that the best solution to be posed throughout our story in either country was posed at the very start – in China. That solution is that of Ricci. It may be formulated as follows: regard the indigenous culture with respect; assume that it has viability among the people concerned, unless the contrary can be shown, and that it is worthy of the interest of people in other countries; seek unity only in the major assumptions of religious thought, and leave all other areas of thought to develop by way of the free exchange of ideas within countries and across frontiers. The arguments for such a solution are partly moral and partly practical – and indeed any question that involves what is right and just must look to both types of argument for resolution. It is right not to trample down non-Western cultures from the standpoint of arrogant assumptions that what the West has is a *a priori* best for all peoples; it is practical not to try to do so, for even though those cultures may suffer severe damage, the results will not be psychologically or morally successful – as Communist Russia and Communist China show. It is right (though here there will doubtless be less agreement) to attempt unity in the religious realm, properly understood, because all men, in the West or non-West, have the same value, and their relation to each other and to God needs to be secured and buttressed by acceptance of the proper kind of religious principles (whether or not of the same kind of ecclesiastical institutions); it is practical to do so, for men will constantly strive for recognition of human dignity in themselves and in others, and only if such recognition is granted will free and creative action be forthcoming from all men in such a manner as to maximize the contribution of every man. In both areas – in safeguarding cultural pluralism and in seeking religious unity – compulsion must not be used; it is not right, it is not practical, and most important, it is self-defeating. The solution of Ricci never envisaged compulsion.

The solution of Ricci must not be identified with the Roman Catholic Church or the Society of Jesus, if for no other reason than the fact that the Church repudiated it and the Society was thereafter unable to employ it. That solution was rediscovered later by James Legge, whose gifts did not extend very far into the practical realm, and Timothy Richard, whose intellectual qualities were not of the first order, and neither had the advantage of a like-minded group working toward that solution as Ricci did in his lifetime and as his successors did until, say, 1722. Thereafter the secularists largely abandoned the Ricci solution, for it was based on a distinction between religion and culture that they did not make, and their vague feeling that some kind of moral unity of mankind was necessary left little room for protection of indigenous cultures against the imperialism of thought which they themselves often exemplified and practiced. Nevertheless some of them had moments of perception of the rightness of the Ricci solution; Russell's disavowal of 'men who wished to introduce all the good and evil of the West' is an important example, even though he did little to protect Chinese culture from the onslaught of his Chinese admirers and fellow-socialists (as he acknowledged the Communists to be) in succeeding decades. The solution of Ricci, from the Western side, and syncretism, from the side of the non-West, converge and produce similar results. Indeed, Ricci's solution is one of the noblest variants of syncretism.

Origen quotes Celsus as denying the possibility 'that all the inhabitants of Asia, Europe, and Africa [Asiae, Europae, Africae gentes, tam Graecas quam barbaras], Greeks and barbarians, all to the uttermost ends of the earth, were to come under one law [nomos]'. Origen[17] replies that rather 'it will surely come to pass, that all who are endowed with reason shall come under one law...Our belief is, that the Word shall prevail over the entire rational creation, and change every soul into His own perfection.' In the sense Origen no doubt intended, such a fulfillment lies far from realization; in a broader sense, it is very close to being realized, for the thought of the West, in one form or another, is carrying everything before it, for better or worse.

CONCLUSION

The Christian teaching of the absolute value of the individual has corollary practical doctrines of his freedom and responsibility. Each man capable of doing so is bound to decide for himself how best to deal with questions of truth, goodness, and beauty in his own culture and in his relations with other cultures. Everyone who believes in the existence of his responsibility, whether he accepts one of the higher religions or not, will not be deterred from exercising it by what seems the likelihood that his best efforts will be of slight effect.

Voegelin declares, 'no one is obliged to take part in the spiritual crisis of a society; on the contrary, everyone is obliged to avoid this folly and live his life in order'.[18]

Ricci was not deterred from acting by his perception of the ailments of the Ming dynasty; Lenin was not paralyzed by the failures of the regime of Nicholas II or the problems of Russia in 1917. The Marxists are right to remind us that the circumstances must be of a certain order for one person to have such an effect on events, but we ought not to be deceived by the insistence of influential men – often tactically quite wisely – that it is not they themselves but only circumstances that are bringing about the change they are seeking. The world today is filled with people who do not recognize their own freedom or their own responsibility, and shackle themselves thereby – one of the consequences of man's freedom is that he is able to deny his possession of it. Many such people do not realize that in the twentieth century as in the sixteenth, groups in the non-West with significant or even decisive influence still follow the lead of the West in deciding which ideas and which values are the proper ones to consider borrowing and which are excluded from serious consideration.

The confusion on this point results in large part from persistence in the unfortunate habit of looking only or chiefly at relations between 'nations' instead of relations between individuals and groups in those nations, which are the only ones that are ultimately significant. It is obvious that many Indians attacked British rule on the basis of mentorship given them by individual Britishers and ideas that had taken shape in Britain; the same is true of Indonesians and the Netherlands, the peoples of Indo-China and France, and in many other cases. The attack on Western imperialism and colonialism today originated in the West, not outside it; the aggressive adoption of nationalism with anti-Western or xenophobic overtones in many parts of the world reflects the acceptance of Western ideas, not action based on indigenous ones; the exclusion of Christianity from serious consideration by intellectuals in developing countries is a result of such exclusion within the Western intellectual community; the contempt for the values of their own peoples exhibited by many non-Western intellectuals was faithfully learned in the West and imitated. 'Caliban' learned 'Prospero's' language well.

For the apparent victory of cultural monism in our time, Westerners bear a grave responsibility. Although many anthropologists, humanists in various disciplines, and others object, some of them vehemently, it is to this day frequently public policy of important and powerful Western governments to act on a usually unvoiced assumption that the differences among cultures may be overlooked and that the sorts of measures applicable in the West are applicable everywhere else. Benevolently appropriated American aid money inundates indigenous cultures and instead of assisting an American-style economy which does not exist in the countries concerned) or creating one intensifies some of the undesirable tendencies to be found there and does little or nothing to develop the desirable ones; such countries are then blamed and an excuse may therein be found for yielding to the selfish and isolationist tendencies always latent in America or any other country. Economists and political scientists are called in to consult, and if they are kept on long enough may stumble onto recognition of some of these facts, but at the outset there is little recognition of the cultural divergences which make wholesale exportation of Western methods to the non-West gravely hazardous.

Not only do bird and animal species perish, but peoples and cultures die. The deculturalized Mayan remnant surviving in Mexico, the ruins of Egypt and Rome bear witness. Some such historical crimes may be so difficult to avoid or undo that correction may approach the realm of practical impossibility; but it is still not too late to try so far as much of the world is concerned. The study of culture, and in particular the interaction between high cultures, is curiously enough in its infancy. The reason is at least partly that although only intellectuals will study such problems, intellectuals (like many other people) are reluctant to reflect upon and study themselves – especially their own mistakes. It is much easier to study others – and to blame them.

A world that is desperately thirsting for values and beliefs is told what it needs is dollars and machines, or 'studies' of how to allocate them. The material has blotted out the non-material in much of our consciousness, but that does not mean that we can dispense with it; we shall merely condemn ourselves to satisfy our non-material needs in grotesque and inadequate ways or lead others in desperation to satisfy them by using grossly inacceptable methods, which may perhaps even ultimately endanger the foundations of civilized society. The problem, like others, may be reduced or even solved; the problem, like others, cannot be attacked until it is recognized and examined in its proper historical context; the problem, like others, cannot be avoided. As Walter Lippmann once wrote: 'Whether we wish it or not we are involved in the world's problems, and all the winds of heaven blow through our land.'[19]

ABBREVIATIONS

In the manuscript prepared for the volume on China every Chinese personal place name and term and every work cited in Chinese was accompanied by characters. With reluctance I had to accept the impracticability of printing them, knowing in any case that scholars would need few of them and persons not knowing Chinese would not benefit from any of them, but I invite correspondence from anyone uncertain about any given Chinese reference.

BDRC *Biographical Dictionary of Republican China*
FEQ   *Far Eastern Quarterly*
JAOS *Journal of the American Oriental Society*
JAS   *Journal of Asian Studies*
MP   Morrison Pamphlets (a collection of mostly printed documents of
      every kind, in 273 large binders, in 14 languages by my count, to be
      found in Toyo Bunko, Tokyo)

NOTES

Preface

1. Benjamin I. Schwartz, *Communism and China: Ideology in Flux* (Harvard, 1968), 39.

Foreword to volume 2: the high culture of old China

1. Edwin O. Reischauer and John K. Fairbank, *East Asia: The Great Tradition* (Boston, 1960), 146. Other basic works on the problems of this brief and presumptuous chapter include Fung Yu-lan, *A History of Chinese Philosophy* (trans., 2 vols, Princeton, 1952–3); Wm Theodore de Bary (ed.), *Sources of Chinese Tradition* (New York, 1960); Arthur F. Wright, *Buddhism in Chinese History* (Stanford, 1959); E. Zürcher, *The Buddhist Conquest of China* (Leiden, 1959), which does not go beyond the mid-fifth century; and the five volumes published by the Committee on Chinese Thought: two by the University of Chicago Press – *Studies in Chinese Thought* (1953), and *Chinese Thought and Institutions* (1957) – and three by Stanford University Press – *Confucianism in Action* (1959), *The Confucian Persuasion* (1960), and *Confucian Personalities* (1962).
2. Wright, *Buddhism in Chinese History*, 82–3.
3. *Ibid.*, 91.
4. *Ibid.*, 98.
5. Hisayuki Miyakawa, 'The Confucianization of South China', in Arthur F. Wright (ed.), *The Confucian Persuasion*, 44–5.
6. Yuji Muramatsu, 'Some Themes in Chinese Rebel Ideologies', in *The Confucian Persuasion*.
7. Nivison's introduction in David S. Nivison and Arthur F. Wright (eds), *Confucianism in Action*, 23; the phrase quoted refers to the Ming, when the process was complete.
8. Frederick W. Mote, 'Confucian Eremitism in the Yuan Period', in *The Confucian Persuasion*.
9. Charles O. Hucker, 'The Tung-lin Movement of the Late Ming Period', in John K. Fairbank (ed.), *Chinese Thought and Institutions*.
10. W. T. de Bary, 'Chinese Despotism and the Confucian Ideal: A Seventeenth Century View', in *Chinese Thought and Institutions*.
11. De Bary (ed.), *Sources of Chinese Tradition*, 615.
12. Liang Ch'i-ch'ao, *Intellectual Trends in the Ch'ing Period* (trans. Harvard, 1959), 26–7.
13. Not including the 'standard' Ch'ing history recently published in Taiwan.
14. Fung Yu-lan, *A History of Chinese Philosophy*, I, 1.
15. *Mencius*, Legge trans., book III, pt I, Ch. IV, 12.

1: Christian humanism: the Jesuits (1582–1774)

1. The King James version reads: 'Behold, these shall come from afar: and, lo, these from the north and from the west; and these from the land of Sinim.' The Revised Standard version substitutes for 'Sinim' the name 'Syene', which refers to the modern Aswan in Egypt. *The Interpreter's Bible* (New York,

1956; V, 575) declares that identification of this place as China is 'the least probable'; Syene is said to be 'the best solution'. Modern scholarship thus relieves the student of China of the task of speculating concerning the exact nature of the relations with the place, since it was most probably not China at all.

2. A. C. Moule, *Christians in China before the Year 1550* (London, 1930), Introduction.

3. Bertold Spuler, 'Die Thomas-Christen in Süd-Indien', *Handbuch der Orientalistik*, first part, VIII, section 2 (Leiden, 1961), 227.

4. G. F. Hudson, *Europe & China: A Survey of their Relations from the Earliest Times to 1800* (London, 1931), Ch. 1 and 125–6.

5. See Donald F. Lach, *Asia in the Making of Europe*, I (Chicago, 1965), bk 1, p. 7, fn. 5.

6. G. Pauthier in 'Documents officiels chinois sur les ambassades étrangères envoyées prés de l'empereur de la Chine', *Revue de l'Orient* (1843) (Morrison Pamphlets, vol. 83, no. 1,108), lists five embassies from Western monarchs prior to Thomas Pires of Portugal, 1521. They date from 166, 284, 643 (Constans II), 1081 (Nicephorus Botaniates), and 1371 (Pauthier says 'Mathieu Cantacuzène', but in 1371 John V Paleologus was emperor); that is, they were Roman or Byzantine.

7. Hudson, *Europe & China*, 90, 129–30.

8. In *China and the Roman Orient* (Shanghai and Hongkong, 1885), vi, F. Hirth concludes that both terms referred not to the whole empire but only to 'western Asia' – that is, the portion thereof under Roman or Byzantine rule at the time.

9. Moule, *Christians in China*, 34–52 gives a translation of the inscription. For the Chinese text, see Saeki, *The Nestorian Documents and Relics in China* (Tokyo, 1937), reversed pages 1–96 in back of book. An authoritative essay is Bertold Spuler, 'Die nestorianische Kirche', *Handbuch der Orientalistik*, first part, VIII, section 2 (Leiden, 1961), 120–69.

10. See Pasquale M. D'Élia, SI (ed.), *Fonti Ricciane* (Rome, 1942–9), I, lviii; Saeki, *Nestorian Documents*, 125.

11. Moule, *Christians in China*, 73.

12. *Ibid.*, 94–127, gives extracts from the sources that contain an account of the journey of Rabban Sauma and Rabban Mark, who later became Chaldean (Nestorian) Patriarch Mar Jaballaha III. See also James A. Montgomery (ed.), *The History of Yaballaha III, Nestorian Patriarch, and of His Vicar Bar Sauma* (New York, 1927). Donald F. Lach, forgetting that Rabban Sauma was a Uighur, calls him 'the first identified Chinese to reach Europe'; *Asia in the Making of Europe*, I, bk 1, 39.

13. See A. van den Wyngaert, *Sinica Franciscana* (Quaracchi, 1929) and Christopher Dawson, *The Mongol Mission* (New York, 1955).

14. A scholarly study is A. C. Moule and Paul Pelliot, *Marco Polo: The Description of the World* (London, 1938).

15. Namio Egami, 'Olon-Sume et la découverte de l'église catholique romaine de Jean de Montecorvino', *Journal asiatique*, CCXL (1952), fasc. 2, 155–67.

16. See below for two isolated groups of Christians discovered later.

17. The foremost authority on China missions, Father Francis A. Rouleau, writes, 'Judging by their letters, these modern [that is, seventeenth century] missionaries would not even have recognized the name John of Montecorvino.' Letter to me of 6 January 1966.

18. Dawson, *The Mongol Mission*, 128.

19. Quoted in D'Élia (ed.), *Fonti Ricciane*, I, lxxx.

20. Antoine Mostaert, CICM, 'Ordosica', *Bulletin, Catholic University of Peking*, no. 9 (November 1934), 1–20.

21. D'Élia (ed.), *Fonti Ricciane*, II, 323.

22. *China in the Sixteenth Century: The Journals of Matthew Ricci, 1583–1610*, trans. from Latin by Louis J. Gallagher, SJ (New York, 1953), 113–14. D'Élia comments on lib. I, cap. x, of the Ricci diary that 'if Ricci had accepted the story of St. Thomas' preaching in China, as did his Latin translator, Nicolas Trigault... he would certainly have spoken of it at this point...' *Fonti Ricciane*, I, 123.

23. George H. Dunne, SJ, *Generation of Giants: The Story of the Jesuits in China in the Last Decades of the Ming Dynasty* (Notre Dame, 1962), 193–7.

24. There were, to be sure, voices which, suspicious of the Jesuits, accused them of faking the Nestorian monument. See Edward E. Salisbury, 'On the Genuineness of the So-called Nestorian Monument of Singan-fu', *JAOS*, III, no. 2 (1853), 401–49 (MP vol. 114, no. 1,454). But such men as Alexander Wylie immediately repudiated such attacks; *JAOS*, V, no. 2 (1856), 277–336 (MP vol. 114, no. 1,460).

25. *Forty-Five Years in China: Reminiscences by Timothy Richard* (London, 1916), 339. Even Richard's sympathetic biographer feels compelled to note that such hypotheses need 'more careful research'. William E. Soothill, *Timothy Richard of China: Seer, Statesman, Missionary & the Most Disinterested Adviser the Chinese Ever Had* (London, 1924), 114–15.

26. D'Élia (ed.), *Fonti Ricciane*, I, xviii.

27. Dunne, *Generation of Giants*, Prologue. See also Johannes Bettray, *Die Akkommodationsmethode des P. Matteo Ricci S.I. in China* (Rome, 1955).

28. *China in the Sixteenth Century*, xix.

29. Joseph Needham, *Science and Civilisation in China*, I (Cambridge, England, 1954), 148.

30. An adequate biography is James Brodrick, SJ, *St. Francis Xavier (1506–1552)* (London, 1952). Georg Schurhammer, SI, *Franz Xaver, sein Leben und seine Zeit*, I: *Europa, 1506–41* (Freiburg, 1955) deals only with his career in Europe, and the continuation of the work must be awaited.

31. C. R. Boxer, *The Christian Century in Japan, 1549–1650* (Berkeley and Los Angeles, 1951).

32. Boxer, *Christian Century*, 78, 187, 320.

33. See Francis A. Rouleau, SJ, 'Matteo Ricci', *New Catholic Encyclopedia* XII, 470–2; Dunne, *Generation of Giants*, 23–108, and Henri Bernard, *Le Père Matthieu Ricci et la société chinoise de son temps (1552–1610)* (2 vols, Tientsin, 1937).

34. Rouleau, 'Ricci'.

35. Dunne, *Generation of Giants*, 28.

36. Considine, *Across a World* (Toronto and New York, 1942), 147; Dunne, *Generation of Giants*, 43.

37. Rowbotham, *Missionary and Mandarin: The Jesuits at the Court of China* (Berkeley and Los Angeles, 1942), 213, 63, 54. The same Rowbotham who speaks of the Jesuits' preoccupation with the 'top' turns a few pages later to decry Jesuit efforts at baptizing abandoned, sometimes moribund children, few of whom were presumably the children of scholars or officials. Another work which treats the whole period of the Jesuit mission is Antonio Sisto Rosso, OFM, *Apostolic Legations to China of the Eighteenth Century* (P.D. and Ione

Perkins; South Pasadena, 1948). It contains almost 200 pages of documents.

38. Of great interest is the manner in which Protestants (and Catholics) in the nineteenth and twentieth centuries fought their way painfully through to the independent discovery of the effectiveness and, many of them came to think, validity of Ricci's methods, as will be discussed later.

39. The fullest treatment is Heinrich Busch, 'The Tung-lin Shu-yüan and Its Political and Philosophical Significance', *Monumenta Serica*, XIV (1949/55), 1–163. See also Charles O. Hucker, 'The Tung-lin Movement of the Late Ming Period', in John K. Fairbank (ed.), *Chinese Thought and Institutions*, 132–62. Busch treats the question of Jesuit influence on the Tung-lin school in an appendix (156–63); Hucker does not mention it.

40. Maurus Fang Hao, 'Notes on Matteo Ricci's *De Amicitia*', *Monumenta Serica*, XIV (1949/55), 574–83.

41. Ricci, *Opere storiche* (ed. by Pietro Tacchi Venturi), II, 243–50, as quoted in Dunne, *Generation of Giants*, 44. The second volume of the Venturi edition of Ricci's works, containing his correspondence, was not superseded by D'Élia's *Fonti Ricciane*, since the latter lacks the letters.

42. C. A. Montalto de Jesus's pamphlet, *The Rise of Shanghai* (Shanghai, 1906) (MP vol. 21, no. 242), discusses Hsü at length.

In Hsü's and other cases the conversion of the father meant the conversion of the family. Hsü's works were first published by a Christian grandson, republished by a priest who was a descendant of the eleventh generation, and again reprinted (1933) by a priest who was a descendant of the twelfth generation. Much zeal was exhibited by women relatives of the converts. Candida Hsü, Kuang-ch'i's granddaughter, made so many gifts to help establish or maintain churches and chapels that she was called 'Mother of the Church'. Other examples were Agnès Yang, daughter of Yang T'ing-yün, and Agathe T'ung, wife of the Christian official T'ung Kuo-ch'i (actually she became a convert before he did).

43. See D'Élia (ed.), *Fonti Ricciane*, I, 379, n. 4 and II, 292, n. 1 for the relationship between the new volume and the earlier catechism of Ruggieri's bearing the title *T'ien-chu Shih-lu*, and the contributions of other scholars to the revision.

44. Rouleau, 'Ricci'.

45. D'Élia (ed.), *Fonti Ricciane*, I and II, contain them in the original Italian form, *Storia dell'introduzione del Cristianesimo in Cina*; the Latin version produced by Trigault as *De Christiana Expeditione apud Sinas suscepta ab Societate Iesu* in 1615 is translated into English as *China in the Sixteenth Century: The Journals of Matthew Ricci, 1583–1610*, by Louis J. Gallagher.

46. *China in the Sixteenth Century*, 82–99.

47. *Ibid.*, 448.

48. Quoted in *Fang Hao wen-lu* (Peiping, 1948), 153.

49. Quoted in *ibid.*, 166.

50. *Ibid.*, pp. 166–7 and 214.

57. *Ibid.*, p. 218. On Ricci's influence on the scholars see Wolfgang Franke, 'Matteo Ricci in den Augen eines chinesischen Zeitgenossen' in Herbert Franke (ed.), *Studia Sino-Altaica* (Wiesbaden, 1961), 72–5.

52. Wei Chün, 'Li shuo huang-t'ang huo-shih p'ien', as quoted in George Ho Ching Wong, 'China's Oppositions to Western Religion and Science During Late Ming and Early Ch'ing' (unpublished Ph.D. dissertation, University of Washington, 1958), 170.

53. *China in the Sixteenth Century*, 582.

54. Hudson, *Europe & China*, 301. Other Catholics continued there until 1838.

55. Needham, *Science and Civilisation in China*, III (Cambridge, England, 1959), 443.

56. J. J. L. Duyvendak in *T'oung Pao* (1948), XXXVIII, 328, reviewing Pasquale M. D'Élia, SI, *Galileo in Cina* (Rome, 1947).

57. D'Élia, SJ, *Galileo in China*, trans. by Rufus Suter and Matthew Sciascia (Harvard, 1960), 52. D'Élia thus replies in the English edition to Duyvendak's review of the original Italian edition.

58. J. J. Langford, 'Galileo Galilei', in *New Catholic Encyclopedia*, VI, 252.

59. Needham, *Science and Civilisation in China*, III, 446.

60. Langford, 'Galileo Galilei', 254.

61. Needham assigns six merits and five demerits to them; *Science and Civilisation in China*, III, 437–8.

62. Needham, *Science and Civilisation in China*, III, 457.

63. *Ibid*.

64. Texts given in E. H. Parker, 'Letters from a Chinese Empress and a Chinese Eunuch to the Pope in the Year 1650', *Contemporary Review* (January 1912), 79–83 (MP vol. 44, No. 575). See Boleslaw Szczesniak, 'The Writings of Michael Boym', *Monumenta Serica*, XIV (1949/55), 481–538.

65. The only biography is Alfons Väth SJ, *Johann Adam Schall von Bell S.J.: Missionar in China, Kaiserlicher Astronom und Ratgeber am Hofe von Peking, 1592–1666* (Köln, 1933). Writings are in *Lettres et mémoires d'Adam Schall S.J.*, edités par le P. Henri Bernard SJ (Tientsin, 1942).

66. Väth, *Schall*, 124.

67. *Ibid.*, 172.

68. Dunne, *Generation of Giants*, 359–60.

69. There is no biography, See R. B. Alb. Gueluy, 'Un mandarin belge: Ferdinand Verbiest', *Bulletin de la Société Belge d'Études Coloniales* (November 1911), 825–41 (MP vol. 67, no. 914). Texts in Latin are in H. Josson SI and L. Willaert SI (eds), *Correspondance de Ferdinand Verbiest* (Bruxelles, 1938).

70. For the following discussion I am indebted to Father Francis A. Rouleau's article, 'Chinese Rites Controversy', in *New Catholic Encyclopedia*, III, 610–17.

71. Dunne, *Generation of Giants*, 269ff.

72. Father Rouleau, in a letter to me, 31 August 1966, states that juridically no reversal occurred. Both decrees gave opinions merely on the basis of the exposition of the petitioner in question, leaving to each missionary the task of deciding for himself what the facts were regarding the Rites, in the form, '*If* this is the sense of the rites, then...' Since, however, not only did the Jesuit position receive this kind of authoritative approval in the decree of 1656 but it also was subsequently widely followed by non-Jesuits, as Father Rouleau himself points out in the 'Chinese Rites Controversy' article, I believe that the present wording of this sentence is accurate.

73. The decree did reaffirm both the 1645 and 1656 decisions in the sense explained by n. 72.

74. H. Chappoulie, *Rome et les Missions d'Indochine au 17ᵉ siècle (1943–48)*, I, 119, as quoted in Malcolm Hay, *Failure in the Far East* (Wetteren, Belgium, 1956), 105.

75. Chappoulie, *Rome et les Missions*, I, 268, as quoted in Hay, *Failure in the Far East*, 106.

76. Josson and Willaert (eds), *Correspondance de Ferdinand Verbiest*, 413–14.

77. Rowbotham, *Missionary and Mandarin*, 146.

78. K. M. Panikkar, *Asia and Western Dominance* (London, 1953), 406.

79. Broomhall, *The Bible in China* (London, 1934), 36.

80. Father Francis Rouleau, in a seven-page commentary on this sentence of mine, kindly dispatched to me 31 August 1966, has questioned it. Given my deep respect for his scholarship and his great knowledge of the subject of this chapter, it pains me to state that although I acknowledge the justice of many of his points, I still believe that in seven years of the juridical proceeding which antedated the decree of 1704 the papacy assumed a competence on questions of fact which it did not have and proceeded to prove its lack of competence by an erroneous decision. It then added, in 1710, a prohibition on further critical discussion of the arguments *pro and contra* which still binds Roman Catholics.

81. Needham, *Science and Civilisation in China*, II (1956), 501. Compare the passage from *The True Doctrine of the Lord of Heaven* quoted earlier; Chu Hsi, therein cited by Ricci, was the chief 'Neo-Confucian' referred to; compare also the remark of Maigrot cited below that China was a land of atheists. The intellectual alliances were interesting: Confucius and Ricci, Chu Hsi and Maigrot. (To be sure, the issues were not that simple; intellectual issues never are.)

82. See Francis A. Rouleau, 'Maillard de Tournon: Papal Legate at the Court of Peking', *Archivum Historicum Societatis Iesu*, XXXI (Rome, 1962), 264–323.

83. Giuseppe Bettinelli, *Memorie storiche dell' Eminentiss. Mgr. Cardinale di Tournon...*, III, 69, as quoted in Rowbotham, *Missionary and Mandarin*, 157.

84. *Memorie storiche...*, II, 68, as quoted in Hay, *Failure in the Far East*, 138.

85. Text of oath is given in Rowbotham, *Missionary and Mandarin*, 174–5.

86. See, for example, Ch'en Yüan, 'Tsung-chiao wai-tien chi-chien Ming-mo Ch'ing-chu chih T'ien-chu-chiao' *Kuo-li Pei-p'ing T'u-shu-kuan Kuan-k'an*, vol. 8, no. 2 (March–April 1934).

87. Rowbotham, *Missionary and Mandarin*, 103.

88. Dunne, *Generation of Giants*, 368.

89. H. Bosmans, SJ, 'Le problème des relations de Verbiest avec la Cour de Russie', *Annales de la Société d'Émulation pour l'étude de l'histoire et des antiquités de la Flandre*, fasc. 3–4 (1913), pp. 193–223 (MP vol. 58, no. 780).

90. Joseph Sebes, SJ, *The Jesuits and the Sino-Russian Treaty of Nerchinsk (1689): The Diary of Thomas Pereira, S.J.* (Bibliotheca Institute Historici SI, XVIII; Rome, 1961), 103, 109.

91. *Ibid.*, 105.

92. See vol. 1, chs 3 and 4.

93. Sebes, *Nerchinsk*, 109.

94. Quoted in Rowbotham, *Missionary and Mandarin*, 110. The last phrase is worthy of note. The emperor's decree read, 'to worship God'–not the 'Christian' God. If ancient Chinese monotheism remained in some question, there was no question about the monotheism of the K'ang-hsi emperor by this time. The question of how near he was to becoming a baptized Christian may have been allowed to obscure this capital point.

95. As shown by the fact, already mentioned, that the Yung-cheng emperor chose to treat this decree as a dead letter and instead revived the 'Sacred Edict' of 1691 which, though it simply termed Christianity 'uncanonical', could serve if desired as a basis for measures against Christians.

96. Sebes, *Nerchinsk*, 135–41, on Pereira; M. F. Feuillet de Conches, 'Les

peintres européens en Chine et les peintres chinois', *Revue contemporaine*, xxv (1856) (MP vol. 90, no. 1,208), which is by no means confined to painting; *Relazione di un viaggio fatto alla China nel 1698 da Giovanni Gherardini, pittore bolognese* (Bologna, 1854) (MP vol. 9, no. 102). Visdelou was one Jesuit who opposed the Chinese Rites.

97. The Figurists represented a distorted and exaggerated variant, rejected by most Jesuits, of the view that the Confucian classics contained monotheism (which underlay the Jesuit position in the Rites Controversy). They held that the *Book of Changes* (*I Ching*) and other texts contained hidden cabalistic meanings which could be deciphered to reveal such Christian mysteries as the Trinity, Incarnation, and Redemption.

98. This subject was debated in Rome and China from the 1650's on; Verbiest tried in 1678 to obtain sanction for a Chinese liturgy; his assistant Anton Thomas tried again in 1695; Julien-Placide Hervieu, superior of the French Jesuits, tried again in 1724. For this information I am indebted to Fr Rouleau in a letter of August 1966.

99. Francis A. Rouleau, 'The First Chinese Priest of the Society of Jesus: Emmanuel de Siquiera, 1633–1673', *Archivum Historicum Societatis Iesu*, XXVIII (1959), 3–50.

100. Arthur W. Hummel (ed.), *Eminent Chinese of the Ch'ing Period (1644–1912)* (Washington, 1944), II, 875–7.

101. Personal letter, August 1966.

102. Quoted from *Shih-chien lu* in Ch'en Yüan, 'Yung-Ch'ien-chien feng-T'ien-chu-chiao chih tsung-shih', *Fu-jen Hsüeh-chih* (July 1932), 24–5.

103. Quoted in *Fang Hao wen-lu*, 166. An inkling of the qualities of Aleni, termed by some Chinese 'the Western Confucius', which produced such reactions, may be gained from his efforts to dispel the doubts of a certain Ts'ai Wen-hsüeh concerning Christianity in the following passage:

'In reading *Daily Notes on Oral Instruction*, I learned how Ch'eng T'ang went to pray in the mulberry grove, with his hair cut short and his nails trimmed, clothed in white reed garments, to make a sacrifice. Seeing the Son of Heaven prostrate in the position of sacrifice, what would a bystander have thought? T'ang even forgot that his was the honor due to the trigrams 9 and 5 [that is, the honor due him as emperor], and his pity for his people was sincere. As for the honor due the Lord of Heaven, mighty is He as he guides his people. He restrained his mighty power in order to suffer and bring salvation, for the people of ancient times and ours, for me, and also for you.'

(Quoted *ibid.*, p. 155.)

104. According to the *Tso Chuan*, when T'an Tzu, the prince of T'an, came to the court of Lu and showed that he was versed in statecraft, Confucius took him as a teacher. The meaning seems to be that Confucianists are justified in learning from anyone who can teach them.

105. The poem, entitled, 'Chi-huai Ching-chou Hsüeh I-fu hsien-sheng', is quoted in Ch'en Yüan, 'Tsung-chiao wai-tien...,' p. 11.

106. Hummel (ed.), *Eminent Chinese*, I, 571.

107. Quoted in Chang Hsing-lang (ed.), *Chung-hsi chiao-t'ung shih-liao hui-p'ien* (Peiping, 1930), II, 418.

108. T'ang Leang-li, *China in Revolt: How a Civilisation Became a Nation* (London, 1927), 43.

109. Rowbotham, *Missionary and Mandarin*, 296.

110. Neither were Buddhism, which spread from India as far as Japan, or Islam, which today extends from Morocco to Indonesia. More precise comparisons of the great 'world religions' in this respect need not be made here.

111. Text of the decree appears in Hay, *Failure in the Far East*, 190-2. My respected colleague Father Rouleau takes exception to my view in the following words: 'When Propaganda (or better, the Holy See) permits as licit these several rites as the present generation of Chinese understands them, one cannot thereby infer that Ricci was right in allowing as morally licit the same rites as his generation three centuries and more ago practiced them.' (Personal letter, August 1966.) In Christian ethics, he of course correctly states, what makes a social practice licit is the intention of the persons concerned, which is 'subject in the process of time to intellectual and moral evolution'; he sees 'a profound transformation' in this respect 'since the end of the nineteenth century'. One may doubt that the papacy in 1704 was as well informed about the current intention in regard to the rites of Chinese Christians (or even non-Christian Chinese such as the emperor himself who had become thoroughly cognizant of Jesuit views on the matter) as the K'ang-hsi emperor was, or that such intentions (always under Ricci's policy subject to being publicly explained, if they were thought likely to be misinterpreted, for the benefit of non-Christians) might not in fact have developed further in the direction visible by 1700 if the papal decision had been otherwise. With the fullest respect for the viewpoint of Fr Rouleau, I regard the 1939 decision as fundamentally a tragically belated recognition of a several-times-reiterated mistake.

112. Rowbotham, *Missionary and Mandarin*, 274.

113. Henri Bernard, SJ, 'Whence the Philosophic Movement at the Close of the Ming (1580-1640)?' *Bulletin, Catholic University of Peking*, no. 8 (December 1931), 67-73. See also Heinrich Busch, 'The Tung-lin Academy and the Catholic Church', *Monumenta Serica*, XIV (1949/55), 156-63; Busch treats Bernard's chief source, Bartoli's *Istoria della compania di Gesu*, with respect but also with caution.

114. H. G. Creel, *Chinese Thought from Confucius to Mao Tse-tung* (Chicago, 1953), 219-20. See Foreword to this volume.

115. George L. Harris points to the need for further research in the Chinese sources in 'The Mission of Matteo Ricci, S.J.: A Case Study of an Effort at Guided Culture Change in China in the Sixteenth Century', *Monumenta Serica*, XXV (1966), 3.

116. Liang Ch'i-ch'ao, *Intellectual Trends in the Ch'ing Period*, esp. 42-8; the quote is on 46.

117. Needham, *Science and Civilisation*, III, 585.

118. Donald F. Lach, *The Preface to Leibniz' Novissima Sinica* (Honolulu, 1957), 32. Incidentally, Leibniz took the Jesuit side in the Rites Controversy (*ibid.*, 25). See also David E. Mungello, 'Leibnitz's Interpretation of Neo-Confucianism', *Philosophy East and West*, XXI (January 1971), 3-22.

119. Rowbotham, *Missionary and Mandarin*, 298.

120. Joseph de Moyriac de Mailla, SJ, *Histoire générale de la Chine...* (13 vols, Paris, 1777-85), XI, 392, quoted by Rowbotham, *Missionary and Mandarin*, 178.

121. Olivier de Beaumont, *Huit Jours à Pékin en 1865* (Paris, 1866) (MP vol. 17, no. 196).

2: *Christian pietism: the fundamentalist Protestants (1807–1900)*

1. Kenneth Scott Latourette, *A History of Christian Missions in China* (New York, 1929), 44. See also his more recent *The Great Century in Northern Africa and Asia, A.D. 1800–A.D. 1914* (vol. VI of *A History of the Expansion of Christianity*, New York, 1944).

2. *Opere storiche del P. Matteo Ricci S.I.* (Macerata, 1913), I, 246–7, in letter from Nanking, 14 August 1599, to P. Girolamo Costa SI in Rome. Since the end of the passage may appear puzzling in view of Ricci's general missionary strategy as described in Chapter X, it may be well to quote what immediately follows: '[However, they are very fearful of foreigners] so that any large number of Christians who might join with us would be in China the most suspicious thing that there could be; and this is the reason why it appears to us the most dependable advantage and the wisest counsel little by little to attempt to gain credit with this people and to remove every suspicion, and then to undertake their conversion.' Ten years of further experience did not make Ricci alter these views. See his letter to P. Claudio Acquaviva from Peking, 22 August 1608, in *ibid.*, 368.

3. Latourette, *History of Missions*, 260.

4. James Hastings Nichols, *History of Christianity, 1650–1950* (New York, 1956), 81.

5. See Chapter 5 of vol. I, which treats pietism in Russia.

6. Columba Cary-Elwes, OSB, *China and the Cross: A Survey of Missionary History* (New York, 1957), 212.

7. Leslie R. Marchant, *A Guide to the Archives and Records of Protestant Christian Missions from the British Isles to China, 1796–1914* (Nedlands, Australia, 1966), contains reference material on all British missionary societies and their periodicals as well as their archival records.

8. Unsigned, in *Edinburgh Review*, X (January 1805), 259–88, reviewing *Travels in China...* by John Barrow Esq. (MP vol. 9, no. 108).

9. Fr Ripa had been sent to China as a member of the mission carrying a cardinal's hat to Tournon (see p. 24), established a seminary in Jehol for a time, and in 1724, having to abandon it, returned to Europe with four of his students. In 1732 Rome authorized him to found a college in Naples to train Chinese clergy. It was suppressed by the Italian government in 1860.

10. *Ta Tsing Leu Lee; being the Fundamental Laws, and a Selection from the Supplementary Statutes of the Penal Code of China* (London, 1810); see review in *Quarterly Review* (May 1810) (MP vol. 136, no. 1,748).

11. 'Sir George Thomas Staunton', *Dictionary of National Biography*, XVIII (1909), 1,001–2. On the eve of the Opium War he wrote a pamphlet foreseeing resort to arms, in which he denied 'the expediency of measures of hostile aggression upon the Chinese' which many were advocating. Sir George Thomas Staunton, Bart., *Remarks on the British Relations with China, and the Proposed Plans for Improving Them* (2nd ed., London, 1836) (MP vol. 84, no. 1,121).

12. William Mosely, *A Memoir on the Importance and Practicability of Translating and Printing the Holy Scriptures in the Chinese Language; and of Circulating Them in That Vast Empire...* (2nd ed., Coventry, n.d.) (MP vol. 112, no. 1,424).

13. Brief biographies and full lists of publications for Morrison and his successors up to the date of publication are to be found in Anon., *Memorials of Protestant Missionaries to the Chinese* (Shanghai, 1867; Taipei reprint, 1967).

14. See passages quoted in Marshall Broomhall, *Robert Morrison: A Master Builder* (New York [1924?]), 17–21.

15. See the devastating review by W. Lauterbach, 'Méprises singulières de quelques sinologues', *Journal Asiatique* (1827) (MP vol. 72, no. 985): 'L'indulgence accordée aux méprises de M. Marshman ne doit pas s'étendre a celles de M. Morrison...' Morrison's dictionary, which he wished to be regarded as superior to the K'ang-hsi one, 'fourmille des fautes les plus grossières'.

16. Broomhall, *Morrison*, 158.

17. Letter written 18 December 1812, quoted in R.T.S. Memorial, *Foreign Operations: China* [1850], 471–2 (MP vol. 204, no. 2,584).

18. *Ibid.*, 481.

19. Lindsay Ride, *Robert Morrison: The Scholar and the Man* (Hong Kong, 1957), 32–9.

20. Robert Philip, *The Life and Opinions of the Rev. William Milne, D.D.* (London, 1840), 111, 112, 115.

21. *Ibid.*, 114, 256.

22. James Legge, *The Nestorian Monument of Hsi-an Fu in Shen-Hsi, China* (London, 1888), 60.

23. Helen Edith Legge, *James Legge: Missionary and Scholar* (London, 1905), 25. See also Gilbert T. Sadler, *Who Translated the Chinese Classics? A Short Life of Dr. James Legge* (London, n.d.) (MP vol. 55, no. 728).

24. The following is a list of the most important translations of the Bible in China by Protestant missionaries.

Wen-li: Marshman, 1822.
           Morrison, 1823.
           Medhurst-Gützlaff New Testament 1837, Old Testament 1838.
           Delegates' Version (mostly Medhurst) New Testament 1852, Old Testament 1855.

Mandarin: Medhurst-Stronach, 1856.
           Peking Committee New Testament 1872, Schereschewsky Old Testament 1875 (who also published, in 1905, the first referenced Bible in Chinese, in both Mandarin and 'easy Wen-li').

See John R. Hykes, *List of Translations of the Scriptures into the Chinese Language* (Yokohama, 1915) (MP vol. 193, no. 2,423); G. H. Bondfield, *The Bible in China* (London, [1904]) (MP vol. 112, no. 1,423); John R. Hykes, *The American Bible Society in China: The Story of Eighty-Two Years' Work* (Shanghai, [1915]) (MP vol. 250, no. 3,112); (title-page missing) *A Brief Account of the Work of the British and Foreign Bible Society* (MP vol. 253, no. 3,146); *Memorials of Protestant Missionaries*.

25. Helen Legge, *James Legge*, Ch. vi.

26. Ricci's choice; see p. 21.

27. William J. Boone, *An Essay on the Proper Rendering of the Words Elohim and Theos in the Chinese Language* (Canton, 1848) (MP vol. 115, no. 1,471); H. Blodget, *The Use of T'ien Chu for God in Chinese* (Shanghai, 1893) (MP vol. 115, no. 1,474).

28. It has been said that Legge's change of mind came in his little book *Notions of the Chinese Concerning God and the Spirits* in 1852 (Helen Legge, *James Legge*, Ch. vi, for example), but he published a pamphlet in 1850 which tells the whole story of the change: James Legge, *An Argument for Shang Te as*

the Proper Rendering of the Words Elohim and Theos in the Chinese Language (Hong Kong, 1850) (MP vol. 117, no. 1,491). See also James Legge, *Letters on the Rendering of the Name God in the Chinese Language* (Hong Kong, 1850) (MP vol. 117, no. 1,495).

29. Sir George Thomas Staunton, Bart., *An Inquiry into the Proper Mode of Rendering the Word 'God', in Translating the Sacred Scripture into the Chinese Language*...(London, 1849) (MP vol. 117, no. 1,498).

30. Evidently the reference is to Joseph Butler (1692–1752), bishop of Durham. See Legge, *The Chinese Classics* (Taipei reprint), II, 56ff.

31. James Legge, *Confucianism in Relation to Christianity* (Shanghai and London, 1877) (MP vol. 90, no. 1,205).

32. (Anon.) Review of *Records of the General Conference of Protestant Missionaries of China, Shanghai, May 10–24, 1877*, in London *Quarterly Review* (April 1879) (MP vol. 231, no. 2,914).

33. Inquirer [pseud.], [*Shang Ti*] (Shanghai, 1877) (MP vol. 115, no. 1,473).

34. Inquirer [pseud.], *A Letter to Prof. F. Max Muller on the Sacred Books of China, Part I* (Shanghai, 1880) (MP vol. 72, no. 984); Legge's reply (London, 1880) is MP vol. 115, no. 1,469.

35. Inquirer [pseud.], *The State Religion of China* (Shanghai, 1881) (MP vol. 89, no, 1,198). This was somewhat misleading, as the anti-Ricci Catholics did not at all favor *shen*, as Happer did, but *T'ien-chu*. The irony of a Protestant evangelical's appealing to the authority of a seventeenth-century pope perhaps does not need pointing out.

36. The controversy up to 1878 is summarized by a zealous partisan of *shen*, but in a fair manner, in S. Wells Williams, 'The Controversy Among the Protestant missionaries on the Proper Translation of the Words God and Spirit into Chinese', *Bibliotheca Sacra* (Oct. 1878), 732–78 (MP vol. 194, no. 2,443). In 1865 Williams had joined a group led by Alexander Williamson which had signed a statement expressing willingness to accept *T'ien-chu*. The signers included Joseph Edkins, W. A. P. Martin, H. Blodget, and Bishop Schereschewsky and Bishop Burdon would have signed if they had not been out of Peking when the statement was composed.

37. Unsigned letter from Hankow of May 1893 (MP vol. 115, no. 1,467).

38. Apparently this incident occurred in 1873 when he was on his way back to England. He could scarcely have chosen a more effective way of scandalizing his critics.

39. A. P. Happer's pamphlet of 1877 had asked, 'Is the Shang-Ti of the Chinese Classics the same being as Jehovah of the Sacred Scriptures?' and replied in the negative.

40. James Legge, *The Nestorian Monument*, 58.

41. *Ibid.*, 52.

42. Helen Legge, *Legge*, 228.

43. *Ibid.*, 97–101.

44. Franz Michael in collaboration with Chung-li Chang, *The Taiping Rebellion: History and Documents* (3 vols), I: *History* (Seattle, 1966), is the most recent and authoritative study; see 3–20.

45. It is uncertain whether Liang himself handed Hung the tracts; *ibid.*, 24, fn. 10.

46. Eugene Powers Boardman in *Christian Influence Upon the Ideology of the Taiping Rebellion, 1851–1864* (Madison, 1952), 30, fn. 21, appears to suggest that the later story (that the tracts when re-examined confirmed that Hung's dream

had been of a Christian heaven) was invented. This seems to go too far, and leaves unexplained the fact that the ideology did not take form until Hung had reread the tracts six years later. If he had remembered the tracts, one would have expected him to go back to them soon after awaking from his trance.

47. Quoted from the *Taiping Heavenly Chronicle* (*T'ai-ping t'ien-jih*) in Chin Yü-fu and T'ien Yü-ch'ing (eds), *T'ai-p'ing T'ien-kuo shih-liao* (Peking, 1955), 10-11.

48. Michael, *Taiping Rebellion*, 1, 78-9.

49. *Ibid.*, 130-1.

50. *Ibid.*, 150. See p. 44.

51. Quoted *ibid.*, 100-1.

52. *Ibid.*, 194-7, 46-7.

53. Anon., *The Religious Precepts of the Tae-Ping Dynasty, with a Brief Account of the Chinese Revolution* (London, 1853) (MP vol. 56, no. 752), 15.

54. 'Political Disturbances in China', *Edinburgh Review* (October 1855) (MP vol. 57, no. 764), 366.

55. Thomas Taylor Meadows, *The Chinese and Their Rebellions* (London, 1856), 446.

56. Lin-le, *Ti-Ping Tien-Kwoh* (2 vols, London, 1866), 1, 147.

57. Meadows, *The Chinese and Their Rebellions*, 324.

58. Helen Legge, *Legge*, 97.

59. Charles C. Stelle, 'Ideologies of the T'ai-P'ing Insurrection', *Chinese Social and Political Science Review*, xx (April 1936), 141.

60. Vincent Y. C. Shih, *The Taiping Ideology: Its Sources, Interpretations, and Influences* (Seattle, 1967), 43-4.

61. *Ibid.*, 472.

62. *Ibid.*, 26-7.

63. The literature on the so-called Triads is unsatisfactory. Gustave Schlegel in *Thian Ti Hwui; the Hung-League or Heaven–Earth-League* (Batavia, 1866), is convinced that the Triads (San-ho-hui, referring to Heaven, Earth, and Man) are a 'sister-society' to the Masons. It is true that many points of Masonic ritual are very strikingly similar to the ritual of the Triads; but no possible route of borrowing in either direction has been proposed. As for Hung, Schlegel writes that 'as his name already indicates' he was a member of the Hung League, but after studying Christianity changed the name of the League to Shang-ti-hui – which is all nonsense. William Stanton in *The Triad Society or Heaven and Earth Association* (Hong Kong, 1900; noted portion is on 14) writes briefly and inconclusively. J. S. M. Ward and W. G. Stirling in *The Hung Society or the Society of Heaven and Earth* (3 vols, London, 1925-6) manage to say very little indeed about China. About the subject of their three-volume work, as Paul Pelliot says in his review in *T'oung Pao*, iie série, xxv, 444-8, 'we still know almost nothing'; and the situation is no better today. What little is known is summed up intelligently by Lt-Col. B. Favre, *Les sociétés secrètes en Chine* (Paris, 1933). In 1960 the Police Commissioner of Hong Kong estimated that one in six of the colony's Chinese population 'had some connection' with the Triads (*New York Times*, 5 August 1968, 76).

64. Michael, *Taiping Rebellion*, 32.

65. Vincent Shih writes, 'in short, they destroyed everything which to them was symbolic of the life of the gentry, who represented a tradition ruthless to the people'. *Taiping Ideology*, 471.

66. Naturally all sorts of elements of the traditional culture are to be found in

the conscious or unconscious behavior, speech, and writing of the T'ai-p'ing leaders. The same phenomenon may be observed in the case of conversions throughout history to all higher religions and to Communism in our own day. Innumerable mistakes have been made, however, by those who do not distinguish the imperious and often integrated demands of ideologies from the inconsistencies and frailties of human beings. The 'old Adam' has always been present, which never proves that a man does not believe in the 'new Jerusalem'. Of course, not all religions and ideologies are equally demanding of the totality of man's allegiance, mental or moral.

67. Boardman does remind his readers that 'Protestant missionaries in China in the first half of the 19th century were much more what may be termed fundamentalist in their beliefs than are many such missionaries in the 20th century'; *Christian Influence*, 52. But he nowhere defines or explains the term 'fundamentalist', does not investigate any specific influences of fundamentalism, and says explicitly: 'It is not my object to discuss the particulars wherein the Taiping religion fails to satisfy the requirements of this or that creed. It is my purpose, rather, to outline a series of general propositions common to Christian belief and based upon the Gospels the complete absence of which no creed can justify' (*ibid.*, 107). In other words, his aim is to test T'ai-p'ing orthodoxy (though he interprets orthodoxy in a gentle and non-denominational manner); there is no reason why he should not do so, and I attempt the same thing below. However, the historical question Boardman, Stelle, Foster, and others set themselves is to assess Christian *influence* on the T'ai-p'ings, and the only possible way to do that is to consider the nature of the particular currents in Christianity which influenced them.

68. Shih, *Taiping Ideology*, 66. 'No sin is unpardonable except the violation of the seventh commandment...', Hung wrote.

69. *Ibid.*, 77. Vincent Shih does not identify the vulgar style as an evangelical borrowing, but there is ample reason to believe that it was.

70. Boardman, *Christian Influence*, 114.

71. Shih, *Taiping Ideology*, 432.

72. What Hung meant by claiming to be 'younger brother' is not quite clear. He certainly claimed divine inspiration. He and his fellows, however, often used the notion of the Trinity, to which he did not claim to belong. His sympathizers among the missionaries defended him against attacks on this point. In one contemporary pamphlet, a critic of the rebels is severely taken to task for translating the phrase 'elder brother' (applied to Christ by Hung) as 'uterine elder brother', which the writer thought implied claims to divinity which Hung had not in fact made. John Scarth, *Is Our War with the Tartars or the Chinese?* (London, 1860) (MP vol. 63, no. 862), 25.

73. Favre, *Les sociétés secrètes en Chine*, 11.

74. Franz Michael has described the Shield King's efforts sympathetically in *Taiping Rebellion*, esp. I, 134–52; see also Documents 202, 203, 205, 210, and 385, in III (1971). Earlier, he writes that it is 'totally unrealistic' to argue that the rebels might have succeeded if they had been more Confucian and could thereby have gained the support of the scholar-gentry; 'the Taiping Rebellion was based on its revolutionary system, and any such revolutionary attempt had to lead to a battle with the leading stratum in Chinese society, the scholar gentry. The Taipings were not and could not be Confucians...' (I, 102–3). It is difficult to see why, in the light of what he writes later about the Shield King's program, Michael is so categorical on this point.

Teng Ssu-yü's biography in Arthur W. Hummel (ed.), *Eminent Chinese of the Ch'ing Period* (Washington, 1944), 367-9, is critical of Hung's effectiveness as a leader, but pays little attention to his ideology.

75. Meadows, *The Chinese and Their Rebellions*, 439.

76. Basic works include T. F. O'Dea, *The Mormons* (Chicago, 1957), and L. J. Arrington, *Great Basin Kingdom: An Economic History of the Latter Day Saints, 1830-1900* (Harvard, 1958). O'Dea is a non-Mormon who strives to give the Mormons the benefit of most doubts; Arrington is a Mormon seeking to use an idiom acceptable to non-Mormon historians.

77. The fact that what appears to be the closest parallel to T'ai-p'ing Christianity is Mormonism may prompt some reflection among institutional historians. The basis of Mormon society in Utah was irrigation agriculture, using a complex network of canals. Many students of China have pointed to the fundamental or even, it has been contended, determining importance of irrigation agriculture to the kind of government and society persistently characteristic of the Chinese Empire throughout the two millennia of its existence. The Mormons, starting with their own version of Christianity, added irrigation; the T'ai-p'ings, starting with the conditions of irrigation agriculture, added their own version of Christianity; the convergence of the results is considerable. To the extent this circumstance may be taken as more than amusing or exotic coincidence, it may suggest that neither the determinism of ideas nor economic determinism is a safe guide to what may happen in human history. See Karl A. Wittfogel, *Oriental Despotism* (New Haven, 1963), 12.

78. An authoritative Roman Catholic distinction is: 'Heretics violate the faith by thinking falsely about God, while schismatics break away from fraternal love by their wicked separation, although they believe as we do' (quoted in F. X. Lawlor, 'Heresy', in *New Catholic Encyclopedia*, VI, 1,062). Protestants (to the extent they are still willing to use either term) and Eastern Orthodox make a similar distinction between denial of dogma and organizational separation.

79. *Ibid.*, 1,063.

80. Michael, *Taiping Rebellion*, 106, citing Meadows's account; see Legge's remarks as quoted p. 45.

81. E. D. McShane, 'History of Heresy', *New Catholic Encyclopedia*, VI, 1,066.

82. This was true from the very first; *Good Words to Admonish the Age* in fact consisted largely of translations of whole chapters from the Bible interspersed helter-skelter with a few admonitory sermons and essays. See account in Theodore Hamberg, *The Visions of Hung-Siu-Tshuen, and Origin of the Kwangsi Insurrection* (Hongkong, 1854) (MP vol. 56, no. 751), 14-19. Hung and his colleagues soon obtained copies of the Bible, probably in the Medhurst–Gützlaff translation, for this was the one they reprinted in 1853. Boardman, *Christian Influence*, 47-8.

83. Stelle, 'Ideologies...', 149.

84. See Ch. 1.

85. Parker himself soon became an interpreter, secretary of legation, and in 1855 US Commissioner. If he was the only American Commissioner or Minister until well into the twentieth century to know any Chinese, he did not distinguish himself in his rapport with the Chinese people. After he repeatedly urged the United States to seize Formosa (1857), he was relieved of his duties.

86. *Chinese Recorder* (May 1913, 283), as cited in Paul A. Varg, *Missionaries, Chinese, and Diplomats* (Princeton, 1958), 28.

87. *Ninth Annual Report of the Peking Hospital* [of the London Missionary Society] *for 1870* (Peking, 1871) (MP vol. 153, no. 1,912), 7.

88. *Report of the London Mission Hospitals, Hankow, for 1898* (MP vol. 148, no. 1,874).

89. *Annual Report of the Hangchow Medical Mission* [of the Church Missionary Society] *for 1907* (Shanghai, 1908) (MP vol. 151, no. 1,901), 20–1.

90. The Treaty of Tientsin with Britain and the parallel treaties with the United States, France, and Russia guaranteed toleration of Christianity, and the British treaty at least specified that the character *i* meaning barbarian was not to be applied to the British government or any British subject by any Chinese official in the capital or in the provinces. Text in MP vol. 63, no. 851. The way that certain missionaries capitalized on their treaty prerogatives during the following decade and the antipathy this provoked are studied by Paul A. Cohen in *China and Christianity: The Missionary Movement and the Growth of Chinese Antiforeignism, 1860–1870* (Harvard, 1963).

91. Eugene Stock, 'Hudson Taylor and the China Inland Mission', *The East and the West* (April 1919), 97–114 (MP vol. 70, no. 946).

92. D. MacGillivray (ed.) *A Century of Protestant Missions in China (1807–1907)* (Shanghai, 1907), 127.

93. *Ibid.*, 88.

94. Marshall Broomhall, *The Bible in China* (London, 1934), 4.

95. A minority view was presented at the 1890 conference by W. A. P. Martin; see p. 66.

96. Samuel Couling, *Encyclopedia Sinica* (Shanghai, 1917), 464.

97. William E. Soothill, *Timothy Richard of China* (London, 1924), 37. Another respectable biography is B. Reeve, *Timothy Richard, D.D.: China Missionary, Statesman, and Reformer* (London, n.d.).

98. Quoted from the *Collected Writings of Edward Irving*, I, in Soothill, *Richard*, 77–8.

99. *Forty-Five Years in China. Reminiscences by Timothy Richard* (London, 1916), 110–11.

100. *Ibid.*, 123.

101. *Ibid.*, 107.

102. Quoted from unidentified source in Soothill, *Richard*, 151.

103. See Richard, *Conversion by the Million in China* (2 vols, Shanghai, 1907), esp. Chs III (a paper by Mrs Richard), X, XVI, and XVII. Even Soothill dissociates himself from these views in *Richard*, 114–15.

104. *Forty-Five Years*, 205.

105. *Ibid.*, 199.

106. *Ibid.*, 145.

107. Quoted in Soothill, *Richard*, 98.

108. *Ibid.*, 156.

109. Richard, *Conversion by the Million*, I, 122.

110. *Ibid.*, I, 172.

111. *Ibid.*, I, 226.

112. *Ibid.*, II, 67.

113. *Ibid.*, II, 69.

114. *Ibid.*, I, 228; II, 73.

115. See Rev. A. Williamson, *The Literati of China and How to Meet Them* (Glasgow, n.d. [1887?]) (MP vol. 142, no. 1,818); the pamphlet makes clear that his views were similar to Richard's in many respects. The tracts currently

distributed by missionaries in 'easy Wen-li', he noted, were on a low level; material should be either in Mandarin or Wen-li. The only way to reach the literati was through books, since the missionaries were too few and the literati too scattered.

116. *Forty-Five Years*, 236.

117. Dwight Goddard, *A Chapter of Chinese History and a Plea* (Cleveland, 1906) (MP vol. 48, no. 623). Goddard was in Peking in 1898.

118. See Ch. 4.

119. Quoted in Soothill, *Richard*, 219.

120. Goddard, *A Chapter*, 20.

121. *Ibid.*, 21. On both publications called *Wan-kuo Kung-pao*, see Roswell S. Britton, *The Chinese Periodical Press, 1800–1912* (reprint, Taipei, 1966), 53–6 and 90–1.

122. See *Forty-Five Years*, 265–6.

123. From the report on the Christian Literature Society for China (formerly the SDK) in MacGillivray, *A Century of Protestant Missions*, 633.

124. *Forty-Five Years*, 291. Further study is needed of the question of Western influence, and specifically of Richard and other like-minded missionaries, on the movement that led to the 'Hundred Days'. Unfortunately Kwan-wai So's 'Western Influence and the Chinese Reform Movement of 1898' (University of Wisconsin Ph.D. thesis, 1950), despite its title and its merits, pays little attention to that question.

125. In his biography of T'an Ssu-t'ung; Hummel (ed.), *Eminent Chinese of the Ch'ing Period*, II, 703.

126. *Forty-Five Years*, 299.

127. Soothill, *Richard*, 268–70.

128. Soothill writes, 'Had Mrs Richard lived, much of his later work, valuable though it is, would have been better done because of her revision. She was the guardian angel of his eager mind, and her opinion weighed with him when that of others would have been ignored' – *Richard*, 280.

129. Richard, *Conversion by the Million*, II, 218.

130. *Ibid.*, 255.

131. *Forty-Five Years*, 371.

132. Soothill, *Richard*, 76–7.

133. *Ibid.*, 149.

134. Richard, *Conversion by the Million*, II, 189.

135. Soothill, *Richard*, 280.

136. Latourette, *History of Missions*, 651–2.

137. Soothill, *Richard*, 98.

138. A good example may be found in the Rev. Arthur J. Brown's *Report of a Visitation of the China Mission* (3rd ed., New York, 1902) (MP vol. 247, no. 3,078), wherein the author declares that the SDK is doing a good deal, that it deserves emulation, and that 'larger use' must be made of the printed word. But these paragraphs get lost in the multitude of topics minor and major through which the report ranges.

139. See Gilbert Reid, 'Confucianism, an Appreciation', *Harvard Theological Review* (January 1916) (MP vol. 78, no. 1,043), in which he repeats Richard's appraisal: it is wrong to think Confucianism and Christianity either identical or antagonistic to each other; between them there should be 'harmony and mutual regard'.

140. The majority view is expressed in Pastor P. Kranz, 'Can the Christian

Church Supply the Wants of the Chinese with Regard to the Reverence for Ancestors?' *Morrison Society Papers*, no. 3 (June 1904), in which he like Legge's critics (see p. 43) invoked the authority of the decisions of Clement XI and answered his own question with a resounding negative. Martin's view is stated in the article that follows, 'The Worship of Ancestors – How Shall We Deal With It?' (MP vol. 218, no. 2,771). He also discusses the K'ang-hsi period, declares that the crucial mistakes were made then, with regard to the rites to ancestors, emperor, and Confucius and in adopting the phrase *T'ien-chu* for God. He confesses to his shame that he once demanded an ancestral tablet (in order to destroy it), but only once. Richard once said to a missionary who came triumphantly bearing a new convert's ancestral tablet, destined for the fire: 'When he burns his tablet, I suppose you will at the same time burn your parents' photographs?' The tablet was not burned. *Forty-Five Years*, 146.

One other scandal was created at the 1890 conference when John L. Nevius questioned the soundness of the work of the Bible societies. To a people to whom sheep were either unknown or regarded as one of the lowest of beasts, the left hand was the seat of honor, white the color of mourning, and the serpent (dragon) the most honored cultural symbol, missionaries had been distributing broadcast materials assuming the opposite values in each case. The Bible societies could scarcely think of adding explanatory notes to the Scriptures they distributed, since any conceivable gloss might give offense to one or more of the multifarious denominations at work in China. The first referenced Bible thus did not appear in Chinese until 1905 (see n. 24).

141. Latourette, *History of Missions*, 414.

142. Cary-Elwes, *China and the Cross*, 204.

143. *Ibid.*, 232.

144. Anon., *China: Or a Few Facts Regarding Canton, Hongkong, and Macao...*(Bombay, 1846) (MP vol. 23, no. 266), 77. The author was a Protestant bewailing Catholic successes in the mission field; he reported the ordinary Catholic salary as $100 per year, the Protestant at $100–$150 per month.

145. The typical Protestant evangelical was often, as in the case of I. J. Roberts's treatment of Hung Hsiu-ch'üan, inclined to postpone baptism. By no means an exceptional missionary reported as late as 1911: 'With respect of receiving members, the rule of the year has been to baptize only such as no excuse could be found for not baptizing.' *Station Reports* of Hunan Mission, China, of the Presbyterian Church in USA, 1911 (MP vol. 246, no. 3,075), 27.

146. The exact figures are elusive. Élisée Reclus in 'La Chine et la Diplomatie européenne', *L'Humanité Nouvelle* (Paris, 1900) (MP vol. 86, no. 1,148), gives for 1899 550,000 Roman Catholic converts, scarcely 25,000 Protestants. Latourette, *History of Missions*, 680 and 537, gives about 100,000 Protestants and 720,000 Catholics.

147. Sir Robert Hart, 'China, Reform, and the Powers', *Fortnightly Review*, CCCCXIII, new series (1 May 1901) (MP vol. 85, no. 1,138), 778–9.

148. Gen Tcheng-ki-tong, in a lecture (in French) in Paris, 12 August 1889 (MP vol. 185, no. 2,316), 430 (taken from unknown periodical).

149. Quoted in Sir Robert Hart, Bart., *The Peking Legations: A National Uprising and International Episode* (Shanghai, 1900), 35.

150. See Ch. 3 for discussion.

151. See *Classified Catalogue* of the Christian Literature Society for China for 1908 and same for 1911 (MP vol. 196, nos. 2,471 and 2,470 respectively).

3: Christian modernism: Sun Yat-sen (1895–1925)

1. James Hastings Nichols, *History of Christianity, 1650–1950* (New York, 1956), 270 and 269.

2. J. J. Heaney, 'Modernism', in *New Catholic Encyclopedia*, IX, 991–5.

3. Karl Barth, *Protestant Thought: From Rousseau to Ritschl* (New York, 1959), 392–4.

4. Nichols, *History of Christianity*, 284–5.

5. Charles Howard Hopkins, *The Rise of the Social Gospel in American Protestantism, 1865–1915* (New Haven, 1940), 3.

6. Walter M. Horton, 'Systematic Theology', in Arnold S. Nash (ed.), *Protestant Thought in the Twentieth Century: Whence and Whither?* (New York, 1951), 108.

7. Quoted in Hopkins, *Rise of the Social Gospel*, 28.

8. *Ibid.*, 60.

9. *Ibid.*, 142–3.

10. Quoted *ibid.*, 233.

11. *Ibid.*, 303–4.

12. Robert Morrison, on his voyage home in 1823, notes in his diary after reading some unspecified books in history (but apparently Gibbon and Hume): 'From these there is little instruction to be derived for the direction of one's conduct in ordinary life...Oh beware of false philosophy, which casts off the restraints of religion, and scriptural morality.' *Memoirs of the Life and Labours of Robert Morrison, D.D., Compiled By His Widow* (2 vols, London, 1839), II, 238.

13. Ray Ginger, *Six Days or Forever? Tennessee v. John Thomas Scopes* (Boston, 1958), Ch. 9. Bryan's sole concession, that perhaps the world was not created in 'six days of twenty-four hours each', was enough to bring down on his head the wrath of his own fundamentalist claque.

14. A. T. Piry, 'Le peuple chinois et la réforme', *Revue des deux Mondes*, III (1901), 656–76 (MP vol. 44, no. 583). Piry specifically referred to Ricci in his peroration.

15. A. R. O'Hara, 'Frederic Vincent Lebbe' *New Catholic Encyclopedia*, VIII, 595; Cary-Elwes, *China and the Cross*, 236–40.

16. He was almost the first Westerner since his great Jesuit predecessors to do so. Apparently Karl Gützlaff became a naturalized Chinese subject under the name Kuo Shih-li; RTS Memorial, *Foreign Operations: China* [1850] (MP vol. 204, no. 2,585), 487. Gützlaff must have done so in a very different spirit from Lebbe, for like his fundamentalist confrères he took a sharply negative view of China and the Chinese; see review of his *Journal of Three Voyages along the Coast of China...*(London, 1834) in *Quarterly Review* (1834) (MP vol. 9, no. 103).

17. See p. 32.

18. R. F. Johnston, 'A League of the Sacred Hills', *The Nineteenth Century* (February 1913) (MP vol. 47, no. 612), 306.

19. The fortunes of Roman Catholicism in China enjoyed, indeed, numerically spectacular improvement. By 1918 there were almost 2,000,000 Chinese Catholics; in 1924 the figure was nearly two and a quarter million. Latourette, *History of Missions*, 740. That only proves that numbers are not the most important thing when one deals with the realm of culture. In 1922 Chinese Protestant communicants numbered just over 400,000. *Ibid.*, 780. Protestants were,

despite their smaller numbers, more influential than Catholics in China, though the influence of either group was very limited. It might be added here that subsequently the statistics did not change very much. In 1936–7 Protestant communicants were not many more than 500,000; in 1939 Roman Catholics were just under 3,200,000. Cary-Elwes, *China and the Cross*, 265 and 292.

20. Alexander Michie, *Missionaries in China* (London, 1891), 3.

21. *Ibid.*, 40.

22. *Ibid.*, 51. On Martin's paper, see p. 66.

23. Rev. Arthur Elwin, *Confucianism* (paper read at Victoria Institute, 2 January 1905; MP vol. 77, no. 1,036), 20.

24. *Catalogue* of the Nanking Bible Training School (Shanghai, 1912) (MP vol. 138, no. 1,771), 12.

25. *Annual Register and Report* of the Shantung Christian University (Shanghai, 1915) (MP vol. 139, no. 1,780), 11.

26. Chiang Monlin, *Tides From the West* (reprint, Taipei, 1957), 46–7. The year was apparently 1902. Soon afterward Chiang came to California to study.

27. Miss Pingsa Hu, 'American Influence on Chinese Students', *China's Young Men* (Shanghai) vol. VI, no. 4 (October 1911), 117.

28. Nathaniel Peffer in 1924 spoke of the 'basic change' from fundamentalism to modernism as having begun in China missions 'in the past fifteen years', or since about 1909. Precise dating of such a phenomenon is, of course, difficult, but his conclusion seems to accord with the evidence given here. Peffer, 'The Uniqueness of Missionaries', *Asia*, XXIV (May 1924), 353ff.

29. Latourette, *History of Missions*, 584–94; Shirley Garrett, *Social Reformers in Urban China: The Chinese Y.M.C.A., 1895–1926* (Harvard, 1970).

30. Soothill, *Richard*, 291. It is probably true that most of the YMCA members and friends did not care for 'profound lectures'; but the general statement, in a book written after the May Fourth Movement, does little credit to Soothill's perception of Chinese realities.

31. *Some Tools for Student Work* (Shanghai, 1912) (MP vol. 250, no. 3,107).

32. Rev. Wilbert W. White, 'A Right Life an Essential Factor in Understanding the Word of God and in Maintaining Faith in It', *Chinese Recorder and Missionary Journal*, XLI (October 1910), 638.

33. Sherwood Eddy, *A Pilgrimage of Ideas* (London, 1935), 44, 43, 54, 116.

34. Since Dr Sun was President only from 1 January to 12 February 1912, and apparently not in Canton during that period, it appears that the story may have been embellished. *Ibid.*, 124.

35. G. Sherwood Eddy, 'Chinese Students and the Gospel', *International Review of Missions* (July 1915) (MP vol. 218, no. 2,774), 372.

36. Eddy, *A Pilgrimage of Ideas*, 336; this is the concluding phrase in the book.

37. *Ibid.*, 54.

38. See, for example, Daniel Johnson Fleming, 'Open-Minded Christianity', *Asia*, XXIV (June 1924), 472ff.

39. 'The National Christian Conference', *Missionary Herald* (July 1922) (MP vol. 232, no. 2,920), 264–5.

40. This is the Cantonese form of the style (*tzu*) Sun I-hsien, whose original name was Sun Wen and who while in Japan adopted the name Sun Chungshan.

41. A possible challenger of this title was Emmanuel de Siquiera. See page 28.

42. Lyon Sharman, *Sun Yat-sen: His Life and its Meaning* (New York, 1934), ix.

43. Wu Hsiang-hsiang, *Sun I-hsien Hsien-sheng*, 1 (Taipei, 1965), 34.

44. *Ibid.*, second plate following bibliography reproduces the baptismal record.

45. Chün-tu Hsüeh, *Huang Hsing and the Chinese Revolution* (Stanford, 1961), 27–8, and 'Sun Yat-sen, Yang Ch'ü-yün, and the Early Revolutionary Movement in China', *JAS*, xix (May 1960), 307–18; Harold Z. Schiffrin, *Sun Yat-sen and the Origins of the Chinese Revolution* (Berkeley, 1968), 46–8.

46. Schiffrin, *Sun*, 52; the quote is from Feng Kuei-fen, an official of the 'self-strengthening' school, in which he expressed his distrust of such Westernized people.

47. *Ibid.*, 89.

48. Wu, *Sun I-hsien*, 156, 158.

49. Quoted in Sharman, *Sun*, 48.

50. Not two years, as he later wrote; Schiffrin, *Sun*, 134–8.

51. *Ibid.*, 308.

52. *Ibid.*, 362–3.

53. In an editorial signed by Sun in the first issue of the organization's new journal, *Min Pao* (20 October 1905), Hu Han-min, the real author, for the first time expounded what later were called the Three People's Principles; 'Fa K'an Ts'u' (photographic ed. of the Scientific Publication Society, Peking, 1957), 1–3. In 1910 a new oath was substituted for one that had incorporated the original slogan. It read: 'to wipe out the Ch'ing dynasty of the Manchus, create a Republic of China, and implement the doctrine of people's livelihood'. It is curious that although Sun, in writing to Teng Tse-ju on 16 August 1910, explained that 'its former four parts had been changed to three, each of which ends in "-ism" (*chu-i*)...' (Hu Han-min [ed.], *Tsung-li ch'üan-chi*, 4 vols in 5, Shanghai [1930] iii, 166), in fact only the third of the three terms used in the 20 October 1905 editorial was used in the new oath, and that one without the '-ism' ending.

54. Shelley Hsien Cheng in 'The T'ung-Meng-Hui: Its Organization, Leadership and Finances, 1905–1912' (Ph.D. dissertation; University of Washington, 1962), 38–42, shows that even that early Hu Han-min and other associates of Sun's had in mind not Henry George's scheme but real land nationalization (*t'u ti kuo-yu*).

55. Sharman, *Sun*, 126.

56. Jansen, *The Japanese and Sun Yat-sen* (Harvard, 1954), 189.

57. George T. Yu, *Party Politics in Republican China: The Kuomintang, 1912–1924* (Berkeley, 1966), 122, 152.

58. Thus Nathaniel Peffer, in a review of Maurice William's *Sun Yat-sen versus Communism*, wrote that Dr Sun was 'one of the great men of our times. But he never attained intellectual maturity, and he was completely devoid of the faculty of reason. He functioned mentally in sporadic hunches. It was typical of him that he met Joffe, read the Communist Manifesto, and turned Communist, and then read one book by an American of whom he knew nothing and rejected communism all in a few months.' *The Nation*, cxxxiv (11 May 1932), 548. The statement is a half-truth. Sun had had some acquaintanceship with Marxism since the 1890's; he never either fully accepted nor fully rejected Communism; but the book Peffer refers to, William's *The Social Interpretation of History*, did have a profound influence on him, as shown below. Paul Myron

Anthony Linebarger, in *The Political Doctrines of Sun Yat-sen* (Johns Hopkins, 1937), 135, fn. 19, goes too far in challenging Peffer's remark.

59. Maurice William, *The Social Interpretation of History: a Refutation of the Marxian Economic Interpretation of History* (London, 1921). William's conclusions, which doubtless were influenced by the conclusions of such post-Marxian economists as Jevons and Menger that value was determined not by production (labor value) but by consumption (marginal utility), were that 'Marxian principles can be applied only through a class movement of *producers*, whereas democratic principles are the agency of a social movement of *consumers*...Marxian Socialism is based upon the theory that class conflict is the propelling motive force of history. The Social Interpretation of History is based upon the theory that man's effort to solve his problem of existence is the propelling motive force in history' (ix).

60. John Dewey, *Human Nature and Conduct: An Introduction to Social Psychology* (New York, 1922), 273.

61. I have not been able to locate a copy.

62. James T. Shotwell, 'Sun Yat-sen and Maurice William', *Political Science Quarterly*, XLVII (March 1932), 22–3.

63. Maurice William, *Sun Yat-sen versus Communism* (Baltimore, 1932), 54–70ff. Shu-Chin Tsui (Ts'ui Shu-ch'in) tries valiantly to argue that William and his admirers were wrong in alleging that Sun reversed himself on Marxism and the USSR because he had read William's *The Social Interpretation of History*. It must be said that Tsui makes very little headway, except to show that Sun had read the book *before* he began the Canton lectures on 27 January 1924, since he referred to it by title and discussed it (though he did not mention William's name as he was to do in the August lectures) in a speech to the I National Congress of the Kuomintang on 21 January, characteristically contending that William had come to 'join him in advocating' *min-sheng*. (Shu-Chin Tsui, 'The Influence of the Canton–Moscow Entente Upon Sun Yat-sen's Political Philosophy', *Chinese Social and Political Science Review*, XVIII [April 1934], 121–3. The passage is in Hu Han-min (ed.), *Tsung-li ch'üan-chi*, II, 393–4.) But this discovery does not alter the significance of the texts William has assembled. All it shows is that there is no intellectual justification for the discrepancy between the views about Marx and the USSR set forth in the lectures on *min-tsu* and in those on *min-sheng*; it tells us nothing new about the lack of coherence in Sun's doctrines.

64. He quoted Mill, presumably John Stuart (as both L. T. Chen and Pascal M. D'Élia agree), as saying 'that only individual liberty which did not interfere with the liberty of others can be considered true liberty. If one's liberty is incompatible with another's sphere of liberty, it is no longer liberty. Before that, Westerners had set no limits upon freedom, but when Mill proposed his theory of a limited freedom, the measure of personal liberty was considerably reduced.' (Price trans., 204; cf. D'Élia trans., 200; see page 86 for full citations.) D'Élia (201 n. and 503) comments that Mill cannot be considered the originator of such restrictions on liberty, tracing the doctrine Sun cites back to the Declaration of the Rights of Man of 1789. Paul Myron Anthony Linebarger in *Political Doctrines of Sun*, 98, declares that Sun was really referring to 'John Millar's definition of liberty, given in *The Progress of Science Relative to Law and Government*, 1787', and declares that D'Élia, in the passage mentioned, 'discusses the reasons which made it seem more probable that Sun was transliterating the name Millar into Chinese rather than (John Stuart) Mill'. Here we have muddle

upon muddle. D'Élia did not mention Millar at all in the original French edition, but added a footnote to this effect in the English edition. Millar's essay (reprinted in William C. Lehmann, *John Millar of Glasgow, 1735–1801* [Cambridge, Eng., 1960], 340–57) contains no such ideas as those of Sun's. John Stuart Mill was indeed influenced by John Millar (see Lehmann, *Millar*, 153), but in the present context that fact seems to lead nowhere. In his essay *On Liberty*, Mill writes: 'The liberty of the individual must be thus far limited; he must not make himself a nuisance to other people' (Ch. 3). But that is one of only two or three sentences in the entire essay which make any reference whatever to limitations on liberty; the piece is devoted to the relationship of individual liberty to government, and his argument, the classic statement in defense of individual liberty in modern Western literature, is entirely against the justifiability of limitations on it. Sun's rendering of the name Mill (Mi-le) makes it highly improbable that he intended instead to refer to Millar. The instance may well serve to illustrate the perils of reverent exegesis of the works of Sun, a man who had not only just lost all his notes (in the burning of his residence of Ch'en Ch'iung-ming) but was not a systematic scholar or thinker.

65. Linebarger, *Political Doctrines of Sun*, 18. Perhaps Linebarger should have been considered the precedent of Mark Twain, who, confronted with a French translation of his work, translated the translation back into English with ludicrous results. Translating Sun's Chinese back into American English may be a comparable endeavor.

66. *Ibid.*, 53.

67. *Ibid.*, 67. See D'Élia (ed. and trans.), *Triple Démisme*, 171. The source of the phrase is the *Li Chi*.

68. Shao Chuan Leng and Norman D. Palmer, *Sun Yat-sen and Communism* (New York, 1960), 23.

69. The arrangement has been suggested by Leonard Shihlien Hsü in *Sun Yat-sen: His Political and Social Ideals* (Los Angeles, 1933), 38–40, and Paul Myron Anthony Linebarger, *Political Doctrines of Sun*, 4–5, but is not identical with that of either. The standard Chinese edition of Sun's works, which I have used except for an item or two not found therein, is Hu Han-min (ed.), *Tsung-li ch'üan-chi* (4 vols in 5; Shanghai, [1930]).

70. Sun Yat-sen, *The International Development of China*, 231.

71. Dr Sun Yat-sen, *The Cult of Dr Sun*, 2. The book is almost identical with Sun Yat-sen, *Memoirs of a Chinese Revolutionary* (London, [1927]), although the minor differences are interesting. Whereas the opening chapter of the original deals with diet, the translator puts the second first, thus making Sun begin as Marx does with a discussion of money and capital. The word 'revolutionary' has been arbitrarily put in the title and inserted here and there in the chapter headings and text by the translator. Obviously he was writing with the needs of the Canton–Moscow *entente* in mind. There are many errors; for example, on page 41 he translates the Chinese name of a certain Mr Hayes [Ho Shih], who traveled in the interior of China during the nineteenth century, as 'the Portuguese Matthew Ricci'. The ancient maxim Sun challenges is found in the *Shu Ching*, part IV, book VIII, and is there attributed to the Great Yü.

72. *Ibid.*, 95.

73. *Ibid.*, 51 and 66.

74. *Ibid.*, 93–4. The brief account of what Dewey said about Europeans and Americans has been omitted by the leftist translator from *Memoirs of a Revolutionary*.

75. See p. 78.

76. Sun states, 'although there was a separation of powers in the English government at the time of Montesquieu, the present government of England is really not a government of distinct separation of powers but a government of parliamentary dictatorship' (Hsü, *Sun*, 103). This is a statement characteristic of Sun's partial understanding of what he was talking about; it is true that in Sun's time there was no separation of powers in England, but parliamentary supremacy was also firmly established in Montesquieu's day.

77. Hsü, *Sun*, 94.

78. Hsü, *Sun*, 92 and 106. Hsü omits the name both times. The translator of *Memoirs of a Revolutionary* includes this lecture as Appendix II, and gives the name as 'Burgess'. Sun refers to the title of the book once as *Liberty*, once as *Liberty and Government*. It is true that Burgess praises the Chinese censorate, as Sun claims. See John W. Burgess, *The Reconciliation of Government with Liberty* (New York, 1915), 5–6. The other view Sun quotes from Burgess, that America should add a fourth power, that of the censorate, cannot be documented from anything Burgess has said, but probably represents a misreading of page 379.

79. D'Élia (ed. and trans.), *Triple Démisme*, 74.

80. D'Élia (ed. and trans.), *Triple Démisme*, 129. D'Élia is at pains to point out in a footnote that they are not the same thing. But time and again when Sun says something Chinese is 'the same thing' as something Western, he simply means that something Western that has caught his fancy can be shown to have some more or less remote analogue somewhere in the rich heritage of China or, perhaps, in something he himself has been saying before.

81. All the evidence Leng and Palmer (*Sun Yat-sen and Communism*, 133) bring to support their view that Sun 'derived many of his ideas from Confucianism' (along with those he took from the West) consists of the enumeration of Chinese virtues, the quotation from the *Ta Hsüeh*, and the contention that the realization of *min-sheng* would be 'the same' as Confucius's *Ta Tung* or Great Commonwealth – that is, all the evidence comes from five pages and two additional paragraphs of one section of the *San Min Chu I*. But at least it would be evidence, if the passages were shown to have any integral relationship to Sun's argument; this is more than can be said of the conclusions of some of the other writers on the subject.

82. In a speech at Kuomintang headquarters in Canton in June 1921 Sun had said: 'From the time of the end of the European War, the American President, Wilson, perceived the great influence of *min-tsu*. He strongly advocated the theory of the "self-determination of nations". This theory...is just our party's *min-tsu chu-i*.' (Hu Han-min [ed.], *Tsung-li ch'üan-chi*, II, 215). Lenin also found the phrase useful; whether Sun was indebted to Wilson directly or indirectly through Lenin is a question not requiring solution here.

83. See p. 86.

84. D'Élia (ed. and trans.), *Triple Démisme*, 208. It is in this connection that he misquotes John Stuart Mill; see n. 64 above.

85. My native state's single contribution to modern Chinese history; the 'Oregon system'.

86. See p. 84.

87. Henry Bond Restarick, *Sun Yat Sen: Liberator of China* (Yale, 1931), 99–101, reports an interview with the Rev. Teiichi Hori, pastor of a Japanese Congregational Church in Yokohama, in which the latter describes how he was

brought into contact with Sun: 'After Sun Yat Sen left [Japan] in 1906, the agent of the American Bible Society brought to my house and introduced to me Mr Chun, the secretary of Dr Sun...' Hori hid Chun, dressed him as a Japanese, and saw to his safe lodging nearby. Hori continues: 'The Japanese Christians, especially, were in favor of Sun because they believed that he stood for the rights of man and was opposed to oppression and cruelty, as shown in the policy of the Manchus.'

88. He addressed the Chinese YMCA's national convention in Canton in October 1923 and Canton Christian (Lingnan) College the same fall.

89. Sharman, *Sun*, 153.

90. James Cantlie and C. Sheridan Jones, *Sun Yat Sen and the Awakening of China* (2nd ed., London, [1912]), 247–8.

91. Paul Linebarger, *Sun Yat Sen and the Chinese Republic* (New York, 1925), 304. Aboard the ship carrying Sun and a few fellow-revolutionaries to Yokohama after the 'second' revolution of 1913, on an occasion when they were alone Sun asked Hu Han-min, 'Do you know who I am?' Hu replied, 'What? You, sir, are Mr Sun'. Sun said, 'No, I am Jesus Christ'. Hu's fears for Sun's sanity were dispelled by his continuing to explain that as Christ had been betrayed by his disciples, so he had been; the Kuomintang men who had sided with Yüan Shih-k'ai were the same as Judas; as Christ suffered for mankind, so Sun had suffered for the masses; and so forth. Personal letter from Winston Hsieh, 24 November 1969, based on the records of the Oral History Project of the Institute of Modern History, Academia Sinica, Taipei, which are not yet subject to direct quotation.

92. If the paragraph seems too strong, a complete reading is suggested of the books of Restarick, Cantlie, and Judge Linebarger cited; *The Gospel of Chung Shan According to Paul Linebarger* (Paris, 1932); and even the restrained and disciplined but still laically pious preface by the great student of the Jesuit missions in China, Pascal M. D'Élia, to *Le Triple Démisme*, which concludes not with a panegyric of Sun but with the triumphant report of the presence of the envoy of the Holy See at the ceremonies for Sun's reburial in Nanking in 1929, possible 'par le caractère purement civil des cérémonies et par l'absence des rites superstitieux' (30). If what Rome had denied to the Ch'ing emperors had finally been granted to their successor, Sun Yat-sen, was it not difficult to renounce hope?

93. *Kuo-fu ch'üan-chi* (Taipei, 1957), VI, 211.

94. So he told Bishop Roots; see Restarick, *Sun*, 153.

95. Cheng, 'T'ung-Meng-Hui', 3, 46, 50 n. 16, 63–4 n. 152. This sort of evangelical–Christian evaluation of the question of whether someone is a Christian on the part of a non-evangelical non-Christian is reminiscent of an eminent agnostic professor of modern literature who, shortly after the appearance of *Doctor Zhivago* and during the discussion of Pasternak's Christianity, told a class of his that Zhivago's and Lara's sexual misconduct in the novel raised grave doubts whether Pasternak was a Christian. (He was.)

96. At least some of those who remained partly evangelical in their outlook were greatly troubled by his dubious second marriage to Soong Ch'ing-ling. But Bishop Restarick comments succinctly: 'his action was not essentially different from that of thousands of men and women in Christian America' (*Sun*, 130); he might have specifically mentioned the chief modernist preacher of the 1890's, George Herron – see page 72.

97. It is difficult to believe, but apparently true, that he intended no self-satire

by entitling his book of speeches, which was the only substitute he could produce for the manuscripts destroyed in the Japanese bombing of the Commercial Press in Shanghai in January 1932: *The Gospel of Chung Shan According to Paul Linebarger*.

98. Paul Myron Anthony Linebarger (ed.), *The Gospel of Chung Shan According to Paul Linebarger* (Paris, 1932), 8.

99. *Ibid.*, 26, 50, 56.

100. Thus Sherwood Eddy wrote, 'after much bitter experience I came gradually to the conclusion that religion has not only its personal, universal, satisfying and social elements, but that it is a *rational* experience as well'. He decided, 'I must come to terms with modern science... I must rigorously purge from my belief all elements of superstition and of irrationality...' *A Pilgrimage of Ideas*, 81–2.

101. Cantlie and Jones, *Sun*, 180. Of course a few decades earlier the statement would have been quite false.

102. Restarick, *Sun*, 44.

103. Quoted in *ibid.*, 60–1. Eddy had written of the new order that 'by violence or non-violence, *it will surely come*'. See page 78 above. For both Sun and Eddy, violence and bloodshed were to be avoided if possible, but they thought it might not be possible.

104. See the characteristically titled chapter (XXIII) 'Sun and the Bible – the Painted Gods of Blue Valley', in Linebarger, *Sun Yat Sen and the Chinese Republic*, in which Sun's apparently believing and Linebarger's certainly unbelieving kind of Christianity as pertaining to personal conduct is summarized.

105. As reported by his son; Paul Myron Anthony Linebarger, *Political Doctrines of Sun*, 155n. And yet Linebarger *fils* does virtually ignore it, relegating it to a footnote.

106. D'Élia (ed.), *Triple Demism*, Appendix III, 718. This appendix does not appear in the French edition.

107. *Ibid.*

108. In 1906 among an estimated 8,620 Chinese students in Japan, of whom 6,000 were within a mile and a half radius of a point in Tokyo (doubtless the Kanda district), it was reported (with pride?) that there were 'at least twenty Christian men'. Rev. Burton St John, 'The Chinese Students in Japan', *China's Young Men* (vol. 1, no. 1, new series, April 1906), 8–9.

109. Restarick, *Sun*, 159.

110. Leng and Palmer, *Sun and Communism*, 23, write, 'it should be stressed that Sun was deeply rooted in Chinese culture and never advocated wholesale Westernization'. All that need be said is that it is one thing to stress something and quite another to demonstrate it; see n. 81. It is only fair to note that their treatment of their subject, Sun's relation to Communism, is an excellent one.

111. *Wu Chih-hui Hsien-sheng wen-ts'ui* (4 vols in 2; [Shanghai], 1928), I, 171.

112. Chu Ho-chung, 'Ou-chou T'ung-meng-hui chi-shih', in Lo Chia-lun (ed.), *Ke-ming wen-hsien* (2nd ed. Taipei, 1958), II, 117.

113. Cantlie and Jones, *Sun*, 33. On the adjoining page appears a photograph of a group of literati. The caption gently reproves their heathenish slothfulness: 'Not only young men, but middle-aged and quite old men continue their studies in order to gain a higher status in literary circles.'

114. *Ibid.*, 249.

115. Sharman, *Sun*, 317.

116. *Ibid.*, 328, 329, 330, 331-2, 337.

117. *Ibid.*, 342.

118. Dr Henry S. Martin's account as quoted in Sharman, *Sun*, 148.

119. Reference has already been made to Sun's discussions with John Dewey. One should distinguish the formative influences of the modernist Protestants on Sun from such later and casual encounters, which may well have reinforced certain tenets which Sun had long held, but obviously did not provide him with new intellectual foundations.

120. See p. 76.

121. Fleming, 'Open-Minded Christianity', *Asia*, XXIV (June 1924), 472ff.

122. E. R. Hughes, *The Invasion of China by the Western World* (New York, 1938), 98.

4: Syncretism: K'ang Yu-wei, T'an Ssu-t'ung, and Liang Ch'i-ch'ao (1890–1929)

1. 'Sou', as my colleague Professor K. C. Hsiao points out, is the correct form and the way in which Liang himself pronounced it; Matthews's dictionary (No. 5483) gives it correctly. A number of writers err in giving the name as 'Shu'.

2. Der Ling, *Two Years in the Forbidden City*, 175, as quoted in Kung-chuan Hsiao, 'Weng T'ung-ho and the Reform Movement of 1898', *Tsing Hua Journal of Chinese Studies*, new series, I, no. 2 (April 1957), 142. As noted above, the best missionaries did not preach that Christianity required chopping up ancestral tablets, but the overwhelming majority of fundamentalists did.

3. Benjamin Schwartz asserts that Yen Fu was 'the first Chinese literatus who relates himself seriously, rigorously, and in a sustained fashion to modern Western thought', *In Search of Wealth and Power: Yen Fu and the West* (Harvard, 1964), 3. If the early modern period is to be excluded, the statement is cogent; but if the term 'modern' is to include the seventeenth and eighteenth centuries, at least as good a case could be made for so characterizing Hsü Kuang-ch'i and one or two others of that period.

4. Mary Clabaugh Wright, *The Last Stand of Chinese Conservatism: The T'ung Chih Restoration, 1862–1874* (Stanford, 1957), 65-6 and 326-7; Knight Biggerstaff, *The Earliest Modern Government Schools in China* (Ithaca, 1961), 12-15; extracts from Feng's essays are translated in Ssu-yü Teng and John K. Fairbank (eds), *China's Response to the West: A Documentary Survey, 1839–1923* (Harvard, 1954), 51-4.

5. Teng and Fairbank, *China's Response*, 63.

6. *Ibid.*, 137-40.

7. See biography in Arthur W. Hummel (ed.), *Eminent Chinese of the Ch'ing Period* (Washington, 1944), I, 402-5; Yung Wing, *My Life in China and America* (New York, 1909).

8. According to Y. C. Wang in *Chinese Intellectuals and the West, 1872–1949* (Chapel Hill, 1966), 76, the slogan was originated not by Chang but by Sun Chia-nai in his memorial on the establishment of Peking University in 1896. At any rate it became associated in most minds with Chang.

9. *Ibid.*, 64. See also John R. Mott, *The Chinese Student Migration to Tokyo* (New York, 1908) (MP vol. 137. no. 1,764).

10. *Ibid.*, 119-20.

11. See p. 76.

12. Hsiao, 'Weng T'ung-ho and the Reform Movement of 1898', 195, 163; see his concluding paragraph on 198.

13. 'Chronological Autobiography of K'ang Yu-wei', in Jung-pang Lo (ed.), *K'ang Yu-wei: A Biography and a Symposium* (Tucson, 1967), 30.

14. Quoted by Laurence G. Thompson in *Ta T'ung Shu: The One-World Philosophy of K'ang Yu-wei* (London, 1958), 12–13.

15. See p. 62.

16. Kung-ch'üan Hsiao, 'K'ang Yu-wei and Confucianism', *Monumenta Serica*, XVIII (1959), 166–75.

17. See p. 62.

18. *K'ang Nan-hai hsien-sheng mo-chi*, III (no pagination), as quoted in Hsiao, 'The Philosophical Thought of K'ang Yu-wei', *Monumenta Serica*, XXI (1962), 174–5.

19. Carsun Chang, *The Development of Neo-Confucian Thought* (2 vols, New York, 1962), II, 419.

20. Hsiao, 'K'ang Yu-wei and Confucianism', 200.

21. Hsiao, 'K'ang Yu-wei', *Encyclopedia Britannica* (1968), XII, 208.

22. Fung Yu-lan, *A History of Chinese Philosophy* (trans. by Derk Bodde; 2 vols, Princeton, 1953), II, 674. In this passage Fung speaks not of K'ang but of 'the Chinese mind'; but the context deals entirely with K'ang and applies in particular to the work called here *Confucius as a Reformer*.

23. In this period K'ang's efforts in this direction were by no means unique. A certain Ch'en Huan-chang, who wrote a Ph.D. dissertation for Columbia University on 'The Economic Principles of Confucius and His School', wished to apply the organizational principles of the Christian Church to Confucianism, creating a Confucian Church. Timothy Richard wrote a preface to the Chinese edition, *K'ung-chiao lun*, in which he stated: 'Although I belong to the Christian Church, I also am very fond of hearing about the essence of Confucianism. The organization of the states of the world must first be one of division and later one of unity. As for religion, I believe the same will be true' (7th printing; Hong Kong, 1940, p. 3). See W. H. Elwin, 'China as Contemplated from Tokyo', *Church Missionary Review* (March 1914) (MP vol. 5, no. 56), 168.

24. As quoted by Hsiao, 'Weng T'ung-ho and the Reform Movement of 1898', 142. Timothy Richard organized a presentation of a copy of the New Testament to the empress dowager on her birthday in 1894, and the next day the emperor had a copy of the whole Bible purchased for him and studied it diligently. Whether the empress believed that K'ang Yu-wei was behind that gesture or pretended to believe it is impossible to say.

25. (See Ch. 2 for a discussion of Richard's impact on the political and social side of the Hundred Days of 1898 and its background.) The only study I have encountered that opens up the question is Chi-yun Chen, 'Liang Ch'i-ch'ao's "Missionary Education": A Case Study of Missionary Influence on the Reformers', *Papers on China* of the Harvard East Asian Research Center, XVI, 66–125. It is a student paper that could profit from greater clarity and better organization, but it rightly notes the need for 'detailed studies from the Chinese side' of missionary influences that 'have been ignored or even expressly denied...'

26. Quoted *ibid.*, 83–5. Liang repeated the message of the last letter in a second of the same period.

27. *Ibid.*, 79.

28. *Ibid.*, 89–90.

29. Liang, *Intellectual Trends in the Ch'ing Period*, 95.

30. Quoted in Fung Yu-lan, *History of Chinese Philosophy*, II, 675.

31. Chang, *Development of Neo-Confucian Thought*, II, 420.

32. Kung-chuan Hsiao, 'In and Out of Utopia: K'ang Yu-wei's Social Thought', *Chung Chi Journal* (vol. VII, nos 1 & 2, and vol. VIII, no. 1), VII (May 1968), 104.

33. It should not be supposed that at this stage, in which he worked out his distant Utopia, K'ang abandoned thought of the needs of the day. In *Discussions of the Official System* (*Kuan-chih*), finished in 1903, he advanced several proposals for reform, dealing chiefly with the desirability of effective administrative centralization and of instituting a system of new institutions for local self-government at the village (*hsiang*) and district (*hsien*) levels. The province would be abolished. Within each village and district there would be a bureau (*chü*) and assembly (*i-shih hui*), elected by qualified voters. K. C. Hsiao, 'Administrative Modernization', *Tsing Hua Journal of Chinese Studies* (August 1970), 18–19. The whole scheme for democratic institutions on the local level under autocratic central government but intended as a preparation for constitutionalism was remarkably similar to the zemstvo institutions introduced in Russia from 1864, but there seems to be no reason to believe that K'ang knew of the latter or was inspired by them. To be sure, K'ang's proposal was not realized; the zemstvos were.

34. K'ang's enthusiasm for what Laurence G. Thompson calls the 'One World' idea, in choosing that phrase consciously evoking the slogan of Wendell Willkie (*Ta T'ung Shu*, 30–1), seems difficult to explain. Thompson goes so far as to say, 'it appears that to him [K'ang] must go the honour of being the first to plan such a world government' (*ibid.*, 53), and marvels that the first draft of the book (1884–5) antedates the first Hague Conference (1898). He continues, 'Our wonder at this great leap of the imagination must be redoubled, when we think of the environment in which his thinking developed. One could scarcely think of a less likely place than the China of the late nineteenth century for the birth of a scheme for One World.' But perhaps our wonder may be tempered somewhat when faced with a fact no one seems to have mentioned in this connection: Timothy Richard had become a zealous apostle for the idea of 'One World'. In 1897 he wrote a 'Prospectus of a Society for Aiding China to Fall in with Right Principles of Universal Progress', in which he discussed how to end poverty, war, ignorance, and 'devilry' in the world (*Conversion by the Million*, II, Ch. XXIV); in 1899 he sent a circular to all 'leading princes of Christendom...in order to prepare their minds for the coming federation of the world' (*ibid.*, II, Ch. XL); and this theme was very much on his mind at the turn of the century and later (see p. 64). The idea of an international polity was very old in the West, but in the case of K'ang, who read Western books only in translation, one looks for a mediator. K'ang's draft of 1884–5 was called merely *Common Principles of Mankind* (*Jen-lei kung-li*), not *The Great Community*. Since neither it nor any other draft is known to survive, the extent of K'ang's debt to Richard in respect to the idea of world government cannot be determined. Nevertheless, since K'ang told Richard on 17 October 1895, that he believed in the Fatherhood of God and 'the brotherhood of nations as we had taught in our publications' (*Forty-Five Years*, 254) the facts seem to require a more cautious view of K'ang's originality in this respect than Thompson has expressed.

35. Thompson, *Ta T'ung Shu*, 211, and note 5, 228. Thompson seems to forget that he himself has pointed this out, for he elsewhere asserts that 'there is

not the slightest indication that he [K'ang] ever heard of any of the writings of the Western utopians...' (*ibid.*, 55).

36. Hsiao, 'In and Out of Utopia', VII, 130–2.

37. Bodde's note is in Fung, *History of Chinese Philosophy*, II, 690.

38. Hsiao, 'In and Out of Utopia', VII, 131.

39. S. L. Tikhvinskii, *Dvizhenie za reformy v Kitae v kontse XIX veka i Kan Iu-vei* (Moscow, 1959). His faulty interpretations are pointed out in Hsiao, 'In and Out of Utopia', VII, 130.

40. As quoted in Hsiao, 'In and Out of Utopia', VIII (November 1968), 3.

41. *Ibid.*, 5.

42. *Ibid.*

43. See Kung-chuan Hsiao, 'K'ang Yu-wei's Excursion into Science', in Lo (ed.), *K'ang*, 378.

44. Quoted in *ibid.*, 386.

45. See Kung-chuan Hsiao, 'The Philosophical Thought of K'ang Yu-wei', *Monumenta Serica*, XXI (1962), 193.

46. Wang Shu-huai, *Wai-jen yü wu-hsü pien-fa* (Taipei, 1965), 104.

47. Yang I-feng, *T'an Ssu-t'ung* (Taipei, 1959), 13–14.

48. Teng Ssu-yü, 'T'an Ssu-t'ung', in Hummel (ed.), *Eminent Chinese*, 703. See also Nathan M. Talbott, 'Intellectual Origins and Aspects of Political Thought in the *Jen Hsüeh* of T'an Ssu-t'ung, Martyr of the 1898 Reform' (unpublished Ph.D. dissertation, University of Washington, 1956).

49. In an essay on T'an, Liang Ch'i-ch'ao wrote: 'When I first met him, he was extremely attracted to the doctrine of Jesus' mutual love, and he paid no attention to Buddha or Confucius'; but thereafter he encountered K'ang Yu-wei's work and became interested in Confucianism and Buddhism. *T'an Ssu-t'ung ch'üan-chi* (Peking, 1954), 525.

50. *Ibid.*, 8.

51. *Ibid.*, 321.

52. *Ibid.*, 324.

53. *Ibid.*, 334. I owe the identification of the Britisher to Professor Herbert Franke.

54. Wang, *Wai-jen yü wu-hsü pien-fa*, 109.

55. Quoted in *ibid.*, 110.

56. Wing-tsit Chan in *Religious Trends in Modern China* (New York, 1953), 99, declares the Richard–Yang translation, *The Awakening of Faith in the Mahayana Doctrine*, to be a 'very poor one'.

57. Chang Te-chün in 'T'an Ssu-t'ung ssu-hsiang shu-p'ing', *Li-shih Yen-chiu* #3 (1962), 58, discusses T'an's debt to Richard.

58. In 1895 Liang wrote to K'ang of T'an that in his talent, knowledge, and capacity to manage affairs 'no one can compare with him. [The only thing that is] unfortunate is that he is too involved with Western learning, but he would still be a fit choice for the highest leadership.' Cited in Ting Wen-chiang, *Liang Jen-kung hsien-sheng nien-p'u ch'ang-p'ien ch'u-kao* (3 vols, Taipei, 1958), I, 28.

59. Pascal M. D'Élia, SJ, 'Un maître de la jeune Chine: Liang K'i-tch'ao', *T'oung Pao*, ser. 2, XVIII (1917), 252.

60. As quoted in Philip Chung-chih Huang, 'A Confucian Liberal: Liang Ch'i-ch'ao in Action and Thought' (University of Washington dissertation, 1966), 55. A revised version is to be published by the University of Washington Press.

61. Hsiao Kung-ch'üan, 'Liang Ch'i-ch'ao', in Howard L. Boorman (ed.), *BDRC*, II (1968).

62. D'Élia, 'Un maître de la jeune Chine', 253.

63. Hu Shih, *The Chinese Renaissance* (Chicago, 1934), 37.

64. See p. 104.

65. Huang, 'Liang', 31–2.

66. *Ibid.*, 34. See p. 62.

67. *Ibid.*, 42.

68. *Forty-Five Years*, 255.

69. *Ibid.*, 72. Chapters I–XVII were published in the newspaper *The New Citizen (Hsin-min ts'ung-pao)* from February 1902 to April 1903; (the last three chapters were written after his trip to the United States in 1903). *Ibid.*, 115.

70. See p. 94.

71. Quoted in Huang, 'Liang', 126.

72. Robert A. Scalapino and Harold Schiffrin, 'Early Socialist Currents in the Chinese Revolutionary Movement: Sun Yat-sen versus Liang Ch'i-ch'ao', *JAS* XVIII (May 1959), 337–8.

73. Huang, 'Liang', 212.

74. Liang, *Intellectual Trends in the Ch'ing Period*, 103.

75. Quoted in Huang, 'Liang', 213.

76. *Ibid.*, 218.

77. Joseph R. Levenson, *Liang Ch'i-ch'ao and the Mind of Modern China* (Harvard, 1959), 85.

78. Arthur W. Hummel's review in *FEQ*, XIV (November 1954), 112.

79. As quoted in D'Élia, 'Un maître de la jeune Chine', 279.

80. As quoted, *ibid.*, 269.

81. *Ibid.*, 273–4.

82. *Ibid.*, 277.

83. See passages quoted in Léon Wieger SJ, *Chine moderne*, I, *Prodromes* (Hienhien, 1931), 198–9.

84. D'Élia, 'Un maître de la jeune Chine', 293–4.

5: Liberalism: Toward the May fourth incident (1898–1923)

1. 'Pokhorony eks-imperatritsy Lun-iui', *Viestnik Azii*, nos. 16–17 (April–May 1913), 99–100; no. 15 (March 1913), 57–8.

2. Ssu-yü Teng and John K. Fairbank (eds), *China's Response to the West* (Harvard, 1954), 'Postface', 276.

3. Benjamin Schwartz, *In Search of Wealth and Power: Yen Fu and the West* (Cambridge, 1964), 29.

4. As quoted *ibid.*, 43.

5. *Ibid.*, 72–5. Nevertheless, Schwartz plausibly speculates whether 'Yen Fu's unexpected perspective actually illumines some of the anomalous features of the Master's [Spencer's] teachings not obvious to his Western disciples'. *Ibid.*, 80.

6. In 'On Our Salvation' ('Chiu-wang chüeh-lun') (1895), he denounced the examination system and rejected as alternatives Sung Neo-Confucianism, the 'empirical research' school, and K'ang Yu-wei's New Text approach. *Ibid.*, 86.

7. *Ibid.*, 99.

8. *Ibid.*, 212.

9. As quoted *ibid.*, 217.

10. D. Willard Lyon, *Chinese Students in Japan* (Shanghai, 1906) (MP vol. 137, no. 1,765), 7. This item is the only book mentioned by name.

11. John Stewart Burgess, 'What Chinese Students are Reading', *China's Young Men*, VI, no. 1 (January 1911); it was subsequently reprinted in a number of other places. Burgess' suggested list was one of books admired or written by Christian modernists (see Ch. 3), many of which gave the 'underlying social message' of Jesus.

12. John Stewart Burgess, 'Introducing Non-Christian Students to Christianity', *China's Young Men*, XI, nos. 1 and 2 (September 1 and October 1), 1915.

13. See my essay, 'Lu Hsü and Chaadaev: A Comparative Study in Westernization', published in Chinese translation in *Ta-hsüeh Sheng-huo*, vol. V, no. 6 (June 1970); an English version is forthcoming in a much-delayed *Festschrift*.

14. Lin Shu can scarcely be called a translator, since he knew no Western languages. However, he operated successfully by having assistants who did read aloud to him and then writing, in classical Chinese, his understanding of the (mostly) novels he was 'translating'. Dumas, Dickens, Scott, and many other Western novelists were thereby introduced to the Chinese reader. See Leo Ou-fan Lee, 'Lin Shu and His Translations: Western Fiction in Chinese Perspective', *Papers on China* (Harvard East Asian Research Center), XIX (December 1965), 159–93.

15. Hsü Shou-ch'ang, *Wang-yu Lu Hsün yin-hsiang chi* (Shanghai, 1947), 23.

16. Wang Shih-ch'ing, *Lu Hsün chuan* (Shanghai, 1948), 49.

17. 'Wen-hua pien-chih lun,' *Lu Hsün ch'üan-chi*, I, 39–41.

18. 'Mo Lo Shih-li shuo', *ibid.*, I, 55ff.

19. See p. 131.

20. As quoted in Chi-chen Wang's introduction to *Ah Q and Others: Selected Stories of Lusin* [Lu Hsün] (New York, 1941), xiv–xv.

21. C. T. Hsia, *A History of Modern Chinese Fiction, 1917–1957* (New Haven, 1961), 33.

22. Wang, *Ah Q and Others*, xv.

23. I am indebted to Hsiao Kung-ch'üan for the information that there is at least one possible Chinese source for the plot. In the history of the Sung of the Southern Dynasties, in the biography of Yüan Ts'an (420–77), there is a tale of a certain state in which all the inhabitants but the king went mad as a result of drinking water from a certain well. 'Since the people of the country had already gone mad, they called the non-madness of the king madness', and tried by various painful treatments to cure him. In desperation he sneaked off and drank also from the well, and thus harmony was restored in the kingdom (*Sung Shu* in T'ung-wen edition [Shanghai, 1884]; chüan 89, p. 2b). Lu Hsün, who had considerable knowledge of traditional literature, may have read this tale, although I know of no indication that he had it in mind when writing 'The Diary of a Madman'.

24. See O. Brière, 'Un écrivain populaire: Lou Sin', *Bulletin de l'Université l'Aurore*, série III, VII, no. 1 (Shanghai, 1946), 56–7. For example, Wu Yü, in 'Ch'ih jen yü li chiao', *Hsin Ch'ing-nien*, VI, no. 6 (1 November 1919), 578–80, assembles several cases of cannibalism from ancient Chinese history and, after savoring the implications of each one, triumphantly concludes, 'we must understand: the cannibals are those who expound the *li chiao* [the teachings of Confucius]; those who expound the *li chiao* are cannibals!'

25. See William Rudolph Schultz, 'Lu Hsün: The Creative Years' (Ph.D. dissertation, University of Washington, 1955), 203 and 344.

26. *Lu Hsün ch'üan-chi*, VI, 242. The comment was made in a preface written in March 1935 to a literary anthology.

27. Most critics today would not regard the problem as open to serious debate. Vladimir Nabokov in *Nikolai Gogol* (Norfolk, Conn., 1944), 41, writing specifically about the play *The Government Inspector* (*Revizor*), puts the matter thus: 'Even in his worst writings Gogol was always good at creating his reader, which is the privilege of great writers. Thus we have a circle, a closed family-circle, one might say. It does not open into the world. Treating the play as a social satire (the public view) or as a moral one (Gogol's belated amendment), meant missing the point completely.' Much the same thing could be said of the 'The Diary of a Madman' and a good deal of Gogol's other belletristic writing. Despite its merits, J. D. Chinnery's article, 'The Influence of Western Literature on Lu Xun's "Diary of a Madman"', *Bulletin of the School of Oriental African Studies*, XXIII (1960); 309–22, misunderstands Gogol.

28. 'Jen chih li-shih', *Lu Hsün ch'üan-chi*, I, 13–23.

29. *Ibid.*, I, 41.

30. See p. 153.

31. Roswell S. Britton, *The Chinese Periodical Press, 1800–1912* (reprint, Taipei, 1966), 18, 22, 42.

32. D. W. Y. Kwok, *Scientism in Chinese Thought, 1900–1950* (New Haven, 1965), Ch. 3; Benjamin Schwartz, 'Ch'en Tu-hsiu and the Acceptance of the Modern West', *Journal of the History of Ideas*, XII (January 1951), 61–72.

33. There may be some question of the best English rendering of the title of the magazine. At first it was called *Ch'ing-nien Tsa-chih*, which means '*Youth Magazine*'. After several months' suspension, it reappeared on 1 September 1916, under the title *Hsin Ch'ing-nien*, which means '*New Youth*'. From 15 January 1919, the French title *La Jeunesse* was added – not '*New Youth*', but simply '*Youth*'. It seems better to use the English translation of the Chinese name it bore for the whole period of its existence except for the first five months. Chow Tse-tsung, *The May Fourth Movement: Intellectual Revolution in Modern China* (Harvard, 1960), 44, summarizes the facts.

34. Chow, *May Fourth Movement*, 46.

35. Ch'en Tu-hsiu, 'Ching-kao ch'ing-nien', *Hsin Ch'ing-nien*, I, 1 (1915), 6.

36. Ch'en Tu-hsiu, 'Fa-lan-hsi jen yü chin-tai wen-ming', *ibid.*, I, 1 (1915), 1–3.

37. Quoted in Benjamin I. Schwartz, *Chinese Communism and the Rise of Mao* (Harvard, 1952), 15. See vol. 1, pp. 168–9.

38. I am indebted to a study of the contents of a set of *Hsin Ch'ing-nien* running from II, 1 (1916) to VII, 5 (1920) made by Philip Huang.

39. Jerome B. Grieder, *Hu Shih and the Chinese Renaissance: Liberalism in the Chinese Revolution, 1917–1937* (Harvard, 1970), 4; see Vincent Shih, 'A Talk with Hu Shih', *China Quarterly*, no. 10 (April–June 1962); and Kwok, *Scientism*, Ch. 4.

40. Grieder, *Hu Shih*, 18.

41. Y. C. Wang, *Chinese Intellectuals and the West, 1872–1949* (Chapel Hill, 1966), 206.

42. Chow, *May Fourth Movement*, 29–30.

43. Grieder, *Hu Shih*, 79, citing Hu's autobiography.

44. See Ch. 3.

45. Kwok, *Scientism*, 94, well says: 'Hu Shih's equation of the modern scientific method with the Ch'ing scholars' empiricism seems strained.'

46. Grieder discusses Hu's debt to Dewey in *Hu Shih*, 112–21. Grieder argues that Hu owed more to the 'unsophisticated skepticism' of Fan Chen, Ssu-ma Kuang, Spencer, and Huxley than to Dewey's subtler thought. He declares that Dewey in his experimentalism was not revolutionary but sought harmonious ties between past and present; Hu was 'at war with his own past' while Dewey was not. The last point is quite true, but irrelevant to the determination of the influence of Dewey's ideas on Hu, for it deals not with ideas but personal attitudes. This book contains many instances of the transplantation to China of ideas intended instead for the West, with results quite different from those intended by Western thinkers; Hu Shih's (perhaps not always sophisticated) use of Dewey's ideas provides an excellent illustration.

47. *Ibid.*, 175.

48. *Ibid.*, 194–5, 212–13, 232.

49. As Chow points out in *May Fourth Movement*, 221–2. J. Gray, in 'Historical Writing in Twentieth Century China: Notes on its Background and Development', in W. G. Beasley and E. G. Pulleyblank, *Historians of China and Japan* (London, 1961), 204, writes: 'Hu Shih proclaimed his freedom from devotion to either [East or West] and his adherence to a completely pragmatic approach to the problems of China, and incidentally to the study of the past.' But a person devoted to Western pragmatism can scarcely claim 'freedom from devotion' to the West.

50. Chow, *May Fourth Movement*, 55. Chow points to the influence of the example of a number of Japanese journals appearing from 1904 and bearing similar names.

51. *Ibid.*, 59.

52. *Ibid.*, 60.

53. Chow identifies two writers as having great influence on Lo Chia-lun at that period: Walter E. Weyl, author of *The New Democracy* (1912), and Stephen B. Leacock, who wrote *Elements of Political Science* (1906). *Ibid.*, 61.

54. Maurice Meisner, *Li Ta-chao and the Origins of Chinese Marxism* (Harvard, 1967), 74. On 1 May 1919, Li published in *New Youth* an article entitled, 'My View of Marxism'. Meisner has translated the title, 'My Marxist Views', in a somewhat misleading manner.

55. Kwok declares that scientism, 'in general, assumes that all aspects of the universe are knowable through the methods of science. Proponents of the scientific outlook in China were not always scientists or even philosophers of science. They were intellectuals interested in using science, and the values and assumptions to which it had given rise, to discredit and eventually to replace the traditional body of values. Scientism can thus be considered as the tendency to use the respectability of science in areas having little bearing on science itself.' *Scientism*, 3. A sharper definition might read: scientism is the attempt to use the supposed methods of natural science in areas outside of natural science.

56. Chow, *May Fourth Movement*, 201.

57. John Dewey and Alice Chipman Dewey, *Letters from China and Japan* (Evelyn Dewey [ed.], New York, 1920), 209 and 247. Two letters of John Dewey's are quoted, both from Peking, one from 1 June and the other from 20 June.

58. As quoted in Chow, *May Fourth Movement*, 228–30.

59. Quoted *ibid.*, 234.

60. Bertrand Russell, *The Problem of China* (New York, 1922), 260.

61. *Ibid.*, 235.

62. *Ibid.*, 4 and 233–4. Russell apparently could find no good words to say of Confucianism, but he did praise what he conceived to be the Taoist teachings of 'production without possession, action without self-assertion, development without domination'. *Ibid.*, 235.

63. *Ibid.*, 194.

64. See Chow, *May Fourth Movement*, 234.

65. Like many other periodicals of this era, it bore a second title in a Western language; in this case the title was *La Rekonstruo*, which is Esperanto. Other second titles were, as noted above, in French, English, and other languages.

66. Chow Tse-tsung plausibly points out the similarity of such views with those of the Russian Legal Marxists of the 1890's.

67. Chow, *May Fourth Movement*, 241. Grieder in *Hu Shih*, 190, terms the May 1922 statement the 'first systematic summary of opinions that can be identified as "liberal"...' Plainly he has in mind political liberalism.

68. E. R. Hughes, *The Invasion of China by the Western World* (New York, 1938), 185.

69. Chow, *May Fourth Movement*, 359.

70. Chiang Monlin, *Tides from the West* (reprint, Taipei, 1947), 139–40.

71. *Ibid.*, 243.

72. *Ibid.*, 272.

73. Personal letter to the author, 26 August 1962. Lord Russell courteously requested me in a subsequent letter to quote all that he said if I quoted at all, and I am glad to do so:

'China today has abandoned the atmosphere of quiet rationalism characteristic of the eighteenth century which I found present during my stay. The values then in evidence are no longer so. I believe that the West bears considerable responsibility for this development. The extraordinary poverty and misery have brought a regime impatient of traditional Chinese humanism. The current regime draws upon impulses which have long existed in potential in Chinese culture – impulses which reflect long-suffering, inordinate willingness to endure hardship and capacity for intense dedication. The extremity of the regime is also a reflection of the hostility it experiences from outside its borders.

I feel that a significant element in the nationalism evident in the behaviour of the regime at the moment is a consequence of the indignity experienced by China as a weak state, parcelled out for exploitation by various imperialist interests. The developed sense of personal liberty among the cultured has succumbed to the more compelling fact of mass misery.

I do not believe that "Bolshevism" has overcome the values which I once thought to represent obstacles to so doctrinaire a regime. It is more a nationalist and centralised Chinese regime, providing an external rationale for innate conditions: pride in national strength and rebuff to those powers who once treated China with the contempt shown the weak by the strong. The attraction of Marxist–Leninist ideas among Chinese youth combines the appeal of a theory of emancipation from such indignity, the obvious call to industrialisation as an answer to economic hardship, and the emotional buttress of a quasi-religious and hysterical metaphysics.

This development could have been infinitely softer and more liberating in its effects had men of power been less greedy and more conscious of the consequences of their behaviour. The attitude of the West has reinforced all the authoritarian impulses available in the Chinese Communist Government.

I am afraid I lost contact with Dr Hu Shih. I do not envy him the dilemma of his choice. China was a great and rewarding experience for me. I retain my affection and admiration for the Chinese people. I am sorry that Chinese rationalism is engulfed in the processes of industrialisation and the surge of national pride.'

There follows the sentence quoted in the text, which is the last in the letter.

6: Socialism: anarchism (1907–1922) and Marxism–Leninism (1920–1949)

1. Robert A. Scalapino and George T. Yu, *The Chinese Anarchist Movement* (Berkeley, 1961), 1.
2. *Ibid.*, 69.
3. Michael Gasster, *Chinese Intellectuals and the Revolution of 1911* (Seattle, 1969), Ch. 5, esp. 163–4.
4. Quoted in D. W. Y. Kwok, *Scientism in Chinese Thought, 1900–1950* (New Haven, 1965), 48.
5. Quoted in *ibid.*, 37.
6. Quoted in *ibid.*, 41–2.
7. See Ch. 5.
8. Scalapino and Yu, *Chinese Anarchist Movement*, 30–1.
9. *Ibid.*, 57; the summary is derived from the collection of the Ch'en-Ou exchanges published as *She-hui-chu-i t'ao-lun chi* (Canton, 1922).
10. However, many Chinese anarchists called themselves Communists (for example, the Society of Anarchist Communist Comrades formed in Canton in 1914), as they did elsewhere; Mao Tse-tung was probably influenced for a time by anarchism; and Ch'ü Ch'iu-pai was an anarchist before he became a Communist.
11. It appeared in *Hsin Ch'ing-nien* on 1 February 1920, and in *The Chinese Recorder* in July 1920; it is discussed in Chow Tse-tsung, *The May Fourth Movement* (Harvard, 1960), 321.
12. Quoted by C. S. Chang, 'The Anti-Religious Movement', *Chinese Recorder*, LV, no. 8 (August 1923), 462ff.
13. Tatsuro and Sumiko Yamamoto, 'The Anti-Christian Movement in China, 1922–1927', *Far Eastern Quarterly*, XII (February 1953), 133–47.
14. Chang, 'The Anti-Religious Movement'.
15. Rev. Henry S. Leiper, 'Steering Student Strikers in China', *Missionary Herald* (December 1919) (MP vol. 144, no. 1,836), 494.
16. T'ang Leang-li, *China in Revolt* (London, 1927), 153.
17. Kidd (1858–1916) was an English writer whose books included *Social Evolution* (1894) and *The Principles of Western Civilization* (1902).
18. Maurice Meisner, *Li Ta-chao and the Origins of Chinese Marxism* (Harvard, 1967), 52–3.
19. *Ibid.*, 115–16.
20. *Ibid.*, xiii.
21. *Ibid.*, 21, 26; Benjamin I. Schwartz, *Chinese Communism and the Rise of*

Mao (Harvard, 1952), 10–11; Young-tsu Wong, 'Formation of a Marxist: A Study in the Intellectual Development of Li Ta-chao, 1913–1920', unpublished paper, Seattle, 1967.

22. Quoted in Meisner, *Li Ta-chao*, 184.

23. Chow, *May Fourth Movement*, 243–4.

24. *Ibid.*, 248–9.

25. Meisner, *Li*, 168–74, 237–40; 'Li Ta-chao', in Howard L. Boorman (ed.), *BDRC*, II, 329–33.

26. 'Ch'en Tu-hsiu', in *BDRC*, I, 240–8.

27. William Ayers, 'The Society for Literary Studies, 1921–1930', *Harvard Papers on China*, no. 7 (February 1953); P. Henri van Boven CICM, *Histoire de la littérature chinoise moderne* (Tientsin, 1946), 39ff.; Amitendranath Tagore, *Literary Debates in Modern China, 1918–1937* (Tokyo, 1967), 48–52; Chow, *May Fourth Movement*, 283–4.

28. Quoted in Ayers, 'Society for Literary Studies', 54.

29. Quoted in van Boven, *Histoire*, 41.

30. Ayers, 'Society for Literary Studies', 59.

31. Tagore, *Literary Debates*, 59–64; Chow, *May Fourth Movement*, 287.

32. David Tod Roy, *Kuo Mo-jo: The Early Years* (Harvard, 1971), 9.

33. Tagore, *Literary Debates*, 70.

34. Van Boven, *Histoire*, Ch. 14.

35. 'Chou Shu-jen', *BDRC*, I, 1967.

36. Despite the fact that he was in Japan from 1928 to 1937, taking part in Chinese literary debates by mail, until Chiang K'ai-shek allowed him to return to China. 'Kuo Mo-jo', *BDRC*, II, 271–6.

37. Tagore, *Literary Debates*, 145ff. For an account remarkable for its combination of warm sympathy for the person and detachment from the leftist dogmatics he espoused, see Tsi-an Hsia's essay on Ch'ü Ch'iu-pai (which he spells in the variant 'Ch'ü Ch'iu-po') in *The Gate of Darkness* (Seattle, 1968). His two essays on Lu Hsün are also notable for the same features.

38. 'Hu Feng', *BDRC*, II, 158.

39. See Kwok, *Scientism*, 137–8. Chun-jo Liu, *Controversies in Modern Chinese Intellectual History: An Analytic Bibliography of Periodical Articles, Mainly of the May Fourth and Post-May Fourth Era* (Harvard, 1964), gives bibliographies of the debates on 'science and metaphysics' (131–7), Eastern and Western civilizations (138–43), and Chinese social history (146–59).

40. Summarized in Harry J. Lamley, 'Liang Shu-ming: The Thought and Action of a Reformer' (unpublished MA thesis, University of Washington, 1960), 100–4. See also 'Liang Shu-ming', *BDRC*, II. See n. 1 to Chapter IV on the spelling of the name.

41. Quoted in Kwok, *Scientism*, 140.

42. As quoted *ibid.*, 141. Kwok rather unfairly declares that by the statement quoted Chang 'revealed himself as unwilling to accept either the social implications of science for the modern age or the changes in Western thinking modern science has fostered'. In general Kwok, a critic of 'scientism' and therefore by no means biased against Chang, is admirably fair to the persons of varying viewpoints whom he studies.

43. See pp. 101–2.

44. Quoted in Kwok, *Scientism*, 155–7.

45. *Ibid.*, 159–60. Bernard Le Bovier de Fontenelle's *Digression sur les anciens et les modernes* was published in 1688.

46. Arthur W. Hummel (trans.), *The Autobiography of a Chinese Historian* (reprint, Taipei, 1966), which is the autobiographical preface Ku Chieh-kang wrote for the 1926 collection, traces in an interesting way the development of the critical spirit in one modern Chinese scholar.

47. Benjamin Schwartz, 'A Marxist Controversy on China', *FEQ*, XIII (February 1954), 143–53; I am indebted to Mr Wong Young-tsu for preparing a calendar of the chief contributions to the debate.

48. Schwartz goes to some pains to show that this, the Stalinist view, could not be clearly reconciled with *Das Kapital*. He does not, by the way, mention Kuo in his article.

49. 'Kuo-min-tang fan-tung cheng-fu ch'a-ching p'u-lo wen-i mi-ling', *Chung-kuo hsien-tai ch'u-pan shih-liao* (Shanghai, 1955), II, 171–2. Many leftist works were indeed prohibited; in 1936, for example, 676 social-scientific publications were banned – though not necessarily with complete effectiveness; *ibid.*, 205.

50. John Israel, *Student Nationalism in China, 1927–1937* (Stanford, 1966), 39.

51. Kwok, *Scientism*, 161.

52. Mary C. Wright, 'From Revolution to Restoration: The Transformation of Kuomintang Ideology', *FEQ*, XIV (August, 1955), 515–32 (518).

53. Quoted in O. Brière, SJ, *Fifty Years of Chinese Philosophy, 1898–1948* (trans., New York, 1965), 36.

54. Israel, *Student Nationalism*, 96.

55. Brière, *Fifty Years*, 36–7, 60–3.

56. Chiang K'ai-shek, *China's Destiny* (trans., New York, 1947), 78.

57. Wright, 'From Revolution to Restoration', 530.

58. Israel, *Student Nationalism*, 46.

59. Quoted in *ibid.*, 102.

60. *Ibid.*, 189.

61. 'Li Ta', *Who's Who in Communist China* (Hong Kong, 1969), 1.

62. Little is known of his early years. See 'Ai Ssu-ch'i', *BDRC*, I, and Ai Szu-ch'i [sic]', in Donald W. Klein and Anne B. Clark (eds), *Biographic Dictionary of Chinese Communism* (Harvard, 1971), I.

63. Stuart R. Schram, *The Political Thought of Mao Tse-tung* (rev. ed.; New York, 1969), and *Mao Tse-tung* (New York, 1966) contain some of the most recent scholarship. Much work remains to be done on the problems of Mao's ideology, as Schram makes quite clear.

64. Schram, *Political Thought of Mao*, 43.

65. *Ibid.*, 50.

66. No attempt will be made here to disentangle the polemics that have engulfed this document and the whole issue of Mao and the peasantry. See the exchanges between Karl A. Wittfogel and Benjamin Schwartz in *The China Quarterly* (1960), nos. 1, 2, and 4.

67. Schram, *Mao Tse-tung*, 174. The leading elements of the Red Army reached Shensi in the fall of 1935.

68. Professor Schwartz in his comments in the *China Quarterly* debate plausibly urges that the term 'Maoism' no more necessarily implies originality on Mao's part than the term 'Stalinism' implies originality on Stalin's. This point deserves consideration; so does contemporary Communist Chinese usage, however.

69. For evidence that the published texts do not in fact date from 1937, see Arthur A. Cohen, *The Communism of Mao Tse-tung* (Chicago, 1964), 22–8.

70. Some of the problems in using the various editions of Mao's writings are discussed in the bibliography to Schram's *Political Thought of Mao* and in the footnotes of Cohen, *Communism of Mao*.

71. For example: 'as everybody knows, war and peace transform themselves into each other. War is transformed into peace: for example, the First World War was transformed into the post-war peace...'

72. See Cohen, *Communism of Mao*, 26.

73. Jerome Ch'en, *Mao and the Chinese Revolution* (London, 1965), 188–9; Mao's assumption of leadership dates from the Tsunyi Conference conducted during the Long March.

74. Boyd Compton (trans. and ed.), *Mao's China: Party Reform Documents, 1942–44* (reprint, Seattle, 1966), xlii, xliii.

75. Cohen, *Communism of Mao*, 82–97.

76. Wing-tsit Chan (comp.), *A Source Book in Chinese Philosophy* (Princeton, 1963), 754.

77. Quoted in Roy, *Kuo Mo-jo*, 166–7.

7: The West and the Chinese tradition

1. In the epilogue to his book *La Chine à travers les âges*, as quoted in André Duboscq, 'Le chaos chinois', *La Revue universelle* (n.d.) (MP vol. 53, no. 708), 91.

2. A recent interesting attempt to deal with the whole West–China confrontation, not exclusively or mainly in the cultural realm, by way of a set of deftly composed biographical vignettes, is Jonathan Spence, *To Change China: Western Advisers in China, 1620–1960* (Boston, 1969).

3. In Yugoslavia, especially, toleration has developed that exceeds such limits, though within the ranks of even Yugoslav Communists vigilance is still emphasized.

4. Robert N. Bellah (ed.), *Religion and Progress in Modern Asia* (New York, 1965), 224.

5. An attempt to study the extent of survival of 'religion' – chiefly Christianity, but also briefly Confucianism, Buddhism, and Taoism – is Richard C. Bush Jr, *Religion in Communist China* (Nashville, Tenn., 1970).

Conclusion: The West in Russia and China

1. As quoted in Eric Voegelin, *Science, Politics and Gnosticism* (Chicago, 1968), 35.

2. Voegelin, *The New Science of Politics* (1952; reprint, Chicago, 1966), 175.

3. Voegelin, *Science, Politics and Gnosticism*, 21.

4. Voegelin, *The New Science of Politics*, 107.

5. See Introduction.

6. Voegelin, *Science, Politics and Gnosticism*, 9.

7. *Ibid.*, 88–99.

8. *Ibid.*, 109.

9. Voegelin, *The New Science of Politics*, 164.

10. The term 'humanism' may not be thought ideal to cover the varieties of Roman Catholic influence described in Russia and China; it may have special applicability to the Jesuits in China and to some of the fifteenth- and sixteenth-century influences traced in Russia, though the seventeenth-century influence in

Russia might be better described by using the term 'scholasticism' (which of course appeared first within the undivided, pre-Reformation Roman Catholic Church, not in Protestant churches). The main point is that there were never strong competing influences within Roman Catholicism at work in either Russian or Chinese thought, and thus a single term seems indicated – in contrast to the case of Protestantism, which gave rise to three quite different, often actively opposed tendencies in our story.

11. See Billington, *The Icon and the Axe*, esp. 550–89.

12. See p. 131 and vol. 1, p. 235.

13. See Introduction.

14. A slightly different list is given by Carl J. Friedrich and Zbigniew K. Brzezinski in *Totalitarian Dictatorship and Autocracy* (2nd ed., Harvard, 1965), 21–2.

15. I myself heard him say this, though I have been unable to find it in any of his works.

16. A striking instance is the remark Leon Trotsky made about Ramon Mercader: though 'rather light-minded...nevertheless, he can be won closer. In order to build the party we must have confidence that people can be changed.' (Quoted in Isaac Don Levine, *The Mind of an Assassin* (New York, 1959), 104.) Mercader proceeded to assassinate Trotsky.

17. Origenes, *Contra Celsum*, Book 8, Ch. 72, translation by W. H. Cairns in *Ante-Nicene Christian Library*, XXIII (1910).

18. Voegelin, *Science, Politics and Gnosticism*, 22–3.

19. Lippmann, *A Preface to Politics* (New York, 1913), 105.

ADDITIONAL BIBLIOGRAPHY

Arkush, R. David. 'Ku Hung-ming (1857–1928)'. *Harvard Papers on China*, XIX (December 1965), 194–238.

Barker, J. Ellis. 'Doctor Sun Yat-Sen and the Chinese Revolution'. *Fortnightly Review*, XCVI (old series) (1 November 1911), 778–92.

Barnett, Suzanne Wilson. 'Wei-Yüan and Westerners: Notes on the Sources of the *Hai-kuo t'u-chih'*. *Ch'ing-shih wen-ti* (New Haven and St Louis), II, no. 4 (November 1970), 1–20.

Baudet, Henri. *Paradise on Earth: Some Thoughts on European Images of Non-European Man*. Trans. New Haven, 1965.

Bennett, Adrian Arthur. *John Fryer: The Introduction of Western Science and Technology into Nineteenth-Century China*. Harvard, 1967.

Benz, Ernst. 'On Understanding Non-Christian Religions', in Mircea Eliade and Joseph M. Kitagawa (eds), *The History of Religions: Essays in Methodology*. Chicago, 1959.

Bryant, Albert H. 'Liang Sou-ming: His Response to the West'. *Harvard Papers on China*, (February 1953), 1–33.

Buck, Pearl S. 'Is There a Case for Foreign Missions?' *Harper's*, CLXVI, (January 1933), 143–55.

Bykov, F. S. *Zarozhdenie obshchestvenno-politicheskoi i filosofskoi mysli v Kitae*. Moscow, 1966.

Cameron, Meribeth E. *The Reform Movement in China, 1898–1912*. New York, reprint, 1963.

Chambre, Henri, SJ. *From Karl Marx to Mao Tse-tung*. Trans. by Robert J. Olsen. New York, 1963.

Chan Wing-tsit. 'Trends in Contemporary Philosophy', in Harley Farnsworth McNair (ed.) *China*. Berkeley, 1946.

Chang Ching-lu (ed.). *Chung-kuo hsien-tai ch'u-pan shih-liao*. Vol. 2, Shanghai, 1955.

Chung-kuo hsien-tai ch'u-pan shih-liao pu-p'ien. Shanghai, 1957.

Chang Te-chün. 'T'an Ssu-t'ung ssu-hsiang shu-p'ing'. *Li-shih yen-chiu*, no. 3 (1962), 27–60.

Chao, T. C. 'The Future of the Church in Social and Economic Thought and Action'. *Chinese Recorder*, LXIX (July–August 1938), 345–54 and (September 1938), 437–47.

Ch'en Hsü-ching. *Chung-kuo wen-hua ti ch'u-lu*. n.p., 1934.

Chen, Stephen and Robert Payne. *Sun Yat-sen: A Portrait*. New York, 1946.

Chien Yu-wen. *T'ai-p'ing T'ien-kuo tien-chih t'ung-k'ao*. 3 vols, Hong Kong, 1958.

China Mission Year Book. Shanghai. First issue, 1910–ninth issue, 1918.

Ch'üan Tseng-ku. 'Shih-nien-lai ti Chung-kuo che-hsüeh chieh', in Ch'en Li-fu (ed.), *Shih-nien-lai ti Chung-kuo*. Shanghai, 1937.

Chung-kuo hsien-tai wen-hsüeh shih ts'an-k'ao tzu-liao. Vol. I, Peking, 1959.

Chung-kuo hsien-tai wen-i tzu-liao ts'ung-k'an. Vol. I, Shanghai, 1962.

'Chung-kuo she-hui k'e-hsüeh-chia lien-meng kang-liang' (1930), reprinted in *Chung-kuo hsien-tai ch'u-pan shih-liao*. Vol. 2, Peking, 1955.

Cronin, Vincent. *The Wise Man From the West*. New York, 1955.

Cumming, C. F. Gordon. *Wanderings in China*. 2 vols, Edinburgh and London, 1886.

Curzon, George N. *Problems of the Far East*. 3rd ed., London, 1894.

Danton, George H. *The Culture Contacts of the United States and China: The Earliest Sino-American Culture Contacts, 1784–1844*. New York, 1931.

Dennett, Tyler. *Americans in Eastern Asia*. New York, 1922.

Dewey, John. *Impressions of Soviet Russia and the Revolutionary World: Mexico–China–Turkey*. New York, 1932.

'New Culture in China'. *Asia*, XXI (July 1921), 581–6, 642.

Drake, Fred W. 'A Nineteenth-Century View of the United States of America from Hsü Chi-yü's *Ying-huan chih-lüeh*'. *Harvard Papers on China*, XIX (December 1965), 30–54.

Fairbank, John King. *Trade and Diplomacy on the China Coast: The Opening of the Treaty Ports, 1842–1854*. 2 vols., Harvard, 1953.

Fang Hao. 'Ming-mo Ch'ing-chu t'ien-chu-chiao pi-fu ju-chia hsüeh-shuo chih yen-chiu'. *Wen-shih che-hsüeh pao*, no. 11 (September 1962), 147–202.

Feng Hsüeh-feng. 'Lu Hsün: His Life and Thought'. *Chinese Literature* (Peking), no. 2 (Spring 1952).

Fitzgerald, C. P. *China: A Short Cultural History*. 3rd ed., New York, 1961.

Foster, John, DD 'The Christian Origins of the Taiping Rebellion'. *International Review of Missions*, XL (April 1951), 156–67.

Franke, Wolfgang. *China and the West*. Trans. R. A. Wilson. Oxford, 1967.

Frenz, Horst (ed.). *Asia and the Humanities*. Bloomington, 1959.

Fung Yu-lan. *The Spirit of Chinese Philosophy*. Trans. E. R. Hughes. Boston, 1962.

Furth, Charlotte. *Ting Wen-chiang: Science and China's New Culture*. Harvard, 1970.

Giles, Herbert A. *Freemasonry in China*. Amoy, 1880.

Gregory, J. S. 'British Missionary Reaction to the Taiping Movement in China'. *Journal of Religious History*. Vol. 2, no. 3 (June 1963), 204–18.

Hodous, Lewis. 'A Precursor of the Modern Renaissance in China'. *Chinese Recorder*, LVIII (July 1927), 422–5.

Holcombe, Arthur N. *The Chinese Revolution: A Phase in the Regeneration of a World Power*. Harvard, 1930.

Hsia, T. A. 'Ch'ü Ch'iu-pai's Autobiographical Writings: The Making and Destruction of a "Tender-hearted" Communist'. *China Quarterly* no. 25 (January–March 1966), 176–212.

Hsiao Kung-chuan. 'Legalism and Autocracy in Traditional China'. *Tsing Hua Journal of Chinese Studies*, new series IV, no. 2 (February 1964), 108–21.

Hu Shih. 'China and Christianity'. *The Forum*, LXXVIII (July 1927), 1–2.

Huang Sung-k'ang. *Lu Hsün and the New Culture Movement of Modern China*. Djambatan/Amsterdam, 1957.

Kiang Wen-han. *The Chinese Student Movement*. New York, 1948.

Kotenev, Anatol M. *New Lamps for Old: An Interpretation of Events in Modern China and Whither They Lead*. Shanghai, 1931.

Kuo Chan-po. *Chin wu-shih nien Chung-kuo ssu-hsiang shih*. 2nd printing, Peiping, 1935.

Last, Jef. *Lu Hsün – Dichter und Idol: Ein Beitrag zur Geistesgeschichte des neuen China*. Frankfurt, 1959.

Li Ao. *Sun I-hsien ho Chung-kuo hsi-hua i-hsüeh*. Hong Kong, 1968.

Michie, Alexander. *China and Christianity*. Tientsin, 1892.

Moule, A. C. 'The Primitive Failure of Christianity in China'. *International Review of Missions*, XX (July 1931), 456–9.

Levenson, Joseph R. *Confucian China and its Modern Fate: The Problem of Intellectual Continuity*. Berkeley, 1958.

Lund, Renville Clifton. 'The Imperial University of Peking'. Unpublished Ph.D. dissertation, University of Washington, 1956.

Lyon, David Willard. 'The Past Decade in Chinese Literature'. *Journal of the North China Branch of the Royal Asiatic Society*, LXV (1934), 62–72.

Papers Relating to the Rebellion in China and the Trade in the Yang-tze-kiang River. Presented to the House of Lords by Command of Her Majesty, 1862. No. 4. Mr Bruce, 6 April 1861.

Pickering, W. A. 'Chinese Secret Societies and Their Origin'. *Journal of the Straits Branch of the Royal Asiatic Society* (Singapore), no. 1 (July 1878), 63–84, and no. 3 (July 1879), 1–18.

Price, Maurice T. *Christian Missions and Oriental Civilizations: A Study in Culture Contact*. Shanghai, 1924.

Reichwein, Adolf. *China and Europe: Intellectual and Artistic Contacts in the Eighteenth Century*. Trans. J. C. Powell. London, 1925.

Reinsch, Paul S. *Intellectual and Political Currents in the Far East*. Boston, 1911.

Rowbotham, Arnold H. 'Oriental–Western Cultural Relations in a Changing World', in *Indiana University Conference on Oriental–Western Literary Relations; Papers edited by Horst Frenz and G. L. Anderson*. Chapel Hill, 1955.

Scalapino, Robert A. 'Prelude to Marxism: The Chinese Student Movement in Japan, 1900–1910', in Albert Feuerwerker, Rhoads Murphey, and Mary C. Wright (eds), *Approaches to Modern Chinese History*. Berkeley, 1967.

Schiffrin, Harold. 'Sun Yat-sen's Early Land Policy'. *Journal of Asian Studies*, XVI (August 1957), 549–64.

Senin, N. G. *Obshchestvenno-politicheskie i filosofskie vzgliady Sun' Iat-sena*. Moscow, 1956.

Shen, Nelson Nai-cheng. 'The Changing Chinese Social Mind (From 1911 to 1922)'. *Chinese Social and Political Science Review*, VIII, no. 1 (January 1924), 68–87, and no. 2 (April 1924), 125–66.

'Shih-an [Ch'en Tu-hsiu's *hao*] tzu-chuan. Ch'en Tu-hsiu yüan-chu'. *Chuan-chi wen-hsüeh*, vol. 5, no. 3 (September 1964).

Shih Tsün (ed.). *Chung-kuo chin-tai ssu-hsiang shih ts'an-k'ao tzu-liao chien-pien*. Peking, 1957.

Shu Hsin-ch'eng. *Chin-tai Chung-kuo liu-hsüeh shih*. Shanghai, 1933.

So Kwan-wai. 'Western Influence and the Chinese Reform Movement of 1898'. Unpublished University of Wisconsin Ph.D. dissertation, 1950.

Spence, Jonathan D. *Ts'ao Yin and the K'ang-hsi Emperor, Bondservant and Master*. New Haven, 1966.

Su Hsüeh-lin. 'P'i-p'a pao-yü chih cheng-shen che – Lu Hsün'. *Wu-ssu yün-tung lun-tsung*. Taipei, 1961.

Sun Ju-ling (ed.). *San-shih nien wen-i lun-ts'ung*. Taipei, 1966.

T'ao-yüan wen-lu wai-p'ien. Hongkong, 1883.

Teng Ssu-yü. *Historiography of the Taiping Rebellion*. Harvard, 1962.

Tsien Tsuen-hsuin. 'Western Impact on China Through Translation'. *Far Eastern Quarterly*, XIII (May 1954), 305–27.

Tu-shu tsa-chih. Four symposia on the debate on Chinese social history appear in vol. I, nos. 4–5, vol. II, nos. 2–3 and 7–8, and vol. III, nos. 3–4, April 1932 to April 1933.

Vargas, Ph. de. 'Some Elements in the Chinese Renaissance'. *New China Review* (Shanghai), IV, no. 2 (April 1922), 115–27, and no. 3 (June 1922), 234–47.

Viestnik Azii. Kharbin. No. 1, July 1909–no. 51, 1923 (no. 52/3 (1925), missing from run used).

Volokhova, A. A. *Inostrannye missionery v Kitae (1901–1920 gg.)*. Moscow, 1969.

Wang, Tsi C. *The Youth Movement in China*. New York, 1927.

Weber, Max. *The Religion of China: Confucianism and Taoism*. Trans. and ed. Hans H. Gerth. Glencoe, Ill., 1951.

Wilhelm, Hellmut. 'Chinese Confucianism on the Eve of the Great Encounter'. Ch. VIII in Marius B. Jansen (ed.), *Changing Japanese Attitudes Toward Modernization*. Princeton, 1965.

Wilhelm, Richard. *The Soul of China*. Text trans. John Holroyd Reece, the poems by Arthur Waley. New York, 1928.

Wong Young-tsu. 'Formation of a Marxist: A Study in the Intellectual Development of Li Ta-chao, 1913–1920'. Unpublished paper (1967).

Wong Young-tsu. 'Remolders of Tradition: Reformist Thought in Nineteenth Century China'. Unpublished Ph.D. dissertation, University of Washington, 1971.

Wood, Alan. *Bertrand Russell: The Passionate Skeptic*. London, 1957.

Yang T'ing-fu. *T'an Ssu-t'ung nien-p'u*. Peking, 1957.

INDEX

Ai Ssu-ch'i, 159, 162
Aleni, Giulio, 17, 29, 203
Alexander VII, pope, 18, 22
Alexander I of Russia, 182
Alexis Petrovich, 179, 185
Allen, Young J., 62, 81, 101, 103, 105, 106
American missions in China, 38, 71
Anabaptists, 53
Anarchism, 142, 143–5, 148, 152
Andreev, Leonid, 128, 150, 152
Andrew of Longjumeau, 3
Andrew of Perugia, 4
Anna, empress, 18
anti-religious movement, 145–7
Aristaeus of Proconnesus, 1
Arrington, L. J., 210
Artsybashev, M. P., 150
Asiatic mode of production, idea of, 155
Auden, W. H., quoted, 111
Augustine, St, 15, 54, 177
Augustinians, 22
Aurora University, 74
Ayers, William, 232

Bakunin, Michael, 143, 183
Baptists, 37, 57, 58, 60, 61
Barbusse, Henri, 146
Barrow, John, 205
Barth, Karl, 214
Batu, khan, 4
Beasley, W. G., 229
Beaumont, Olivier de, 204
Bellah, Robert N., quoted, 171; 234
Bellarmine, Robert Cardinal, 6, 16
Benedict XII, pope, 4
Benedict XIV, pope, 25
Benedict XV, pope, 75
Benevente, Alvaro, 22
Benoît, Michel, 28
Berdiaev, Nicholas, quoted, 176
Bergson, Henri, 111, 148, 153, 157
Bernard, Henri, quoted, 32; 199, 201, 204
Bettinelli, Giuseppe, 202
Bettray, Johannes, 199
Bible, 36–7, 57, 61, 73, 81, 93, 96; trans-

lations of into Chinese, 39, 40, 206; use
of by T'ai-p'ings, 48, 49, 51, 54–5
Biggerstaff, Knight, 222
Billington, James H., ix; 235
Biondo, Flavio, 177
Blanc, Louis, 136
Blodget, H., 206, 207
Bluntschli, J. K., 119, 121
Boardman, Eugene P., quoted, 50, 53;
207, 209, 210
Bodde, Derk, quoted, 108
Bogdanov (A. A. Malinovsky), 152
Bondfield, G. H., 206
Boone, William J., 206
Boorman, Howard L., 226, 232
Bornhak, Konrad, 119, 121
Borodin, Michael, 84, 86, 185
Bosmans, H., 202
Bouglé, Célestin, 146
Bouvet, Joachim, 28
Boven, Henri van, 232
Boxer, C. R., 199
Boxer Rebellion and resultant indemnity,
57, 63, 67, 95, 101, 102, 126, 134
Boym, Michel, 18
Bridgman, Elijah, 40, 48
Brière, O., quoted, 157; 227, 233
British missions in China, 38, 69
Britton, Roswell S., 212, 228
Brodrick, James, 199
Broomhall, Marshall, quoted, 23, 58; 202,
206, 211
Brown, Arthur J., 212
Bryan, William Jennings, 73
Brzezinski, Zbigniew K., 235
Buddhism, xv–xvii, xviii, xx, xxi, 5, 9, 11,
12, 31, 33, 49, 60, 61, 79, 165, 192, 204;
Kang Yu-wei and, 103, 104, 107, 108,
111; T'an Ssu-t'ung and, 112–4;
Liang Ch'i-ch'ao and, 121; Hu Shih
rejects, 133
Buglio, Ludovico, 19
Bulgakov, Sergei, 187
Burdon, Bishop, 207
Burgess, John Stewart, 77, 127–8; 227

Burgess, John W., 87; 219
Busch, Heinrich, 200, 204
Bush, Richard C., Jr, 234
Bushnell, Horace, 72
Butler, Joseph, 43, 207
Byron, George Gordon, Baron 129
Byzantium, relations with China of, *see* Rome

Cabet, Étienne, 108
Calendar, Bureau of the, 15, 17, 18, 27
Campbell, R. J., 72
Cantlie, James, 81, 89, 90, 92, 94, 95; 220, 221
Canton Christian (Lingnan) College, 76, 220
Cary-Elwes, Columba, quoted, 66; 205, 213, 214, 215
Castiglione, Joseph, 28
Catherine II of Russia, 182
Cattaneo, Lazzaro, 11, 13
Celsus, 193
Ch'an school of Buddhism, xvi, 19
Chan Wing-tsit, 225, 234
Chang, C. S., 146; 231
Chang, Carsun (Chang Chün-mai), quoted, 104, 107; 122, 153–4, 162, 169; 223, 224
Chang Chi, 144, 145
Chang Chih-tung, 62, 97, 101, 102, 117, 154, 186
Chang Ching-chiang, 143
Chang Hsing-lang, 203
Chang Hsün, 104, 116
Chang Te-chün, 225
Chang Tso-lin, 149
Chang Tung-sun, 139, 154, 162
Chao Yuen-ren, 134
Chappoulie, H., 201
Chekhov, Anton, 128
Chen, Chi-yun, 105; 223
Ch'en Ch'iung-ming, 218
Ch'en Hsü-ching, 155
Ch'en Huan-chang, 223
Ch'en, Jerome, 234
Ch'en Li-fu, 157, 158
Ch'en Po-ta, 159
Ch'en Tu-hsiu, 97, 124, 129, 132, 133, 134, 135, 136, 137, 145, 146, 148, 149, 152, 154, 159, 160, 169, 185; 228
Ch'en T'ung-p'u, 103, 106, 115
Ch'en Yüan, quoted, 29; 202, 203
Cheng Chen-to, 150
Ch'eng Fang-wu, 151, 152, 163
Ch'eng Hao, xix
Cheng Hsüan, xix

Cheng, Shelley Hsien, 216, 220
Cheng Wei-hsin (Emmanuel de Siquiera), 28–9, 215
Chia-ch'ing emperor (1796–1820), 45
Ch'iang Hsüeh Hui, 62, 112, 113, 115
Chiang K'ai-shek, 83, 97, 99, 124, 149, 156–8, 160; 233
Chiang Monlin, 77, 140–1; 215, 230
Chicherin, B. N., 182
Ch'ien Hsüan-t'ung, 129, 133, 151, 154
Ch'ien Mu, 162
Ch'ien-lung emperor (1736–96), 28, 32, 45
Ch'in dynasty, *see* Ch'in Shih Huang-ti
Chin P'ing Mei, xx
Ch'in Shih Huang-ti, xiv, xv, xviii
Chin Yü-fu, 208
Chin-pu Tang (Progressive Party), 116, 139
chin-shih (third degree in examination system), 62, 103, 115
Chin-te Hui, 145
China Inland Mission, 57
China's social history, controversy on (1928), 155
Ch'ing dynasty, xviii, 17, 18, 35, 48, 55, 68, 81, 86
Ch'ing (Richard's secretary), 59
Ch'ing, Prince, 64
Ching-tu school of Buddhism, xvi
Chinnery, J. D., 228
Chou dynasty, xiii, xv
Chou Chen-fu, 127
Chou Tso-jen, 130, 133, 146, 150, 151
Chou Yang, 152, 153
Chou Yüan-piao, 13
Chow Tse-tsung, quoted, 140; 228, 229, 230, 231, 232
Chu Ch'i-hua, 155
Chu Chih-hsin, 147
Chu Chiu-chiang, 103
Ch'ü Ch'iu-pai, 149, 152, 231, 232
Chu Ho-chung, 94, 95; 221
Chu Hsi, xvi, xvii, xviii, xix, 119; quoted, 13
Ch'ü T'ai-su, 10, 11
chu-jen (second degree in examination system), 62, 64
Chuang Ts'un-yü, xix, 103
Chuang-tzu, xv, 127
Ch'un Ch'iu, xiv
Chung Yung, quoted, xiii, 13; xiv, 43, 110
Ch'ung-chen emperor (1628–44), 15, 17, 18
Ch'ung-fu-ssu, 3
Civil War, Chinese, 162

Clark, Anne B., 233
Clarke, Arthur C., quoted, 111
Clavius, Christopher, 6, 15, 16
Clement VIII, pope, 21
Clement IX, pope, 22
Clement XI, pope, 24, 25, 43, 213
Clement XIV, pope, 28
Cohen, Arthur A., 233, 234
Cohen, Paul A., 211
Comintern, *see* International, Third
Communism, Chinese, 93, 109, 124, 129, 135, 139, 142, 145, 148, 152, 153, 155, 156, 157, 158–63, 168, 170
Communism, Soviet, 124, 138, 156, 168, 189
Compton, Boyd, quoted, 161; 234
Comte, Auguste, 176, 177
Condorcet, M. J. A. N. Caritat, Marquis de, 177
Confucianism, xiii–xv, xvi; attitudes toward of: Jesuits, 9, 12, 13, 21, 31; Legge, 43–4; T'ai-p'ings, 47–8, 49, 51, 52; Richard, 60–1; Martin, 76; Eddy, 79; Sun Yat-sen, 85–9; K'ang Yu-wei, 106; T'an Ssu-t'ung, 113–14; Liang Ch'i-ch'ao, 117, 121; Chiang K'ai-shek, 157. *See also* Neo-Confucianism
Confucius, xiii, xiv, xv, xix, 12, 91, 106–7, 109, 120, 121, 157, 203; quoted, 13; his 'negative Golden Rule', xiv, 43; rites to, 21, 23, 44, 66, 74
Congregationalists, 80
conservatism, 190–1
Considine, John J., quoted, 10; 199
Constantine, prince, 18
Copernicus, Nikolaus, 15, 131
Couling, Samuel, 211
Creation Society, 150, 151
Creel, H. G., quoted, 32; 204
Crescent Moon Society, 151
Cruz, Gaspar da, 8

Darrow, Clarence, 73
Darwin, Charles, and Darwinism, 71, 77, 84, 85, 86, 89, 118, 121, 126, 127, 128
Dawson, Christopher, 198
De Bary, Wm Theodore, 197
Decembrists, 182
D'Élia, Pasquale, quoted, 5, 15; 86, 96, 116, 121–2, 198, 199, 200, 201, 217, 218, 219, 220, 221, 225, 226
Democratic League, 162
Der Ling, Princess, quoted, 105; 222
Dewey, Alice Chipman, 229
Dewey, John, 85, 87, 125, 134, 135, 137–8, 139, 140, 146, 147, 148, 169, 183, 217, 218, 222, 229
Diaz, Emmanuel, 32
Dickens, Charles, 227
Diderot, Denis, 125
Dimitrov, G., 161
Dominicans, 3, 20, 21, 22, 74
Dostoevsky, F. M., 150, 185
Driesch, Hans, 157
Duboscq, André, 234
Dumas, Alexandre, 227
Dunne, George H., quoted, 5, 10, 26, 199, 200, 201, 202
Dutch, 7, 12, 26, 38
Duyvendak, J. J. L., quoted, 15; 201
'dynastic cycle', 45
dynastic histories, xx

East India Company, British, 38, 39
Eddington, Sir Arthur, 111
Eddy, George Sherwood, 78, 97; 215, 221
Edict of Toleration (1692), 20, 23, 25; quoted, 27
Edkins, Joseph, 47, 52, 207
Edward I of England, 2
Egami, Namio, 198
Élia, Pasquale d', *see* D'Élia, Pasquale
Eliot, George (Mary Ann Evans), quoted, 70
Elwin, Arthur, 215
Elwin, W. H., 223
Emerson, Ralph Waldo, 148
Engels, Friedrich, 147, 155, 177
Erh Ya, xiv
Ethiopia, 7
Eucken, Rudolf, 71
Euclid, 11
examination system, xvii, 63, 87, 117, 122, 152, 164

Fairbank, John K., 197, 200, 222, 226
Fan Chen, 229
Fan Shou-k'ang, 154
Fang Hao, Maurus, 200, 203
Favre, B., 208, 209
Federal Council of Churches, 73
Feng Kuei-fen, 100, 216
Feng Yü-hsiang, 84
Feng Yün-shan, 46
Feuerbach, Ludwig, 161
Feuillet de Conches, M. F., 202
Figurists, 28, 203
Fitzgerald, C. P., ix
Five Classics, xiii, 114
'Five Elements' school, xv
Fleming, Daniel Johnson, 215, 222

Florovsky, Georges, xi, 185
Fogazzaro, Antonio, 72
Fontenelle, Bernard Le Bouvier de, 154, 232
Formosa, see Taiwan
Foster, John, 209
Four Books, xiv, xvii, 114, 157
Fourier, F. M. C., 108
Francis of Assisi, St, 177
Franciscans, 3–5, 20, 21, 22, 66
Franke, Herbert, 200, 225
Franke, Wolfgang, 200
Friedrich, Carl J., 235
Fryer, John, 112
Fu Ssu-nien, 133, 136
Fu-jen University, 74
Fukuzawa Yūkichi, 118, 119
Fung Yu-lan, ix, 100, 162, 197; quoted, xxi, 104, 105; 223, 224, 225

Galileo Galilei, 15, 16
Gallagher, Louis J., quoted, 6; 200
Garrett, Shirley, 215
Garshin, V. M., 128
Gasster, Michael, 231
Gaubil, Antoine, 28
Gautama, Siddhārtha, xvi
Genghis Khan, 3, 188
Geoffroy St Hilaire, Isidore, 131
George, Henry, 72–3, 81, 82, 84, 89, 216
Gerbillon, Jean François, 26, 27
Gherardini, Giovanni, 27
Gibbon, Edward, 214
Giles, H. A., 91
Ginger, Ray, 214
Gladden, Washington, 72
Gnosticism, 53, 176, 177–8
Goddard, Dwight, quoted, 62; 212
Goethe, J. W. von, 151, 177
Gogol, N. V., 128, 129, 130, 150
Golovin, F. A., 27
Goodnow, F. J., 83
Gordon, Charles George, 47, 51, 56
Granet, Marcel, 146
Grave, Jean, 143
Gray, J., 229
Great Proletarian Cultural Revolution, 162, 186
Greece, xx, 1, 89
Gregory X, pope, 3
Gregory XIII, pope, 21
Grieder, Jerome B., 228, 229, 230
Grimaldi, Filippo Maria, 27
Gueluy, R. B. Alb., 201
Gützlaff, Mr and Mrs Karl, 42, 101, 131, 214

Hadley, Arthur T., 78
Hager, Charles R., 80, 89
Hallerstein, Augustin de, 28
Hamberg, Theodore, 210
Han dynasty, xiv, xv, xix; see also Han Learning, school of
Han Learning, school of, xviii, 32, 33, 106, 135
Han-fei-tzu, xiv
Happer, Andrew P., 43; 207
Hardie, James Keir, 72
Harnack, Adolf, 72
Harris, George L., 204
Hart, Sir Robert, 67, 101; 213
Hay, Malcolm, quoted, 22; 201, 202, 204
Heaney, J. J., 214
Hegel, G. W. F., 148, 177
Heidegger, K. W. (Baron von Heideck), 177
Helena, dowager empress, 18
heliocentric theory, 15
Herodotus, 1
Herron, George D., 72, 73, 81, 220
Hervieu, Julien-Placide, 203
Herzen, Alexander I., 132, 183, 184, 188
Hīnayāna tendency of Buddhism, xvi
Hirth, F., 198
Hitler, Adolf, 177
Ho Chen, 144
Ho Kai, quoted, 164, 171
Holtzmann, Heinrich, 71
Hopkins, Charles Howard, 214
Horton, Walter M., 214
Hsia, C. T., quoted, 129; 227
Hsia Tsi-an, xi; 232
Hsiao Ching, xiv
Hsiao Kung-ch'üan, quoted, 104, 107, 108; xi, 222, 223, 224, 225, 226, 227
Hsieh Chao-chih, 13
Hsieh Tsuan-t'ai, 81
Hsieh, Winston, 220
Hsien-feng emperor (1851–61), 45, 46
Hsin Ch'ao (New Tide), circle and journal, 136, 137, 139, 148
Hsin Ch'ing-nien (New Youth), circle and journal, 129, 132–3, 134–5, 136, 139, 144, 145, 148, 151, 159
Hsing Chung Hui, 81, 82
hsiu-ts'ai (first degree in examination system), 59, 64
Hsü Chi-yü, 103
Hsü Chih-mo, 151, 152
Hsü Kuang-ch'i (Paul Hsü), 11, 14, 15, 17, 31, 32, 33, 186, 200, 222
Hsü, Leonard Shihlien, 218, 219
Hsü Shen, xix

Hsü Shou-ch'ang, 227
Hsü Yen-chih, 136
Hsüeh, Chün-tu, 216
Hsüeh I-fu, 29, 30
Hsün-tzu, xiv, 120
Hu Ch'iu-yüan, 152
Hu Feng, 153
Hu Han-min, 216, 217, 218, 219, 220
Hu Li-yüan, quoted, 164, 171
Hu Lin-i, 157
Hu, Pingsa, 215
Hu Shih, 97, 116, 124, 132, 133–6, 137,
    139, 140, 151, 154, 155, 158, 162, 169,
    182, 183; 226
Hua-yen school of Buddhism, xvi
Huang Ching-fang, 29
Huang, Philip Chung-chih, quoted, 119;
    225, 226, 228
Huang Tsung-hsi, xviii
Huang Yung-shang, 81
Hucker, Charles O., 197, 200
Hudson, G. F., quoted, 1, 2; 198, 201
Hügel, Friedrich von, 72
Hughes, E. R., 222, 230
humanism, 234
Hume, David, 214
Hummel, Arthur W., 203, 210, 212, 222,
    225, 226, 232
Hunan Report, Mao Tse-tung's, 160
'Hundred Days' (1898), 38, 63, 104, 105,
    112, 126, 167, 169
'Hundred Flowers', 171
'Hundred Schools', xiii
Hung Hsiu-ch'üan, 45–7, 49, 51, 52, 54,
    56, 80, 90, 97, 166, 213
Hung Jen-kan, 44, 47, 48, 51–2, 55, 56,
    102, 166, 180, 186
Hung-lou meng, xx
Huxley, T. H., 77, 126, 127, 128, 131,
    133, 229
Hyde, William DeWitt, 77
Hykes, John R., 206

I Ching, xiii, xiv, 13, 203
Ibsen, Henrik, 129, 134, 150
Ignatius of Loyola, 6
Incarnation, doctrine of, 12
India, xvi, xxi; Portuguese in, 7; as
    Roman Catholic base for Asian mis-
    sions, 8
Innocent X, pope, 22
International Workingmen's Association:
    Second, 124, 136; Third, 89, 124, 136,
    147, 148, 149
Ireland, 7
Irving, Edward 58–9

Isaiah, Book of, question of its reference
    to China, 1
Islam, xx, 191–2, 204
Israel, John, quoted, 158; 233

James, William, 71
Jansen, Marius B., 216
Jansenists, 21, 22, 23
Japan, xiii, xix–xx, 32, 63, 71, 168; Xavier
    in, 7; Sun Yat-sen and, 81, 82, 83;
    Chinese students in, 101, 124; Chinese
    war (1894–5) with, 115; Liang Ch'i-
    ch'ao and, 115, 117, 118; Lu Hsün
    and, 128; anarchists in, 143; Creation
    Society and, 151. See also Sino-
    Japanese War (1937–45)
Jardines, 42
Jaricot, Pauline, 66
Jeans, Sir James, 111
Jenks, Edward, 126, 127
Jesuits, xx, 4, 5–34, 58, 60, 66, 74, 100,
    126, 142, 164, 165, 166, 167, 170, 178–
    9, 182, 184
Jevons, W. S., 126, 217
Jews, 1, 5
Joachim of Floris, 177
John of Marignolli, 4
John of Montecorvino, 3, 4, 5, 198
John of Plano Carpini, 3
Johnston, R. F., quoted, 75; 214
Jones, C. Sheridan, 220, 221
Jordan, Sir John, 64
Josson, H., 201
Juan Yüan, 106
Judaism, xx

Kadets (Constitutional Democrats) in
    Russia, 182–3
K'ang Yu-wei, xix, 62, 63, 82, 83, 94, 95,
    97, 99, 100, 102–12, 113, 114, 115, 116,
    117, 118, 119, 120, 121, 122, 123, 132,
    159, 164, 168, 169, 186, 226
K'ang-hsi emperor (1662–1722), 20, 23,
    24, 25, 26, 28, 32, 33, 165, 166
Kant, Immanuel, 111, 126, 177
Kao I-han, 133
Katō Hiroyuki, 118
Kavelin, K. D., 182
Kawakami Hajime, 151
Ke-ming-tang, 83
Kepler, Johannes, 15
Keresnky, Alexander, 185
Kerr, Dr John G., 80, 89
Kidd, Benjamin, 127, 147, 231
Kidd, Samuel, 40, 42
Kierkegaard, Søren, 129

Klein, Donald W., 233
Koffler, Andreas, 18
Korea, xiii, 11
Korolenko, Vladimir, 128
Kōtoku Shūsui, 144
Kranz, P., 212
Križanić, Jaraj, 179
Kropotkin, Prince Peter, 87, 89, 121, 143
Ku Chieh-kang, 136, 151, 154, 233
Ku Yen-wu, xviii, xix, 33
Kuang-hsü emperor (1875–1908), 63
Kuang-wu emperor (25–57 AD), xix
Kublai Khan (ruled in China 1260–94), 3, 182
Kuei Wang, 18
Kung, H. H. (K'ung Hsiang-hsi), 83
Kung Tzu-chen, xix
Kung-yang commentary to Ch'un Ch'iu, xix, 103, 107, 119
Kuo Mo-jo, 151, 152, 155, 162, 163
Kuo Sung-t'ao, 101, 125
Kuomintang, 71, 79, 83, 84, 87, 96, 97, 99, 123–4, 143, 144, 147, 148–9, 152, 153, 155, 156–9, 160, 162, 167, 170, 171, 186
Kwok, D. W. Y., quoted, 136, 154, 156; 228, 229, 231, 232, 233

Lach, Donald F., 198, 204
Lamarck, J. B. de Monet, Chevalier de, 132
Lambert de la Motte, 22
Lamley, Harry J., 232
Langford, J. J., 201
Lao-tzu, xv, 126
Latourette, Kenneth S., quoted, 35, 36, 66; 205, 212, 213, 214, 215
Latter-Day Saints, 53–4
Lauterbach, W., 206
Lavrov, P. L., 183
Lawlor, F. X., quoted, 54; 210
Lazarists, 66, 74
Lea, Homer, 82
Leacock, Stephen B., 229
Lebbe, Vincent, 74–6
Lee, Leo Ou-fan, 227
Leeuwen, Arend Th. van, quoted, 188
Le Fèvre (Étienne Fabre), 19, 29
Leftist Writers, League of, 152, 170
Legal Marxists in Russia, 230
Legge, Helen Edith, 206, 207, 208
Legge, James, quoted, xv, 41; 41–5, 47, 48, 49, 52–3, 56, 57, 58, 60, 61, 66, 68, 101, 102, 132, 166, 167, 170, 180, 186, 193; 206, 207, 210, 213
Legists, xiv, xv

Lehmann, William C., 218
Leibniz, G. W., Freiherr von, 34, 36, 191, 204
Leiper, Henry S., 231
Leng, Shao Chuan, quoted, 86; 218, 219, 221
Lenin, Vladimir I., 88, 89, 147, 152, 155, 161, 177, 183, 185, 188, 194, 219
Lermontov, M. Yu., 128, 129
Levenson, Joseph R., quoted, 120; 226
Levine, Isaac Don, 235
Li Chi, xiv, 107, 218
Li Chi, publicist, 155, 159
Li Chih-tsao (Leo Li), 11, 17, 32
Li Huang, 146
Li Hung-chang, 60, 62, 66, 80, 101
Li Po, xx
Li Shih-tseng, 143, 145, 146
Li Ta, 159, 162
Li Ta-chao, 124, 132, 133, 135, 136, 137, 139, 147–9, 159, 160, 185
Li Tzu-ch'eng, 17
Li Ying-shih (Paul Li), 12, 26
Li Yüan-hung, 116
Liang A-fa, 40, 45, 46, 166
Liang Ch'i-ch'ao, quoted, xix, 33, 99, 123; 62, 63, 82, 94, 95, 97, 99, 100, 102, 103, 105, 106, 107, 112, 114–22, 123, 127, 132, 133, 147, 153, 154, 159, 168, 169, 186; 197, 204, 224, 225, 226
Liang Shih-ch'iu, 151, 158
Liang Sou-ming, 100, 122, 139, 153, 162, 169
liberalism, Ch. 5, 173
Liberty, League for, 152
Lin Shu, 128, 227
Lin Tse-hsü, 117
Lin Yutang, 162
Lincoln, Abraham, 82
Lindley, Augustus F., 48; 208
Linebarger, Paul, Judge, 82, 86, 90, 91–2, 93; 220, 221
Linebarger, Paul Myron Anthony, quoted, 85; 216–17, 217, 218, 221
Lippmann, Walter, quoted, 195; 235
liturgy, use of Chinese in, 28
Liu, Chun-jo, 232
Liu Feng-lu, xix, 103
Liu Hsin, xix, 103
Liu Meng-yüan, 155
Liu Pan-nung, 133, 151
Liu Shao-ch'i, 162
Liu Shih-p'ei, 144
Liu Ssu-fu (Shih Fu), 144
Liu-Fa Chien-hsüeh Hui, 145
Lo Chia-lun, 136

Lo Jung-pang, 223
Lo T'ang, 114
Lo Wen-tsao (Gregorio Lopez), 22, 23, 28, 29, 75
Loisy, Alfred, 72
London Missionary Society, 41
Longobardo, Nicolò, 17
Louis IX of France, 3
Louis XIV of France, 70
Lu, state of, xiv, 172, 203
Lu Hao-tung, 80
Lu Hsün (Chou Shu-jen), 125, 128–31, 133, 135, 136, 151, 152, 153, 169, 187; 227, 228, 232
Lun Yü, xiii, xiv, xviii
Lung-yü, 123
Luther, Martin, 106
Lyon, D. Willard, 227

Macartney, George, Earl, 38, 39
McCall, Professor, 140
MacGillivray, D., 211, 212
Mackenzie, Robert, 62, 63, 117
McShane, E. D., 210
Magalhães, Gabriel de, 19
Mahāyāna tendency of Buddhism, xvi, xvii
Maigrot, Charles, 23, 24, 25, 31
Mailla, Joseph de Moyriac de, 204
'Malabar rites', 24
Manchus, 17, 18, 19, 45. See also Ch'ing dynasty
'Mandate of Heaven', xiv
Manicheanism, xx
Mao Tse-tung, 133, 148, 159–62
Maoism, 160
Mar Jaballaha III, patriarch, 198
Marchant, Leslie R., 205
Marcus Aurelius Antoninus, 1
Maria, 18
Marin, Jerónimo, 8
Marshman, Joshua, 40, 42
Martin, Henry S., 222
Martin, W. A. P., 66, 76, 101, 207, 211, 213
Martini, Martino, 22
Marx, Karl, 81, 84, 85, 89, 147, 155, 161, 174, 176, 177, 184, 189, 190, 217, 218
Marxism, 124, 147, 159, 160, 163, 178, 194
Marxism–Leninism, 142, 143, 145, 147–8, 151, 152, 155, 156, 158, 159, 160, 161, 162, 170, 184, 189, 190, 230
Mathews, Shailer, 77
Maupassant, Guy de, 150
May 4th incident and movement (1919),

99, 124, 130, 131, 136, 137, 139, 142, 183, 184
May 30th incident (1925), 150, 151
Meadows, T. T., 48, 50, 53; 208, 209
Medhurst, W. E., 42
Mei Wen-ting, 29, 30
Meisner, Maurice, 229, 231, 232
Mencius, xiv, xix, 43, 108, 157; quoted, xxi
Meng-tzu, xiv, xvii, 43
Menger, Carl 217
Mensheviks, 152, 183
Mercader, Ramon, 235
Methodists, 37, 57, 91
Mezzabarba, George Ambrose de, 25
Michael, Franz, quoted, 47, 48, 49; 207, 208, 209, 210
Michie, Alexander, quoted, 76; 215
Mickiewicz, Adam, 129
Miliukov, P. N., 182
Mill, James, 190
Mill, John Stuart, 77, 85, 114, 119, 121, 126, 127, 140, 175, 190, 217–18
Millar, John, 217–18
Milne, Dr William, 40, 41, 45, 131
Ming dynastic history, quoted, 30
Ming dynasty, xvii, xviii, xx, 4, 7, 9, 16, 17–18, 32, 36
Missionary Conference of 1877, 42–3, 58, 66
Missionary Conference of 1890, 43, 58, 66, 76
Missions Étrangères, 22, 66
Miyakawa, Hisayuki, 197
Mo-tzu, xv, 88
Modernism, Protestant, 38, 68, 69, ch. 3, 99
Mongols, 2–4, 5. See also Yüan dynasty
Monroe, Harriet, 134
Monroe, Paul, 140
Montesquieu, Charles de Secondat, Baron de, 87, 117, 126, 219
Morales, Juan Bautista, 22
More, Thomas, 177
Morgan, Lewis Henry, 155
Mormons, see Latter-Day Saints
Morrison, Robert, 37, 38–41, 42, 45, 52, 56, 57, 97, 166, 180, 205, 214
Mosely, William, 39, 40; 205
Mostaert, Antoine, quoted, 5; 199
Mote, Frederick W., 197
Mott, John R., 78, 97; 222
Moule, A. C., quoted, 2; 198
Mu Shu, 172
Muller, Max, 42
Mungello, David E., 204
Muramatsu, Yuji, 197

Nabokov, Vladimir, 228
Nakamura Masanao, 118
Nan Hsüeh Hui, 112, 114
Nash, Arnold S., 214
National Socialism, German, 176, 189
nationalism, 71, 88
Nationalists, Chinese, see Kuomintang
Nearing, Scott, 73
Needham, Joseph, quoted, 6, 15, 16, 23–4, 166; ix, 199, 201, 202, 204
neo-Confucianism, xvi–xviii, xx, 32–3, 103, 142
Nerchinsk, Treaty of (1689), 20, 26–7
Nestorian Christianity, xx, 2, 3, 4, 5, 32, 60
Nevius, John L., 59, 213
New Culture movement, 142, 146
New Life movement (1934), 157
New Texts, xviii, xix, 103, 105, 106
Nicholas IV, pope, 2, 3
Nichols, James Hastings, quoted, 71, 72; 205, 214
Nien rebellion, 47
Nietzsche, Friedrich, 129, 177
Nivison, David S., 197
No-name Society, 151
Nobili, Roberto di, 24
Nunes Barreto, Melchior, 8
Nurhaci, 17

Octobrist party in Russia, 119
O'Dea, T. F., 210
O'Hara, A. R., 214
Old Texts, xviii, xix, 103
Olopen, 5
Öngüts, 4
Opium War, 41
'Oregon system', 219
Origen, 193; 235
Ōsugi Sakae, 144
Ōu Sheng-pai, 145
Ou-yang Hsiu, xvi
Ou-yang Pan-chiang, 113
Oxford Movement, Milne's attitude toward, 41

pai hua (vernacular) movement, 124, 134, 139
Pai Shang-ti Hui, 46
Pallu, François, 22, 23
Palmer, Norman D., quoted, 86; 218, 219, 221
Pan Ku, xxi
P'ang T'ien-shou (Achilles P'ang), 18
Panikkar, K. M., quoted, 23; 202
Pao Huang Hui, 104

Parennin, Dominique, 28
Parker, E. H., 201
Parker, Peter, 56
Paul, St: Acts quoted, 1; 34, 174
Paul V, pope, 21, 28
Pauthier, G., 198
Peabody, Francis G., 77
Peace Congress, Lucerne, 1905, 64
Peffer, Nathaniel, 215, 216, 217
Peking: Imperial University of, 66; National University of, 99, 123, 124, 126, 129, 133, 134, 135, 169
Pelliot, Paul, 198, 208
Peregrino da Castello, Fra, 5
Pereira, Thomas, 26, 27
Persians, 2
Peter I of Russia, 179, 180
Petöfi, Sandor, 128
Petrashevtsy, 183
Philip IV of France, 2
Philip, Robert, 206
Philippines, 7, 165
pietism, defined, 36
Pires, Thomas, 198
Piry, A. T., quoted, 74; 214
Pius XI, pope, 75
Plato, 109
Plekhanov, G. V., 152
Polanco, Juan, 22
Polevoi, Sergei, 148
Polo, Marco, 3, 4
Polo, Nicolò and Maffeo, 3
Portuguese, 6–7, 25, 70
Possevino, Antonio, 179, 182
Prémare, J. H. M. de, 28
Presbyterians, 39
Propaganda Fide, de (Congregation for the Propagation of the Faith), 22, 28, 32
Protestants, numbers in China, 66, 214–15
P'u-i, emperor (1909–12), 83, 104, 110, 116, 164
Pulleyblank, E. G., 229
Puritans, 53
Pushkin, A. S., 129

'quarrel between ancients and moderns' in France, 154

Rada, Martin de, 8
Rand, Ayn, 176
Rauschenbusch, Walter, 72, 73, 77, 81
Reclus, Elisée, 143; 213
Reeve, B., 211
Reid, Gilbert, 62, 66; 212
Reischauer, Edwin O., 197

Renaissance: in Europe, 6, 34, 70; 'Chinese Renaissance', 133
Renan, Ernest, quoted, 173
Research Clique, 116
Restarick, Henry Bond, quoted, 92, 94; 219, 220, 221
Revolution of 1911, 82–3, 105, 110
Revolution, October (1917), in Russia, 124, 136, 142, 147, 160
Rhodes, Alexandre de, 28
Rhodes, lay brother, 27
Ribera, Juan Bautista, 8
Ricci, Matteo (Li Ma-tou), 5–14, 15, 16, 17, 18, 19, 20, 21, 22, 24, 25, 26, 30, 32, 33, 34, 35, 36, 41, 43, 44, 49, 60, 64, 65, 69, 74, 75, 76, 102, 165, 167, 174, 179, 180, 181, 186, 191, 192, 193, 194, 214
Richard, Timothy (Li T'i-mo-t'ai), 5, 12, 36, 58–66, 67, 68, 69, 77, 95, 102, 104, 105, 106, 107, 112, 114, 115, 117–18, 120, 121, 167, 170, 174, 180, 186, 193, 199; 211, 212, 213, 223, 224, 225, 226
Ride, Lindsay, 206
Ripa, Matteo, 39
Rites Controversy, Chinese, 14, 20–6, 31, 33, 34, 43, 44, 56, 61, 66, 75, 165, 167, 186
Ritschl, Albrecht, 72, 77, 92
Roberts, Issachar J., 46, 47, 54, 213
Roman Catholics, numbers in China, 12, 19, 66, 214–15
Rome, relations with China of, 1–2
Rouleau, Francis A., quoted, 29; 198, 199, 200, 201, 202, 203, 204
Rousseau, Jean Jacques, 85, 108, 119, 127
Rowbotham, Arnold H., quoted, 10, 23, 26, 32, 34; 199, 202, 203, 204
Roy, David Tod, 232, 234
Roy, M. N., 86
Royal Asiatic Society, 39
Ruge, Arnold, 132
Ruggieri, Michele, 8, 9, 200
Russell, Bertrand, 125, 138–9, 141, 147, 169, 173, 183, 187, 193; 230–1
Russia, China's relations with, 26–7

Sadler, Gilbert T., 206
Saeki, 198
St John, Burton, 221
St John's College, Shanghai, 76
Saionji, Marquis, 64
Salisbury, Edward E., 199
Sambiasi, Francesco, 18
Sauma, Rabban, 2, 198
Scalapino, Robert A., 226, 231

Scarth, John, 209
Schall von Bell, Johann Adam, 14, 15, 17–19, 20, 26, 34, 165
Schelling, F. W. J. von, 177
Schereschewsky, Samuel Isaac, 206, 207
Schiffrin, Harold Z., 216, 226
Schlegel, Gustave, 208
Schleiermacher, Friedrich, 71, 72
scholasticism, 235
Schopenhauer, Arthur, 129
Schram, Stuart R., 233, 234
Schreck, Johann (Terrentius), 17
Schultz, William Rudolph, 228
Schumpeter, Joseph, quoted, 189
Schurhammer, Georg, 199
Schurman, Jacob Gould, 83
Schwartz, Benjamin I., quoted, x, 126, 127; 197, 222, 225, 228, 231, 233
Schweitzer, Albert, 72
'science and metaphysics', debate between (1923), 119, 142, 153–4
Scopes trial, 73
Scott, Sir Walter, 227
Sebes, Joseph, 202
secret societies, xvii, 49
'self-strengthening' (tzu-ch'iang), 100–1
Shang dynasty, xiii
Shang-ti (to translate 'God' into Chinese or to be translated as 'God' in English), 12, 13, 21, 23, 42, 43
Sharman, Lyon, quoted, 95; 216, 220, 222
Sheldon, Charles Monroe, 73
Shen Ch'üeh, 17
Shen Yen-ping (Mao Tun), 149, 150, 152
Shen Yin-mo, 133
Shiba Shirō, 118
Shih Ching, xiv
Shih Ta-k'ai, 47
Shih, Vincent Y. C., quoted, 49, 50; 208, 209, 228
Shih-shih Hsin-lun (New Tracts for the Times), 63
Shimada Saburō, 143
Shimonoseki, Treaty of (1895), 62, 115
Shotwell, James T., 85, 217
Shu Ching, xiii, 218
Shui-hu chuan, xx
Shun-chih emperor (1644–62), 17, 18–19, 20
Sienkiewicz, Henryk, 128
Simon Magus, 177
Sino-Japanese War (1937–45), 75, 135, 156, 157
Siquiera, Emmanuel de, see Cheng Wei-hsin
Sisto Rosso, Antonio, 199

Slavophiles, 185
Smenovekhovtsy in Russia, 163
Smith, Adam, 86, 126, 127, 140, 190
Smogułęcki, Jean-Nicolas, 29, 30
So, Kwan-wai, 212
Social Democrats in Russia, 183
'social gospel', 72–3, 92
Socialism, Christian, 73
Socialism, guild, 139
Socialism, state, 138
Socialist Revolutionaries, 183
Society for Diffusion of Christian and General Knowledge (SDK, later Christian Literature Society), 61, 63, 64, 112
Society for Literary Research, 149–51
Society for the Study of Marxist Theory, 148
Society for the Study of Socialism, 144
Society, Marxist Research, 148
Society, Socialist Research, 148
Soloviev, Vladimir, 181, 185
Songgotu, Prince, 27
Soong (Sung) Ch'ing-ling, 83, 220
Soothill, William E., 64, 65, 77; 199, 211, 212, 215
Spaniards, 7, 12, 21, 22
Spence, Jonathan, 234
Spencer, Herbert, 77, 125, 126, 127, 128, 229
Spener, Philipp Jakob, 37
Spengler, Oswald, 85, 121
Spuler, Bertold, 198
Ssu-ma Ch'ien, xxi
Ssu-ma Kuang, 133, 229
Stalin, Joseph, and Stalinism, 149, 155, 160, 161, 171, 175, 186, 190
Stanton, William, quoted, 49; 208
Staunton, Sir George Thomas, 39, 42; 205, 207
Stelle, Charles C., quoted, 55; 208, 209, 210
Stephen of Perm, St, 174
Stirling, W. G., 208
Stock, Eugene, 211
Strindberg, Johan August, 150
Strong, Anna Louise, 162
Sun Chia-nai, 63, 222
Sun Ching-ya, 86
Sun Yat-sen, 71, 73, 78, 79–98, 99, 100, 104, 105, 118, 119, 123–4, 130, 131, 133, 135, 140, 143, 144, 149, 156, 158, 167–8, 169, 170, 181, 186; 218, 219, 220, 221
Sung dynasty, xvi, xvii, xviii, xx, 3, 33
Sung Chiao-jen, 83, 148
Swedenborg, Emanuel, 53

syncretism, 31, Ch. 4, 123, 143, 165, 168, 171, 185–7, 192–3
Szczesniak, Boleslaw, 201

Ta Hsüeh, xiv, 88, 219
Ta T'ung Shu of K'ang Yu-wei, 104, 107–9, 118, 119
Tagore, Amitendranath, quoted, 152; 232
Tagore, Rabindranath, 151
Tai Chen, xviii, xix
Tai Chi-t'ao, 86
T'ai-p'ing rebellion, 37, 41, 44, 45–56, 59, 68, 80, 90, 92, 95, 96, 100, 101, 157, 166, 180, 185
Taiwan, xvii, 38, 97, 135, 156, 163, 164, 186
Talbott, Nathan M., 225
T'an Ssu-t'ung, xix, 99, 102, 105, 112–14, 115, 116, 120, 122, 123, 168; 225
T'an Tzu, 30, 203
T'ang dynasty, xv, xvi, xx, 2, 165
T'ang Leang-li, 203; 231
T'ang Ts'ai-ch'ang, 118
T'ang Wang, 18
T'ao Hsi-sheng, 155, 156, 158
Tao Te Ching, xv
Tao-kuang emperor (1821–50), 45
Taoism, xiii, xv, xvi, xvii, xviii, xx, 12, 49, 60, 61, 79, 145; K'ang Yu-wei and, 103, 108; Yen Fu and, 126, 127; Russell and, 230
Taylor, Charles, 48
Taylor, Hudson, 57
Te P'ei, Prince, 29
Ten Commandments: translated into Chinese, 8, use of by T'ai-p'ings, 50
Teng Ssu-yü, quoted, 63; 210, 222, 225, 226
Teng Tse-ju, 216
Tengchow College, Shantung, 76
'term question': among Catholics, 21; among Protestants, 42–4, 166
Thales, 131
Theravāda tendency of Buddhism, see Hīnayāna
Third-Party Men, Literature of, 152
Third Rome, idea of Moscow as the, 177
Thirteen Classics, xiv
Thomas, St, the Apostle, 1, 5
Thomas Aquinas, St, 15
Thomas, Anton, 24, 203
Thompson, Laurence G., 223, 224
Thread of Talk Society, 151
Three People's Principles, 82, 84, 86, 87, 123, 156, 157, 158, 216
T'ien Han, 146

T'ien Yü-ch'ing, 208
T'ien-t'ai school of Buddhism, xvi
Tikhvinsky, S. L., quoted, 109; 225
Ting Ling, 152
Ting, V. K. (Ting Wen-chiang), 154, 155; 225
Tolstoy, Count Leo N., 150
totalitarianism, 177, 188–9
Tournon, Charles Thomas Maillard de, 24–5
Triad society, 49, 208
Trigault, Nicolas, quoted, 5; 17, 18, 200
Triple Demism, see Three People's Principles
Troeltsch, Ernst, 72
Trotsky, Leon, and Trotskyism, 149, 152, 235
True Doctrine of the Lord of Heaven (T'ien-chu Shih I), of Ricci, 11, 24, 32, 60; quoted, 13
Ts'ai Wen-hsüeh, 203
Ts'ai Yüan-p'ei, 99, 124, 133, 146, 152
Tsai-li, Prince Regent, 144
Ts'ao K'un, 139
Ts'ao O, 157
Tseng Chi-tse, 62
Tseng Kuo-fan, xviii, 47, 55, 97, 100, 101, 117, 157
Tso Chuan, xiv, 172, 203
Tso Tsung-t'ang, 60, 157
Ts'ui Shu, xviii
Tsui, Shu-Chin, 217
Tu Fu, xx
Tuan Ch'i-jui, 84, 116, 119
Tung Chung-shu, xix, 103
T'ung-chih emperor (1862–74), 45, 67, 100, 157
Tung-lin academy, xviii, 11, 32
T'ung-meng Hui, 82, 83, 133, 143, 144, 167
Turgenev, Ivan S., 150
Turgot, A. R. J., Baron de l'Aulne, 177
Twenty-One Demands (1915), 83, 137
Twiss, Professor, 140
Tyau, Min-ch'ien T. Z., 86
Tytler, Alexander Fraser, 150
Tz'u Hsi, empress, 63, 100, 105

Uighurs, 2
Urban VIII, pope, 16, 21
USSR, Sun Yat-sen's relations with, 83–4, 85, 88, 97, 100

Vagnani, Alfonso, 30
Valentinus, 177
Valignano, Alessandro, 8, 9, 10, 21

Varg, Paul A., 210
Väth, Alfons, 201
Vatican Council of 1870, 61
Vekhi, 185
Verbiest, Ferdinand, 19, 20, 23, 26, 33, 34, 64, 165, 203
Vietnam, xiii, 31, 165
Visdelou, Claude de, 28, 203
Voegelin, Eric, quoted, 175, 176, 177, 178, 194; 234, 235
Voitinsky, Gregory, 148, 185
Voltaire (François-Marie Arouet), 28
Vucinich, Alexander, ix

Waldensians, 53
Wan-kuo Kung-pao (The Globe Magazine), 62, 81, 103
Wan-li emperor (1573–1620), 11
Wang, Chi-chen, 129; 227
Wang Ching-wei, 84, 86, 145
Wang Mang, xix
Wang Shih-ch'ing, 227
Wang Shu-huai, 225
Wang T'ao, 100, 132
Wang T'ing-na, 13
Wang, Y. C., quoted, 101; 222, 228
Wang Yang-ming, xvii, xviii, xix, 87
Ward, Frederick T., 47, 56
Ward, Harry F., 73
Ward, J. S. M., 208
Wei (T'o-pa) dynasty, xv, xvi
Wei Chün, 14, 200
Wei Yüan, xix, 100
Wellhausen, Julius, 71
Wen I-to, 151
Wen T'ien-hsiang, v
Wen Hsiang, 67
Weng T'ung-ho, 102
Wesley, John, 37
Western response to China, 33–4
Wetter, Gustav, quoted, 176
Weyl, Walter E., 229
Whampoa Military Academy, 157
White Lotus Society, xvii
White, Wilbert W., 215
Whitman, Walt, 151
Wieger, Léon, quoted, 164; 226
Wilhelm, Richard, 86
Willaert, L., 201
William of Ruisbroek, 3, 4
William, Maurice, 84–5, 89, 216, 217
Williams, S. Wells, 207
Williamson, Alexander, 61–2, 113, 207, 211
Wilson, Woodrow, 88, 219
Wittfogel, K. A., 210, 233

Wolff, Christian, 36
Wong, George Ho Ching, 200
Wong, Young-tsu, 231, 233
World War I, 116
Wright, Arthur, quoted, xvii; 197
Wright, Mary Clabaugh, 222, 233
Writers' Association, 152
Wu Chih-hui, 94, 95, 132, 133, 136, 143–4, 145, 146, 154; 221
Wu Hsiang-hsiang, 216
Wu Li, 29
Wu Wang, 13
Wu Yü, 133; 227
Wylie, Alexander, 47, 52, 199
Wyngaert, A. van den, 198

Xavier, St Francis, 7

Yamamoto, Tatsuro and Sumiko, 231
Yang Ch'ang-chi, 160
Yang Ch'ü-yün, 81
Yang Hsiu-ch'ing, 46, 47
Yang I-feng, 225
Yang Kuang-hsien, 19
Yang Ming-chai, 148
Yang T'ing-yün (Michael Yang), 11, 17, 32, 200
Yang Wen-hui, 114
Yavorsky, Stefan, 179
Yeh Shao-chün, 150

Yen Fu, 99, 105, 118, 124, 125–8, 130, 133, 136, 169, 183
Yen Jo-chü, xviii
Yen Yüan, xviii
Yin dynasty, see Shang dynasty
yin-yang school, xv, xix
YMCA (Young Men's Christian Association). 38, 77, 78, 83, 89, 94, 127, 138, 146, 168, 215, 220
Yoffe, Adolf, 83, 149, 185, 216
Young China Association, 146
Yu, George T., 216, 231
Yü Ta-fu, 151, 152
Yü-keng, 101
Yüan dynasty, xvii, xx, 2, 3, 4, 36
Yüan Shih-k'ai, 83, 90, 110, 116, 119, 127, 132, 148, 164, 169, 220
Yüan Ts'an, 227
Yung Wing (Jung Hung), 101, 223
Yung-cheng emperor (1722–35), 25, 28, 31, 34, 55, 202
YWCA (Young Women's Christian Association), 77, 168

Zasulich, Vera, 184
Zen school of Buddhism, see Ch'an
Zenkovsky, V. V., ix
Zola, Émile, 150
Zoroastrianism, xx
Zürcher, E., 197